MW00581032

CREATING GLOBAL SHIPPING

Shipping has been the international business par excellence in many national economies, one that preceded trends in other, more highly visible sectors of international economic activity. Nevertheless, in both business and economic history, shipping has remained relatively overlooked. That gap is filled by this exploration of the evolution of European shipping through the study of two Greek shipping firms. They provide a prime example of the regional European maritime businesses that evolved to serve Europe's international trade and, eventually, the global economy. By the end of the twentieth century, Greeks owned more ships than any other nationality. The story of the Vagliano brothers traces the transformation of Greek shipping from local shipping and trading to international shipping and ship management, while the case of Aristotle Onassis reveals how international shipping was transformed into a global business.

GELINA HARLAFTIS is the director of the Institute for Mediterranean Studies of the Foundation of Research and Technology–Hellas (FORTH) in Crete, and is a professor of maritime history at the University of Crete. She was president of the International Maritime Economic History Association, visiting fellow at All Souls College, Oxford University, and an Alfred D. Chandler Jr. International Visiting Scholar at the Harvard Business School. She has published many books, including *The World's Key Industry: History and Economics of International Shipping*, a collection coedited with Stig Tenold and Jésus M. Valdaliso.

CAMBRIDGE STUDIES IN THE EMERGENCE
OF GLOBAL ENTERPRISE

The world economy has experienced a series of globalizations in the past two centuries, and each has been accompanied and shaped by business enterprises, their national political contexts, and new sets of international institutions. Cambridge Studies in the Emergence of Global Enterprise focuses on those business firms that have given the global economy many of its most salient characteristics, particularly regarding how they have fostered new technology, new corporate cultures, new networks of communication, and new strategies and structures designed to meet global competition. All the while, they have accommodated changes in national and international regulations, environmental standards, and cultural norms. This is a history that needs to be understood because we all have a stake in the performance and problems of global enterprise.

Editors
Louis Galambos, The Johns Hopkins University
Geoffrey Jones, Harvard Business School

Other Books in the Series

Teresa da Silva Lopes, *Global Brands: The Evolution of Multinationals in Alcoholic Beverages*

Christof Dejung and Niels P. Petersson, *The Foundations of Worldwide Economic Integration: Power, Institutions, and Global Markets, 1850–1930*

William J. Hausman, *Global Electrification: Multinational Enterprise and International Finance in the History of Light and Power, 1878–2007*

Christopher Kobrak, *Banking on Global Markets: Deutsche Bank and the United States, 1870 to the Present*

Christopher Kobrak, *National Cultures and International Competition: The Experience of Schering AC, 1851–1950*

Christopher D. McKenna, *The World's Newest Profession: Management Consulting in the Twentieth Century*

Johann Peter Murmann, *Knowledge and Competitive Advantage: The Coevolution of Firms, Technology, and National Institutions*

Neil Rollings, *British Business in the Formative Years of European Integration, 1945–1973*

Andrew L. Russell, *Open Standards and the Digital Age: History, Ideology, and Networks*

Jonathan Silberstein-Loeb, *The International Distribution of News: The Associated Press, Press Association, and Reuters, 1848–1947*

CREATING
GLOBAL SHIPPING

Aristotle Onassis, the Vagliano Brothers, and the
Business of Shipping, c.1820–1970

GELINA HARLAFTIS

IMS-FORTH and University of Crete

CAMBRIDGE
UNIVERSITY PRESS

CAMBRIDGE
UNIVERSITY PRESS

University Printing House, Cambridge CB2 8BS, United Kingdom

One Liberty Plaza, 20th Floor, New York, NY 10006, USA

477 Williamstown Road, Port Melbourne, VIC 3207, Australia

314–321, 3rd Floor, Plot 3, Splendor Forum, Jasola District Centre, New Delhi – 110025, India

79 Anson Road, #06–04/06, Singapore 079906

Cambridge University Press is part of the University of Cambridge.

It furthers the University's mission by disseminating knowledge in the pursuit of education, learning, and research at the highest international levels of excellence.

www.cambridge.org
Information on this title: www.cambridge.org/9781108475396
DOI: 10.1017/9781108573009

© Gelina Harlaftis 2019

This publication is in copyright. Subject to statutory exception and to the provisions of relevant collective licensing agreements, no reproduction of any part may take place without the written permission of Cambridge University Press.

First published 2019

Printed in the United Kingdom by TJ International Ltd. Padstow Cornwall

A catalogue record for this publication is available from the British Library.

Library of Congress Cataloging-in-Publication Data
Names: Harlaftis, Gelina, 1958- author.
Title: Creating global shipping : Aristotle Onassis, the Vagliano Brothers, and the business of shipping, c.1820-1970 / Gelina Harlaftis, IMS-FORTH and University of Crete.
Description: Cambridge, United Kingdom ; New York, NY : Cambridge University Press, 2018. | Series: Cambridge studies in the emergence of global enterprise | Includes bibliographical references and index.
Identifiers: LCCN 2018048302 | ISBN 9781108475396 (hardback : alk. paper) | ISBN 9781108466783 (pbk. : alk. paper)
Subjects: LCSH: Shipping–Europe–History. | Shipping–Greece–History. | Onassis, Aristotle Socrates, 1906-1975. | Vagliano, Marinos, 1804-
Classification: LCC HE821 .H36 2018 | DDC 387.5/4409409034–dc23
LC record available at https://lccn.loc.gov/2018048302

ISBN 978-1-108-47539-6 Hardback

Cambridge University Press has no responsibility for the persistence or accuracy of URLs for external or third-party internet websites referred to in this publication and does not guarantee that any content on such websites is, or will remain, accurate or appropriate.

For Chrysiida and Niko

CONTENTS

FIGURES

MAPS

TABLES

PREFACE

Shipping has been a leading sector in European economic growth for centuries. By the end of the twentieth century, Greeks owned more ships than any other nationality in the world, and shipowners played a fundamental role in global connectivity and economic growth. Shipping integrates world markets. For centuries, it has been the international business par excellence in most national economies, and it preceded trends that later became visible in many other sectors of international economic activity.

Nevertheless, shipping remains invisible in the global business arena as its products – transport services – cannot be seen among the cargoes carried across the vast oceans. It is equally invisible in economic and business history, for several reasons. First, mainstream studies of the emergence of modern economic and business growth in industrializing economies usually focus on manufacturing; if they emphasize the service sector, they usually privilege banking and finance and neglect trade and shipping. Some historians have pushed back on this trend recently, notably Geoffrey Jones, Gordon Boyce, and Michael Miller, but their work is a relative trickle amid the flood of research on manufacturing and finance. The study of shipping and shipping firms has long remained on the periphery, isolated within the disciplines of maritime history and maritime economics. Second, the international character of shipping firms, which blurs their links to individual economies, has made them difficult for mainstream research to assimilate. The production of shipping and sea transportation takes place beyond national boundaries, and its income is earned abroad and is thus often removed from the economic structures a one specific country. Shipping companies thus reside in a liminal space that is difficult for most historians to adapt to their nation-based conceptions.

The third reason for the underexamination of global shipping is that the evolution of shipping firms has been overshadowed by the history of trading companies. For example, the European-chartered companies serving colonial expansion in the early modern era and the international European trading companies of the nineteenth century were also major shipping firms, but the latter function has been overshadowed by their trading and financial activities.

Large, specialized shipping corporations, meanwhile, are a product of the twentieth century and remain understudied.

A fourth reason shipping has been neglected by historians is that prior to the twentieth century, in the era of sailing ships, the shipping sector was comprised mainly of small-scale firms known as free traders. Free traders were shipowners who usually captained their own vessels, engaged in both trade and sea transport. Theirs were essentially family firms that developed in maritime regions around small towns and island ports on Europe's coastline. There they developed their own maritime traditions, practices that were only fitfully connected to the main economic centers or ports of their respective countries. In the same way that early industrial districts were established (in Italy, for example), maritime districts developed with the emergence of hundreds of small firms. The sheer numbers of shipping firms, and the elusive character of the businesses at sea and in foreign lands beyond their home waters and land base, makes their historical study particularly difficult.

That elusiveness is related to the fifth reason for the invisibility of the business of shipping: its intangible nature. The economic output of a ship is not as easy to see or value as the output of a factory or a plot of land – even the historical remains and ruins of such a space are more palpable. The fact that the ship and its crew spend most of their time at sea further contributes to shipping's evanescence. Ships are demolished; they live and die like people and they leave only indirect traces.

Finally, the large, independent shipowners that created the global shipping business groups of the twentieth century based them on global institutions like offshore companies and open registries, thus allowing them to remain shrouded in secrecy in a world that still focused on national economies.

This book explores the evolution of the European shipping company through the study of two Greek shipping firms, which provide a prime example of the regional European maritime businesses that evolved to serve Europe's international trade and eventually the global economy. The Vagliano Brothers case traces the transformation of Greek shipping from local sea transport and trading to international shipping and ship management, while the Onassis case shows how international shipping was transformed into a global business.

The book contributes to the understanding of the shipping business during two major waves of globalization. The Vaglianos were active during the first wave, which started in the second half of the nineteenth century and receded during the interwar period. The Onassis business emerged from the explosion of the second wave of globalization in the second half of the twentieth century. These two firms contributed to the process of global economic integration by inventing and reinventing a Greek and ultimately a wider, southern, and northern European maritime tradition. For this story is not only about of the Greeks: it can also be read as the history of the evolution of the European maritime tradition in tramp/bulk shipping. It follows that this book should draw on the field of maritime business history, developed in the past few decades by maritime, economic, and business historians, and that it has benefited from discussions in the international fora facilitated by the European Business History Association and the International Maritime Economic History Association.

ACKNOWLEDGMENTS

With the kind support of Panagi A. Vagliano and S. F. Antypa Bequests in Cephalonia.
This book has taken me on a long and happy journey to many port cities. It "set sail" from Argostoli, in Cephalonia, continued to Taganrog and Rostov-on-Don, in Russia, proceeded on land to Kiev, St. Petersburg, and Moscow, and then took to the sea again: to Marseille, London, Bergen, New York, and Boston. Each time I discovered a new source, a new piece of the mosaic, it gave me more enthusiasm and impetus to continue. A large number of friends and colleagues came on board to sail alongside me on various legs of the journey. They showed me the way, described the winds and currents, in every sea and ocean, and tolerated my driving the boat, showing patience and great interest while I talked to them endlessly of my long-term relationship with four men: Mari, Andrea, Panagi, and Aristotle. I am thankful to all.

I have long studied the Greek shipping industry, identifying its actors and, in most of my studies, incorporating the big picture. Then a time came when I needed to return to the microlevel before drawing the big picture again – to examine, that is, the activities of the shipping businesses themselves. This time I decided to choose the biggest shipping business of the nineteenth century, the Vagliano Brothers, and the best-known shipping business of the twentieth century, the Onassis group. I decided to write about the Vaglianos in the summer of 2006 in Cephalonia, in Argostoli, while sitting on the balcony of the Ainos Hotel overlooking the statue of the Vaglianos in the main square. At the local branch of the General Archives I had just "discovered" a fragmented Vagliano Archive. I decided to write about Onassis in connection to the Vaglianos at the Harvard Business School (HBS), in Cambridge, Massachusetts, sitting in my office overlooking the gardens. It was in the fall of 2008, during which I spent part of my sabbatical as an Alfred D. Chandler Jr. International Visiting Scholar in the Business History program. I had just recently uncovered, through electronic sources, more archival evidence on Onassis (this time from the FBI), which gave me enough evidence to proceed. The concept of the book was presented for the first time in November 2008, at an HBS seminar organized by Geoffrey Jones and Walter Friedman. I would like to thank them both very much for their inspiration and support.

It was in February 2009, while I was a visiting fellow at All Souls College, Oxford University, that I continued my research in the Archives of the Bank of England. I would like to thank the warden of All Souls, Professor Sir John Vickers, for facilitating my research there. Many thanks are owed to the archivist of the Bank of England, Sarah Millard, who assisted me in tracing all the necessary collections. I thank Heather Gibson, my flatmate in Oxford back in 1986, for presenting me with the connection between the Vaglianos and the Bank of England; she had heard about this link from her professor of banking at Glasgow University. It was information that remained in my memory for more than twenty years before I searched for evidence to support it. It was the historian and museographer Eleanna Vlachou who had told me of the existence of the Vagliano Archive back in 1997. The archive lay in the basement of the Korgialeneio Historical and Folklore Museum of Cephalonia, beyond the grasp of researchers for many years. When the archive was moved to the Greek State Archives for the Prefecture of Cephalonia, it was more easily accessible, although it had not been catalogued at the time. My most sincere thanks go to the director at that time, Stamatoula Zapanti-Pentogalou, for allowing me open access and study of the as-yet unclassified archive. The next director, Dora Zafeiratou, has proved equally obliging and I would like to thank her very much for facilitating my research during my visit to Argostoli.

I would also like to thank the Management Committee of the Panagi A. Vagliano and S. F. Antypa Bequests in Cephalonia and, in particular, the committee's president in 2008, George Kouris, for the financial support they provided for my research on Mari Vagliano in Kiev. Warm thanks go to the next president of the Bequest's Management Committee, Spyridon Hourmouzis, board member Nikolaos Boukas and secretary Maria Choida for their time and interviews and for access to the minutes of the committee. Many thanks are also due to the current president, Ilariani Tzanetatou, for financial support for the editing of this volume. At the Nursery Home-Charity Foundations of Lixouri, in Cephalonia, I am grateful to Gerasimos Geroulanos and to the president, Christina Tsangaratou-Valsamou, for their hospitality and for providing me access to the only existing photo of Panagi Vagliano. I am also grateful to the Korgialeneio Historical and Folklore Museum of Cephalonia for giving me permission to photograph the Vagliano portraits and other archival material from the Collection of Francis and Stephan Vagliano, and I wish to extend special thanks to the curator of the museum, Theotokoula Moulinou, for facilitating everything. Many thanks also to Eleni Lykiardopoulou for the valuable tour in Keramies and to the photographer Vassilis Loukatos for making it possible to take the pictures from Lixouri and Argostoli.

Meeting and conversing with the members of the Vagliano family in the United States, France, England, and Greece was very rewarding. Making Andre Marino Vagliano's quasi-metaphysical acquaintance in cyberspace made it possible to meet the "lost" French branch of the Vagliano family.

Before that, however, the research of his son Jason Vagliano on the family history, along with the accessibility of his interview with Francis Vagliano, gave me the first window onto the grandsons of Mari Vagliano. I am very grateful to Marina Eloy, Sonia de Panafieu, and Jean Marc de le Bédoyère for providing me with details and photographic material on the descendants of the Vagliano family in France. Sophia Kostomeni, Irene Matiatou Facon, Athanassios Akrivos, and Ioannis Dimitriadis-Vaglianos provided me with valuable photographic material and details on the genealogical tree of the Vaglianos who remained in Greece.

Meeting the "Onassis business family" was another delight. I am indebted to the president of the Alexander S. Onassis Foundation, Dr. Anthony Papadimitriou, for his trust and for opening the "magic door" to the Onassis business archives. The unconditional access to the Onassis business records was an unexpected gift. Research for this book in the unclassified but systematically amassed Onassis archive, gathered carefully over the years by the Onassis Foundation, triggered his interest. Through the initiative of Dr. Papadimitriou, the "Onassis Business Archive" is currently under construction. It classifies the Onassis business documents to make them accessible to the public.[1] This is a pioneering endeavor not only for Greek shipping but also for the Greek business world, as extremely few business archives exist in Greece, and these are usually connected either with banking or state enterprises. Its formation will set an excellent example that I believe will prove a landmark in the course of maritime business history in my country and in the greater understanding of the global shipping community.

I am also obliged to Paul Ioannidis for the long and numerous discussions of the Onassis business and the early, formative years of the Alexander S. Onassis Foundation. Ioannidis is a respected figure and the only surviving member of the permanent board of directors appointed by Aristotle Onassis in his will. At ninety-six years old, he retains his lucidity, memory, and passion for the continuation of the Onassis shipping business and the Alexander S. Onassis Foundation. I am extremely privileged for the time I was able to spend with him.

The staff of the Onassis Foundation were also more than obliging and helpful. Effie Tsiotsiou, executive director of the Alexander S. Onassis Public Benefit Foundation, facilitated the research in all the storage areas of the Onassis archives in Athens and New York. My sincere thanks to Clare Nelson, of the Onassis Public Benefit Foundation in New York, a trusted employee of the

---

[1] The organization and classification of the Onassis Business Archive is undertaken by a research team from the Institute for Mediterranean Studies at the Foundation of Research and Technology-Hellas and is financed by the Alexander S. Onassis Foundation. The team aims to complete the project by 2020. It will be led by the author; the main collaborators are Amalia Pappa, the deputy director of the General State Archives of Greece, and postdoctoral researcher Alexandra Papadopoulou.

Onassis business and Onassis Foundation since the 1970s, who made my research there possible. The diachronic presence of the Onassis shipping business was nowhere more evident than at the Olympic Shipping and Management, the Onassis shipping company, headquartered in Paleo Phalero. I am very grateful to John Ioannidis, the general manager at the time and also a member of the executive committee of the Alexander S. Onassis Foundation, for his account of their work in the shipping business and the teamwork since the 1990s.

Springfield Co. was the company Aristotle Onassis set up in 1963 in Greece; today it is the main subagency of Olympic Shipping and Management. I am greatly indebted to its general manager, Dimitris Patrikios, for his time, openness, and friendliness. Thanos Krassaris, his predecessor, and a member of the Onassis company since the 1960s, gave me invaluable information about the organization of Onassis companies around the world and their intercompany communication; I would like to thank him heartily. The interviews from all heads of departments at Springfield greatly illuminated the continuity of the maritime tradition of the company. I would also like to sincerely thank Captain Dionysis Siganakis, head of the Operations Department; Captain Gerassimos Barkas, head of the Marine Department; Captain Thanasis Apostolopoulos, head of the Manning Department; and naval architect Dimitris Makris, head of the Technical Department. Needless to say, the contribution of Emmy Adali in facilitating everything was invaluable.

The only real surviving relatives of the Onassis family that I was able to meet were from the side of Aristotle Onassis's first cousins, the Konialidises. Ritsa Konialidis, wife of Constantino Konialidis, and her brother, Professor George Hartofilakidis-Garofalidis, provided me with the fullest genealogical tree I could find and with photographic material. Nicolas Const. Konialidis, the son of Constantino and Ritsa Konialidis, helped me to complete many gaps and I would like to thank him very much for his kindness in Montevideo. The son of Nikos Konialidis, Marios Chrysostomos Konialidis contributed substantially in filling the gaps in the genealogy and gave me valuable information after the completion of this book which I hope to use in a future study; unfortunately he passed away in March 2019. I would like to thank all of them very much for their time and contributions.

The beautiful painting of Konstantinos Volanakis that is on the cover of the book was generously provided by Panos Laskaridis; my warmest thanks. I would also like to thank Roger Kvarsvik, of the Bergen Maritime Museum, for his help with Norwegian bibliographies and archives. Julia Kysla, in Kiev, was very helpful during my research in the Ukrainian State Archives. Dimitra Kardakari in Corfu did the difficult and exhausting job of furnishing a database from the thousands of transactions of the Vaglianos in the Bank of England. And, as always, I am indebted to Dr. Mitia Frumin for the maps in the book. Jim Ashton edited this volume and I would like to thank him for his efforts and collaboration.

There are a number of colleagues and friends with whom I have discussed this project and whose advice, inspiration, and support have been invaluable. I am indebted, as always, to a special person and colleague, Ioannis Theotokas, for discussions, comments, and ideas on Onassis' entrepreneurship. My thanks also to Stig Tenold for being my Norwegian "co-sailor." I collaborated with my good colleague Maria Damilakou, a specialist in Latin American history, to present a paper on the early Onassis professional life in Buenos Aires at the sixteenth annual EBHA conference in Paris in 2012 and she provided valuable evidence from her own research, which has been incorporated in Chapter 6. I would very much like to thank another special friend and colleague, Nikolaos Chrissidis, whose help and guidance in Russian history, archives, and research in Kiev, Odessa, and Rostov-on-Don have been decisive. Equally, without Oksana Iurkova I would not have been able to trace the archives on the trial of Mari Vagliano in the Russian courts; her help in the State Ukrainian Archives in Kiev was fundamental. My dear friends and colleagues Evrydiki Sifneos (1957–2015) and Evdokia Olympitou (1962–2011) heard a lot about this book over the years and gave me valuable advice; their premature absence has left an unfilled gap.

I have profited from the discussions, research assistance, and archival data furnished over the years by a number of young scholars who were PhD students when I began and, by the time this book was finished, had already received their doctorates. As they were all doing research in various archives in Greece and abroad, wherever they found the name "Vagliano" they would send me the evidence. Apostolos Delis provided me with evidence on the Vaglianos building or buying of ships from the Syros shipyards. Panayotis Kapetanakis gave me access to his database "Odysseas," concerning ships arriving to the Ionian Islands, along with some evidence from the National Archives in the United Kingdom. Dimitris Kontogeorgis brought to my attention evidence on the Vaglianos from the Archives of the National Bank of Greece. Alexandra Papadopoulou gave me, from her own research in the Coutsis Archive, on the island of Spetses, a few hundred transliterated letters from the valuable correspondence between the Coutsis shipping firm and all three Vaglianos. With Katerina Galani, we did research in the Archives of the Bank of England on Greek merchants in the City of London. Together with both Alexandra Papadopoulou and Katerina Galani we discussed theoretical approaches and presented papers at the European Business History Conferences. Anna Sydorenko helped me identify and process evidence from the Ukrainian and Russian archives and has given me another perspective of the nineteenth-century northern Black Sea ports, trade, and shipping. All of them have proved valued collaborators along the way, and I cannot thank them enough for how much they have taught me.

I would like to thank my two closest friends, Katerina Tsakona and Thaleia Spanou, for always being there. Writing this book (and others!) means that I have neglected them from time to time, and I would like to express my gratitude to both for their patience, love, and support and to tell them how much I value their friendship.

And then there is Dimitri, my husband. It is he who gives me the space, the place, the embrace, and the peace to write. This book is dedicated to our children, who have spent almost a third of their lives listening to my stories about Vagliano and Onassis and have endured a "spaced-out" mother. It is for Chrysiida, who is twenty-eight, and Niko, who is twenty-five, who have both finished their studies and are out there, to explore and conquer the world.

ABBREVIATIONS

DWT	Deadweight Tonnage
FBI	Federal Bureau of Investigation
FO	Foreign Office
GARO	Государственный архив Rostov области [State Archive of the Rostov Region, Russia]
GRT	Gross Registered Tonnage
NRT	Net Registered Tonnage
TsDIAK	Центральний державний історичний архів України [Central State Historical Archive of Ukraine in Kiev]

~

Introduction

In 1893, Panagi Vagliano foresaw the future of Greek shipping. In an interview conducted in his office in London and published in a Greek newspaper, a reporter described a casual and confident Vagliano, his "right leg folded on his left one, as he usually did, looking towards the window with a childish laugh." Vagliano told the reporter, "I imagine the Greek steam shipping colossal and the Greek shipowner so big that you cannot imagine."[1] When Vagliano gave this interview, Greek nationals owned only 1 percent of the world's shipping fleet. Eighty years later he was proved right: by the 1970s, Greeks owned the largest fleet in the world and Greek shipping tycoons were among the wealthiest people on earth. In the mid-1970s, the Onassis group of shipping companies was one of the world's ten largest independent tanker-owning companies, along with a number of other Greek shipowners.[2] According to the *Review of Maritime Transport* 2018, "Greece with 17.3% of world tonnage expanded its lead."[3]

The Greek shipping industry originated in networked family enterprises dating back to eighteenth- and nineteenth-century island shipping companies. These small, family-owned companies evolved into international trading companies like Panagi Vagliano's, and then reinvented themselves during the twentieth century into ship management and global maritime business groups like Aristotle Onassis's. *Creating Global Shipping* follows these two leading Greek firms, Vagliano's in the nineteenth century and Onassis's in the twentieth, to explain how Greek firms evolved, survived, and thrived between the 1820s and 1970s, eventually gaining international competitive advantage within the shipping sector.

---

[1] Andreas Lemos, *Η εμπορική ναυτιλία της Χίου* [*The Commercial Shipping of Chios Island*] (Chios: privately published, 1963), 407.
[2] *The Role of Independent Tanker Owners*, H. P. Drewry Shipping Consultants Ltd, London, 1976.
[3] *Review of Maritime Transport* (New York: UNCTAD, 2018), 22,29. Greece was followed in 2018 by Japan, China, Germany, and Singapore. Together, the top five shipowning countries control more than half of the world tonnage (dwt). Five of the top ten shipowning countries are from Asia, four are European, and one (the United States) is from the Americas.

The Vagliano brothers, though generally unknown to the wider public, were the first Greek tycoons of the nineteenth century. They were major ship-owners, bankers, and traders with Imperial Russia, and, in the City of London, were comparable to the Schröders and the Rothschilds. Aristotle Onassis, a more recognizable name, was the quintessence of a twentieth-century shipping tycoon. He became a household name globally, mostly through his marriage to Jacqueline Kennedy, widow of President John F. Kennedy. Both the Vaglianos and Aristotle Onassis left assets of about $2.8 billion each (in 2018 values) when they died.

My study shows how these two companies evolved as agents of the integra-tion and globalization of the world economy. Shipping enterprises have always been important agents of globalization, and the Vagliano and Onassis enter-prises reveal this crucial context. They opened new markets and linked them with the international economy, working in multiple states and surviving confrontations with many different political regimes. They managed to become competitive in the international economy by creating new business methods and organizational models, and through the formation of networks of shipping, trade, and finance. Meanwhile, Vagliano and Onassis were busy inventing – and continually reinventing – their own maritime business culture and institutions, all designed to fit global norms. Their story identifies the mechanisms, interfirm family networks, and institutional flexibility that underpinned the survival of Greek shipping. Both the Vagliano and Onassis business activities demonstrate how Greeks, by serving the sea routes of the major economic powers of the time (the British and the Russians from the 1820s and then the United States from the 1940s onwards), created the global shipping industry.

My book builds on the recent work of Michael Miller, who has sought to locate shipping and ports in the prevailing historical narratives of global business.[4] He highlights how Europeans ran the maritime world by weaving local maritime regions into an interconnected whole – a global system. Miller has provided the first integrated approach to the study of the mechanisms of shipping businesses and the contribution of maritime industry to globalization. However, Miller's work has focused on liner/container shipping, big ports, and northern European enterprises. The plethora of small-, medium-, and large-scale tramp and bulk shipping, traditionally connected with localized maritime communities and ports from the Baltic to the eastern Mediterranean and the Black Sea, has escaped the attention of historians writing about shipping. These smaller shipping communities, acting outside of the big maritime centers, are an integral and understudied part of the maritime industry.

---

[4] Michael Miller, *Europe and the Maritime World: A Twentieth-Century History* (Cam-bridge: Cambridge University Press, 2012).

Tramp and bulk shipping made possible a global supply line for basic resources like food, energy, and raw materials for industry. This book reveals how Greeks in the south of Europe contributed to the evolution of regional European maritime businesses to serve the global economy. Historically, tramp shipping, the part of the industry which carries bulk cargoes on demand, consisted of multiple small companies which were either too difficult to research or else considered marginal.[5] Tramp ships also did the dirty work of carrying bulk cargoes like coal, fertilizers, minerals, grain, cotton, or oil.[6] They carry more than two-thirds of the world's sea trade and they are highly significant in the running of the world economy. Yet despite their importance, there has been remarkably little research on tramp- or bulk-shipping companies in the last twenty-five years, with a few notable exceptions.[7] Moreover, there have been no scholarly studies of individual Greek shipping companies, partly because these were family companies with scattered, fragmented archival resources.[8] Moreover, many of the important shipowners are not easily accessible, or have not been open concerning their private lives or their business practices. It is no wonder that there are extremely few scholarly accounts of Onassis's business.[9]

Such lacunae in historical scholarship make even more glaring the fact that the history of modern bulk and tramp shipping (and, as we shall see, the global economy itself) simply cannot be written without the Greek example. Local ports and islands – small-scale loci for regional trade – triggered regional development by acting as cradles for the development of larger maritime firms,

---

[5] Gelina Harlaftis and Ioannis Theotokas, "European Family Firms in International Business: British and Greek Tramp-Shipping Firms," *Business History* 46, no. 2 (April 2004): 219–255.

[6] Gelina Harlaftis and John Theotokas, "Maritime Business during the Twentieth Century: Continuity and Change," in C. T. Grammenos, ed., *Handbook of Maritime Economics and Business* (London: Lloyd's of London Press, 2002), 9–34.

[7] With the important exception of Gordon Boyce in his *Information, Mediation and Institutional Development: The Rise of Large-scale Enterprise in British Shipping, 1870–1919* (Manchester: Manchester University Press, 1995). See also Forbes Munro and Tony Slaven, "Networks and Markets in Clyde Shipping: The Donaldsons and the Hogarths, 1870–1939," *Business History* 43, no. 2 (April 2001): 9–50. For the Norwegians, Atle Thowsen and Stig Tenold, *Odfjell: The History of a Shipping Company* (Bergen: Odfjell ASA, 2006).

[8] The only study that exists contains 150 short maritime business family histories. See Ioannis Theotokas and Gelina Harlaftis, *Leadership in World Shipping: Greek Family Firms in International Business* (Houndmills, Basingstoke: Palgrave Macmillan, 2009).

[9] See Gelina Harlaftis, "The Onassis Global Shipping Business: 1920s–1950s," *Business History Review* 88, no. 2 (summer 2014): 241–271; Geoffrey Jones and Paul Gomopoulos, "Aristotle Onassis and the Greek Shipping Industry," 9–805-141, rev. October 18, 2008, Harvard Business School; Theotokas and Harlaftis, *Leadership in World Shipping*; Gelina Harlaftis, *Greek Shipowners and Greece, 1945–1975: From Separate Development to Mutual Interdependence* (London: Athlone Press, 1993).

and through shipping articulated connections to larger financial and commercial centers. The vehicle of shipping is the European shipping enterprise, which played a key role in the promotion of regional and intercontinental trade and economic development. Ultimately, Greek ships were the vehicles of the global economy.

Creating Global Shipping begins by tracing the evolution of European shipping firms. Given that maritime Europe ran world shipping up to the end of the twentieth century, it is remarkable that the evolution of European shipping companies is still understudied. However, its "invisibility" in academic discourse is not just the result of maritime historians and economists failing to highlight their field of study in the context of more traditional analyses of economic and development. It is also a reflection of the nature of shipping itself.[10] Shipping is not easy to research. Its production (sea transport) takes place beyond national boundaries, and its income is earned abroad and thus usually removed from the economic structures of a specific country. Furthermore, the earnings of shipping companies are difficult to estimate and analyze since their activities are global. In some cases, historians have studied major shipping companies in the context of the growth of trading companies and business groups, but these histories tend to marginalize the shipping component.[11] Furthermore, the analysis of European maritime businesses has until recently been fragmented either by nation or by sector. This study places shipping at the center of the story of global economic development, and demonstrates how Greek shipping exemplified the crucial shift from regional economies to a global whole.

I identify four stages of development in the history of European shipping, the transitions between them stemming from a series of exogenous and endogenous factors. Greek shipping follows the same path. The exogenous factors come from the evolution of world shipping: in other words, the various economic, technological, and political developments that led to the specialization of world markets in liner and tramp shipping and the appropriate development of shipping firms to serve those markets.

The endogenous factors, meanwhile, can be traced within the "black box" of shipping companies themselves; "mysterious" mechanisms which this book partially pries open. My purpose, by focusing on the two case studies of the Vaglianos and Onassis, is to identify the factors that led to the creation of global shipping – in other words, the path from local to global. These factors, not surprisingly, highlight the success of the Vaglianos and Onassis as entrepreneurs. First, both recognized important opportunities and made decisive

---

[10] Gelina Harlaftis, Stig Tenold, and Jésus M. Valdaliso, eds., *"World's Key Industry": History and Economics of International Shipping* (London: Palgrave MacMillan, 2012).

[11] Geoffrey Jones, *Merchants to Multinationals: British Trading Companies in the Nineteenth and Twentieth Centuries* (Oxford: Oxford University Press, 2000), 1.

judgments, usually ones connected with risk and uncertainty. Second, each came from an institutional environment that formed and determined individual entrepreneurial ability; environments on which each tended to rely. Third, the Vaglianos and Onassis each adapted and used effective social networking in order to collect and disseminate information and use it accordingly. These personal networks were systems of information that decreased uncertainty and transaction costs. Fourth, they innovated – not only in technology but also in management. Fifth, they demonstrated the ability to raise finance. And last but not least, each displayed a distinctive business philosophy and culture, characteristic of the entrepreneur, that determined the management and organization of their material and human resources. In order to trace entrepreneurship historically one has to trace a businessman's entrepreneurial activities within the market system and within his own business; to investigate how he identified opportunities and how he assembled resources to exploit those opportunities.[12]

The Vagliano brothers represented an archetypal multinational family firm of the Greek diaspora, developing a Russian and then a British international trading company, which led the way in international networking and pioneered the business practices that continue to be used in Greek shipping companies today. They were a prime example of leadership, innovation, expansion, and readjustment of business networks. From the Ionian island of Cephalonia, then a semi-British colony, the Vaglianos started their careers as merchant captains in the 1820s, following the long maritime tradition of their island, and were able to exploit the opportunities available during the era of *Pax Brittanica* and the First Industrial Revolution. Entering into business during a transitional era for eastern Europe, they seized opportunities offered by the Russian colonization of the northern and eastern coasts of the Black Sea, which transformed the area into the world's preeminent grain-exporting market during the course of the nineteenth century. The Vaglianos were

[12] For all aspects of approaching a business see Geoffrey Jones and Jonathan Zeitlin, eds., *The Oxford Handbook of Business History* (Oxford: Oxford University Press, 2008). For entrepreneurship in Greek shipping companies see Ioannis Theotokas, "On the Top of World Shipping: Greek Shipping Companies' Organization and Management," *Research in Transportation Economics* 21 (2007): 63–93; Robert F. Hébert and Albert N. Link, "In Search of the Meaning of Entrepreneurship," *Small Business Economics* 1 (1989): 39–49; Gordon Boyce and Simon Ville, *The Development of Modern Business* (Basingstoke: Palgrave, 2002), 264–268. Also for networks in the shipping industry see Gordon Boyce, *Co-operative Structures in Global Business* (London: Routledge, 2001). See also Mark Casson, *The Entrepreneur. An Economic Theory*, 2nd edn (Cheltenham: Edward Elgar, 2005, repr. 2008), 43; Mark Casson, Bernard Yeung, Anuradha Basu, and Nigel Wadeson, "Introduction," in Mark Casson et al., *The Oxford Handbook of Entrepreneurship* (Oxford: Oxford University Press, 2006), 1–30; Mark Casson, "Entrepreneurship and the Theory of the Firm," *Journal of Economic Behavior & Organization* 58 (2005): 327–348.

among the pioneers that integrated the Black Sea grain market with the West. As they transformed themselves into a top Russian exporting house, they opened up routes to the frontier markets of Russia. They were owners of dozens of sailing ships involved in bulk shipping, invested in the new technology of steam, and invented business methods that affected not only the path of their own firm but also the entrepreneurial Greek network that they led.

The Vagliano brothers' business administration helped them to develop the necessary mechanisms to construct strong links with the powerful British economy and its infrastructure. The adoption of new technology, in the form of steamships and their operations, had long-lasting effects within the circle of their cluster group: it diffused expertise and connected it with the pulse of British economic development and industrialization. Ultimately, the choices made by this one company charted the course of their home country's national fleet in the transition from sail to steam. The Vagliano House provides a paradigm of the transformation of an island shipping company to an international trading house. The firm later reinvented itself into a major shipowning and ship-management firm based in London, providing a model for imitation by others, thus opening the path to the global routes of twentieth-century Greek-owned shipping.

Almost all analyses of Greek shipping tycoons and of the post–World War II Greek shipping "miracle" disregard the long continuity of a business in which Greeks had already developed and shown remarkable entrepreneurship and expertise. The Onassis story, presented as a paradigm of the Western capitalist rags-to-riches tale, is part of this long tradition. Born in 1904, in the cosmopolitan Ottoman port city of Smyrna, Onassis, a son of a tobacco merchant, was raised in a bourgeois milieu. He emigrated to Argentina and seized the opportunities offered by the tobacco trade there. This tranche of capital facilitated his timely entrance into shipping in the early 1930s. Onassis ensconced himself in the community of Greek ship-management offices based in London and was able to take advantage of their human resources expertise by employing experienced managers and seamen from the Ionian island of Ithaca. As an outsider in the shipping industry, he was able to recognize the strengths of traditional Greek and Norwegian shipping practices and thereby reinvent the business of oil transportation through the infrastructures of London and New York markets, as world financial and maritime power shifted from Britain to the United States. In this way, he provided a new model of exceptional organization and administration for his shipping business that remained untouched by the conflicts he later encountered. Consequently, his business organization became a model for imitation.

Onassis's entry into the shipping industry in the 1930s coincided with a transitional era for shipping within the world economy. The decline of the gigantic British shipping groups (battered as they were by the economic crisis of the 1930s), the decolonization that brought an end to the British Empire,

World War II, and the rise of oil as the world's primary energy source, all combined to transform the world's sea-transport systems, and at the same time created opportunities for the Greek shipping industry. In the immediate postwar era, Onassis was among the prime movers in tankers, ready to exploit opportunities offered by the outcome of the massive American shipbuilding programs during World War II and the spectacular rise of the global oil trade. Greek shipowners were able to exploit these opportunities far better than was the case for their main competitors, the Norwegians, who were handicapped by their nation's decision to prohibit the purchase of foreign vessels. The Greeks engaged with the United States, the world's new economic power in the wake of war, as their main trading partners, as they had done with Great Britain and Russia in an earlier period. This was the advantage of cross-border traders and of tramp owners: by serving international trade rather than the needs of a particular nation, they were able to adjust rapidly to changes in the world environment.

This book aspires to tell a new story: the emergence of global shipping enterprise through the paradigm of the growth and transformation of two Greek enterprises. It is partly due to the pioneering activities and remarkable metamorphosis of these two businesses that at the turn of the twenty-first century Greek shipowners still had the largest fleet in the world. These Greek companies were responsible for carrying on the European maritime tradition and reinventing it with their British and American partners to create the global shipping sector.

The Archival Odyssey

The first great challenge of the research into these two businesses was that there were no available and organized archives; I had to construct them. As these were network firms engaged in activities from Russia to the Americas, and therefore characterized by great mobility, I had to travel to discover their traces. In the course of a few decades of my research into Greek shipping, the Vaglianos had repeatedly caught my interest. Whether I was in Athens or London, or on whatever Greek island I wanted to research in local state or private archives for the period from the 1830s to the 1900s, there would be a Vagliano: a charter party, a letter, a crew list, a logbook, or an insurance contract. Indeed, it seemed that there was not a single part of the development of the shipping industry in the nineteenth century that was not influenced by these brothers. However, despite the Vaglianos' importance, nothing had been written apart from short biographies on their business. Greeks knew that they were important, but nobody knew their true significance. It was in the summer of 2006 at the General State Archives of the Prefecture of Cephalonia that I discovered a Vagliano Archive that included mostly business archival material from the last years of the Vaglianos' London shipping office. It contained books of correspondence of Panagi Vagliano and his nephews, leather-bound large-format books containing insurance contracts drafted by the Vagliano Bros for their own ships and for those of clients, double-entry ledgers of transactions conducted at the London office, ledgers with the transactions of the company's clients and collaborators in shipping, trade, finance, etc. There were also some twenty files relating to cases of claims from the insurance companies of several steamships, insurance contracts, excerpts from logbooks, payments of invoices for compensations, bills of lading, freight agreements, court rulings on averages, correspondence between Greek captains and the Vagliano office, receipts of suppliers, and more. The archive also contained documents on the function of the Vagliano Bequest in Cephalonia during the first half of the twentieth century. Consequently, despite its fragmentation, the Vagliano Archive provided the foundation for my research needs.

Next, to England. There was some material to be found about the Vaglianos in the National Archives at Kew Gardens, including British censuses, consular reports, naturalization of members of the Vagliano family, documents on steamship companies, and other similar historical documents. However, the most valuable find was at the Archive of the Bank of England. In huge volumes, there were tens of thousands of transactions of the accounts of the Vagliano Brothers from 1858 to 1887 – a completely unexpected harvest.[13]

I found more material in the Archives of the National Bank of Greece, where there are files with the correspondence from Andrea Vagliano in Constantinople, as he was an agent of the National Bank of Greece. The private archives of Captain Anastasis Syrmas (from the island of Andros) and Captain Alexandros Arvanitis (from Galaxidi) found in the Hellenic Literary and Historical Archive also confirmed the connections of various captains with the Vagliano family. Most precious proved to be the Coutsis Archive on the island of Spetses, which held a few hundred letters of correspondence from the Coutsis shipping firm with all three Vagliano brothers. However, the evidence above provided mainly evidence on Panagi and Andrea Vagliano. Mari Vagliano, the eldest brother and the one who initially set up the business, seemed to be lost in Russia.

It was in September 2007 that I traveled for the first time to Russia. There, in Taganrog, the adopted hometown of Mari Vagliano, I saw his house and traced his story through local and popular historical books. Mari Vagliano was referred to as the multimillionaire, the "Tsar," the great capitalist of the

---

[13] Based on the wealth of information found in the Bank of England's Archives for Greek merchant bankers who were established in the City of London, I decided to continue the research with Dr Katerina Galani in a postdoctoral research project in 2013–2015, "From Constantinople to the City of London: Greek Merchant Bankers, 1820–1880." The project was co-funded by the EU, and the Greek Ministry of Research and Development, in which I was the scientific advisor.

area. In the State Archives of the Rostov-on-Don region, I discovered details about a major trial that took place sometime in the 1880s or 1890s but nothing more, and the libraries did not have any newspaper archives for me to review. Although Russians had not forgotten Mari Vagliano, a larger-than-life figure to whom was attributed all the negative connotations of capitalism during the Soviet and post-Soviet era, there was little research about him, and hard data was frustratingly thin on the ground. What there was, was parochial and journalistic.

After correspondence with the Kharkov and Kiev archives in Ukraine, I decided to head to Kiev in June 2009. There I discovered more traces of Mari Vagliano. From 1881 to 1886, he featured in the headlines of Russian newspapers in Odessa, Moscow, St. Petersburg, Kiev, and Kharkov, to name but a few cities. There was a large file related to a court case in the Kiev Archives on "Taganrog Customs" with documents from interrogations and examinations, along with commercial documents of the daily work of the merchants and the Customs employees under accusation. Further research in Taganrog, Rostov-on-Don, Kiev, Odessa, Moscow, and St. Petersburg provided rich material and valuable statistics on the overall importance and participation of all exporters from southern Russia in value and quantity from the 1810s to 1910s. This material placed Mari Vagliano in perspective and documented his importance not only in the Black Sea region but also in the whole of Russia.[14]

---

[14] This material was further enhanced from the major research interdisciplinary and interuniversity project "The Black Sea and its Port-Cities, 1774–1914: Development, Convergence and Linkages with the Global Economy" that took place from 2012 to 2015; the project was included in the Action "Thales," financed by the Greek National Strategic Reference Framework, the EU and the Greek Ministry of Education. The project was led by the Department of History of the Ionian University, with Gelina Harlaftis as project leader. It was a collaboration, on a national level, with the University of Crete, the National Hellenic Research Foundation, the Institute for Mediterranean Studies-FORTH, the University of Thessaly, and the University of the Aegean. On an international level, it collaborated with twenty-three academic institutions – universities, research institutes, and archives – from the Black Sea countries, that is Turkey, Bulgaria, Romania, Ukraine, Russia, and Georgia, as well as from Moldavia, Norway, Italy, Israel and the United States. The collaborating group consisted of the following academic institutions: Boğaziçi University, Bilkent University, Düzce University, and 19 May University from Turkey, Bulgarian Academy of Sciences and Varna University from Bulgaria, Dunarea De Jos University of Galati from Romania, Moldavian Academy of Sciences from Moldavia, State Archives of Odessa, State Archives of Nikolaev, National Academy of Sciences of Ukraine, University of Berdiansk, University of Mariupol, and University of Kharkov from Ukraine, Russian Academy of Sciences (Moscow), Southern Russia Academy of Sciences (Rostov-on-Don), State Russian University of Human Studies, European University of St. Petersburg, and State University of St. Petersburg from Russia, Elia State University (Tiblisi) from Georgia, Jerusalem University from Israel, Southern State

My engagement with Aristotle Onassis and his shipping company was more experiential than that with the Vaglianos. In October 1968, at the age of ten, I was in the Naval Hospital of Athens recovering from tonsil surgery (my father was a naval officer). My mother brought magazines to pass the time while sitting with me. I "met" Onassis, who at the time was getting married to Jackie O on the island of Skorpios, through the lengthy articles on his life contained in the magazines. Ever since then I, along with millions of other Greeks, have followed his life.

However, writing about Onassis for this project has proved both fascinating and frustrating. As he attracted the world's attention, he was featured in the headlines of newspapers and magazines around the world for years, which means there are stories about him everywhere. There are thousands of articles (the *New York Times* alone has more than 4,000 columns on Onassis), with still more being produced more than forty years after his death. Reporters, journalists, gossip columnists, novelists, storytellers, popular writers, and moviemakers have turned Onassis into an important figure in the world's popular culture. A mythology has been built around Onassis and reproduced over the years. But for the scholar, this is problematic. Almost none of the books on Onassis are based on scholarly research; their authors include only the most general and vague references. How should the academic approach this mythology?

It was not easy, as it turned out. No company archives were available on the Onassis business, as far as I knew when I started this book. I needed to find archives elsewhere, such as those of the Federal Bureau of Investigation and the Congressional Committees on Onassis companies, along with the Lloyd's Register and those available from press organizations.[15] It was only in 2015 that I decided to apply to the Onassis foundation in the event they had any archives. I held out little hope of a response, as Greek shipping firms are notorious for being suspicious of researchers. There is no culture of maritime business archives and the knowledge related to the largest shipping fleet in the world is in danger of falling into oblivion, as it does not take care of its recent history. There is not a single shipping archive from the mid-twentieth century to the present day that is appropriately organized and open for research, in Greece or abroad. Hoping against hope, I wrote to Dr. Anthony S. Papadimitriou, President of the Alexander S. Onassis Foundation. To my amazement, he responded positively and asked me to meet him at the Foundation. What followed was beyond my expectations.

Connecticut University from the United States, and Maritime Museum of Bergen from Norway. The website is www.blacksea.gr.

[15] The FBI archives consist of two main files of about 1,000 pages each: Archives of the Federal Bureau of Investigation (FBI), "Aristotle Onassis," part 1, Bufile 100-125834 and parts 2, 3, and 4, Bufile 46-17783.

I found that he, his predecessors, and the Board of Directors of the Onassis Foundation, with respect to their heritage, have saved an impressively rich body of archival evidence from the Onassis business companies around the world. In fact they kept the records of the Onassis business from 1939 to 1975 (and after) and have gathered them together from the offices in Montevideo, New York, and Monte Carlo to Athens. The archival material, in hundreds of boxes, contained corporate books with statutes and minutes of Board Meetings of more than 200 Panamanian and Liberian companies, ledgers of monthly accounts of companies, crew and wage lists, technical specifications of ships, insurance contracts, charter parties, loan agreements, sales and purchases of ships, court cases, and the general balances of all companies. There was also the internal and external correspondence of CEOs and other high-level employees, ship logbooks and medical logbooks, indemnities of seamen, photographic material (for example photographs and booklets of ship launchings), and extracts of publications on the Onassis family. I could have drowned in all this material, to which I was given unrestricted access; it would need a few years to systematically study and process. Nonetheless, in a few months of research I was able to gather a valuable sample of the material that proved clearly what Aristotle Onassis did, how he structured his business empire, and the importance of his role in the creation of the global shipping business.

Fellow historians can understand the excitement of opening dusty boxes of unseen documents of the Onassis business for the first time after a few decades of concealment. The financial results of his ledgers were exciting enough, but it was also amusing and moving to find other, more personal, material. For example, in the files of the company that dealt with his personal expenses were the bills for Jacky O's Valentino dresses in 1970, or the monthly allowance he sent to his Norwegian first partner, Ingeborg Dedichen, in 1966, more than twenty years after their separation. In full detail, there are records of his family and house accounts around the world, while the logbook of his flagship *Christina* is also there from the beginning to the end, with detailed lists of its famous passengers. In another box, there were several books that belonged to Christina Onassis. As I was browsing a copy of Carl Bernstein and Bob Woodward's *All the Presidents' Men*, published in New York in 1974, a small note escaped the pages and fell. It was from a concierge in a hotel in New York: "RM 3903 . . . Miss Onassis. Your father called from Paris. 10.10 pm." Could it be that her father called her from the hospital in Paris? But as fascinating as they are, none of these personal items will be included in this book. What needs to be produced is not another popular interpretation and exposé of his well-known personal life, but a serious effort to understand the significance of his shipping business, and through it his contribution to global economic growth.

Many times I have thought that I should have written a novel, not an academic history, about the Vagliano family and Aristotle Onassis. A novel based on real facts, such as the excellent *The Hare with Amber Eyes* by

Edmund de Waal who, through an art collection, unfolds the history of the
Ephrussi, a Jewish diaspora trading family that started its business in southern
Russia (and, incidentally, a business collaborator of Mari Vagliano). Alterna-
tively, perhaps I could have written something like John Galsworthy's *Forsyte
Saga*. The Vaglianos resided in Kensington, and had a lifestyle equivalent to
the Forsytes, being one of the commercial upper-middle-class families of
Victorian London. Writing a multigenerational saga of rich families scattered
around the world, with descendants living on the founders' money, would
have been tantalizing.

I could also have written a novel about those family businesses in Taganrog,
Constantinople, Cephalonia, Marseilles, London, Oslo, Buenos Aires, New
York, or Monte Carlo. This is the familiar Onassis legend: lavish homes,
enormous fortunes, balls, receptions, private yachts, private islands, love
stories, and scandals. I would certainly have loved to visit the houses of my
four protagonists. To drink tea from the samovar with Mari Vagliano in
Taganrog, or coffee with Andrea in Constantinople, or in London with Panagi,
or go and listen with Ari Onassis to the Diva in the Scala di Milano. Spending
so many years immersed in the activities of these four men, I feel I have
penetrated their daily lives, walked in and out of the myth and the reality, lived
in the romance and the ferocity of more than one bygone era.

This book could also have been a good detective story. It would take place in
the Imperial Russia of the Tsars, in Victorian England, and in the Cold War
era of the United States and Soviet Union. It would follow the Russian
Imperial police putting the multimillionaire Mari Vagliano in jail and under
scrutiny, and watch his celebrated trial in the Russian courts advertised all
around Russia. It would then follow FBI and CIA agents spying on Aristotle
Onassis, or British detectives following Panagi Vagliano in the City of London.

But history can transcend the imagination of the novelist – unless we make
it so serious and scientific as to dry it out. As R. W. Southern wrote, when
historians "began to take a more prosaic view of historical facts and to
distinguish more rigorously between fact and fancy ... the end was in sight
for history as an art conceived in terms borrowed from the ancient world:
Romance became separated from History. Art and science went their different
ways to separate heavens, and history flees between the two."[16]

This book is the story of the life voyages of citizens of the world, of "polites"
(citizens, in Greek) of "cosmos" (world, in Greek), that is of cosmopolitan
people. These were citizens of a pan-cosmian (all-world, in Greek), or global
society. As the Vagliano brothers and Aristotle Onassis are connected with the
islands that claim Ulysses, Cephalonia and Ithaca, they are connected with the

---

[16] R. J. Bartlett, *History and Historians: Selected Papers of R. W. Southern* (Oxford: Blackwell
Publishing, 2004), 29.

periplous, the continuous wandering along the sea routes searching for business and profit. They all had boldness: the nerve to reach out to foreign lands and to sail in unchartered waters. Their business life stories, I submit, link us with Hellenic myth, as hands touching across a vast gulf. Myths and heroes can be prototypes to be admired or hated, and can become stereotypes and paradigms to follow or avoid. Mari, Panagi, and Andrea Vagliano managed to do this on a local, regional, national, and international basis. Aristotle Onassis made it global.

This book has taken a very long time to complete, not least because I had such good fun traveling and doing research tracing their activities that I did not want it to end. A book, however, becomes alive when it ends and follows its own path into the world. A hundred and six years after the last Vagliano's death and forty-three years after Aristotle Onassis's, I realized it is time to let it go. May the reader enjoy reading it as much as I enjoyed writing it.

1

The European and Greek Shipping Firm

The Greek shipping firm is an integral part of Europe's maritime tradition. This chapter follows the evolution of European shipping business by focusing on the Greek experience. Embedded in the distinctive Mediterranean maritime entrepreneurship, Greek shipping firms reinvented and transformed it from local to global during the last three centuries. Europe's shipping businesses thrived in small- and medium-sized ports concentrated in specific maritime regions with common characteristics and transactions, from the northern and Baltic seas all the way to the Atlantic and Mediterranean seas. As these localized shipping centers were transformed as part of the overall shift to a globalized maritime economy, some shipping firms handled the change better than others. Greek firms responded swiftly to the new economic conditions, becoming the most dynamic, flexible, and eventually the most important group of European shipping firms of the twentieth century. In the new millennium, they still are.

Remarkably, the shipping industry of southern Europe replaced northern leadership in the twentieth century. By the 1970s, the gigantic British companies that were the main international players in the shipping business in the early 1900s had been replaced by the Greeks.[1] In 1976, the list of the world's ten largest independent tanker owners and tanker-owning companies comprised five European companies, three of which were Greek: the Greek Onassis shipping group, Costas Lemos (Nereus Shipping), and Petros Goulandris sons (United Shipping and Trading).[2]

---

[1] Gordon Boyce, *The Growth and Dissolution of a Large-Scale Business Enterprise: The Furness Interest 1892–1919*, Research in Maritime History 49 (St. John's, Newfoundland: International Maritime Economic History Association, 2012): 10–11. See also Harlaftis and Theotokas, "European Family Firms." There is also a large bibliography on the big British shipping companies. For a recent overview, see Boyce, The Growth, 12; Miller, *Europe and the Maritime World*, 70–103.

[2] The other European firms were the Norwegian Sigval Bergesen (Bergesen d.y.) and the Danish A. P. Møller-Maersk Group. The five non-European shipping companies consisted of one American firm (National Bulk Carriers, led by Daniel Ludwig) and four from East Asia, indicating the dynamism of shipping development in this part of the world. These consisted of two Hong Kong shipping tycoons: Chao Yung Tung (Island Navigation

A shipping firm is the economic unit that uses the factors of production to produce and provide sea transport services.[3] It consists of a person or group of people that take the decisions for the employment (or not) of the factors of production.[4] In this context, shipowners have to decide which markets they will enter, the types of ships needed in these markets, the timing of ship investments, the sources to be mobilized to draw finance and human labor, and the kind of administration they are going to follow. Because a shipping firm is a business that operates beyond national borders and beyond its own land base, trust and communication with people of different nationalities and cultures has always been of prime importance. At the same time, the depth of knowledge required for dangerous ocean voyages meant that shipping firms initially grew and flourished in particular regions – places that developed a maritime tradition and the know-how to run ships. Maritime business grew from local, to national, to international.

Unfortunately, most histories of shipping firms have concentrated on the national perspective. Their research, for the most part, has focused on the developed northern countries and on the few large-scale liner shipping companies, with little attention paid to the smaller-scale but multiple tramp-shipping firms of both the north and south of Europe. As to more recent international developments, Michael Miller has brought out Europe's maritime tradition and the continuation of its supremacy in world shipping in the twentieth century. He has examined globalization through maritime business connections, demonstrating the dramatic changes in the organization and mechanisms of European and world shipping during the second half of the twentieth century. Miller emphasizes the importance of new leaders in the shipping industry who became agents of change, the "world connectors" and "architects of transport" of the new oil transportation era. Transporting oil safely and on schedule across the seas on ships that were huge floating reservoirs required new expertise, organization, and business processes – a metamorphosis in shipping practices.[5] The combination of new practices and new leaders transformed the shipping world.[6] The new men leaped at the opportunities inherent to oil; furthermore, Miller stresses, the "movers and shakers in tankers" were the Greeks, among them Aristotle Onassis.[7] Just as in the twentieth century, the Greek shipping firms of the nineteenth century were at the

---

Corporation), often described as the "Onassis of the Orient," and Yue-Kong Pao (World Wide Shipping Group); as well as the Japanese shipping companies NYK and Sanko. Drewry Shipping Consultants, *Tanker Shipping Report 1976*, www.drewry.co.uk (accessed September 14, 2013).
[3] Ioannis Theotokas, Management of Shipping Companies (London: Routledge, 2018), 10–12.
[4] Basil N. Metaxas, *Flags of Convenience* (London: Gower Press, 1985), 11.
[5] Miller, *Europe and the Maritime World*, 161, 95.   [6] Ibid., 377.   [7] Ibid., 309.

forefront of new modes of operation. The Vaglianos (and others) developed articulated networks and sea transport production systems in local maritime regions throughout an area encompassing the Ottoman, Habsburg, and Russian Empires. The Vaglianos, living in the age of sail and steam, anticipated and in a way prepared for the globalized maritime world of Aristotle Onassis in the twentieth century. Conduits for the integration of the economies of the eastern Mediterranean and Black Sea regions in the international economy of the nineteenth century, Greek shipping businesses expanded to all oceans in the twentieth century. From the 1820s to the 1970s, Greeks crested the wave of maritime transformation.

The changing environment of world shipping during the past two centuries puts the development of the Vagliano and Onassis businesses in perspective. The Vaglianos grew their business during the First Industrial Revolution, with its dizzying technological advances as well as unprecedented rates of trade and shipping growth. The advent of the new technology of steamships, consolidated in the last third of the nineteenth century, brought the division of world shipping into tramp and liner shipping markets. The Vaglianos were able to exploit these developments, specializing in tramp shipping and steamships.

Aristotle Onassis' business had its growing pains during the 1930s, as the world economy was torn by depression and war, and it came of age during the golden years of the period from the late 1940s to the early 1970s. During this period, Onassis leveraged his experience in the tramp-shipping sector to benefit from the oil transportation and ship gigantism that emerged after the end of World War II. He foresaw these developments in the 1930s, and was the first Greek to build oil tankers and continue to invest in them. Imitators soon flocked to try to copy his success. Indeed, Greek shipowners still represent the world's largest group of tanker owners today.

World Shipping and Shipping Markets

The basis of the global trade system at the start of the twentieth century had been consolidated in the nineteenth: industrial goods flowed from Europe to the rest of the world, while raw materials poured from all over the world into Europe. Because of these two-way flows, a small number of bulk commodities carried in massive quantities increasingly dominated deep-seagoing trade throughout the maritime world; in the last third of the nineteenth century, grain, cotton, and coal were the main bulk cargoes that filled the holds of the world fleet.[8]

Just as importantly, the ships of that fleet were increasingly powered by steam instead of wind. New technology, as was so often the case during the

---

[8] Harlaftis and Theotokas, "Maritime Business during the Twentieth Century."

First Industrial Revolution, transformed the shipping industry; the transition from sail to steam, apart from increasing the availability of cargo space at sea, caused a revolutionary decline in freight rates.[9] Europe remained at the core of the system: until the eve of World War I, three-quarters of world exports in value and almost two-thirds of world imports flowed into or out of Europe.[10] Because of steam, European ships, the largest part of the world fleet, were able to carry an increasing volume of cargo between continents with greater speed and at lower cost. By the turn of the twentieth century, Great Britain was the undisputed world maritime power, owning 45 percent of the world fleet, followed by the United States, Germany, Norway, France, and Japan. Over 95 percent of the world fleet belonged to the fifteen countries that formed the so-called Atlantic Economy; Greece was among those countries, with 2 percent of the world fleet in 1914.[11]

The Vaglianos, as Ionian British citizens, had a hand in both of these large-scale developments. They were among the first to open the south Russian frontier and eventually became the largest exporters and shipowners in an area that was the granary of Europe by the latter part of the nineteenth century. In the Mediterranean, apart from state-subsidized corporate liner-steamship navigation companies, the Vagliano brothers were the first Greek shipowners (and the largest of the independent shipowners in the eastern Mediterranean and Black Sea) to invest massively in large cargo steamships. They bought their own steamships and also financed other Greek shipowners to help them invest in steam. During World War I, the withdrawal of British ships from trade routes not directly related to the Allied cause opened Atlantic routes to

[9] See the classic studies of C. Knick Harley, "Ocean Freight Rates and Productivity, 1740-1913: The Primacy of Mechanical Invention Reaffirmed," *Journal of Economic History* 48 (December 1988): 851–875; and Douglass C. North, "Ocean Freight Rates and Economic Development, 1750-1913," *The Journal of Economic History* 18, no. 4 (December 1958): 537–555. For more recent studies, Y. Kaukiainen, "Journey Costs, Terminal Costs and Ocean Tramp Freights: How the Price of Distance Declined from the 1870s to 2000," *International Journal of Maritime History* 18, no. 2 (2006): 17–64; and Mohammed I. Saif and Jeffrey G. Williamson, "Freight Rates and Productivity Gains in British Tramp Shipping 1869-1950," *Explorations in Economic History* 41, no. 2 (April 2004): 172–203.
[10] Lewis R. Fischer and Helge W. Nordvik, "Maritime Transport and the Integration of the North Atlantic Economy, 1850-1914," in Wolfram Fischer, R. Marvin McInnis, and Jurgen Schneider, eds., *The Emergence of a World Economy, 1500-1914* (Wiesbaden: Franz Steiner Verlag, 1986), 519–544. See also Gelina Harlaftis and Vassilis Kardasis, "International Bulk Trade and Shipping in the Eastern Mediterranean and the Black Sea," in Jeffrey Williamson and Sevket Pamuk, eds., *The Mediterranean Response to Globalization* (London: Routledge, 2000), 233–265.
[11] See also Gelina Harlaftis, "The Evolution of the European Shipping Firm: From Local to Global," in Teresa da Silva Lopes, Christina Lubinski, and Heidi Tworek, eds., *The Routledge Companion to Global Business* (London: Routledge, 2019).

the neutral Norwegians and Greeks, which meant that their fleets were able to profit from high wartime freight rates (Greece entered the war in 1917). Shipping, as a derived demand, depends on trade and can suffer (but also profit) from sharp freight-rate fluctuations. Timing is extremely important to losing or amassing wealth.[12]

During the interwar period, world shipping faced severe problems stemming from contracting sea trade worldwide, as well as decreasing immigration and increasing protectionism.[13] British shipping companies were particularly hard hit, starting the long eclipse of their fleet (although it would be another forty years before Britain lost its primacy in global shipping).[14] From 1918 to 1936, the absolute size of the British fleet decreased only slightly, but as a percentage of the world fleet it plummeted from 43 to 31 percent. The decrease continued in the postwar period: by 1963, it had declined to 15 percent and by the turn of the twenty-first century to just 3 percent of the world fleet.

Other countries rushed to fill the void left by the British. The United States handed out costly subsidies to shipping entrepreneurs, raising its world share from 11 to 18 percent. In the Pacific, Japanese companies took over trade routes abandoned by the British, almost doubling their fleet in the process.[15] The Norwegians and Greeks (in tramp shipping), and the Italians and the Dutch (in liner shipping), made moderate increases.[16]

After World War II, the world fleet witnessed an exponential and unprecedented expansion: from 67 million Gross Register Tonnage (GRT) in 1937 to 146 million in 1963 and 444 million in 1992. The Greek-owned fleet led the way, rocketing from 3 percent of the world fleet in 1937 to 10 percent in 1963 and 14.5 percent in 1992.[17] The Greeks, along with the Norwegians and Japanese, gradually replaced the old guard (the British, Germans, and Americans) as the decades passed, and proved the most dynamic fleets of the second half of the century.[18]

---

[12] Basil N. Metaxas, *The Economics of Tramp Shipping*, 2nd edn (London: Athlone Press, 1981).

[13] Stanley G. Sturmey, *British Shipping and World Competition* (London: Macmillan, 1962).

[14] Sarah Palmer, "British Shipping from the Late Nineteenth Century to the Present," in Lewis R. Fischer and Evan Lange, eds., *International Merchant Shipping in the Nineteenth and Twentieth Centuries: The Comparative Dimension*, Research in Maritime History 37 (St. John's, Newfoundland: International Maritime Economic History Association, 2008).

[15] As in the Atlantic, during World War I Britain had abandoned trade routes not directly related to the conflict.

[16] Harlaftis, "The Evolution of the European Shipping Firm."

[17] Ibid. The Norwegians rose from 6 percent in 1937 to 9 percent thereafter, and the Japanese from 7 percent on the eve of World War II to more than 12 percent after the 1990s.

[18] We will examine the relative picture in the twenty-first century in Chapter 9 (see Table 9.5). Despite the growth of Asian shipping, Europe still leads the world today, and the Greeks have increased their volume and percentage even further.

The growth of the Greek shipping industry was interconnected with the most important change in global trade during the interwar period: the replacement of coal by oil as the world's leading source of energy. In 1900, coal was king, and the British, as in shipping, were the power behind the throne. The United Kingdom produced 225 million metric tons of coal in 1900, or 51 percent of Europe's production. On the eve of World War II, Britain still led the way in the coal industry, producing 42 percent of total European output in 1937. By comparison, in 1870 the production of oil was less than a million tons, and thirty years later it was still an insignificant source of energy; in 1900, world production of 20 million tons of oil met only 2.5 percent of world energy consumption.

All this changed in the interwar period. By 1938, oil production had increased more than fifteen times; it was 273 million tons and accounted for 26 percent of world energy consumption.[19] In 1900, because production was so limited, there had been little need for specialized vessels; oil tankers, mostly owned by Europeans, accounted for a tiny 1.5 percent of world merchant tonnage. Four decades later, the tanker fleet had grown to 16 percent of world tonnage. Although these ships were mostly owned by oil companies, independent tanker owners started to appear after the worldwide depression of the 1930s, when oil companies discovered it was less costly to charter tankers than to own them. The largest independent owners of the interwar period were the Norwegians.[20] It was through Norwegian shipowners that Aristotle Onassis was introduced to the oil market and its tankers during the 1930s; he was the first Greek shipowner to invest in the tanker business and led the way for the rest. The entry of other Greek shipowners into tankers defined their future in the second half of the twentieth century.

The choices and exploitation of technological advances by shipping entrepreneurs determined the path of world shipping. The first half of the twentieth century was characterized on the one hand by the use of steam engines and their gradual replacement by diesel engines, and on the other by massive standardized shipbuilding projects during the two world wars. From 1914 to 1918, 50 percent of the Allied merchant fleet was sunk (5,861 ships in total). US and British shipyards replaced this sunken fleet between 1918 and 1921 with "standard" ships that became the main cargo ship during the interwar period; these were steamships of a standard type of 5,500 grt, built on a large

---

[19] R. Eden, M. Posner, R. Bending, Edmund Crouch, and Joe Stanislaw, eds., *Energy Economics, Growth, Resources and Policies* (Cambridge: Cambridge University Press, 1981); C. Knick Harley, "Coal Exports and British Shipping, 1850–1913," *Explorations in Economic History* 26, no. 3 (February 1989): 311–338.

[20] Sturmey, *British Shipping*, 75–79. See the new book of Stig Tenold who provides the first full and comprehensive account of Norwegian shipping in the twentieth century. For the interwar period see Stig Tenold, *Norwegian Shipping in the 20th Century. Norway's Successful Navigation of the World's Most Global Industry*, (Cham, Switzerland: Palgrave, 2018): 100–115.

scale. It was these standard ships that Greek, Japanese, and Norwegian tramp operators purchased en masse from the British secondhand market in the 1930s, expanding their fleets even amid the world economic crisis. The first two steamships that Onassis bought in the early 1930s were of this kind.

During World War II, faced again with potentially crippling losses of merchant ships to German U-boats, the United States and Canada launched the most massive shipbuilding program the world had known, using new and much faster methods of building ships (the ships were assembled in sections and welded instead of riveted together). In four years, the US Maritime Commission managed to build about 4,700 vessels of all kinds, both commercial and military; out of these about 2,700 were the well-known Liberty ships that formed the standard dry-bulk cargo vessel for the next twenty-five years, and about 500 were tankers of the so-called T2 type.[21] Liberty ships and T2 tankers later formed the basis of the great leap forward of the Onassis shipping business (see Chapter 7).

The world economy grew almost uninterrupted between 1945 and 1975. Seaborne trade between the end of World War II and 1973 expanded more than sixfold by volume, from 490 million metric tons in 1948 to 3,210 million metric tons in 1973. About 60 percent of this massive expansion was caused by an almost ninefold increase in oil shipments.[22] (Tonnage of the five main bulk cargoes – ore, bauxite, coal, phosphates, and grain – also grew impressively.) To carry the enormous volumes required to feed the industries of the West and East Asia, ships carrying liquid and dry cargoes had to get much bigger. And as ships grew gigantic, they also increasingly specialized in single types of cargo and operated under flags of convenience (today called open registries) or under the auspices of offshore companies whose nationality was difficult to trace. In the immediate postwar years, such ships were used most extensively by Greek and American shipowners in the carriage of oil.[23] Aristotle Onassis, as we shall see, pioneered not only ship gigantism, but also used offshore companies and flags of convenience almost exclusively in his fleet.

Until the last third of the nineteenth century the shipping market was unified, meaning that cargoes did not determine either the type of ship or the

---

[21] Rebecca Achee-Thornton and Peter Thomson, "Learning from Experience and Learning from Others: An Exploration of Learning and Spillovers in Wartime Shipbuilding," *The American Economic Review* 91, no. 5 (December 2001): 1350–1368.

[22] Gelina Harlaftis, *A History of Greek-Owned Shipping: The Making of an International Tramp Fleet, 1830 to the Present Day* (London: Routledge 1996), 246–251.

[23] For an insightful analysis, see Alan Cafruny, *Ruling the Waves: The Political Economy of International Shipping* (Berkeley: University of California Press, 1987). For a classic work on flags of convenience, see Metaxas, *Flags of Convenience*. For the resort by the Greeks to flags of convenience, see Gelina Harlaftis, "Greek Shipowners and State Intervention in the 1940s: A Formal Justification for the Resort to Flags-of-Convenience?," *International Journal of Maritime History* 1, no. 2 (December 1989): 37–63.

organization of the trade. In the latter decades of the nineteenth century, the shipping market diverged into two distinct categories: liner shipping and tramp shipping. The type of cargo and ship determined the method of shipment; for example, liner ships carried general cargoes (finished or semifinished manufactured goods) and tramp shipping carried bulk cargoes (like coal, ore, grain, fertilizers, oil, and so forth). Furthermore, liner shipping carried cargo on regular routes, and tramp shipping on demand. Specialization of markets thus led to specialization of shipping firms in serving these two markets.

For the next hundred years, until the 1970s, liner and tramp-shipping markets continued more or less on the same lines. From the 1870s to the 1940s, the cargoes carried by liner and tramp shipping were not always clearly defined: liner ships could carry tramp cargoes and vice versa. Although there was substitution between the two distinct markets, their main structures were diametrically opposed: oligopoly and protectionism for the liner market (after the formation of shipping cartels starting in 1880, called "shipping conferences," in order to regulate freight rates and monopolize certain routes), and almost perfect competition for tramp shipping.[24] By the eve of World War I, 60 percent of the British fleet was employed in tramp shipping and 40 percent in liner shipping; the Germans and the French were primarily involved in liner shipping, while the Italians and the Spanish kept smaller fleets also engaged mainly in liner shipping. The Greeks were involved almost exclusively in tramp shipping, and, along with the Norwegians, they have remained Europe's main tramp operators.

In the postwar era, as world production and trade expanded at an unprecedented rate, more distinct changes in the structure of the markets led to a gradual decrease in substitution between liner and tramp shipping.[25] In the latter, the introduction of new liquid bulk cargoes on a massive scale, like oil, and of a few main dry bulk cargoes (coal, ore, fertilizers, and grain) led to specialization of function: individual bulk markets and ships built to carry specific cargoes.

The introduction of container ships in the 1960s revolutionized the carriage of industrial goods, world transport, and port systems. It also meant a landmark decade for the liner industry in the 1970s. Containerization, uniquely suited to liner transport, meant radically new designs for vessels and cargo-handling

---

[24] Harlaftis and Theotokas, "European Family Firms." On conferences, see Sturmey, *British Shipping*; Peter N. Davies, *The Trade Makers: Elder Dempster in West Africa 1852–1972* (London: George Allen & Unwin, 1973); Sara Palmer, "The British Shipping Industry 1850–1914," in Lewis R. Fischer and Gerald Panting, eds., *Change and Adaptation in Maritime History: The North Atlantic Fleets in the Nineteenth Century* (St. John's: International Maritime Economic History Association, 1985); Peter N. Davies, "Nineteenth Century Ocean Trade and Transport," in Peter Mathias and John A. Davis, eds., *International Trade and British Economic Growth from Eighteenth Century to the Present Day* (Oxford: Blackwell, 1996).
[25] For more on the substitution relationship of the tramp with the liner, see Metaxas, *The Economics of Tramp Shipping*, 111–116.

facilities. It led to global intermodal transportation (use of interconnected multiple modes of transportation, e.g., ship, rail, and truck), some of the earliest uses of modern information technology, and finally structural changes in the industry through the formation of consortia, alliances, and international mega-mergers.[26] Liner shipping companies were the beneficiaries of these far-reaching transformations, and they became the archetype of the globalized, multinational shipping company. If you think of modern shipping, you will likely envision gargantuan container ships and the Brobdingnagian cranes devoted to the loading and unloading of a ceaseless stream of such ships. Ocean transport happens on the largest of scales.

Nevertheless, this book is devoted to tramp/bulk shipping. Despite the importance of liner shipping companies, it is worth mentioning here that, to the present day, more than two-thirds of the volume of world trade is carried by tramp/bulk shipping and less than one-third by liners or container ships. The development of tramp shipping did not involve such innovative techno-logical developments and no dramatic changes in the organization and struc-ture of markets took place. Instead, the tramp ship was replaced by specialized bulk carriers built according to the bulk cargoes they carried, and to highly specialized dry and liquid bulk shipping markets.[27] The great technological innovation in this market was ship gigantism. The general pattern of trading, however, has not changed over the last 130 years and the tramp-shipping companies have remained, to a large extent, family businesses.[28]

The Evolution of the European Shipping Firm

Taking into consideration the above developments, I introduce a rough overall model, centered on the evolution of the European shipping firm as depicted in Figure 1.1 There are four distinct stages in the evolution of the European shipping firm: (1) up to the 1820s; (2) from the 1830s to the 1870s; (3) from the 1880s to the 1930s; and (4) the 1940s–1970s.[29] The transformation of the shipping firm from one stage to another was determined by economic and

[26] See the excellent analysis by Frank Broeze, *The Globalisation of the Oceans: Container-isation from the 1950s to the Present*, Research in Maritime History 23 (St. John's, Newfoundland: International Maritime Economic History Association, 2003). See also Marc Levinson, The Box: How the Shipping Container Made the World Smaller and the World Economy Bigger, (Princeton: Princeton University Press, 2006).
[27] Harlaftis and Theotokas, "Maritime Business during the Twentieth Century," 9–34.
[28] On family business, see Andrea Colli and Mary Rose, "Family Firms in Comparative Perspective," in Franco Amatori and Geoffrey Jones, eds., *Business History around the World at the End of the 20th Century* (Cambridge: Cambridge University Press, 2003); Andrea Colli, *The History of Family Business 1850–2000* (Cambridge: Cambridge University Press, 2003); Geoffrey Jones and Mary Rose, eds., *Family Capitalism* (London: Frank Cass, 1993).
[29] See also Gelina Harlaftis, "The Evolution of the European Shipping Firm."

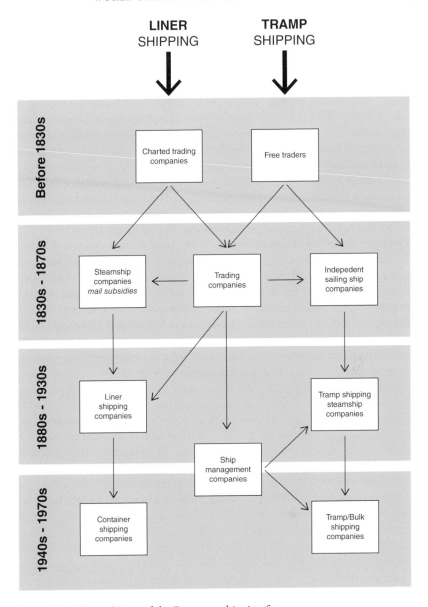

Figure 1.1 The evolution of the European shipping firm
Source: Gelina Harlaftis, "The Evolution of the European Shipping Firm: From Local to Global," in Teresa da Silva Lopes, Christina Lubinski, and Heidi Tworek, eds., *The Routledge Companion to Global Business* (London: Routledge, 2019).

technological developments. The first stage contains the forms of merchant shipping business as it developed during the early modern era. It is interesting to note that until that stage, shipping was not distinctive from trade. In fact, the term "shipowner" did not exist at the beginning of the nineteenth century in Europe's main port cities;[30] shipowning was just one role for the "merchant" or "trader," as they were typically called. Merchants' activities subsumed trade, shipping, and finance. The transition to the second stage happened in the 1820s; the exponential rise in production due to the Industrial Revolution demanded other trading business structures that led to the dissolution of the big chartered trading companies and liberalization of trade. The second stage, from 1830 to the 1870s, is characterized by a peak in sailing ship companies, the formation of big international trading companies, and the formation of the first subsidized steamship companies.

The third stage, from the last third of the nineteenth century to the 1930s, proved an important landmark for the specialization of shipping markets and the introduction of two business models: liner shipping and tramp shipping. At this stage the full effects of the introduction of steam power were evident in the transformation of the shipping industry and consolidation of the liner and tramp-shipping firm. The British, who in many ways invented the modern shipping company, dominated this steam era until the 1930s, after which Britain's loss of the world's maritime hegemony began. It was also marked by the dramatic decrease of British tramp-shipping companies, often led by single shipowners who had passed down local maritime traditions from generation to generation. This did not happen in southeastern Europe: Greek shipowners resisted this trend, as we shall see. The fourth stage was characterized by the "golden years" of the post-World War II period, the consolidation, growth, and gigantism of oil tankers and the new technology of container ships. It also marked the globalization of the shipping firm, with the widespread use of offshore companies and flags of convenience.

Until the 1820s (the first stage, see Figure 1.1), European commercial and shipping businesses in the nineteenth century developed in lockstep with their countries' colonial empires, and the inter-empire and national external trade was operated by close-knit business networks. At the beginning of the nineteenth century there were two types of enterprises in European shipping: chartered companies and free traders. The big chartered merchant companies of the seventeenth and eighteenth centuries, whether British, Dutch, French, or Scandinavian, had special trading privileges in certain countries and maritime regions. They traded, owned fleets, and financed all that mercantile activity, and as their trade became more and more regularized, they

---

[30] Sarah Palmer, "Investors in London Shipping, 1820–1850," Maritime History 2 (1973): 46–68.

increasingly resembled precursors of latter-day liner shipping companies. However, the growth of international trade during the Industrial Revolution brought with it the need for structural changes that most chartered companies were unable or unwilling to make, and by the 1820s most had disappeared.

It was independent shipowners, the so-called free traders, who developed tramp/bulk shipping. In the first stage (before the 1830s) the free-trader sailing ship constituted the first form of shipping firm. Free traders were ships outside the control of the chartered companies and were formed by shipmasters or merchants who attracted investors in partnerships.[31] At that stage, the tramp sailing ship was involved in a dual activity; sailing ships, apart from providing sea transport services, were traders. The sailing vessel was therefore also a merchant trader with two functions: commercial and maritime.[32]

In the second stage, from the 1830s to 1870s, two types of companies filled the vacuum left by the vanished chartered companies. The first type was the international trading company and the other was the steamship companies, which had obtained state subsidies to carry the mail (Figure 1.1). International trading companies followed in the footsteps of the chartered company; they were involved in trade, shipping, and finance, owned large fleets, and exploited trade links between the home country and its colonies during the age of imperialism.[33] The big British trading companies were typical of the species.

---

[31] Davis, *The Rise of the English Shipping Industry*, 84–19. See also Adam W. Kirkaldy, *British Shipping: Its History, Organisation and Importance* (London: David & Charles Reprints, 1970), 151–173.

[32] For the early modern period in Britain, see the classic Davis, *The Rise of the English Shipping Industry*, 82–83; see also the case study of the Henleys during the 1780s–1820s in Simon P. Ville, *English Shipowning during the Industrial Revolution* (Manchester: Manchester University Press, 1987). For the Dutch see Werner Scheltjens, *Dutch Deltas: Emergence, Functions and Structure of the Low Countries' Maritime Transport System, ca. 1300–1850* (Leiden: Brill Studies in Maritime History, 2015). For Venetian Greek shipping, Gerassimos Pagratis indicates that the formation and function of the shipping company in the area of the eastern Mediterranean remained impressively the same from the fifteenth to the eighteenth century. He based his thesis on the study of thousands of notarial documents on ownership, co-ownership, and partnerships of shipping firms in Corfu during 1496. See Gerassimos Pagratis, "Οργάνωση και διαχείριση της ναυτιλιακής επιχείρησης στην Κέρκυρα στο πρώτο ήμισυ του 16ου αιώνα" ["Organisation and Administration of the Shipping Firm in Corfu in the First Half of the Sixteenth Century"], *Μνήμων [Mnimon]* 30 (2009): 9–35; and also Gerassimos Pagratis, *Κοινωνία και οικονομία στο βενετικό "Κράτος της Θάλασσας": Οι ναυτιλιακές επιχειρήσεις της Κέρκυρας (1496–1538) [Society and Economy in the Venetian Stato del Mar: The Shipping Firms of Corfu (1496–1538)]* (Athens: Pedio, 2013). For Ottoman Greek shipping see Gelina Harlaftis and Sophia Laiou, "Ottoman State Policy in Mediterranean Trade and Shipping, c. 1780–c. 1820: The Rise of the Greek-Owned Ottoman Merchant Fleet," in Mark Mazower, ed., *Networks of Power in Modern Greece: Essays in Honour of John Campbell* (London: Hurst & Company, 2008), 1–44.

[33] Miller, *Europe and the Maritime World*, 112.

Although the majority of them evolved, in the twentieth century, into important multinationals with diversified and multifaceted activities, some decided to specialize in shipping. Furthermore, the fact that they started as international trading companies sometimes disguised their significant shipping dimension. For example, this was the case when Mackinnon Mackenzie founded the British India Steam Navigation Company, known as BI, one of Britain's giant shipping concerns, based in Glasgow. The same thing happened with the China Navigation Company of the Swires, based in Liverpool.[34]

The introduction of steamships and their evident advantages over sailing ships induced most European nations into a wild competition for the control of the seas. State-subsidized steamship companies sprang up all around the continent's rim, and subsidies were given mostly in the form of mail subventions by their states. These steamship companies, the second descendants of the chartered company, did not charge for carrying the mail of particular countries with which they traded, in return enjoying certain tax exemptions within these countries; their obligation was to serve a particular route a certain number of times per week or month. All European nations established steamship companies which competed in cargo and passenger transportation in both European waters and the world's oceans.[35]

"Free traders" that combined trade and sea transport sometimes evolved into international trading companies (thus overlapping in some cases with the descendants of the charter companies), but more often became independent shipping companies specializing in sea transport, owning a large number of ships, and drawing capital from their hometowns through co-ownership. Joint ownership practices were usual in the sailing ship era all over Europe. Greeks, British, Norwegians, Dutch, French, Italians, and Spanish – anywhere in Europe with a traditionally strong maritime culture – all relied on joint ownership, with its strong kinship ties and local merchant family networks.[36]

---

[34] Jones, *Merchants to Multinationals*, 31, 37–38, 166, 221; Miller, *Europe and the Maritime World*, 108; Forbes J. Munro, *Maritime Enterprise and Empire: Sir William Mackinnon and his Business Network, 1823–1893* (Woodbridge: Boydell, 2003); Sheila Marriner and Francis E. Hyde, *The Senior: John Samuel Swire 1825–98: Management in Far Eastern Shipping Trades* (Liverpool: Liverpool University Press, 1967).

[35] Ibid.

[36] Palmer, "Investors in London Shipping, Helge Nordvik, "The Shipping Industries of the Scandinavian Countries," in Lewis R. Fischer and Gerald E. Panting, eds., *Change and Adaptation in Maritime History: The North Atlantic Fleets in the Nineteenth Century* (St. John's, Newfoundland: International Maritime History Association, 1985); R. Caty and E. Richard, *Armateurs Marseillais au XIXe siecle* (Marseilles: Chambre de Commerce et d'Industrie de Marseilles, 1986), 45–46; Jesus Valdaliso, "Spanish Shipowners in the British Mirror: Patterns of Investment, Ownership and Finance in the Bilbao Shipping Industry, 1879–1913," *International Journal of Maritime History* 5, no. 2 (December 1993): 1–30; Harlaftis, *A History of Greek-Owned Shipping*, 130–142.

The watershed in the evolution of the European shipping firm happened in the third stage: the advent of steam for shipping of all types. During the last several decades of the nineteenth century, shipping companies coalesced into tramp-shipping companies on one hand and liner companies on the other – all using steam.[37] As before, connections with home ports and strong family ties provided regional sources for investment funds, not to mention control over shipping businesses themselves. Moreover, during this stage specialization in shipping, as distinct from trade, was completed. The shipping industry became an independent sector involved exclusively in sea transport services and a number of supporting companies with specialized function developed, including ship management companies, ship broking, and ship agencies, all to serve the needs of the exponential growth of international sea trade.

In order to control growing competition, the existing British steamship liner companies collaborated to form shipping cartels, the so-called conferences.[38] These were coalitions of liner companies trading in specific oceanic regions with the sole purpose of blocking new entrants and keeping the prices at higher levels. Closed entrepreneurial networks on a national and international level proved extremely important. These liner shipping companies were joint-stock companies but, in most cases, control was still in the hands of one family or one person.

---

[37] Yrjö Kaukiainen, "Coal and Canvas: Aspects of the Competition between Steam and Sail, c. 1870–1914," *International Journal of Maritime History* 4, no. 2 (1992): 175–191; John Armstrong and David M. Williams, "The Steamship as an Agent of Modernisation, 1812–1840," *International Journal of Maritime History* 19, no. 1 (2007): 145–160; John Armstrong and David M. Williams, "Technological Advances in the Maritime Sector: Trade, Modernization and the Process of Globalization in the Nineteenth Century," in Maria Fusaro and Amelia Polonia, eds., *Maritime History as Global History*, Research in Maritime History 43 (St. John's Newfoundland: International Association of Maritime Economic History, 2010); Gordon Jackson and David M. Williams, *Shipping, Technology and Imperialism* (Hans: Scolar Press, 1996). Graeme J. Milne, "North East England Shipping in the 1890s: Investment and Entrepreneurship," *International Journal of Maritime History* 21, no. 1 (2009): 1–26; David J. Starkey, "Ownership Structures in the British Shipping Industry: The Case of Hull, 1820–1916,"*International Journal of Maritime History* 8, no. 2 (December 1996): 71–95. Robin Craig, ed., *British Tramp Shipping, 1750–1914*, Research in Maritime History 24 (St. John's, Newfoundland: International Economic History Association, 2003).

[38] Robert G. Greenhill, "Competition or Co-operation in the Global Shipping Industry: The Origins and Impact of the Conference System for British Shipowners before 1914," in D. J. Starkey and G. Harlaftis, eds., *Global Markets: The Internationalization of the Sea Transport Industries since 1850*, Research in Maritime History 14 (St. John's, Newfoundland: International Maritime Economic History Association, 1998), 53–80; For classic studies on the British conference system and its drawbacks see Sturmey, *British Shipping*; Cafruny, *Ruling the Waves*, 38–70.

Tramp shipping grew in Europe's maritime regions, areas that developed fleets in small port-towns, islands, or regional maritime centers. In Britain, for example, until the nineteenth century the traditional areas of free traders were, apart from the London area, the South West ports and the West Country.[39] The Industrial Revolution changed the geography of shipping. In the nineteenth century, the main tramp-shipping areas of Britain developed along with and relied upon coal exports: The North East English ports and Wales became the main hubs of British tramp-operators in combination with those of the Clyde in Scotland, which was traditionally connected with the worldwide trading networks of Scottish merchants. All these areas had been traditional providers of shipping (like Whitby in the North East or Swansea in Wales), producing some of the best master mariners of the British fleet. Tramp sailing and steam shipping thrived and formed the largest part of the British mercantile marine up to World War I, consisting of 55 percent of the fleet.[40]

Other main maritime regions of deep-seagoing tramp sailing vessels in northern Europe, apart from Britain, included Scandinavia, with the southwestern Norwegian coast being the most prominent, and the Dutch deltas in the Low Countries. In southern Europe, deep-seagoing tramp shipping thrived in Spain, along the Basque coastline, and in Italian Liguria and the Sorrento coastline. The Adriatic Dalmatian coastline developed an important maritime culture, but the Ionian and the Aegean islands nourished the most important tramp operators of the eastern Mediterranean.[41]

Most European tramp-shipping companies were family-owned. Intermarriages among ship operators allowed them to keep the business within closed circles and expand regionally. Such strong regional ties resulted in close-knit maritime communities; for example, a shipmaster from a particular port might recruit seamen from the same port in addition to having a partnership with local investors. In Britain, tramp ships were owned by the old method of the "64th system," where the "sixty-fourthers" were shareholders of ships they held with unlimited liability; this system served well during the sailing ship era. But with the advent of steamers the cost of one share became prohibitively high (averaging as much as £300). In the late 1870s, single-ship companies of

---

[39] Craig, *British Tramp Shipping*.

[40] There has been remarkably little research done on British tramp shipping in the last twenty-five years with the important exception of Gordon Boyce in his *Information, Mediation and Institutional Development*; see also Leonidas Argyros, *Burrell and Son of Glasgow: A Tramp Shipping Firm, 1861–1930* (Unpublished PhD thesis, Memorial University of Newfoundland, 2012). The work of the path-breaking maritime historian Robin Craig has revealed the main aspects of tramp shipping; see Craig, *British Tramp Shipping*. See also Harlaftis and Theotokas, "European Family Firms."

[41] For more on the subject see Harlaftis, "The Evolution of the European Shipping Firm."

unlimited liability were introduced, producing a real boom in the market in the main tramp-shipping areas of Britain.[42]

Through this innovation, the British invented the modern form of the tramp-shipping company, which acted as the managing agent of ships owned by joint-stock single-ship companies nominally distinct from each other but with the shipowner in firm control of all. In this way, shrewd entrepreneurs could satisfy their shipowning ambitions at very little cost to themselves, by tapping sources of investment from a wider public.

The British, in their regional maritime areas, further developed the usual practice of joint shipownership during the steamship era of the last third of the nineteenth century.[43] Then, in the early twentieth century, big British firms expanded their sources of finance by exploiting resources beyond their local regions, instead seeking backing from banks that specialized in shipping finance, like the Westminster Bank or the Royal Bank of Scotland.[44] But the single-ship model still ruled in the tramp-shipping sector. In 1931–1932, 53 percent of British shipping companies owned just one ship. In France the number was 56 percent, in Norway 61 percent, and in Greece it was highest of all: fully 74 percent of Greek shipping companies owned only a single ship.[45] In Norway and Greece, the single-ship model has continued to dominate. Single-ship firms have been the basis of shipping business expansion, that is, startups of new business in shipping.

By the end of the interwar period, particularly in Britain, most of the liner and tramp-shipping firms had merged into large conglomerates. The structure of British shipping changed, leaping from private family businesses to the corporate liner companies. The economic crisis of the 1930s hit British shipping and its companies hard. In the liner business, the colossal Royal Mail group, a public company that owned 11 percent of the British fleet, collapsed, while the liner companies that retained their family character (like those belonging to shipping families such as the Holts or Furnesses) were better able to withstand the financial turbulence. British banks intervened heavily to save British shipping.[46] On the eve of World War II, the British fleet, despite

---

[42] The conversion or merger of the sixty-fourthers into firms that owned single fleets was called "consolidation" by shipowners at the end of the nineteenth century; See Boyce, *Information, Mediation and Institutional Development*, chapter four, and Robin Craig, *The Ship: Steam Tramps and Cargo Liners, 1850–1950* (London: HMSO, 1980), 40–41.

[43] See for example the example of the Radcliffe Company in South Wales. See Craig, *British Tramp Shipping*, 187–210.

[44] David Souden, *The Bank and the Sea: The Royal Bank of Scotland Group and the Finance of Shipping since 1753* (Norwich: RBS, 2003).

[45] Gelina Harlaftis and Costas Chlomoudis, "Greek Shipping Offices in London in the Interwar Period," *International Journal of Maritime History* 5, no. 1 (June 1993): 1–40.

[46] Edwin Green and Michael Moss, *A Business of National Importance: The Royal Mail Shipping Group, 1902–1937* (London: Methuen, 1982).

the loss of a large percentage, was still the leader with 28 percent of world tonnage; however, the fleet had lost what proved to be its backbone, its small-scale operators involved in tramp shipping.[47]

The interwar period marked a time of stagnation for British tramp shipping, and saw the gradual contraction of traditional tramp-shipping areas and their concentration to London. Tramp shipping declined from 55 to 39 percent of the British fleet.[48] The most important thing lost, beyond ships and localities, was the human dimension. The self-reproduction of human capital from traditional maritime communities, with their special expertise and unique business cultures, was a *sine qua non* for the continuation and expansion of the shipping industry, which was facing intense international competition during and after World War II. Instead, Britain, for the most part, lost this human capital: tramp owners whose professional origins were either from "the Counting house" or "the Hawse hole" (that is, they were employees from commercial/shipping companies like the Burrels, Jones, or Radcliffes, or master mariners like the Hains, Runcimans, Pymans, or Tatems). Greek tramp operators had similar professional origins, but retained their local knowledge.

In the fourth stage, from the 1940s to the 1970s, a large number of the European liner companies continued to function but faced major challenges due to the reduction of passenger traffic, which increasingly relied on airlines. The advent of container ships revolutionized the business and brought further deep changes. However, most of the major shipping lines still function today as global liner/container shipping groups after having undergone major restructuring in the 1970s.[49]

In the pre-1940s period (the first three stages in Figure 1.1), the tramp-shipping operators fell into two categories: cross-traders like the Greeks or the Norwegians, who carried mainly cargoes for third countries, and "national" traders like the British, Germans, French, or Italians. In both cases capital, flag, and labor came from their national state. Tramp companies had a national character, each with a particular predominant regional dimension, organized around family capitalism; however, many also participated in the international tramp markets.

After the 1940s, international trade transformed tramp shipping. During this time, many tramp operators lost their national culture and became companies of an international character. They drew resources from global capital and labor markets, and took advantage of internationalizing institutions like offshore

---

[47] One of the great failures of British tramp operators has been complacency and the lack of insight leading to a failure to adapt to the rising tanker market. See Sturmey, *British Shipping*, 61–97.

[48] Harlaftis and Theotokas, "European Family Firms."

[49] Broeze, *The Globalisation of the Oceans*; Miller, *Europe and the Maritime World*, 104–145, 319–374.

companies and competitive open registries.[50] Tramp operators were becoming increasingly globalized, losing their national character.

Except for the Greeks. Remarkably, Greek shipowners formed global businesses with a distinct Greek character; they were able to incorporate the local into the global without losing either.

The Stages of Development of the Greek Tramp-Shipping Firm

The Vagliano and Onassis companies, like most Greek tramp shipowners, followed the path of other European tramp-shipping firms, as shown in Figure 1.1; in fact, they survived through all the stages of the transformation of the shipping industry, becoming international players with an indelible Greek character. The three Vaglianos, coming from a traditional maritime family of free traders from the Ionian islands, started their careers as island shipping firms, and were able to make the great leap forward from the first stage to the second stage, becoming a powerful international trading firm involved in trading, shipping, and finance, as well as transforming themselves into a steam-shipping company during the last third of the nineteenth century. A landmark in these transformations was the creation of a hybrid Greek ship management office in London, which opened the way from the second to the third, and eventually to the fourth stages. Aristotle Onassis, meanwhile, started his tramp-steamship business in the 1930s out of a Greek London ship management office, purchased his first two ships, and started a tramp-steamship company. From there he made the great leap forward to becoming a global tramp/bulk-shipping group.

During the eighteenth and nineteenth centuries, Greek shipping fleets from the Ionian and Aegean seas competed successfully against the French, the Spanish, the Italians, and the British in the long-haul Mediterranean trade, supplying their goods and services efficiently and at low cost. Why were they so competitive against these international powers? First, they formed unique institutions and organizational structures. The shipowners of the Ionian and Aegean islands operated in a borderless and economically integrated maritime area, regardless of whether that area was under Ottoman, Venetian, French, Russian, or British control at any given time.[51] The seafarers of the area had to

---

[50] Theotokas, *Management of Shipping Companies*, 282–284.

[51] Until 1800 the Ionian islands were under Venetian control; after becoming a semiautonomous state for a number of years under Russian, Ottoman, or French protection, in 1815 they became a British protectorate and in 1864 part of the Greek state. The Aegean islands were under Ottoman Empire until the formation of the independent Greek state in 1830, when western and central Aegean became part of Greece. Before and after the Balkan wars, Crete (in 1908) and the northeastern Aegean islands (1912) were united with Greece. The southeastern Aegean islands became part of Greece in 1947.

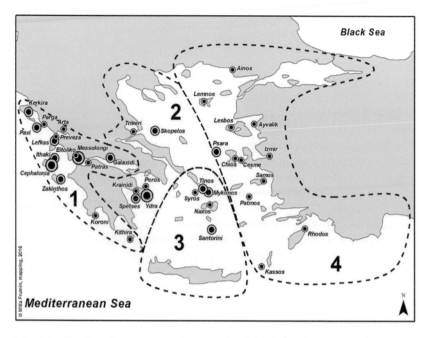

Map 1.1   The four districts of the "maritime city" of the northeastern Mediterranean
Source: Gelina Harlaftis and Katerina Papakonstantinou, eds., *Η ναυτιλία των Ελλήνων, 1700–1821:
Η ακμή πριν την Επανάσταση* [*Greek Shipping, 1700–1821: The Heyday before the Greek War of
Independence*] (Athens: Kedros Publications, 2013).

develop their own institutions and organizational structures on every island
that conformed to Mediterranean shipping practices, without relying on a
national model. As the prominent Greek historian Spyros Asdrachas has
described it, they were part of an economic entity that was, in effect, a
"dispersed maritime city" (Map 1.1). This vast city of islands formed a unified
market.[52] Its four districts, the Ionian Sea and the western, central, and eastern
Aegean, each developed several maritime centers. During the sailing ship era,
as many as forty islands and port cities developed important deep-seagoing

---

[52] In Greece, the historian Spyros Asdrachas coined the phrase "dispersed maritime city" to
stress the unity of these islands; see Vasilis Sphyroeras, Anna Avramea, and Spyros
Asdrahas, *Maps and Map-Makers of the Aegean* (Athens: Olkos, 1985), 235–248. See
also Emile Kolodny, *La population des îles de la Grèce*, Essai de géographie insulaire en
Méditerranée orientale, 1–3 (Aix en Provence: Edisud, 1974).

fleets, owned by prominent local shipping families.[53] The island of Cephalonia in the Ionian Sea had by far the largest fleet of all. It was also the original home base of the Vagliano brothers.[54]

The second factor that led to the increased competitiveness of the Greek-owned fleet was its specialization and verticalization of production, innovations that happened alongside an important technological development: the adaptation of western European sailing ship types. These new types of vessels provided flexibility and better carrying capacity and adaptability; it was during the 1790s that the Greeks began to adopt western ship types like pollacas, brigs, and brigantines.[55] The groups of family shipping firms that Greeks formed in the maritime centers of a certain region functioned as "clusters." Clusters are groups of firms nestled close to each other, their businesses interlinked and their institutional structures appropriate to a very specific economic sector. They are linked by common characteristics and businesses that supplement each other.[56] The galaxy of ancillary businesses that supplied the shipping firms was an integral part of the cluster. Through these interwoven clusters, shipping firms in Greek maritime centers increased their competitiveness via vertical and horizontal production of sea transport services.[57] As these clusters of firms interacted with each other, unifying the local markets of individual maritime regions, their seafarers tended to specialize in certain kinds of trade, or trade with a specific region.

The configuration of a specialized seafaring working force was a third determinant factor in the success of the Greek shipping firm. A stable cadre of about 18,000 seafarers spread throughout the forty islands comprising the

---

[53] Gelina Harlaftis, "Η ναυτιλία των Ελλήνων ως μοχλός ενοποίησης των αγορών. Η μεθοδολογία" ["The Shipping of the Greeks as Leverage for the Unification of Markets: Methodology"], in Gelina Harlaftis and Katerina Papakonstantinou, eds., Η ναυτιλία των Ελλήνων: Η ακμή πριν την επανάσταση, 1700–1821 [Greek Shipping, 1700–1821: The Heyday before the Greek Revolution] (Athens: Kedros Publications, 2013), 72–82.

[54] Gelina Harlaftis, "Η 'ναυτική πολιτεία' του Ιονίου και του Αιγαίου: Ναυτότοποι, ναυτικές οικογένειες και επιχειρήσεις" ["The 'Maritime City' of the Ionian and the Aegean: Maritime Centers, Shipping Families and Firms"], in Harlaftis and Papakonstantinou, eds., Greek Shipping, 353–406; Harlaftis, "The Shipping of the Greeks as Leverage," 72.

[55] Apostolos Delis, "Τύποι πλοίων της ναυτιλίας των Ελλήνων, 1700–1821" ["Types of Ships in Greek Shipping, 1700–1821"], in Harlaftis and Papakonstantinou, eds., Greek Shipping, 469–540; Apostolos Delis, Mediterranean Wooden Shipbuilding: Economy, Technology and Institutions in Syros in the Nineteenth Century (Leiden: Brill, 2016), 146–179.

[56] M. Porter, "Location, Competition and Economic Development: Local Clusters in a Global Economy," Economic Development Quarterly 14, no. 1 (2000): 15–34; Michael Porter, "Locations, Clusters and Company Strategy," in Gordon L. Clark, Maryann P. Feldman, and Meric S. Gertler, eds., The Oxford Handbook of Economic Geography (Oxford: Oxford University Press, 2000), 253–274.

[57] Amy K. Glasmeier, "Economic Geography in Practice: Local Economic Development Policy," in Gordon L. Clark, Maryann P. Feldman, and Meric S. Gertler, eds., The Oxford Handbook of Economic Geography (Oxford: Oxford University Press, 2000), 559–579.

dispersed maritime city in the Ionian and Aegean seas was a key factor in Greek competitiveness. These seafarers specialized in long-haul trips, and were trained in navigational skills onboard vessels alongside their fathers, sons, brothers, cousins, uncles, and friends. Shipping was their only way of life, their sole source of income, and a fount of personal recognition. They proved that cohesion and the flow of information in the "maritime city" gave them increased knowledge and thus the competitive advantage that allowed their vessels to compete with their western European counterparts.[58]

Fourth, Greek entrepreneurs expanded beyond their Aegean and Ionian home base – sometimes far beyond. The geographic expansion beyond the borders of the Ottoman or Venetian dominion proved a fundamental entrepreneurial strategy for the development of the sea trade and the increase in the wealth of the maritime centers. Starting in the eighteenth century, captains imitated their peers in following new and hazardous ventures, leading to a gradual expansion through imitation. When a captain returned to his island with a profit, there were many who were ready to disregard risk and follow his path.

Thus, Greek competitiveness at its heart came from the formation of entrepreneurial networks – the consequence of their creation of sea transport systems and their harnessing of an ever-increasing flow of information. Every maritime region developed information networks regarding, for example, loading places, or the times of arrival of ships. Finding new ways to get such information quickly – and spread it quickly – resulted in faster loading and unloading of cargoes; and succeeded in creating a chain of logistics in combined maritime and land transport.[59] In this way the island business groups linked local entrepreneurial activity with the periphery and with other countries through articulated entrepreneurial networks. The firms of the Aegean/Ionian maritime city exhibited a remarkable dynamism in economic development and institutional formation, as well as the ability to adjust flexibly to accommodate all economic circumstances. From the one side there were the groups of shipping firms of the islands/maritime centers of the "maritime city" of the Ionian and the Aegean seas and, from the other, the diaspora trading

[58] Gelina Harlaftis, "The 'Eastern Invasion': Greeks in the Mediterranean Trade and Shipping in the Eighteenth and Early Nineteenth Centuries," in Maria Fusaro, Colin Heywood, and Mohamed-Salah Omri, eds., *Trade and Cultural Exchange in the Early Modern Mediterranean: Braudel's Maritime Legacy* (London: I. B. Tauris, 2010), 223–252.

[59] Katerina Papakonstantinou, "Θαλάσσιες και χερσαίες μεταφορές και διακινούμενα φορτία τον 18° αιώνα: η συγκρότηση μεταφορικών συστημάτων στην Ανατολική Μεσόγειο" ["Sea and Land Transport and the Movement of Cargoes in the Eighteenth Century: The Formation of Transport Systems in the Eastern Mediterranean"], in Harlaftis and Papakonstantinou, eds., *Greek Shipping*, 283–351.

companies in the merchant communities of the Greeks dispersed along the Mediterranean and the Black Sea.[60] Long before the formation of the Greek state in 1830, Greek subjects of the Ottoman and Venetian states in the Ionian and Aegean islands had developed the so-called *fleet dei Greci* (fleet of the Greeks). By 1821, the year of the beginning of the Greek War of Independence, they owned the biggest fleet in the eastern Mediterranean and the Black Sea, comprising 1,000 deep-seagoing vessels; it was the only substantial fleet of the Levant, and ran mostly under the Ottoman flag. At the same time, the most important western Mediterranean fleets were those of Spain, France, the Italian states, the Habsburgs, and the Republic of Ragusa. The Greek fleet was the fifth largest in the Mediterranean during the last third of the eighteenth century; it underwent a remarkable fivefold growth from the mid-eighteenth century to the 1820s.[61] It was a fleet of free traders combining trade and shipping.

In the second stage of the evolution of tramp shipping, from the 1830s to the 1870s, Greek free traders evolved into international trading houses, on one hand, and sailing ship companies based on individual islands, on the other. International trading companies, the leading ones originating from Chios and Cephalonia, represented some of the most powerful of the Greek diaspora traders, expanding as they did beyond the boundaries of the Ottoman Empire and the Greek state. The international entrepreneurial networks that were formed by Greek international houses in the nineteenth century have been described as the "Chiot" network, which had its heyday during 1830–1860, with the Ralli brothers as a leading family; the "Ionian" network followed from 1870 into the twentieth century and was led by the Vaglianos.[62] Diaspora trading companies conformed to the theory that has

---

[60] Gelina Harlaftis, "Mapping the Greek Maritime Diaspora from the Early Eighteenth to the Late Twentieth Century," in Ina Baghdiantz McCabe, Gelina Harlaftis, and Ioanna Minoglou, eds., *Diaspora Entrepreneurial Networks: Five Centuries of History* (Oxford: Berg Publications, 2005), 147–169.

[61] Gelina Harlaftis, "Η "ναυτική πολιτεία" του Ιονίου και του Αιγαίου. Στόλος και ανταγωνιστικότητα " ["The 'Maritime City' of the Ionian and Aegean Seas: Fleet and Competitiveness"], in Harlaftis and Papakonstantinou, eds., [*Greek Shipping, 1700–1821*], 407–443. See also Harlaftis, "The 'Eastern Invasion'"; Harlaftis and Laiou, "Ottoman State Policy."

[62] I named them as "Chiot" and "Ionian" networks back in 1993; see Gelina Harlaftis, "Εμπόριο και ναυτιλία τον 19ο αιώνα, το επιχειρηματικό δίκτυο των Ελλήνων της διασποράς, η 'χιώτικη' φάση (1830–1860)" ["Trade and Shipping in the Nineteenth Century: The Entrepreneurial Network of the Diaspora Greeks, the 'Chiot' Phase (1830–1860)"], *Μνήμων* [*Mnemon*] 15 (1993): 69–127; and also in Harlaftis, *A History of Greek-Owned Shipping*, 39–69. The Ralli Brothers have been treated as a British trading company. See Stanley Chapman in his *Merchant Enterprise in Britain: From Industrial Revolution to World War I* (Cambridge: Cambridge University Press, 1992), chapter 5, discusses the importance of foreign merchants in British mercantile development. Jones gives us a

been developed about multinational companies, entrepreneurship, and international business.[63]

Greeks proved adept at exploiting local and international political circumstances as they expanded. The rise of the Russians as the most dynamic presence in the Black Sea after their victories against the Ottoman Empire proved very important for the Greeks. Russian dominance consolidated international trade and channeled it through the Straits and the Russian Empire conquered the lands covering the northern and eastern Black Sea coastline, from Odessa to Batoum. Greeks, who excelled in trade, shipping, and finance, handled more than half of all the external trade of the Russian Empire by the mid-nineteenth century.[64] The Greek position in the eastern Mediterranean was strengthened when the Ionian islands became a British protectorate after 1815; moreover, the formation of the newly independent Greek state after 1830 gave them the right to fly their own Greek flag.

The success of the Greek trading companies relied on their human resources. The Greek diaspora's entrepreneurial networks created a production system of close-knit small, medium, and large businesses within a loosely organized network. This commercial and maritime web assumed a triple dimension: the local/regional, the national/peripheral, and the international. It gave access to ports, agents, and financial and human resources, providing the Greek diaspora networks with the ability to internalize many operations and survive international competition. Their cohesion was derived from the business culture they inherited from the island maritime and trading communities, and, through shipping, they were able to reinvent themselves and survive economically in the international arena.[65] The trust that Greek traders

---

global view of British traders' activities and identifies the origin of important traders but still treats them as part of the British trading companies groups. Jones, *Merchants to Multinationals*, 24–25. For the Greek merchants in England see also Maria Christina Chatziioannou, "Greek Merchants in Victorian England," in Dimitris Tziovas, ed., *Greek Diaspora and Migration since 1700: Society Politics and Culture*, 2nd edn (Abingdon: Routledge, 2016), 45–60. See also Katerina Galani, Η Ελληνική Κοινότητα του Λονδίνου τον 19ο αιώνα: Μια Κοινωνική και οικονομική προσέγγιση" ["The Greek Community in London in the Nineteenth Century: A Social and Economic Approach"], *Ιστορικά* [*Istorika*] 63 (April 2016): 43–68.

[63] Mira Wilkins, *The Growth of Multinationals* (Aldershot: Elgar, 1991).

[64] There are detailed archives of the first decades of the establishment of Greeks in South Russia in the States Archives of Odessa and Rostov-on-Don. See Evrydiki Sifneos and Gelina Harlaftis, "Entrepreneurship at the Russian Frontier of International Trade: The Greek Merchant Community/*Paroikia* of Taganrog in the Sea of Azov, 1780s–1830s," in Viktor Zakharov, Gelina Harlaftis, and Olga Katsiardi-Hering, eds., *Merchant "Colonies" in the Early Modern Period (15th–18th Centuries)* (London: Chatto & Pickering, 2012), 157–180.

[65] Gelina Harlaftis, "From Diaspora Traders to Shipping Tycoons: The Vagliano Bros.," *Business History Review* 81, no. 2 (Summer 2007): 237–268. Theotokas and Harlaftis, *Leadership in World Shipping*; Casson, "Entrepreneurship and Business Culture,"

engendered among both clients and ancillary companies was fueled by this complex web of networks, by their allegiance to family and ethnicity, and by pure economic interest.

Greek shipping companies based in the Ionian and Aegean islands, still relying on sailing ships during this second stage, became the sea-carriers for the Greek diaspora trading companies, and profited enormously by the association.[66] At the peak of the sailing-ship fleet in the mid-1870s, there were about 800 shipping families in the forty maritime centers of the Ionian and Aegean seas, operating some 2,500 deep-seagoing sailing ships. Joint partnerships continued to the same degree and Masters were the appointed managers, yet as a rule they were not now the main co-owners. The growth of the fleet and its concentration in international transport altered the structure of shipowning.

During the evolution of the previous period, the island tramp-sailing-ship firms developed in a particular way. Historian Alexandra Papadopoulou, drawing from the paradigm of the maritime tradition of the Aegean island of Spetses in the eighteenth and nineteenth centuries, has distinguished the three phases of development of the family shipping firm of Greek maritime centers.[67] According to her analysis, in the first phase, the shipping firm with one ship took two organizational forms: the independent shipping firm (meaning a single person or entity who owned the ship entirely); and co-ownership of the ship. The two organizational forms are distinguished according to the nominal control of the ship (ownership) and real control (management).[68] Independent shipping firms and co-ownerships formed the "shipping house" in the second phase, its main characteristic being intergenerational continuity: the activity of at least two generations of a family in shipping activities. As she mentions, "with the term 'shipping house' we are referring to the male members of the family that are relatives of first or second rank, have the same surname and form

44–45. See also Ioannis Theotokas, "Organizational and Managerial Patterns of Greek-Owned Shipping Companies and the Internationalization Process from the Postwar Period to 1990," in David J. Starkey and Gelina Harlaftis, eds., *Global Markets: The Internationalization of the Sea Transport Industries since 1850*, Research in Maritime History 14 (St. John's, Newfoundland: International Maritime History Association, 1998), 303–318.

[66] Harlaftis, *History of Greek-Owned Shipping*, 137–139.

[67] Alexandra Papadopoulou, Ναυτιλιακές επιχειρήσεις, διεθνή δίκτυα και θεσμοί στη σπετσιώτικη εμπορική ναυτιλία, 1830–1870: Οργάνωση, διοίκηση και στρατηγική [*Maritime Businesses, International Networks and Institutions in the Merchant Shipping of the Island of Spetses: Organization, Management and Strategy*] (Unpublished PhD thesis, Corfu: Ionian University, 2010), chapter 3. See also Alexandra Papadopoulou, "From Local to Global: The Evolution of Greek Island Shipping Business Groups" (Unpublished ms).

[68] Papadopoulou, *Maritime Businesses, International Networks*, 123.

shipping firms either collaborating exclusively with each other or with the participation of others."[69] The third and final phase of the organization of island shipping companies was the business group of a maritime center, formed by the shipping firms/houses, reflecting the economic and social relations that developed among the shipping houses. The island shipping business group is linked in official and unofficial ways that are characterized by trust relations. The latter acts as a safety valve for the reduction of business risk and, ultimately, of the transaction costs. It was those island shipping business groups that configured the international entrepreneurial networks and ensured the competitiveness of the fleet. As will be indicated later, the Greek London office became a hybrid form of the ship management company of the island business group.

The 1870s marked both the growth and the decline of the Greek sailing-ship fleet; almost at the same time that the fleet peaked in 1875, it started a decline from which it never recovered. Greek deep-sea sailing vessels continued to operate to a limited degree up to World War I, but the future lay with the new technology, steam. Masters of sailing ships and investors had to find ways to enter this capital-intensive market.

In the third stage, the 1880s–1930s, the way opened to the steamship tramp-shipping era. At this stage, the new technology destroyed the old structure of regional maritime centers and brought restructuring. The familiar Greek production system, based on the two pillars of the international diaspora trading companies and the island sailing-ship companies, reinvented itself into hybrid shipping-management offices, the so-called London offices. These were both shipowning companies and shipping agencies.

From the powerful diaspora trading companies of the mid-nineteenth century, based in London, only the Ralli Brothers continued as a British trading company in the twentieth century up to the 1960s. Of the others, some went bankrupt in the 1860s–1870s, some were absorbed by banking institutions in London, and some continued trading from the Black Sea region until World War I on a more limited scale. The traders that survived through to the twentieth century were those that invested in shipping. Eight out of the top ten Greek shipowning companies of 1910 were diaspora international Greek trading companies that had been based in the port cities of the Danube, the Azov Sea, and in Constantinople (these were the family firms of the Embiricos, Stathatos, Svoronos, Scaramangas, Sideridis Dracoulis, and the Lykiardopoulos – and, of course, the Vaglianos). By the early twentieth century, half of these families had opened shipping offices in London.[70]

---

[69] Ibid., 131.   [70] Harlaftis, *A History of Greek-Owned Shipping*, Appendix 6.9–6.10.

The great innovation that the Vagliano Brothers brought about was that they set up the first London office.[71] The last Vagliano died in 1902, yet by the eve of war in 1914, there were eleven London offices that handled 20 percent of the Greek-owned fleet. By 1937, seventeen London offices handled 45 percent of the fleet.[72] These London offices internationalized and modernized parochial shipping companies in the Greek islands. It was from a London office representing the shipping firms of Ithaca that Aristotle Onassis started his fleet.

The transition from island shipping companies to tramp-steamship companies happened after steam shipping destroyed most of the small maritime centers. Out of the forty maritime islands only six managed to make the transition to steam (one or two from every maritime region). From the Ionian sea, it was the shipowners from Cephalonia and Ithaca; from the eastern Aegean, Chios and Kassos; from the central Aegean, Syros and Andros; from the western Aegean, none. Island shipping families pooled together their capital to purchase the first family steamship; individual family capital was not enough.[73]

In 1914 there were 309 Greek shipping companies owning 515 steamships of 861,080 grt. The interwar period and the formation of the Greek London offices brought expansion of the fleet to all oceans. From 1914 to 1938, the Greek merchant fleet soared from thirteenth to ninth place among the ten largest national merchant marines, accounting for 3 percent of world tonnage. More important, however, Greece now owned the second largest dry-cargo tramp fleet; its 16 percent share trailed only Britain (39 percent) and was ahead of Japan (11 percent) and Norway (8 percent). We can safely assume that the shares of the dry-cargo tramp-shipping market enjoyed by Greece, Norway, and Japan came largely at the expense of the declining British tramp fleet.

This massive expansion continued during the post-World War II global shipping period, led by Onassis. If in 1938 the number of Greek shipping offices in Piraeus, London, and other cities numbered around 300, in 1958 they exceeded 350, by 1975 they topped 800, and by the end of the twentieth century numbered more than 1,000.[74] The year Onassis died, in 1975, Greek-owned shipping was the world's largest maritime power, with more than 3,000 ships and about fifty million grt in total.[75]

---

[71] Harlaftis, "From Diaspora Traders to Shipping Tycoons," 237–268.

[72] Ibid., 194–203.   [73] Harlaftis, A History of Greek-Owned Shipping, 93.

[74] Ibid., 270–271, 289.

[75] Theotokas and Harlaftis, Leadership in World Shipping, table 3.1, 59; Gelina Harlaftis, "The Greek Shipping Sector c. 1850–2000," in Lewis R. Fischer and Even Lange, eds., International Merchant Shipping in the Nineteenth and Twentieth Centuries: The Comparative Dimension 37 (St. John's, Newfoundland: International Maritime Economic History Association, 2008), 79–103.

In the period after 1945, most of the Greek London offices were transformed into global shipowning groups, such as the Embiricos Brothers,
Kulukundis Brothers, Livanos Brothers, Goulandris Brothers, and Chandris
Brothers. One should note that all these families had more than three generations' experience in the maritime business, with the Kulukundis and the
Embiricos having at least seven generations of experience. The appearance
of new companies made necessary the distinction between "traditional" and
"non-traditional" or new shipowners. "Traditional" shipowners were at least
second generation; they inherited their shipping enterprises from their
parents. "Non-traditional" shipowners entered the sector only after World
War II and came from other professions.[76]

The only "non-traditional" shipowners in the post-World War II period
that prevailed immediately after entering the market were Aristotle Onassis
and Stavros Niarchos. However, as renewal of the shipowning community
proceeded at a rapid pace throughout the postwar period, new names gradually began to make their presence felt in the forefront of Greek-owned
shipping. The participation of the older shipowning families began to wane
appreciably after the 1980s and, in the last two decades of the twentieth
century, new shipowners held sway.[77] Path dependence provided for the
success of the Greeks in the post–World War II period.[78]

The success of modern Greek shipowners has depended on their established
worldwide networks, which functioned through a sort of exclusive international "club" of Greek shipowners that was crucial to their overall strategy
and their economic survival. Moreover, Greek specialization in tramp
shipping, dry and liquid (dry cargoes included coal, grain, fertilizers, ore etc.;
liquid cargoes included crude oil and its products) made them unique worldwide. Aristotle Onassis triggered the carriage of oil cargoes and the postwar
penetration of the tanker business. However, he was not the first Greek
shipowner to carry oil or the first to buy a tanker. Greek sailing ships and
steamships had been carrying oil from the port of Batoum (coming from the
oilfields of Baku) in the Black Sea since the 1890s.[79] As with the Vaglianos,

---

[76] See Harlaftis, *Greek Shipowners and Greece*, 9–23.

[77] Theotokas and Harlaftis, *Leadership in World Shipping*, 33.

[78] Gelina Harlaftis, Helen Thanopoulou and Ioannis Theotokas, *Το Παρόν και το Μέλλον
της Ελληνικής Ναυτιλίας* [*The Present and the Future of Greek Shipping*], Research Study
no. 10, Office of Economic Studies, Academy of Athens, Athens 2009.

[79] For example Elias Kulukundis's sailing ship *Anastasia* from Batoum to Constantinople in
1897 and the steamship *Marietta Ralli* from Batoum to Calcutta in 1895, in logbook for
sailing ship *Anastasia*, 1882–1898, Private Collection of Elias M. Kulukundis and logbook
of steamship *Marietta Ralli*, 1892–1895, Archive of Captain Anastassios Syrmas, Hellenic
Literary and Historical Archive, Athens, Greece. See also Harlaftis, *History of Greek-
Owned Shipping*, 150 and 158.

modern Greek shipping tycoons built on the rich, complex history of their industry even as they sought new ways to innovate.

Conclusions

Up until around the 1870s, Greek shipping firms in general followed the development of their European counterparts; this was the context in which the Vaglianos and Onassis shipping firms developed. However, this similar track of institutional development masks a rich, varied, and complex history that made Greek firms leaders in world shipping.

Multiple generations of Greek shipping families formed groups of businesses throughout the various maritime regions and islands of the Aegean and Ionian seas in the course of three centuries. Their success lay to a large extent in the fact that they were family businesses that retained an important connection to specific island maritime communities, each one providing a wealth of human resources and preserving a unique maritime cultural tradition. From this solid base, these firms expanded geographically to form extensive entrepreneurial networks. By developing transport systems in local maritime regions in the eighteenth century, they expanded during the new age of industrial revolution through articulated networks and sea transport production systems in a wider peripheral maritime region in the nineteenth century. The case of the Vaglianos indicates how from the first stage of the evolution of the sail-shipping firm, they made the transition to the second stage of the international trading firm, and then led the way in the third stage, to the formation of a ship-management firm.

The Onassis case indicates how, from the third stage of the ship-management firm, there was a great leap forward towards the fourth stage: the creation of the new form of global maritime business in the second half of the twentieth century. Ultimately, Greeks, by functioning as conduits for the integration of the economies of the eastern Mediterranean and Black Sea regions in the international economy of the nineteenth century, expanded in the twentieth century to all oceans, contributing to the globalization of the world's economies. The remainder of this book is about how all this was done.

2

The Vagliano Shipmasters

Creating a Business Empire, 1820s–1850s

The Vagliano Brothers is a classic case of the evolution of the European and Greek shipping firm in the nineteenth century: from free traders, combining trade and sea transport, evolving into independent sail-shipping companies specializing in sea transport by forming large fleets of sailing ships, and finally evolving into international trading companies. All three Vagliano brothers started their professional careers as merchant captains of sailing ships from the Ionian Sea. Each of them traveled for at least one or two decades between the Mediterranean and the Black Sea before settling in the city ports of Russia, France, and England to become shipowners, merchants, and bankers. I distinguish three periods in their career. The first period, which this chapter examines, covers the first thirty years of the business from the 1820s to the 1850s, and indicates its penetration and establishment in the Russian markets. The second period (which I analyze in Chapter 3), covers their geographical expansion and establishment in London, the apogee of their operation as an international trading house serving both the British and Russian empires from the 1860s to 1880s. During the third period (see Chapter 5), from the late 1880s to the beginning of the twentieth century, they specialized in shipping and led the way into the steamship era of Greek-owned shipping.

Research on the Vagliano Brothers as a prime international trading house revealed new archival evidence from the Russian archives that challenges the prevailing historiography on Russian and Greek international trading companies. The evidence it brings out is the fact that, during this period, sixty big Russian international trading companies established by traders who originated from Chios, Cephalonia or elsewhere, were first "Russian" before they were considered British, French, or Italian international trading companies. Henceforth, some of Europe's main international trading houses of Greek origin like the Ralli Brothers, Rodocanachi, or Vagliano made their wealth in southern Russia before moving to western Europe.

This chapter will cover the Vaglianos' business during the first period of their entrepreneurial activities, beginning as island shipping companies and ending as a prime international trading house in southern Russia after the Crimean War. The aim is to investigate the Vaglianos' activities in southern Russia, the Black Sea, and the eastern Mediterranean, identifying the beginnings of their business. The maritime entrepreneurial environment in which they grew marked them, as all three Vaglianos started as seamen and shipmasters, continuing Cephalonia's maritime tradition. They were able to penetrate the established commercial and maritime networks of the Greeks from Chios and Epirus and form their own entrepreneurial networks in Russia, the Ottoman Empire, and Greece. They further extended their business from the Azov to the entire Black Sea region, then into the eastern Mediterranean, the western Mediterranean, and even into northern Europe, by forming strategic entrepreneurial and societal alliances.

The Importance of Maritime Culture: From Cephalonia to the Azov Sea

The Vaglianos hailed from the village of Kerameies on the island of Cephalonia, which has had the longest and strongest Greek maritime tradition since the eighteenth century. Until the beginning of the nineteenth century, the Cephalonians were among the main transporters of the Levant sea trade to the central Mediterranean and particularly the Italian port cities. After the conquest of the northern Black Sea shores by the Russians in 1774, they turned to the maritime transport of the Black Sea and, by following the chain of immigration, they established important merchant colonies in most of the newly formed Russian Black Sea city ports from Odessa to Taganrog.[1]

The great power of the Greek island maritime centers was the transgenealogical continuity of shipping family businesses, in some cases for more than 200 years, which led to the formation of a common maritime culture within the islands. This culture was imbedded in the entrepreneurial environment that fostered the three Vagliano brothers. The centuries-long Venetian conquest of the Ionian islands meant that the Cephalonians had direct and continuous access to Adriatic commerce as well as that of Venice, along with all the Italian ports and Malta. Cephalonia was under Venetian control from 1500 to 1797. Its main wealth depended on the agricultural production of currants and olive oil on the one hand, and on maritime activities on the other. Throughout the eighteenth century, the Cephalonian seafarers managed to create the largest fleet among all the islands of the Ionian and Aegean seas.

By the beginning of the nineteenth century, 170 Greek families owned and operated large deep-seagoing vessels in Cephalonia.[2] It was the largest deep-seagoing fleet of all the islands in the Ionian and Aegean seas and formed

---

[1] On the immigration of the Cephalonians to Taganrog based on the Russian archives of the State Archives of the Rostov-on-Don region, see Sifneos and Harlaftis, "Entrepreneurship at the Russian Frontier of International Trade," 157–179.

[2] Ibid., 361.

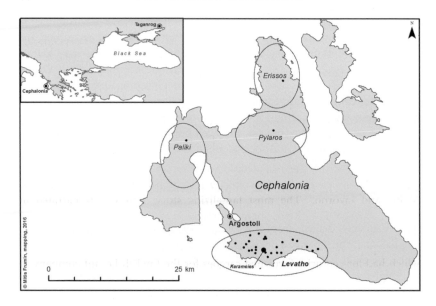

Map 2.1 Maritime Cephalonia: the Levatho region

more than 10 percent of the total deep-seagoing Greek-owned fleet.[3] Cephalonia's shipping families came from four distinct regions across the large island. Half of Cephalonia's seafaring population comes from Levatho, the "mother of seafarers" and the most famous of these regions, which nurtured an "aristocracy" of Greek seafarers (Map 2.1).[4] In the mid-nineteenth century, more than two-thirds of Cephalonian seafarers came from the Levatho region, and it produced some of the top nineteenth- and twentieth-century Greek shipowning families like the Cuppa, Inglessi, Lykiardopoulo, Vagliano, or Vergottis.[5]

By the time the three Vagliano brothers were born, Kerameies, in Cephalonia, was a village of about 500 people where members of five seafaring families lived: the Vaglianos, the Metaxas, the Kambitsis, the Lykiardopoulos,

---

[3] Harlaftis, "The 'Maritime City' of the Ionian and Aegean Seas."
[4] The twenty-five villages of Levatho: Dorizata, Fokata, Kaligata, Kastro, Kerameies, Keravados, Kleismata, Kokolata, Koriana, Kourkoumelata, Koundourata, Lakeithra, Lourdata, Mazarakata, Metaxata, Minies, Moussata, Peratata, Pesades, Sarlata, Simotata, Spartia, Svoronata, Travliata, and Vlahata.
[5] See Panayiotis Kapetanakis, Ναυτιλία και εμπόριο υπό βρετανική προστασία: Ιόνιο Κράτος *(1815–1864)* [*Shipping and Trade under British Protection: Ionian State (1815–1864)*] (Athens: EIE, 2015). For the Cephalonian shipping companies see also Gelina Harlaftis, Helen Beneki, and Manos Haritatos, eds., *Ploto: Greek Shipowners from the Late Eighteenth Century to the Eve of World War II* (Athens: ELIA, 2003) (in Greek and English).

and the Ambatiellos.[6] The Vagliano clan's long tradition of seafaring can be traced back to the eighteenth century archives of Mediterranean port cities, all the way to a Vagliano in the Venetian archives who traded from the Ionian islands to the port of Venice in 1725. There seems to have been substantial activity in Venice, particularly during the Seven Years' War (1756–1763) by a number of captains from the family: in particular Angelos, Andrea, and Theodoris Vagliano.[7] In the 1770s, Captain Dimitri Vagliano, with his vessel *La Beata Vergine di Acatisto*, and Captain Rokos Vagliano, with his ship *Madonna di Scopo e Acatisto*, were regularly plying the routes between Corfu and Venice. During the Napoleonic wars a number of Masters from the Vagliano family were active in shipping trading between the Ionian islands, Malta, and Livorno.[8] The most tantalizing story, however, is narrated in 1801 by Admiral Lord Keith about a Captain Nicholas Vagliano and his ship, flying a Russian flag, suspected of a robbery onboard an English prize.[9]

As Cephalonia was known, along with Zante, for its production of currants, which had for centuries furnished cargoes for the English Levant company, it was a common practice among Cephalonians that some of the members of each family stayed on the island as farmers, while others left to get involved in the maritime business. The father of our Vagliano brothers was Athanasios (1775–1845), who, according to the oral family history, remained on the island as a farmer.[10] Athanasios Vagliano and his wife Kerasia Kambitsi had eight children, six sons and two daughters (see Appendix 1.A, The Vagliano Genealogical Tree). The first three sons, Metaxas, Nikolaos, and Spyridon, became farmers like their father, while the other three became Masters on sailing ships and eventually formed the fraternal triumvirate that created the House of Vagliano Bros.: Marino (known as Mari; 1804–1896), Panagi (1814–1902), and Andrea (1827–1887).

---

[6] Felix Vagliano, "Livre d'or de la Famille Vagliano" (typescript, Athens, 1965), 54. I would like to thank André Marino Vagliano for sending me this typescript. Although the author of the genealogical tree of the Vagliano family, Felix Vagliano, traces the origins of the family to nobility (back to a twelfth-century Crusader French Knight), it is more probable that they are descended from one Zacharias Vagliano in the sixteenth century. For the noble families of Cephalonia see Eugene Rizo Rangabe, *Livre d'or de la noblesses Ionienne*, 3 vols. (Athens: Eleftheroudakis, 1925–1927).

[7] *Amphitrite* Database, Research Programme of the Ionian University "Greek Shipping History, 1700–1821," funded by the European Union and the Greek Ministry of Education and included in the "Pythagoras 1" Operational Programme, 2004–2007.

[8] Ibid.

[9] FO 78/33, 173–174. Letter from Admiral Lord Keith, Commander in Chief of His Majesty's Ships and Vessels in the Mediterranean (Abukir, August 17, 1801) to the British Admiralty. I would like to thank Panayotis Kapetanakis for furnishing me with this information.

[10] Interview with Spyridon Vagliano's great-granddaughters, Sophia Kostomeni and Irene Matiatos Facon, in Kerameies, Cephalonia, September 15, 2006.

By the time the Vagliano brothers were growing up, the daily lives of the villages of Levatho must have teemed with stories of seamen traveling to the Black Sea and bringing back wealth to their homes. Although there is no study available for the Greek seafarers of the early nineteenth century, from data available from the mid-nineteenth century we know that it was usual for young boys to start working onboard the family's or relatives' sailing vessels between the ages of nine and fourteen and, if they were able, to become captains when they reached eighteen or twenty.[11] With little formal education available in the villages, apprenticeship onboard was the best school. On the ships, elder seamen taught navigation and the brighter youngsters learned to communicate in Mediterranean and Black Sea languages, and mastered basic arithmetic and accounting in order to be able to handle bills of lading, charter parties, ships' expenses, basic letter-writing, and logbook entries.[12] This rough-and-ready training enabled them to manage their ships in Ottoman, Russian, Italian, French, Maltese, Spanish, or other ports. Each sailing vessel was a cradle of learning and provided a unique cosmopolitan experience that nurtured and reproduced a maritime culture from one seafaring generation to the next, also transmitting a local island pride. The endless hours onboard provided a perfect environment of self-directed teaching for those who wanted to learn. We have wonderful examples of nineteenth-century captains, supposedly illiterate, who had in fact taught themselves not only perfect Greek but also other languages, and could even translate shipping manuals from English to Greek – all made possible by shipboard education.[13]

In this way, although the three Vagliano brothers were never formally educated, their apprenticeships as seafarers and subsequent development to shipmasters (a process that took about twenty years for each) gave them ample education in the world of international maritime business. They certainly knew how to read and write in Greek and Italian, and they could also communicate basically in Russian, Turkish, French, and English. Their job was to write and read thousands of letters per year, mainly dictated in Greek and Italian. Having the right employees in all the countries where they were established, they worked and adjusted to all the rules and regulations of bookkeeping in their business.

Evidence on the early years of the three Vagliano brothers, from the 1820s to the late 1850s, is scarce, rather blurry, and at times contradictory. Greek historiography repeats the short biographies written in 1904 by a distinguished

---

[11] Harlaftis, *A History of Greek-Owned Shipping*, 171–177.
[12] See the case of Captain Anastasios Syrmas in the last third of the nineteenth century in ibid., 157–166, 172–173.
[13] Ibid.

Cephalonian scholar, Ilias Tsitselis, who was their contemporary.[14] A recent biography has corrected some of the usual mistakes repeated about their lives, mainly by using local Cephalonian archives, but it has only slightly illuminated their professional careers either on the Ionian islands or abroad.[15] I will attempt here to reconstruct the early years of their establishment when, from merchant captains, they became shipowners, merchants, and bankers, as well as providing some information on their personal lives.

A Successful Merchant Captain in the Azov: 1820s–1830s

Marinos Vagliano, known as Mari to the Greeks, "sior Marakis" to the Cephalonians, and also as "Mark" to the Russians, was born in 1804,[16] and established himself in the Azov port of Taganrog in the early 1820s. He almost certainly traveled there onboard a Cephalonian sailing ship belonging to a relative, after having worked for a number of years as a seaman in the eastern Mediterranean and the Black Sea. When he reached Taganrog for the first time in the 1820s, it was a city of 10,000; half of them were Greek, and among these was a large and affluent community of Cephalonians.[17] The destruction of the Republic of Venice in 1797 and the short-lived formation of the Ionian State of Seven Islands (1800–1807), a semi-independent state under the protection of

---

[14] Ilias A. Tsitselis, Κεφαλληνιακά Σύμμικτα: Συμβολαί εις την Ιστορίαν και Λαογραφίαν της Νήσου Κεφαλληνίας [Cephalonian Collection: Contribution to the History and Folklore of the Island of Cephalonia] (Athens: Paraskeua Leoni, 1904), 37–40. All Vagliano biographers are based on this evidence. Εγκυκλοπαιδικόν Λεξικόν Ελευθερουδάκη [Eleutheroudakis Encyclopedic Dictionary] vol. 2 (Athens: Eleutheroudakis, 1927); D. Margari, "Vaglianos," in Constantinos Vovolinis, ed., Μέγα Ελληνικόν Βιογραφικόν Λεξικον [Grand Greek Biographical Dictionary] 1 (Athens: Publication of Industrial Review, 1958]; Lemos, The Commercial Shipping, 401–402; "Vagliano Maris," in Παγκόσμιο Βιογραφικό Λεξικό [World Biographical Dictionary] (Athens: Athens Publishing House, 1984).

[15] Moschona's biography – Panayota Moschona, Παναγής Α. Βαλλιάνος: Από τη μυθοπλασία στην ιστορία [Panagi A. Vagliano: From Myth to History] (Athens: Foundation of Panagi A. Vagliano, 2008) – although it presents some new material mainly on genealogical analysis based on Cephalonian archives, is highly problematic regarding anything concerning their economic and shipping activities.

[16] All Greek sources, based probably on Tsitselis, Cephalonian Collection, 37–40, refer to the date of birth of Mari Vagliano as 1808. Vladimir V. Morozan, Деловая жизнь на юге России, в XIX-начале XX века [Entrepreneurial Life in Southern Russia, Nineteenth-Beginning Twentieth Century] (St. Petersburg: Dmitri Bulanin, 2014), 474, based on Russian Archives, refers to Mari Vagliano's date of birth as the year 1804.

[17] On Russia's southward expansion, see R. E. Jones, "Opening a Window on the South: Russia and the Black Sea, 1695–1792," in L. Hughes and M. di Salvo, eds., A Window on Russia: Papers from the V International Conference of the Study Group on Eighteenth-Century Russia (Rome: La Fenice, 1996), 123–130. See also Sifneos and Harlaftis, "Entrepreneurship at the Russian Frontier," table 9.3.

Russia, and the suzerainty of the Ottoman Empire brought about a wave of immigration to the Russian Black Sea port cities by many members of Cephalonian shipping families.[18]

Throughout the nineteenth century, the large and affluent Greek merchant community of Taganrog grew to dominate the economic and social life of the town, to the extent that in 1877 the Russian novelist Vassili Sleptsov referred to it as a "Greek Kingdom."[19] Greeks brought with them entrepreneurship: in other words, capital, technical know-how, and their networks in trade and shipping. They also promoted the economic development of the area and its integration into the world economy.[20]

The development of the city ports of south Russia was part of the strategic plan of the Russian Empire to expand southwards into the Black Sea and the Mediterranean and to create a new economic zone, specializing in the grain trade. The expansion of Russia along the southern and the eastern coasts of the Black Sea took place during the Age of Empires, a period of intense competition between the colonial western European powers to acquire new lands for exploitation of economic sources. The development of grain exports via the Black Sea was a central choice of its strategy to create a new economic zone.[21] The zone ran along the northern Black Sea coast from west to east and several hundred kilometers into the hinterland and included a fertile strip of "black soil" that was gradually totally cultivated to provide first-class grain.[22] Within a few decades the area was transformed into the granary of Europe, and covered the gubernias (provinces), as presented in the next chapter in Map 3.1, up to Caucasus. Figure 2.1 shows grain exports and ship departures from the south Russian

[18] Sifneos and Harlaftis, "Entrepreneurship at the Russian Frontier," 157–179.

[19] Letter to his wife L. F. Lomofskaya-Nelidova, October 6, 1877, quoted from A. Tsymbal, "Οι Έλληνες ως επικεφαλής της Δημοτικής Δούμας του Ταγκανρόκ" ["Greeks at the Head of the Duma of Taganrog"], in E. Sifneos and G. Harlaftis, eds., Οι Έλληνες της Αζοφικής, 18ος-αρχές 20ου αιώνα [Greeks in the Sea of Azov, Eighteenth–Early Twentieth Centuries] (Athens: EIE/INE, 2005), 181–200. See also G. Harlaftis, "Ο 'πολυεκατομμυριούχος Κύριος Μαράκης' Βαλλιάνος, το σκάνδαλο του Τελωνείου Ταγκανρόκ και οι 144 καταστροφές του Αντόν Τσέχωφ" ["The 'Multimillionaire Mr. Marakis Vagliano,' the Scandal of the Taganrog Customs Office and 144 Disasters of Anton Chekhov"], Ιστορικά [Istorika] 54 (2011): 79–122.

[20] E. Sifneos, "Merchant Enterprises and Strategies in the Sea of Azov Ports," International Journal of Maritime History 22, no. 1 (June 2010): 259–268.

[21] N. V. Riasanovsky, A History of Russia, 5th edn (Oxford: Oxford University Press, 1993), 254–275; V. N. Zakharov, "Внешнеторговая деятельностьё иностранных купцов в портах Азовского и Чёрного морей в середине и второй половине XVIII в" ["The Development of Foreign Trade by Foreign Merchants in the Azov and the Black Sea Ports in the Second Half of the Eighteenth Century"], Vestnik Moskovskogo universiteta, ser. 8, Istoria 4 (2004): 85–102; Patricia Herlihy, Odessa: A History, 1794-1914 (Cambridge, MA: Harvard University Press, 1986).

[22] David Moon, The Plough that Broke the Steppes: Agriculture and Environment on Russia's Grasslands, 1700-2014 (Oxford: Oxford University Press, 2015), 9, 47–88.

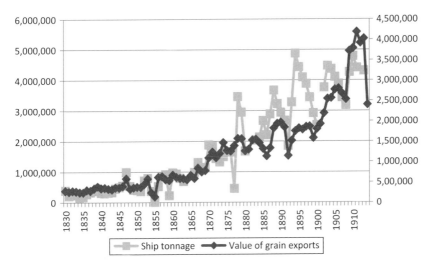

Figure 2.1   Russian Black Sea grain exports (in thousands of French francs) and ship departures (in tons) from Russian Black Sea ports, 1831–1914
Source: Socrates Petmezas and Alexandra Papadopoulou, eds., *Black Sea Historical Statistics, 1812–1914*, www.blacksea.gr.

ports. The exports of grain, with the exception of two years, indicate a steep rise in the 1830s and, after an initial downfall in the 1840s, an almost vertical rise until 1847, followed by deep fluctuations in the 1850s. As grain exports were entirely carried by ships, the same pattern is indicated in the ship departures (Figure 2.1).

The first port city to be established in south Russia was Taganrog, located in the Azov, on the northeastern part of the Black Sea coast, twenty years before the establishment of Odessa in 1794 in the northwest part (see Map 2.2). South Russian port cities became the centers of attraction for economic immigration for the mobile groups of the so-called people of the classic diaspora of the Greeks, Jews, and Armenians, as well as those of other central European groups.[23]

The young Mari Vagliano reached the Azov in the turbulent and revolutionary years of the 1820s that brought fundamental changes in southern Europe, and great opportunities for aspiring businessmen along with those changes. The outbreak of the Greek War of Independence in 1821 on the Greek mainland, which was under Ottoman rule, disrupted sea trade and ship

---

[23] Vassilis Kardasis, *Diaspora Merchants in the Black Sea: The Greeks in Southern Russia, 1775–1861* (Lanham, MD: Lexington Books, 2001); Harlaftis, *A History of Greek-Owned Shipping*, 3–38; Herlihy, *Odessa*.

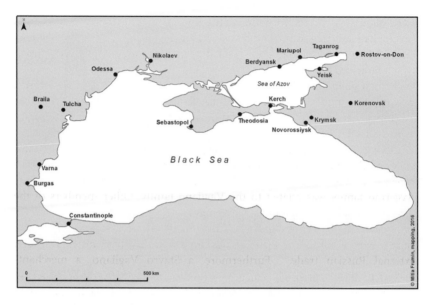

Map 2.2   The main cities from which the Vaglianos exported

employment for the seventeen-year-old Mari, involved in the Ionian/British
trade with the Black Sea. The story related by his biographers suggests that
Mari remained in the early 1820s to work with the grain merchant and
shipowner Anton Avgerinos, who was established in Taganrog.[24] As the
Russian archives reveal, there were many members of the Avgerinos family
in Taganrog during the time Mari was established there, registered to the
various ranks of Russian merchantry.

In Russia in the nineteenth century, the population was divided into four
social estates called *soslovia*: aristocrats, clergy, bourgeoisie, and peasants. The
bourgeoisie were divided into four subgroups (*sostoiania*): honorary citizens
(*pochotny grazhdanin*), merchants, lower middle class, and artisans. In order

---

[24] According to his first biographer, Mari Vagliano arrived in Taganrog in Russia in 1825.
See Tsitseli, *Cephalonian Collection*, 37–40. The same is repeated by Constantinos
Vovolinis, *Μέγα Ελληνικόν Βιογραφικόν Λεξικόν* [*Great Greek Biographical Dictionary*] 1
(Athens: Publication of Viomichaniki Epitheorisis, 1958]; and supported by Nikolaos
B. Metaxas in his *Οι ναυτικοί της της Κεφαλληνίας και Ιθάκης.Βιογραφικά στοιχεία 600
ναυτίλων, 1850–1970* [*The Seamen of Cephalonia and Ithaca: Biographical Evidence for
600 Seafarers, 1850–1970*] (Athens: Etaireia Meletis Elliknikis Istorias, 2002). However,
evidence provided by the archives of the Taganrog port Customs reveals that Mari
Vagliano went to Taganrog earlier, when he was just sixteen. He is found as "Captain
Vagliano" trading iron in the port in 1822; see GARO 584.1.1, 79. Archival evidence from
the State Archives of Rostov-on-Don Region seems to link Vagliano and Avgerino in later
years, in 1848. See GARO 558.518, 141.

to be allowed to engage in trade, a businessman had to show the authorities
that he had sufficient capital each year. According to the amount of capital he
indicated, he was classified and enrolled in the first, second, or third "guild,"
which indicated the classification of merchants. Rich merchants who remained
in the first guild for at least a decade took the title of *honorary citizen*, which
gave them a number of advantages similar to those enjoyed by aristocrats.[25] In
Taganrog there were plenty of Cephalonian merchants belonging to all ranks
of Russian merchantry.

Among the early settlers, we find a Vagliano-Avgerino member of the third
guild of the merchants, established in 1804 with 2,010 rubles as capital,
engaged in the foreign trade.[26] The hyphenated name suggests that the
Avgerino family was related to the Vagliano family. Other members of the
Avgerino family, the merchants Gerassimos and Michael Avgerino, had been
established in Taganrog since 1798; by 1800, they were second guild merchants with a capital of 8,100 rubles, and were involved in internal and
external Russian trade.[27] Furthermore, a Stavro Vagliano, a merchant-
nobleman of the first guild, resided in Taganrog in the 1820s; the same person
is referred to as handling imports and exports in a range of 150,000 to 1 million
rubles between 1832 and 1836.[28] While there is no evidence to connect him
with our Vagliano, this does provide sufficient evidence for the existence of a
thriving familial Cephalonian environment in Taganrog.

Newly ensconced in Taganrog, Mari managed to become captain of a small
coastal vessel, with which he probably worked with the Avgerinos. In the
Taganrog port archives there are multiple references from 1822 to 1830 to
Vagliano as *shkipera*, which refers either to a person responsible for the supplies
of a ship or a captain of coastal vessels involved in various activities concerning
cargoes and small vessels.[29] It seems that Mari first became "lorkatzis," as it was
known in the Greek nautical *argo* of the time – that is, a captain/owner of small
coastal Azov vessels.[30] These small vessels, called *lotka*, brought the cargoes of

[25] Alfred J. Rieber, *Merchants and Entrepreneurs in Imperial Russia* (Chapel Hill: University of North Carolina Press, 1982), xxiii.
[26] GARO 579.3.2, "List of the Merchants of the Greek Magistrate of Taganrog, 1795–1804."
[27] Ibid.
[28] *Государственная внешняя торговля в разных ее видах* [*State Foreign Trade in Differ- ent Categories*] Департамент внешний торговли [Department of Foreign Trade] (St. Petersburg, 1832, 1833, 1835, and 1836).
[29] This evidence is for the 1830s and 1840s; GARO 584.1.1, "Алфавит таганрогской портовой таможни" ["List of Taganrog Port Customs"].
[30] Newspaper Ακρόπολις [Acropolis], January 26, 1896. The article written in the newspaper on the event of his death seems to be the most reliable account on Mari Vagliano. My research in the State Archives of Rostov-on-Don (GARO) corroborated all the events referred to in the article. It seems that the journalist must have interviewed a close collaborator of Mari Vagliano.

grain down the river Don to Rostov and to the *rada* (on the roads) of Taganrog to be loaded onto larger vessels. During the 1820s, Mari Vagliano was able to create a fleet of *lotkas* and became indispensable for the carriage of grain from the river port of Rostov not only to Taganrog but also to Kerch.

Mari Vagliano seems to have had a remarkable ability to recognize opportunities and make timely decisions that defined the future of the business, in three ways. First, he exploited wartime opportunities, as well as the possibilities inherent in alignment with the Russian government and local authorities; second, he collaborated with the Cossacks of the area; and third, he timed his investment in new ships perfectly in the rising Aegean maritime center of Syros.

Mari was able fully to exploit Russian imperialism and the recurrent wars in the area, foreshadowing a particular intuition in taking advantage of all wars that took place throughout his career. The 1820s were turbulent years and there was great advantage to being in a frontier land of a rising imperial power. Russian wars with Persia, the Ottoman Empire, and Poland between 1826 and 1831 provided him with his first commercial success, as a supplier of the Russian Army, acting this time not only as shipowner and captain but also as a merchant. In 1827, "Mark" Vagliano is referred to in the Russian Archives as a "Captain" involved in Russian state sea transports on the Caucasian coast during the Russo-Persian War of 1826–1828, an activity that he must have continued during the Russo-Ottoman War of 1828–1829.[31] The year 1829 was marked by peace between Russia and the Ottoman Empire, and the Treaty of Adrianople in 1829 that opened the Black Sea ports to all vessels. The War of Greek Independence ended at around the same time, leading to the formation of the Greek Kingdom in 1830. Peace came to the eastern Mediterranean and some parts of the Black Sea, and with it a great spurt in the growth of external trade.

Until the 1880s, most of this region remained the frontier zone of the Russian Empire, and it was mainly populated by Cossacks. Cossacks in the Russian Empire were a special military estate (*soslovie*) with special privileges. There they acted as a buffer against the continuous raids of the many Caucasian tribes, and also as a permanent military force for the almost ninety years of war conducted by the Russians to colonize the eastern part of the Black Sea – the Transcaucasian area from Kuban down to Batoum from the 1790s to 1880s. By taking an active part in the Russian conquest of the northern Caucasus, Cossacks of the Don and Kuban area settled in, conquered, and expanded their lands to the south, producing millions of tons of grain (see Map 3.1).

It was with the heads and merchants of the Cossacks that Mari Vagliano seems to have developed close ties. These ties began from the 1820s when, as a

---

[31] GARO 584.1.1.

merchant captain, he provided supplies with his ships. According to the local laws, ammunition was to be traded only by Cossack merchants.[32] Vagliano's connection with the Cossack merchants lasted throughout his lifetime and ensured a constant flow of cargoes, which were directed to the Western markets.

By the 1830s, Mari Vagliano had established himself as a shipowner, merchant, and Master on sailing ships involved in the Black Sea trade serving the local Russian authorities. He is found in the service of the Governor of Taganrog in 1837, where he undertook time-charters for the Russian government, which was trying to establish itself in the Caucasus lands acquired since the Treaty of Adrianople. It seems that the sea transport of the Russian government was taken over by many Cephalonian vessels.[33] By traveling constantly in the Azov, Mari Vagliano, like his fellow Cephalonian seafarers, became familiar with the navigation of the Azov and Black Sea waters, and also came into contact with all agents, ship chandlers, warehouses in Taganrog, Mariupol, Berdyansk, Yeisk, and Kerch.

Mari Vagliano made crucial decisions regarding ship investment and the choice of shipyards during those years. When in 1827 he was in need of more tonnage, Mari turned to the Greek islands for the purchase of new ships. One must not forget that these were turbulent times in the Aegean as the Greek War of Independence (1821–1830) was still ongoing. As he needed vessels for his growing business, Mari was quick to realize the rising importance of the island of Syros in the middle of the Aegean; this is where he turned to purchase and build ships. In 1824, a new town called Ermoupolis (the city of Hermes, named after the ancient Greek god of commerce) grew on a deserted bay, a remarkable urban development formed by the flow of refugees from nearby islands during the time of the Greek revolution.[34] In this way Syros, without any prior tradition in shipping or shipbuilding during the 1820s and afterwards, drew Aegean maritime entrepreneurship and eventually became Greece's biggest economic, commercial, shipping, and shipbuilding center after 1830.[35]

---

[32] O. P. Saveliev, *Очерки по истории торговли на Дону. Общество донскихъ торговыхъ казаковъ, 1804–1904 г.г.* [*Essays on Don Trade History: Society of Don Cosack Merchants*] (Novocherkask: Printing House BN, 1904), 44–45.

[33] John Vlassopoulos, *Οδυσσέας: Ένα καράβι της Ιθάκης* [*Odysseas: A Ship of Ithaca, 1837–1841*] (Athens: Melissa, 1892).

[34] Apostolos Delis, *Ερμούπολη (Σύρος): το ναυπηγικό κέντρο της ιστιοφόρου ναυτιλίας, 1830–1880* [*Hermoupolis (Syros): The Shipbuilding Centre of the Sailing Merchant Marine, 1830–1880*] (Unpublished PhD thesis, Ionian University, 2010); Christina Agriantoni and Aggeliki Fenerli, *Ερμούπολη-Σύρος: Ιστορικό Οδοιπορικό* [*Hermoupolis-Syros: Historical Travelogue*] (Athens: EIE, 2000).

[35] Ibid.; and Vassilis Kardasis, *Σύρος: Το σταυροδρόμι της Ανατολικής Μεσογείου, 1832–1857* [*Syros: Crossroads of the Eastern Mediterranean (1832–1857)*] (Athens: Cultural Foundation of the National Bank, 1987).

Syros' archives reveal that on September 19, 1827 Mari Vagliano purchased a sailing ship of the type martigo, 62 tons from the Hydriots Lucas G. Matheos and Eletherios Eleftheriou for the amount of 9,000 piaster (or 2,070 French francs)[36] at an auction, as it was a piratical prize. Business must have proved highly profitable as in August 1828 he ordered the building of a vessel, huge for its time, in the Syros shipyards – namely, the 422 ton *Achilles*.[37] It was built by Ioannis Pagidas; Pagidas became one of the most renowned shipbuilders of Syros in the following decades. The ship took three months to build, from August to November 1828, and the contract indicates that it was 100 percent owned by Mari Vagliano of Cephalonia. Mari Vagliano was twenty-four years old.

In the 1830s, Captain Mari Vagliano, with his large deep-seagoing merchant vessel *Achilles* flying the Ionian flag, started to ply the routes from the Black Sea to the eastern and western Mediterranean.[38] More specifically, we find that he left Odessa in *Achilles* on May 20, 1830 with a cargo of grain of 2,820 chetwerts and, after calling at Constantinople on June 3, 1830 and Livorno on July 3, 1830, he arrived at Marseille on July 21, 1830.[39] That same year 116 vessels had arrived at Marseille from the Black Sea ports.[40] The purchase was very timely and it seems to have triggered a series of new purchases by Mari Vagliano. Freights in the early 1830s to 1839 increased continuously and secured the profits of his investments in cargoes and ships (see Figure 2.2).

Internal Organization: The First Regional and Peripheral Sea Transport System of the Three Brothers

The 1840s was to be a landmark decade as two of Mari Vagliano's brothers joined him in the business and formed the first internal organization of the company. All three brothers used their ships to develop a regional sea-transport system in the Azov, and a peripheral one in the Black Sea and eastern Mediterranean. Panagi and Andrea proved equally dynamic, shrewd, and successful and all archival evidence indicates a harmonious collaboration

---

[36] General State Archives, Syros, Archive of Notary Maximos Talaslis, contract no. 854, September 19, 1827. I would like to thank Apostolos Delis for this information. The piaster during this period was quite unstable. If we use its value after the 1844 monetary reform, according to which 1 gold lira = 100 piasters = 0.9 Lstg = 23 francs, then 1 franc = 100/23 = 4.35 piasters and 1 piaster = 0.23 francs.

[37] Brig *Achilles*, 422 tons, length 28.8 meters, breadth 9 meters, depth 4.7 meters. See General State Archives, Syros, *Archive of Notary Maximos Talaslis*, no. 2498, December 7, 1828. I would like to thank Apostolos Delis for this information.

[38] The brig *Achilles* was registered in the Classification Society *Bureau Veritas*, where we find it registered in 1830 and 1835 under the name of Mari Vagliano.

[39] This information is verified by the voyage details given by *Semaphore de Marseille*, 1830.

[40] Ibid.

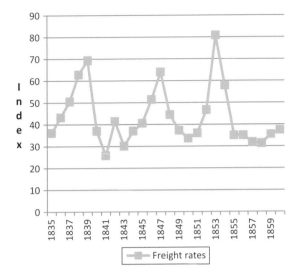

Figure 2.2   Freight rates (in shillings per ton) from Odessa to London, 1835–1860
Source: Gelina Harlaftis and George Kostelenos, "Services and Economic Growth: Estimating
Shipping Income in the 19th Century Greek Economy," working paper available in
http://hdoisto.gr/gr/library/seminar-proceedings, Appendix II; calculations based for the period
1835–1857, The National Archives, Washington, "Despatches from United States Consuls in
Odessa," vols. 1–2, May 1831–January 1858. For the period 1850–1913, C. Knick Harley, "Coal
Exports and British Shipping, 1850–1913," *Explorations in Economic History* 26 (1989): 311–338.
For the period 1869–1914, E. A. V. Angier, *Fifty Years' Freights, 1869–1919* (London:
Fairplay, 1920).

between the brothers. Panagi Vagliano, born in 1814, went to sea in 1828 at
the usual age of fourteen onboard the Cephalonian vessel of Vergottis and
joined his brother in the Azov.[41] By the early 1830s, he was acting as a
merchant captain carrying the cargoes of the trading business his brother
Mari had set up on the axis of the Azov-Constantinople-Ionian islands. In
May 1834, we find him arriving at Taganrog as a merchant captain with the
ship *Rosa*, 196 tons, with a crew of fourteen seamen, bringing wine and oil
from the Ionian islands via Constantinople (Appendix 1.B). For the return
cargo, the ship would be loaded with the new season's grain for the Ionian
islands. The youngest brother, Andrea, born in 1827, left Cephalonia in 1840,
at the age of thirteen, to join Mari in the Azov and soon proved a trusted
Master of his brother's sailing vessels. Andrea "left in secret the house of his
parents, went to Argostoli, and swam, with a bundle of clothes tied on his back

[41] That Panagi joined shortly his brother Mari in the Azov is mentioned by Tsitselis,
Cephalonian Collection, 37–40.

to a sailing ship that was sailing for Russia."[42] When Andrea joined the business in the early 1840s, Panagi spent more time in the Ionian islands trying to sell cargoes to other western Mediterranean and European destinations; he also traveled between Zante, Cephalonia, and Corfu from 1846 to 1849, coordinating the business.[43]

In the 1840s the three brothers, working as merchant captains, created the transport and trading system on which their business was founded. Mari was able through shipping to penetrate the transport system of the Azov Sea and eventually to gather cargoes of grain directly from the hinterland. His brother Panagi, based in Cephalonia and Zante in the 1840s, carried and, more importantly, promoted and sold to the western Mediterranean ports at good prices cargoes sent by his brother to the foreland. Andrea acted for a number of years as a sea transporter of cargoes between his two brothers, as a Master of vessels they owned, until he was established in Constantinople in 1849. In Constantinople he acted as provider, charterer of ships for cargoes on their own account, or on account of others for whom he acted as agent. The Vaglianos owned an ever-growing fleet of sailing vessels. The two vessels purchased and built by Mari Vagliano in 1827 and 1828 had by the 1840s become seven, and the three brothers acted as Masters but also hired others to run the extra vessels (see Appendices 1.B and 1.D). In order to control additional fleets to handle extra cargoes, they lent money to other Cephalonians to purchase vessels and merchandise. Therefore, they acted as financiers not only of their own trade and shipping but also for a large number of other Greeks.

Mari Vagliano was remarkably active and mobile. He learned all the problems of the ports of the Azov Sea, which were muddy and shallow, subject to much wind and bad weather during the winter, and frozen for five months.[44] He developed a system to bypass these problems by establishing an agency in Kerch to control the business both of the big deep-seagoing vessels and various short-sea shipping and lighter vessels. The town of Kerch, opened to external trade in 1822 (almost upon Mari's arrival in the Azov), was highly important; it dominated the straits that allowed communication between the Azov and the Black Sea, and ship captains were forced to load or reload their cargoes in order to pass the straits. Mari appears as "Mark" Vagliano, first guild merchant of Kerch (see Table 2.1).[45] In the 1840s when the city of Yeisk was created, Mari Vagliano also established himself as a merchant enrolled there. A number of other merchants did the same, which

[42] Ibid.   [43] Moschona, *Panagi A. Vagliano*, 30.
[44] Black Sea Pilot, *The Dardanelles, Sea of Marmara, Bosporus, Black Sea and Sea of Azov* (Washington, DC: Washington Printing Office, 1927), 42–43, 45.
[45] From 1847 to 1857 we find him as a "Kertch merchant" in GARO, 584.1.1.

Table 2.1 *Mari Vagliano as a merchant of the Russian Empire, 1851–1863*

	Name[a]	Where registered	Guild	Where traded	Imports	Exports	Total (in rubles)
1851	Vagliano Marko	Kerch	First	Taganrog	131,704	227,330	359,034
1852	Vagliano Marko	Kerch	First	Taganrog	130,182	547,100	677,282
1853	Vagliano Marko	Kerch	First	Taganrog	247,919	670,144	918,063
1854	Vagliano Marko	Kerch	First	Taganrog	314,742	202,818	517,560
1855	Vagliano Mari	Yeisk	First	Ismail	46,290	52,609	159,666
	Vagliano Marko	Kerch	First	Taganrog	60,767	······	
1856	Vagliano Mark	Yeisk	First	Taganrog			2,160,967
1858	Vagliano Mark	Yeisk	First	Taganrog and Ismail	427,781	711,114	1,135,895
1861	Vagliano Mark	Yeisk	First	Rostov	625,398	78,569	2,448,814
		Taganrog	First	Berdyansk, Taganrog		1,744,847	
1862	Vagliano Mark	Taganrog	First	Taganrog, Mariupol, Berdyansk, Rostov	792,364	1,765,613	2,557,977
1863	Vagliano Mark	Taganrog	First	Taganrog, Mariupol, Rostov	1,138,105	1,723,084	2,861,189

[a] In the Russian Archives Mari or Marino Vagliano is mentioned as Mark or Marko Vagliano.

Source: Государственная внешняя торговля в разных ее видах [State Foreign Trade in Different Categories] (St. Petersburg: Department of Foreign Trade, 1851–1862), Список купчам, [List of Merchants], Table XLII, 1851–1862. Виды государственной внешней торговли за 1863 год [Categories of State Foreign Trade, 1863], St. Petersburg.

probably meant that they were given incentives to do so. As Yeisk lies at the western side of the Sea of Azov, near the town of Taganrog, it probably proved highly useful; it has a passage that is suitable only for small coasters and vessels and is a fairway channel to the town of Taganrog.

Merchant shipping during that time involved both carrying cargoes for others on freight rates, and trading on one's own account. During this time, the three brothers were able to develop by trading and transporting their own cargoes on their own ships. The voyages and trade of their own cargoes in the 1840s must have been highly lucrative, particularly during the period of high freight rates during 1844–1847 (see Figure 2.2). Their first breakthrough came in the 1840s and particularly 1847–1848 following the huge rise in demand for grain in western Europe, which consolidated their establishment in the sea-trading route along the Azov-Constantinople-Zante axis. Zante, a known emporium of the Levant trade for the British in the mid-Mediterranean, provided a booming intermediate market, a satellite of Constantinople as a distribution center for the promotion of Black Sea grain cargoes to the West. Zante was also an intermediate port of call for cargoes of the Vagliano House in the so-called cargo trade.

Following the methods of the time then, the three Vagliano brothers developed a synchronized and complementary shipping and trading system.[46] Mari Vagliano, based in Taganrog as shipowner and acting as merchant also from Kerch, Taganrog and Yeisk, provided the grain cargoes to be disposed by Panagi in Zante or other Ionian islands. Mari then prepurchased the harvest of the Azov hinterland from the Cossacks for himself or for other Greeks, which he loaded onto his own ships or chartered others waiting outside the port of Taganrog. He then sent the cargoes to his brother Panagi in Zante, a "port of call" or "port of orders" (i.e., a point where ships were to be notified of their final destination).

Panagi Vagliano must have been very successful in promoting the grain cargoes in the Mediterranean markets. He established his presence in the 1840s in Zante, where he must have traveled with his coastal boat among the islands in search of purchasers and information.[47] The brothers probably also used a warehouse in Zante or Cephalonia to store grain in order to profit from the varying prices. Moreover, the younger brother Andrea proved a reliable captain, able to carry the grain cargoes from the Azov to the Ionian

[46] Harlaftis, *A History of Greek-Owned Shipping*, 59–60.
[47] His presence in Zante is confirmed by a letter from Maris Vagliano on April 4, 1848 to the merchant Petros N. Stamatopoulos from the island of Lefkada, to whom he sends Russian grain and refers to his brother Panagi, "who is present at the islands." This letter lies in the Administrative Panagi Vagliano Bequest in Argostoli and is referred to in Moschona, *Panagi A. Vaglianos*, 32.

Sea on one of their own vessels, and transport them to the Ionian islands. Mari Vagliano was established in Taganrog but also continued carrying his own cargoes on one of his ships as Master, when needed. For example, he commanded the 92-ton brig *Sophia* carrying the Russian flag in June and July of 1850 from Constantinople to Zante and Cephalonia (see Appendix 1.B).

The Crimean War was a turning point in the history of the Vagliano House; this is when Mari Vagliano grabbed the opportunities provided by a fortuitous confluence of historical events. Russia prohibited grain exports in March 1854 from its ports, both to secure grain for its own troops and to cause problems for European markets, where the demand for grain was very high during the bad harvest years of 1853 and 1854. Things became difficult for Greek merchants and shipowners between April 1854 and May 1855, as the Ottomans also prohibited Greek ships from trading in Ottoman ports. The Greek government, however, signed a treaty for trade and shipping with both the Ottoman and Russian Empires in May 1855; in the latter case, Greek ships could carry exports of grain from Russia only under the condition that these went to neutral countries.[48] As there were no alternative sources of grain for Europe, grain prices doubled along with the freight rates (Figure 2.2).

Mari Vagliano profited from the war in three ways. First, he was able to provide the Russian army in Sebastopol with food, clothes (particularly furs), and ammunition.[49] The second way he profited was by illegally directing exports of cereals while war was being waged. The big Greek merchants from south Russia promoted grain from both Russian and Danubian ports to the Greek port of Syros and from there reexported them to the Ottoman Empire or elsewhere as Greek produce. A Constantinople merchant and banker, Andreas Syngros, states in his *Memoirs* that, during the Crimean War, grain from the Danube was allowed to be exported on Greek ships; the Greeks loaded Danubian grain onto sailing ships. From there it was then directed to the Greek port of Syros, which became an intermediary transit port for reexports to Constantinople or to western European ports as Greek produce at very high prices.[50] Although we have no archival evidence for the involvement of the Vaglianos in this, in fact, the whole Greek-owned fleet developed the system and benefited from this wartime business. In this way,

---

[48] Kardasis, *Syros*, 83–84.

[49] Simon Katakouzinos, *Το εμπόριον, η ναυτιλία και αι μεταναστεύσεις των Ελλήνων* [*Trade, Shipping and the Immigration of the Greeks*], 2nd edn (Athens: n.p., 1908). That he provided grain, furs and ammunition for the Russian army is also mentioned in the Greek newspaper *Ακρόπολις* [Akropolis], January 26, 1896.

[50] Andreas Syngros, *Απομνημονεύματα* [*Memoirs*], Alkis Aggelou and Maria Christina Chatziioannou, eds. (Athens: Estia, 1998), 249–255.

the island of Syros was transformed during this period to the most important entrepôt not only of Danubian but also of Russian grain in the eastern Mediterranean.[51]

Third, Vagliano took advantage of low grain prices in the internal market due to the prohibition of grain exports, which resulted in an abundance of unsold grain and led to the decrease of prices. In this way, during the war, the Vaglianos purchased large amounts of grain, which they were able to sell after the war at extremely high prices in comparison to what they had paid for it. At the end of the prohibition of grain exports, they were able to swiftly redirect grain to the hungry western European markets, and sell the cargoes at high prices.[52] They were able to do this probably by sending the cargoes to the British market via their relatives, the Melas Brothers, who had been established in London since 1854. In 1856, the Vaglianos therefore made tremendous profits.

As is indicated in Figure 2.2, freight rates, due to the Crimean War, shot up in 1856. The profits of the Vagliano Brothers reached unprecedented heights: from 360,000 rubles in 1851 they rose dramatically more than seven times, to 2 million rubles. The Vagliano Brothers thus came to be among the top ten of south Russia's tycoons. By 1856, the Vagliano Brothers was among the top twenty Greek exporting houses of southern Russia (see Table 2.2). The Crimean War was really the springboard to the top; earnings kept growing. In 1861, the brothers' earnings grew to 2.5 million rubles and in 1863 to 2.9 million rubles (see Table 2.1). Along with earnings and more cargoes, the fleet also grew; by 1860 it comprised twenty-four vessels. This was already a large fleet by any standards in the area. The brothers owned large brigs of about 200 tons under Ionian or Russian flags, and vessels between 60 and 90 tons mostly under Russian flags registered in Rostov, Kherson, and Taganrog (see Appendix 1.D).

Behind innate entrepreneurial talent, there were significant societal factors at work. A turning point, and a major breakthrough in the expansion and establishment of their business to western Europe, was the successful marriage of young Andrea Vagliano, at twenty-three years old. In 1850 he married Euphrosyne Mela of the well-known Melas merchant family, which not only brought Andrea a bride but also gave the Vagliano family an important connection with a wide network of Greek diaspora commercial families that extended from Moscow and Odessa to Livorno, Marseilles, and London. Andrea met Euphrosyne either in Taganrog or in Constantinople through her father George L. Melas, who ran a branch office of the Melas trading house there. However, it was not only the Melas House that Euphrosyne brought to

[51] Kardasis, *Syros*, 82–94.   [52] Tsitselis, *Cephalonian Collection*, 37–40.

Table 2.2 *The twenty biggest merchants (by value) in the Russian Empire involved in external trade, 1860*

International trading firm	Cities where they traded	Imports and exports (in rubles)	Imports and exports (in pounds sterling)[a]
Rodocanachi Theodor	St. Petersburg, Taganrog, Rostov, and Odessa	7,418,456	1,186,953
Frerichs I. G.	St. Petersburg	6,436,642	960,693
Armstet I. Mitchel & Comp.	Riga	5,778,697	862,492
Scaramanga Ivan	Mariupol, Taganrog, and Rastov	5,311,694	792,790
Gubbard E.	St. Petersburg	4,817,399	719,015
Kapger & Comp.	St. Petersburg and Vierzbolov	4,697,266	701,084
Rikker I. A. & Comp.	Pernov and Riga	4,354,925	649,989
Clements & Comp.	St. Petersburg	4,031,094	601,656
Eliseiev S. under firm Eliseievui Bros	St. Petersburg	3,782,195	564,507
Dei & Comp.	Narv and St. Petersburg	3,610,323	538,854
Ralli Ivan & Comp.	Odessa	3,472,448	518,276
Ephrussi Ioachim & Comp.	Odessa	3,413,912	509,539
Gorin Karl & Comp.	Odessa	3,265,736	487,423
Gauf L. under firm Miller & Gauf	St. Petersburg	3,241,909	483,867
Ferster Roman	Vierzbolov, Moskva, and St. Petersburg	3,118,240	465,409
Gill bros	Riga	3,098,059	462,397
Mahs Ernest & Comp.	Odessa	3,064,271	457,354
Stieglitz A. L. & Comp.	St. Petersburg	3,057,059	456,277
Mari Vagliano	**Taganrog and Rostov**	**2,726,413**	**406,927**

[a] £1 sterling = 6.25 rubles.

Source: *Государственная внешняя торговля в разных ее видах*, Департамент внешний торговли [*State Foreign Trade in Different Categories*] (St. Petersburg: Department of Foreign Trade, 1860).

the Vaglianos. It was also those of her relatives, Mavros, Vasiliou, and Sevastopoulos, from established networks of Greeks from Epirus and Chios.[53]

In the 1850s, the network of the collaborating Mavros, Melas, Basiliou, Sevastopoulos, and Vagliano families extended beyond Constantinople (where Andrea Vagliano and George L. Melas were established). It also included Moscow (Panos D. Melas, Dimitrios L. Melas, and Ioannis St. Melas), Odessa (Spyridon Mavros, Theodosios L. Melas), Taganrog (Mari Vagliano), Braila (Anastassios Petrou Melas), Galatz (Michael G. Melas), Zante (Panagi Vagliano), Livorno (Dimitrios M. Basiliou and Ilias Panas), Marseilles (Alexander M. Basiliou, who was joined in 1857 by Constantine G. Melas and Leon G. Melas), and London (Vasilios G. Melas and Leon G. Melas in 1849).[54] These close relatives and collaborators in London and Marseille were extremely important for the great leap forward by Panagi Vagliano, and his establishment in London in 1858, and that of Andrea Vagliano in Marseille in 1869.

The 1850s were very important for all the Vaglianos' personal lives. Mari, twenty years older than Andrea, who was married to Maria Krassa at least since 1840[55] had a daughter named Aspasia born in 1842. He had his first son, Alcibiades, born in 1850 in Taganrog, and his second son Athanassios, born in 1854. At about the same time, Andrea and Euphrosyne had their first son in 1851; they named him Marinos after Andrea's favorite older brother, who must have been like a father and mentor to him. When they had a girl in 1859, they named her Aspasia, after Mari Vagliano's firstborn child and only daughter, Aspasia, who died that same year at seventeen years old.[56] Andrea and Euphrosyne had ten children: three boys and seven daughters, all of whom

---

[53] The first generation of the commercial House of Melas from Epirus (Ioannina) started from the mid-eighteenth century in Russia. The members of the second generation of the Melas family established branch offices from the late eighteenth century to the 1850s in Moscow (Panos D. Melas, Dimitrios L. Melas, and Ioannis St. Melas), in Odessa (Theodosios L. Melas), Leipsig (Ioannis L. Melas and Pavlos L. Melas), and Constantinople (George L. Melas). It was the daughter of the latter whom Andrea Vagliano married. See L. I. Melas, Ηπειρωτικές μελέτες: Μία οικογένεια, μία ιστορία [Studies of Epirus: A Family, a History] (Athens: n.p., 1967).

[54] Harlaftis, A History of Greek-Owned Shipping, chapter 2.

[55] According to Moschona, Panagi A. Vaglianos, in his father's will written on December 16/28, 1840, "his son Maris married abroad...," 27. There is no more information on Mari's wife Maria Krassa.

[56] The tomb of Aspasia Vagliano (1842–1859) is in the Taganrog cemetery, Russia. It is a beautiful marble sarcophagus and the epitaph is exhibited in the State Literary, Historical and Architectural Museum of Taganrog. It reads: ΑΘΩΑΣ ΠΑΡΘΕΝΟΥ ΕΣΧΑΤΗ ΠΝΟΗ ΑΪΔΙΟΣ ΕΙΝΑΙ ΑΓΓΕΛΟΥ ΖΩΗ ΑΣΠΑΣΙΑ Μ. ΒΑΛΛΙΑΝΟΥ ΔΕΚΑΕΠΤΑΕΤΗ ΚΥΡΙΩ ΑΠΟΔΗΜΗΣΑΣΑ ΕΝ ΤΗ 1Η ΑΠΡΙΛΙΟΥ ΑΩΝΘ ΟΙ ΤΕΘΛΙΜΕΝΟΙ ΓΟΝΕΙΣ [LAST BREATH OF INNOCENT VIRGIN IS ETERNAL ANGEL LIFE. ASPASIA M. VAGLIANO SEVENTEEN YEARS OLD TO THE LORD SHE WENT ON 1ST APRIL 1859. THE SORROWFUL PARENTS].

eventually married into the best Greek and French high society (see Chapter 10 and Appendix 1.A). Andrea opened the Constantinople branch of the firm in 1849, and he remained in charge of this branch until 1869, when he moved with his family to Marseille.

Panagi Vagliano in Zante did not only work for the family business, but also became a commercial and shipping agent of other Black Sea merchants in the 1840s. He was already well connected with Greek Odessan merchants, whose cargoes he promoted via Zante, and particularly the big merchant of Odessa, George Vucina, who remained his close collaborator for the rest of his life.[57] He collaborated with the prosperous merchant family of Bagdatopoulos on the island of Zante, with whom the brothers co-owned the vessel *Andreas Vagliano*.[58] At the age of forty-two, Panagi married the seventeen-year-old Clara Bagdatopoulos, probably in 1856; it is interesting to note that ninety years later, in 1946, the forty-two-year-old Aristotle Onassis married the seventeen-year-old Tina Livanos. Like Onassis, Panagi Vagliano had an unhappy married life. He moved to London in 1858 with his young bride and her brother George Bagdatopoulos. His wife appears in the English censuses of 1861 and 1871. In the 1881 census, she is not in the house, although he does not declare that he is a widower, as he does in 1891. Some biographers claim he had a son who died at a young age. Panagi had no other children and he did not remarry.[59]

Rising to Become the Prime Trading Company in the Russian Black Sea

Starting as merchant captains, the Vagliano brothers climbed their way up and their company became a renowned international trading house from the 1820s to the 1850s. They gradually built regional (in the Azov), peripheral (in the Black Sea), and international (between western and eastern Europe) commercial, shipping, and financial networks. The leader of the triad during this first period was the older brother, Mari Vagliano.

The crucial decisions that brought Mari Vagliano profits and business success gave him the means to build important institutional backup in Russian society. Raising capital gave Mari Vagliano the opportunity to become a member of the Russian system of merchants and gradually climb the ladder of the Russian hierarchy, and eventually became a member of the nobility. As already noted, the rich merchants who remained in the first guild for at least a

---

[57] See more on the relationship between Panagi Vagliano and Vucina in the next chapter.

[58] There is very little information on the Bagdatopoulos. It was a merchant family from the Peloponnese and was established in Zante at the beginning of the nineteenth century. See Leonidas C. Zois, Λεξικόν Ιστορικόν και Λαογραφικόν Ζακύνθου [*Historical and Folklore Dictionary of Zakynthos*] (Athens: Ek tou Ethnikou Typografeiou, 1963).

[59] National Archives, English Censuses, 1861, 1871, 1881, 1891.

decade took the title of *honorary citizen*, and joined the Russian nobility.[60] The first mention that we find of Mari Vagliano as part of the merchant system in Russia is in 1846. In this year, he adopted Russian citizenship as "Mark Vagliano, merchant of Kerch-Yeni Kale." In 1861, he obtained the top honorary title a merchant could get: "Mark Vagliano, Honorary Citizen." This made him a member of the Russian nobility, and the title was hereditary for his sons. From 1861 onwards, he is found as a first guild merchant of Taganrog trading in Taganrog, Rostov, Berdyansk, and Mariupol (see Table 2.1).

Mari Vagliano became one of the Greek traders who grew in distinction in the 1820s in Russia. As is evident from Table 2.3, in 1824, 2 percent of the whole Russian Empire's external trade was handled by Greek trading companies, whereas 22 percent of all southern Russian external trade was carried by them. In 1856, those percentages had skyrocketed: Greeks handled 13 percent of the whole Russian external trade and 66 percent of the total southern Russian external trade. It is thus not surprising that the members of the Greek trading companies of southern Russia who established themselves in the City of London in the 1820s gained access to the Baltic Exchange and the Bank of England, where they were considered to be, and treated as, a tight business group.[61]

A few decades ago, based on French and English archives, I used shipping movements to identify the importance of the Chiot and Ionian networks in the trade and shipping of southern Russia with the western European port cities.[62] The leading Chiot diaspora families have been identified in historiography, particularly because of their importance as trading companies based in London or in the main Mediterranean port cities.[63] Recent research has

[60] Rieber, *Merchants and Entrepreneurs in Imperial Russia*, xxiii.

[61] Katerina Galani and Gelina Harlaftis, "Trade and Finance between London, Constantinople and Southern Russia: The Greek Business Group in the Nineteenth Century," paper presented at the European Business History Association, Utrecht, 2014.

[62] Databases were formed based on British Customs Bills of Trade and the French commercial and shipping journal *Semaphore de Marseille*. See Harlaftis, *A History of Greek-Owned Shipping*, chapters 2 and 3.

[63] For Greeks in London, see footnote 62. There is a large historiography on Greek diaspora communities and trading companies. For an overall treatment of the earlier period see Viktor Zakharov, Gelina Harlaftis, and Olga Katsiardi-Hering, *Merchant "Colonies" in the Early Modern Period (15th–18th Centuries)* (London: Chatto & Pickering, 2012), Introduction *passim*. For more on Greek diaspora trading companies in a comparative perspective, see I. Baghdiantz McCabe, G. Harlaftis, and I. Pepelasis Minoglou, eds., *Diaspora Entrepreneurial Networks: Four Centuries of History* (New York: Berg, 2005); and Olga Katsiardi-Hering, "Central and Peripheral Communities in the Greek Diaspora: Interlocal and Local Economic, Political, and Cultural Networks in the Eighteenth and Nineteenth Centuries," in M. Rozen, ed., *Homelands and Diaspora: Greeks, Jews and Their Migrations* (London: I. B. Tauris, 2008), 169–180, 372–376. See also Katerina Vourkatioti, "The House of Ralli Bros (*c.* 1814–1961)," in Maria Christina Chatziioannou and Gelina Harlaftis, eds., *Following the Nereids: Sea Routes and Maritime Business, 16th–20th Centuries* (Athens: Kerkyra Publications, 2006).

Table 2.3 *Merchants engaged in Russia's external trade, 1824 and 1856*

	1824		1856	
	Number of merchants	Total imports and exports handled (%)	Number of merchants	Total imports and exports handled (%)
Merchants in all Russian cities	279		537	
Greek merchants in all Russian cities	*18*	*2*	*63*	*13*
Merchants in southern Russian port cities	68	10	117	20
Greek merchants in southern Russian port cities	*18*	*22*	*60*	*66*

Source: *Государственная внешняя торговля в разных ее видах*, Департамент внешний торговли [*State Foreign Trade in Different Categories*, Department of Foreign Trade], St. Petersburg, 1824, 1856.

revealed that the Chiots owed their primacy to their importance in the external trade of Russia. So the new archival evidence from the Russian archives indicates that Greek merchants who originated from Chios, Cephalonia, or elsewhere, were established in Russia as big international trading companies first before going to the West.[64] They thrived mainly in Taganrog and Odessa, the most important ports of the southern Russian Empire, during the 1820s to 1860s. It was the big Chiot trading companies that excelled in Russia, with the Ralli, Scaramanga, and Rodocanachi as the leading "Russian" trading companies (Table 2.2). In the 1860s, the Ionians took the lead and surpassed the Chiots, and from the 1860s to the turn of the century remained the prime Greek trading companies of southern Russia; the Vaglianos formed the nucleus of the Ionian group of trading companies.

By 1860, Mari Vagliano figured in the top twenty exporting firms for the whole of the Russian Empire (Table 2.2). In the same year, in the top twenty trading firms in southern Russia 66 percent were Greeks (Table 2.3). Altogether, they carried trade worth more than £3 million. As Table 2.2

---

[64] New research and new evidence has been brought out from the research project titled "The Black Sea and its Port-Cities, 1774–1914: Development, Convergence and Linkages with the Global Economy" during 2012–2015, see www.blacksea.gr (accessed October 5, 2016).

reveals, almost all top exporters of the Russian Empire in 1860 were foreigners. Apart from the Greeks, they were Germans, like Mahs,[65] or German Jews, like Stieglitz, or Sephardic Jews, like the Ephrussi. As Table 2.2 indicates, Mari Vagliano comes in under the trading house of Stieglitz. It is interesting to note that in 1860 Baron Alexander von Stieglitz, who had inherited from his father, Ludwig, the banking house of Stieglitz and Co., which became the Emperor's Bank (the State Bank), was made the first governor of the State Bank of the Russian Empire, the predecessor organization to today's Central Bank of the Russian Federation.

By the 1870s, Rodocanachi and Ralli, who featured in the top ten of 1860, had left the Russian markets; the Ralli expanded to India and the Americas, while the Rodocanachi became bankers in London. Scaramanga was overtaken by Mari Vagliano by 1869 (see Table 3.3). By 1880 Mari Vagliano was by far the largest exporter in all of south Russia and certainly among the top of all Russian exporters.

Conclusions

The Vaglianos evolved from free traders combining trade and sea transport into independent sailing shipping companies specializing in sea transport, forming large fleets of sailing ships, and finally becoming international trading companies. In the evolution of the tramp-shipping firm as it appears in Figure 1.1, it covers the period from the first stage of the shipping firm to the second one, from the stage of the merchant captain and sailing shipowner to the international trading company.

Maritime culture was the first factor that led them to this path. The three Vaglianos came from the island of Cephalonia, which carried a long maritime tradition. Furthermore, as subjects of the Ionian islands since 1815 they were also citizens of a British colony, a position that provided them with even more opportunities in Russia. Through this process, the three Vaglianos continued and expanded the maritime tradition of their ancestors. During the first thirty years of their business, each of them worked as merchant captains for at least twenty years. It was Mari Vagliano, the elder brother who, during this period, exhibited remarkable insight and the ability to penetrate and establish himself in the Russian frontier market of the Azov Sea. He first worked as a seaman and then a merchant captain for the House of his relatives in Taganrog. There he recognized opportunities and was able to make the right and timely decisions, which in less than two years led to him starting his own business.

Mari Vagliano was able to exploit the opportunities offered by war and by the Russian colonization schemes in this frontier zone of the Russian Empire.

---

[65] Wolfgang Sartor, *Das Haus Mahs: Eine international Unternehmerfamilie im Rissischen Reich, 1750–1918* (Moscow: Olearius Press, 2009).

He supplied the Russian Army in the recurring wars of the area in the 1820s, acting as both a shipowner and a merchant. As this was a Cossack area, which formed the Russian Army in this borderland, Mari Vagliano developed close connections with the Cossack leaders and merchants who had trade privileges in the region, and thus penetrated the hinterland. He owned a number of smaller vessels for local transport along the Don River and Azov navigation channels and turned to the Greek island shipyards to build his first large vessel for long-haul trade in 1828. He started carrying cargoes to the western Mediterranean in 1830, establishing linkages with the foreland ports with which he traded beyond the eastern Mediterranean.

His two brothers Panagi and Andrea joined him in the 1830s as merchant captains; they proved equally able and the business took off. The international conjuncture helped. By the 1830s, peace had come to the eastern Mediterranean, after the end of the Greek War of Independence in the 1820s; by 1830, the modern Greek state had been established. The continuing industrialization of western Europe meant great and increasing demand for grain; the Russian steppes became the granary of Europe.

All three Vaglianos not only expanded but also consolidated the business beyond the Azov and formed a system by which Mari provided the cargoes from the Azov Sea, Andrea operated the vessels and carried cargoes himself until 1850, when he was established in Constantinople, and Panagi successfully sold them to Western markets established in Zante. Their first solid network was established within the Black Sea and eastern Mediterranean. Panagi Vagliano, however, was pivotal in reaching out from Zante to western European markets, where he sold the cargoes of grain brought by his brothers; they were now all engaged in trade, shipping, and finance from all three nodes and hired Greek captains to operate their own vessels or chartered other Greek vessels. By the 1840s, the three Vaglianos had a fleet of about eight vessels, which tripled within a decade. The great leap forward that brought them to the top of southern Russia' exporters was during and immediately after the Crimean War. They were able to exploit the high demand for grain, when Russian exports were prohibited to the enemy forces, bypassing the rules by exporting via neutrals, for example through the Danubian ports or to Greece, from where they reexported to the Ottoman Empire or to others.

Societal factors also helped this expansion. The Vaglianos became related to the established Greek entrepreneurial network and, by the 1860s, they had become a powerful international trading company. In the next decades they became the foremost firm of the Greek entrepreneurial network, replacing the leading Chiot trading companies in the Black Sea trade. By the end of the nineteenth century, the region became the world's leading grain-exporting area and an integral part of the group of European international traders, bankers, and shipowners.

3

An International Trading House from Russia to the United Kingdom, 1850s–1880s

The three Vaglianos reached their apogee as an international trading company during the second period of their business. It was during this time that they paved the way for the Greeks to global shipping, and made maritime and commercial transactions on an equal basis with the world's best; in 1881, in London they had a turnover of about £8 million sterling when Schröders had a turnover of £4 million and Rothschild's £12 million (see Appendix 2.F). This chapter analyzes the functioning of their international trading house in trade, finance, and shipping. It reveals how multinational business and multiple identities – British, Russian, French, or Greek – both facilitated their operations and brought them into conflicts.

Their success followed the unprecedented increase of Russian grain exports. The move to London, the world's biggest commercial, maritime, and financial capital, was fundamental for their establishment in the European markets. Just as important, they consolidated in Constantinople, the largest financial, trading, and shipping center of the eastern Mediterranean and the Black Sea,- and expanded into Marseille, the largest commercial and maritime center of the western Mediterranean. By establishing a chain of agencies in the main European port cities linking eastern and western European sea trade and shipping on the one hand, and penetrating the interlocking financial circuits of Europe on the other, they were able to connect the local to the global.

The Vaglianos provided services to a plethora of shipping companies in the Greek islands, and to the few dozen powerful international trading houses they collaborated with, by forming a central shipping agency that operated from many nodal points. The path to the top and the formation of their wealth was not without conflicts with their host countries. Despite their clear success in international business, the 1880s proved to be a troubled era for the Vagliano Brothers. In Russia, Mari Vagliano was sued by the Russian government for fraud in 1881 and was in danger of confiscation of his fortune in the trial that took place in 1885. In Britain, one of Panagi Vagliano's employees defrauded him almost £9 million (in 2018 purchasing power) in 1887. Panagi Vagliano sued Great Britain's major financial institution, the Bank of England which had cashed the forged bills of exchange over the counter to that particular employee without consulting him. On the French front, the youngest Vagliano brother, Andrea, died unexpectedly in 1887.

Figure 3.1   Mari (Marino) Vagliano (1804–1896)
Source: Collection of Stephan and Frances Vagliano, Korgialeneio Historical and Folklore Museum of Cephalonia.

Internal Organization

The internal organization of the Vagliano Brothers House was formed around the four nodes the three brothers established. It continued to depend on kinship and ties of trust that reduced commercial risk and the cost of transactions. All three brothers appeared to be equal to third parties, and all had signing authority.[1]

Mari Vagliano continued to be based in Taganrog during this period (Figure 3.1). Despite his mobility as a captain in the 1820s and 1830s, after the establishment of his family in the early 1840s in Taganrog, and the growth of the business in the 1850s, he probably never moved again. His house, a fine two-story building at 75 Chekhova Street in Taganrog (which still stands), was not pompous or too luxurious.[2] He walked everywhere; only his wife used their carriage, to go to church on Sunday. The lack of pretension, incredible for a millionaire in the epoch of the Russian Empire, lent him the characterization of

---

[1] Private Archive of Coutsis family, Spetses, Letter of Mari Vagliano (Taganrog) to G. I. Coutsis (Spetses), 47/5, April 10, 1869.

[2] O. P. Gabrioushkin, *Мари Вальяно и другие* [*Mari Vagliano and Others*] (Taganrog: MNKM, 2001), 235. Gabrioushkin mentions that he owned more houses and buildings in Chekhova, Alexandrovskaya Street, and also a building in the commercial quarter (Birzha).

a "miser" by Russian novelists after his death. Lacking formal education (as did all three brothers), he was also reported to be "illiterate." An article in a Greek newspaper claimed that he was able only to sign his name, that, despite his long-term residence in Russia, he retained his heavy Cephalonian accent, and that "for the sixty years he was in Russia he was able to speak only about sixty Russian words."[3] Paperwork, a central part of his business, occupied a large part of his time, and he kept his business going by reading and dictating thousands of letters on shipping, trade, and finance every year, in Greek to his Greek business partners and in Italian to non-Greeks. He had learned the importance of this correspondence well as a merchant captain.

Mari Vagliano's office in Taganrog opened with the sunrise and closed at 2 o'clock in the afternoon.[4] Every morning "Sior Marakis," as he was called in the Cephalonian idiom, stood in front of his door as Russian peasants and the employees of landowners paraded in front of him, holding samples of grain that they put on his palm. Grain still in his palm, he would turn and say to his employee who was standing next to him keeping notes: "for purchase," or "not for purchase."[5] In his office in Taganrog, Mari Vagliano had as secretary Lykiardopoulo, a close friend of his, and a trusted employee George A. Kambitsi, both from his village, Kerameies.[6] But Mari managed his colossal business alone. He had the power to affect grain prices by speeding or delaying ships and delivery of cargoes. As one Greek obituary said, "he sent millions of tons of grain to all parts of the globe through his palm."

Mari was highly gifted, albeit difficult and autocratic. Not surprisingly, neither of his two sons remained in Taganrog to work with him. Alcibiades, the firstborn, was sent to London in the early 1870s, to be followed by Athanasse. Mari Vagliano kept the title of the "Tsar of the Azov" for himself as long as he lived. His able nephews, sons of his brother Spyridon who had stayed in Cephalonia, joined him in the 1870s and eventually took over the branch offices of Rostov and Novorossiysk in the 1880s.[7]

Andrea Vagliano, the younger brother, was established by Mari in two nodes: in Constantinople from 1849 to 1869 and in Marseille from 1869 to

---

[3] Theodoros A. Vellianitis, "Οι Εν Ρωσσία Έλληνες" ["Greeks in Russia"], Εστία [Estia] 44 (1893): 273–276.

[4] This report on Mari Vagliano's business was published in his obituary in the newspaper Ακρόπολις [Acropolis] on January 26, 1896. From the detailed evidence it is certain that it was from an interview with a very close associate.

[5] Ibid.

[6] Spyridon Efst. Metaxas-Laskaratos, Εμποροπροξενικοί καταδιωγμοί [Commercial-Consular Prosecutions] (Athens: n.p., 1882), 8.

[7] "Vagliano Mikhail Spiridonovich," in Vladimir Sidorov, Энциклопедия старого Ростова и Нахичевани-на-Дону [Encyclopedia of Old Rostov and Nachichevan-on-Don] vol. 3 (Rostov-on-Don: Gefesy, 1995), 103–106; Metaxas-Laskaratos, Commercial-Consular Prosecutions, 76.

Figure 3.2 Panagi Vagliano (1814–1902)
Source: Collection of Stephan and Frances Vagliano, Korgialeneio Historical and Folklore Museum of Cephalonia.

1886 (Figure 3.3). Andrea set up offices in Constantinople in the familiar and flourishing environment of the large Greek merchant community in the city. In the nineteenth century, Constantinople was an ever-growing city, the capital of the modernizing and Westernizing Ottoman Empire. In 1885, more than half of its 850,000 population belonged to Christians; the largest non-Muslim communities were of Greeks and Armenians, followed by the Jews.[8]

It was also the financial capital of the eastern Mediterranean, dominated by the "Galata Bankers," mainly Greeks, Jews, and Armenians who connected it with the West and provided loans to the Ottoman state.[9] According to an annual Constantinople professional guide, one-third of the bankers and big

---

[8] More specifically, 44.06 percent were Muslim, 17.48 percent Greek Orthodox, 17.12 percent Armenians, and 5.08 percent Jews; the remainder were other western European "foreigners." See Zeynep Celik, *The Remaking of Istanbul: Portrait of an Ottoman City in the Nineteenth Century* (Seattle: University of Washington Press, 1981), 38.

[9] Sevket Pamuk, *A Monetary History of the Ottoman Empire* (Cambridge: Cambridge University Press, 2000), 200–205; Edhem Eldem, *A History of the Ottoman Bank* (Istanbul: Ottoman Bank Historical Research Center, 1999); Z. Toprak, "The Financial Structure of the Stock Exchange in the Late Ottoman Empire," in Philip Cottrell, M. Pohle, and Fraser I. Fraser, eds., *East Meets West: Banking, Commerce and Investment in the Ottoman Empire* (Aldershot: Ashgate, 2008), 145–150.

Figure 3.3 Andrea Vagliano (1827–1887)
Source: Collection of Stephan and Frances Vagliano, Korgialeneio Historical and Folklore Museum of Cephalonia.

traders of Constantinople in 1881 were Greeks.[10] Situated at the chokepoint between Asia and Europe, Constantinople controlled the flow of commodities from the Black Sea and became the transit point for thousands of vessels.[11] Apart from dealing with the chartering, insuring, and supplying of ships and selling cargoes, Andrea was also involved in shipowning and finance.

After twenty years of business in Constantinople, in 1869 Andrea moved with his wife Euphrosyne (Figure 3.4) and his family to Marseille. Marseille, the largest port of the western Mediterranean, was the main recipient of Black Sea grain in the region. A small but prosperous community of members of more than twenty Greek trading families was established in the French port by the 1830s, handling more than one-third of all commerce and shipping entering from the eastern Mediterranean and Black Sea between 1830 and 1860.[12] Among them were Euphrosyne's brothers, Leon and Constantine

---

[10] *L'indicateur Ottoman. Annuaire-Almanach du Commerce de l'Industrie, de l'Administration et de la Magistrature*, 2me années, Cervatti Frères et D. Fatzea, 1881; Galani and Harlaftis, "Trade and Finance between London, Constantinople and Southern Russia."

[11] Harlaftis and Kardasis, "International Bulk Trade and Shipping in the Eastern Mediterranean and the Black Sea," 233–265.

[12] Harlaftis, *A History of Greek-Owned Shipping*, table 2.11, 63.

Figure 3.4   Euphrosyne Vagliano (1837–1908), daughter of George Mela, wife of
Andrea Vagliano
Source: Private collection of Marina Eloy, Paris.

Melas, who had moved to Marseille in 1857.[13] Therefore, when Andrea and
Euphrosyne Vagliano moved to Marseille they were joining family already
there. During the next twenty years of Andrea's business activity in Marseille,
from 1869 to 1887, the House of the Vagliano Brothers reached its apogee.

Panagi Vagliano went to London after the Crimean War (Figure 3.2). An
anecdote has it that when Panagi "was ordered" by Mari in 1856 to go from
Zante to London, where he had never set foot before, he said "I do not want to
go to London because among other things, I know nothing." "Leave immediately," said the older brother, "you'll see you know a lot."[14] Although Panagi
Vagliano was living in a British semicolony and had grown up under British
rule in the Ionian islands, he knew no English – but it seems that he knew
"something," at least.

The move to London, the world's biggest commercial, maritime, and financial center, was fundamental for the consolidation of the House of the
Vagliano Brothers in the European markets. There were two institutions that

[13] Erato Paris, "Les Grecs de Marseille dans la deuxième moitié du XIXe siècle: une
perspective nationale et transnationale," *Revue européenne des migrations internationales*
17, no. 3 (2001): 23–42.
[14] "Panagi Vaglianos," Newspaper Άστυ [*Asty*], January 13, 1902.

Panagi had to penetrate: the Baltic Exchange and the Bank of England. He managed to get access to both in 1858, registering the company as "Vagliano Brothers" in the City.[15] He opened an account for the company with the Bank of England on August 5, 1858, and by 1861 the names of all three brothers appeared in the Bank's book. Panagi, like Andrea in Marseille, had relatives to help him start the business; some of the Melas brothers had moved to London and had opened their own business in 1854.

Goods from the Black Sea, particularly tallow, linseed, and grain, found their way to the British market through the Baltic Exchange.[16] During the course of the nineteenth century, the Baltic became London's central freight market, the main place to exchange information about ships and cargoes. When Panagi Vagliano arrived in the City of London, an affluent community of Greek merchants, particularly from Chios, was already established.[17] In 1854, Pandia Ralli was part of the twenty-member Baltic committee, which made the rules and decided various issues.[18] It was at that time that Panagi Vagliano also became a member of the Baltic. The main foreign merchant houses in Britain were owned by Germans, Jews, Greeks, and Americans.[19]

Family control remained a primary characteristic of the Vagliano business. The first generation of the three brothers, who founded the business, was reinforced from the 1860s to the 1870s and onwards by the second generation, who were formally educated in Russia, Greece, and the Ottoman Empire, acquiring along the way both commercial education and language skills. Furthermore, the first generation directed their sons and daughters to follow strategic marital alliances with prominent and wealthy international trading families such as the Rallis, Petrocochinos, Ballis, Negrepontes, Zarifis, Coupases, and Ambanopouloses. It was into these families that the sons of Mari, and the sons and the daughters of Andrea, were married. Mari, Panagi, and Andrea also made sure that their nephews and nieces, sons and daughters of the brothers who had remained in Cephalonia (Metaxas, Nikolaos, and

---

[15] Archives of the Bank of England, C98/3618, 1858.

[16] See H. Barty-King, *The Baltic Exchange* (London: Hutchinson Benham, 1977). On maritime institutions in London, see Gordon Boyce, "The Development of Commercial Infrastructure for World Shipping," in Gelina Harlaftis, Stig Tenold, and Jesus Valdaliso, eds., *"World's Key Industry": History and Economics of International Shipping* (London: Palgrave Macmillan, 2012), 106–123.

[17] This is what I have called the "Chiot network"; see Harlaftis, "Trade and Shipping in the Nineteenth Century"; see also Harlaftis, *A History of Greek-Owned Shipping*, chapter 2. For the origins of Greek merchants in England and in the British trade see Katerina Galani, *British Shipping and Trade in the Mediterranean in the Age of War, 1770–1815* (Unpublished PhD dissertation, Oxford University, 2011).

[18] Harlaftis, *A History of Greek-Owned Shipping*, 97.

[19] Chapman, *Merchant Enterprise in Britain*, 165.

Spyridon) and of their two sisters (Santina Rosolymos and Maria Kambitsi), also married into important families (Appendix 1.A).

The External Organization: Networks

The network of a merchant consisted of linkages in the hinterland, in the production area where he purchased his cargoes, and in the foreland, the ports where he sent his cargoes for consumption. The Vaglianos strategically set the function of their network. The hinterland, where cargoes were purchased, was controlled by Mari Vagliano; the foreland, the ports where cargoes were dispatched to southern and northern Europe, was handled by Andrea and Panagi Vagliano. Apart from these three, sons, nephews, and trusted collaborators were part of the Vagliano networks, which included the regional network of the Azov and its hinterland, the peripheral network of the Black Sea, and the international network in western Europe

The Azov hinterlands covered the eastern Black Sea coast (see Map 3.1). Most of this area involved a frontier market to which the Russian Empire continuously expanded throughout the nineteenth century and eventually totally conquered in the 1880s. There were three subregions. The first one was the northeast of the Black Sea region, including as hinterland parts of the *gubernias* of Taurida, Ekaterinoslav, Poltava, and Kharkov; Berdyansk and Mariupol were the main ports in this area. The second subregion, which was the most important for grain production in the area, was the eastern Black Sea, the lands of the *gubernias* of Voronezh, Tambov, Saratov, Don, and Kuban, with its main outlets, the ports of Taganrog and Rostov; the latter grew to prominence after the 1880s. The third region was the southern Transcaucasian coastline from Kuban to Kutais, stretching from Novorossiysk down to Batoum. The port of Novorossiysk served this coastline, which did not have any worthy port until 1883, when Batoum was conquered.

Taganrog remained the biggest port of the area. Its hinterland was blessed with the enormous and complex river systems of the Volga and the Don and their tributaries (see Map 3.1). Together, the Volga and Don provided 5,000 km of navigable waterways.[20] Grain cargoes were carried downstream to the ports mainly via river craft and, to a lesser extent, by oxen-wagons. Land transport could only easily take place on the steppes during the dry summer season and with horse-drawn sleighs during the winter, as there was no road system. The mud from the rains and melting of ice of spring and autumn

---

[20] Министерство путей сообщения, Отдел статистики и картографии, Статистический обзор железных дорог и внутренних водных путей [Ministry of Transport, Department of Statistics and Cartography, *Statistical Review of Railways and Internal Waterways of Russia*] (St. Petersburg, 1900), 118–119.

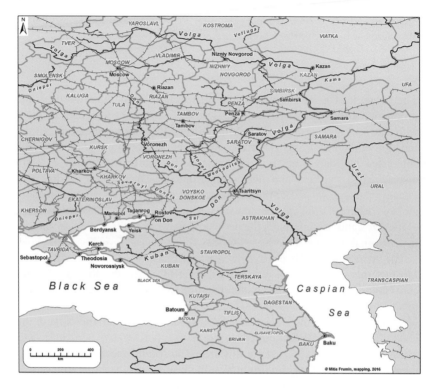

Map 3.1   The exporting port cities and their hinterland, eastern coast of the Russian Empire (*gubernias*, waterways, and railways), 1880s

made roads impassable.[21] Railroads modernized land transport, supplementing river transport and decreasing freight costs. Thus, railway construction in the 1860s and 1870s provided the country with long lines of transportation that connected the internal regions of the country with the sea. In the 1890s and early 1900s, railway construction integrated the countryside and increased the rail network's density.[22]

---

[21] Arcadius Kahan, *Russian Economic History: The Nineteenth Century* (Chicago: University of Chicago Press, 1989), 27–33.

[22] Jacob Metzer, "Railroad Development and Market Integration: The Case of Tsarist Russia," *The Journal of Economic History* 34, no. 3 (September 1974): 529–550; Gelina Harlaftis and Anna Sydorenko, "The Ports between the Hinterland and Foreland: The Transport System of the Maritime Region of the Eastern Coast of the Black Sea," in Gelina Harlaftis, Victoria Konstantinova, and Igor Lyman, eds., *The Port-Cities of the Eastern Coast of the Black Sea: From the Azov to the Caucasus, Late 18th–Early 20th Centuries*, Black Sea History Project Working Papers, vol. 3 (Corfu: Ionian University, 2019).

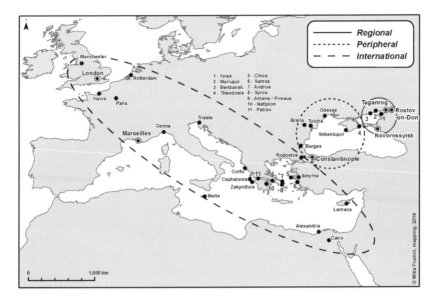

Map 3.2   The regional and peripheral network of the Vagliano Bros. in the
Black Sea

Mari Vagliano maintained offices in Taganrog, Yeisk, and Kerch in order to
keep control of the navigable channel of the shallow and difficult Azov, along
with a chain of agents in the area (Map 3.2). He also had agents in Mariupol
(G. Aloupis[23]), in Berdyansk, where he was collaborating with the Cuppa and
Ambanopoulo families (with whom he became later related through the
marriages of Andrea's daughters to sons of these families), and in Rostov,
where his nephew Michael S. Vagliano was set up in the 1880s. In the
Circassian coast and hinterland, he kept a branch office in the port of
Novorossiysk, establishing his nephew Athanasse S. Vagliano there in the
1870s. It is interesting to note that along the way he placed his agents close
to the railway from Rostov to Novorossiysk (compare Maps 2.2 and 3.1 in the
Kuban area). Mari Vagliano kept agents at the Kuban Cossack towns of
Korenovsk (Andrea Ardavanis), at Krymsk (Petros Papadopoulos), and at
Ust-Labinsk (Grigorios Koundouris).[24] These towns were administrative
centers of their own areas. Mari maintained close relations with all the local
institutions and elites in all of these towns: governors, heads of municipalities,

---

[23] Metaxas-Laskaratos, *Commercial-Consular Prosecutions*, 40.
[24] Dionyssios Metaxas-Laskaratos, Ελληνικαί παροικίαι Ρωσσίας και Ρωμουνίας [*Greek Communities of Russia and Romania*] (Braila: Publishing House Universala of Con.
P. Nikolaou, 1900), 62–63.

police, port masters, Customs officials, and more. He also had close relations with the chain of Greek consuls and vice-consuls in all the Azov towns. For example in the 1870s, Greek Vice-Consul M. Giourdis was the husband of the sister of his wife, and Georgios Vucina, the Greek consul in Odessa, was his close collaborator.

Trustworthiness and efficiency were the main strengths of Mari Vagliano, who was able to establish long-term networks with the Cossacks of the hinterland.[25] His close connections with the Don and Kuban Cossacks of the area had developed since the 1820s, when, as a young shipmaster, he was transporting supplies and ammunition for the wars in the Caucasus. The big Greek merchants developed social connections with elite Cossack families. A number of powerful aristocratic Cossack families, some of questionable origin, proudly claimed Greek descent: the important Cossack families of Ianov, Grekov, Martinov, and Apostolov were all either descended from Greek forebears or married to the daughters of prosperous Greek merchants. For example, Andrei Dimitrievits Martinov (1838–1913), a cavalry general and Commander of the Ataman Regiment, married Ariadne Konstantinova Papudov, daughter of the first guild merchant of Odessa Konstantin Papudov and of Ariadne Eustratievna Sevastopoulo, from the rich Chiot merchant family.[26] The Vaglianos had become closely related to the Sevastopoulos through Euphrosyne Melas, the wife of Andrea.

The peripheral Black Sea network embraced the whole Black Sea coastline, particularly in the north and the western coast of the Black Sea (Map 3.2). The Vaglianos kept agents in the Crimean peninsula (whose ports had the great advantage of not being iced in during the winter), like Antonios Solomos in Sebastopol and C. Koundouris in Theodosia.[27] Both of these ports developed as export gateways and transit ports after the Crimean War.[28] The brothers cooperated with Spyridon Mavro and Georgios Vucina in Odessa and Zissimos Frangopoulos and L. N. Lykiardopoulos in Nikolaev to control grain exports.[29]

[25] Harlaftis, "From Diaspora Traders to Shipping Tycoons"; Harlaftis, "The 'Multimillionaire Mr Marakis' Vagliano."

[26] Z. Chumakhova, "Έγγραφα για την Ελληνική διασπορά του Ντον και της Αζοφικής στο Κρατικό Αρχείο της Περιφέρειας του Ροστόβ-στον-Ντον" ["Documents for the Greek Diaspora of the Don and the Azov in the State Archives of the Rostov Region"], in Evrydiki Sifneos and Gelina Harlaftis, eds., Οι Έλληνες της Αζοφικής, 19ος αιώνας [The Greeks of the Azov, Nineteenth Century] (Athens: National Research Foundation, Institute of Historical Research, Section of Neohellenic Research, 2015), 537–559.

[27] Metaxas-Laskaratos, Greek Communities of Russia, 4.

[28] Anna Sydorenko, The Economic and Social Development of the Crimean Ports in the Second Half of the Nineteenth Century (Unpublished PhD dissertation, Ionian University, Corfu, 2017).

[29] Metaxas-Laskaratos, Greek Communities of Russia, 5; Kardasis, Diaspora Merchants in the Black Sea, 98.

On the Danube in Tulcha and Braila, Mari collaborated closely with the Theofilatos, who were the prime merchants and shipowners of that river.[30] He also exported from the hinterland of Burgas and Varna.[31] Meanwhile, in Constantinople, Andrea operated until 1869, when he was replaced by his nephew Basil M. Vagliano, followed by his first cousins Gerasimos Michael Kambitsis (son of the Vagliano brothers' sister Maria) and Athanasios Lazaros Rosolymos (son of their sister Santina) when Basil moved to the London office in the 1890s.[32] The "inner core" of the Vagliano business depended on the members of the immediate family to extend and run branch offices in the European port cities. The "outer core," however, was not only the Cephallonian but also the wider Greek shipping network and its foreign collaborators.

The international network of the Vaglianos extended beyond the Black Sea: along the Mediterranean, European Atlantic and Northern Sea coastline (Map 3.2). Along the eastern Mediterranean coast the brothers kept business associates in Rodosto (Tekirdag) on the Sea of Marmara, in Smyrna, Samos, Chios, Larnaka, Alexandria, and Cairo. On the Greek mainland there were associates in Athens, Piraeus, Patras, and Galaxidi; more on the Aegean islands of Andros, Syros, Melos, Santorini, Poros, Spetses, Hydra, and the Ionian islands of Cephalonia, Zante, and Corfu; and finally, there were agents in the main Adriatic port of Trieste, the transit port of Malta, and the Ligurian port of Genova. In Marseille, the western Mediterranean node of their international network until 1869, Constantine and Leon Melas were the main agents of the Vagliano House. They were replaced in 1869 by Andrea Vagliano. After the death of Andrea Vagliano in 1887, his son, Marinos, and his nephew, Athanasse Met. Vagliano (son of his brother Metaxas), managed the Marseille branch of the Vagliano House. From 1870, Panagi worked with his nephew Alcibiades Vagliano (son of Mari) in London and in the late 1890s he was joined by Basil Vagliano (son of his brother Metaxas); the other son of Mari, Athanasse Mar. Vagliano was probably sent directly to Paris, although there is no evidence when he exactly went there. The filaments of the Vagliano network extended throughout the Black Sea basin, the Mediterranean, and western Europe, and all of it was tightly controlled by the brothers, whose humble beginnings belied their power in nineteenth-century shipping.

---

[30] Harlaftis, A History of Greek-Owned Shipping, Table 3.4, 74.

[31] "The grain magnate from Cephalonia, Marinos Vagliano, claiming 20,000 Turkish lira from the peasants, had managed as a Russian subject to include himself in the reparation scheme for Russian subjects who suffered during the Russian-Turkish War and received this money from the Ottoman government as compensation." See Andreas Lyberatos, "The Usury Cases of the Black Sea Region: State Legitimation and Bourgeois Rule of Law in Nineteenth Century Dobrudzha," Études Balkaniques XLIX, no. 3–4 (2013): 59–94.

[32] See the Vagliano Genealogical Tree, Appendix 2.A.

Function of the Network

The Vagliano Brothers formed a nodal agency, the center of an entrepreneur-ial network. One of the greatest contributions of this network was that, apart from its own business, the House acted as an agent involved in sale and purchase of cargoes and ships, chartering, insurance, finance, and all other agency business for hundreds of small Ionian and Aegean island shipping companies, charging about 2 percent commission for the transactions carried out for them. An entrepreneurial network can be well described as "a group of agents that pursue repeated, enduring exchange relations with one another."[33] The Vagliano business network facilitated the purchase and sale of goods and their sea transport from the West to the East, and became a system of infor-mation processing that produced and disseminated rules, and ultimately diminished transaction costs. It did so based on personal relations, bypassing official market mechanisms and internalizing their activities in dispersed locations. This network minimized entrepreneurial risk by adopting a timely, unified response to crises. It was based on trust, which was generated by economic interest and by the social-control system of the Greek communities either on the islands or abroad.

Letter writing made the network function smoothly. The letters of two Vagliano associates allow us a glimpse inside their business. George Vucina, a merchant and banker in Odessa, and a merchant captain and shipowner from the island of Spetses, Georgios Coutsis, were respectively a major and minor partner of the Vaglianos.[34] The correspondence of Captain Georgios Coutsis to the three brothers reveals the nature of the business and opens a window to their character: these letters contain mostly business information,

---

[33] Joel Polodny and Karen Page, "Network Forms of Organisation," *Annual Review of Sociology* 24, no. 1 (1998): 57–76. See also Gordon Boyce, "Network Structures, Processes, and Dynamics," in Lewis R. Fischer and Even Lange, eds., *International Merchant Shipping in the Nineteenth and Twentieth Centuries: The Comparative Dimension* (St. John's, Newfoundland: International Maritime Economic History Association, 2008).

[34] The precious Coutsis archive belonged to Georgios Coutsis, a merchant Master and shipowner from the island of Spetses; the archive has been preserved by his great-great-grandsons. The archive has been fully used by Alexandra Papadopoulou in her unpublished PhD thesis "Maritime Businesses," chapter 6. Concerning the Vagliano Brothers, the Coutsis archive contains sixty-two letters from Mari Vagliano in Taganrog, twenty-five letters from Andreas in Constantinople and Marseille, and ten letters from Panagi Vagliano from London during 1869–1872; the letters have been transliterated by Alexandra Papadopoulou. The correspondence of Georgios Vucina concerns exclusively his correspondence with Panagi Vagliano; it has been published for the use of the court case *Vagliano Bros. v. Bank of England*. Invaluable are the ledgers and the letter books of the Vagliano London office in addition to logbooks, charter-parties, and insurance policies found in the Vagliano Archive deposited in the General State Archives of the Prefecture of Cephalonia.

but they are expressed in a personal style.[35] Mari's letters are professional but they always have a couple of more personal sentences at the beginning or the end. Andrea's letters from Marseille are the longest and richest, with an even more distinct personal character, whereas Panagi from London is laconic in his letters to Coutsis. He mentions only what is absolutely necessary and signs off as "Vagliano Bros.," where the others sign with their names. Among the many business activities and transactions described in these letters, it is amusing to see that Andrea Vagliano or Mari Vagliano were also asked to carry out Captain Coutsis' orders for the delivery of fashionable French furniture, or silver candlesticks from Russia for his house on the island of Spetses.[36] Based on the content of these letters, both Andrea and Mari knew Captain Coutsis very well, as he used to travel constantly to Taganrog and Constantinople; they probably had the same relations with all the captains they collaborated with for many years.

The three Vagliano brothers conducted continuous control and rechecking of communication, mostly in Greek and if necessary in Italian (but rarely in French), in their letter writing during this period.[37] They oversaw a vital system of information processing and circulation of information across the network. At the end of their letters, the brothers exchanged information on freight rates, local grain prices, exchange rates, and references to the problems of the new season in their respective parts of the world.[38] They expected feedback from business associates and demanded a steady flow of letters from all sides in case of delays.[39]

The Vaglianos personally handled sales and purchases of cargoes to all destinations. Each of the three brothers, from their end, purchased cargoes for their business associates and/or themselves, chartered vessels to carry them, insured them, supervised their lading, and sold them. They also issued,

---

[35] Private Archive of Coutsis family, Spetses, Letter of Mari Vagliano (Taganrog) to G. I. Coutsis (Spetses), 47/3, September 20, 1869.

[36] Private Archive of Coutsis family, Spetses, Letter of Andreas Vagliano (Marseilles) to G. I. Coutsis (Athens), 46/26, December 31, 1870.

[37] G. Vucina to Vagliano brothers, 24/5, February 1887 in "Minutes of Evidence and Proceedings at the Trial. In the High Court of Justice," appendix 8 in "In the House of Lords. Appeal Case, the Governor and Company of the Bank of England vs Vagliano Bros," Freshfields Papers: Records of Civil Court Actions, 1798–1903, F13.38, Archives of the Bank of England, 225.

[38] Private Archive of Coutsis family, Spetses, Letter of Mari Vagliano (Taganrog) to G. I. Coutsis (Spetses), 43, March 20, 1871. G. Vucina to Vagliano brothers, 10/22, August 1887, in "Minutes of Evidence and Proceedings at the Trial. In the High Court of Justice," appendix 8 in "In the House of Lords. Appeal Case, the Governor and Company of the Bank of England vs Vagliano Bros," Freshfields Papers: Records of Civil Court Actions, 1798–1903, F13.38, Archives of the Bank of England, 237, 241.

[39] Private Archive of Coutsis family, Spetses, Letter of Mari Vagliano (Taganrog) to G.I. Coutsis (Spetses), 47/15, December 6, 1869.

circulated, exchanged, and cashed bills of exchange, and kept detailed accounts of their collaborators. So wrote Panagi in a letter from London to Captain George I. Coutsis in Spetses, on May 16, 1871:

> [W]e confine ourselves with the present [letter] to informing you that our man in Marseilles [Andrea Vagliano] sent us on your behalf a remittance of £1,460 and we gave you from 27th July shortly. On the other hand, you have been indebted with £4,000 from the 19th of the same month, a sum that our man in Taganrog [Mari Vagliano] withdrew ... so that you be pleased to make a report in writing.[40]

Quality control of the produce was also of prime importance. Coutsis, for example, trusted that Mari would choose him for his good-quality grain. In his letters to Coutsis, Mari mentions in detail when each ship arrived, and what kind of grain he purchased to load onto the ship.[41] The Vaglianos sold grain in the Baltic Exchange for their business associates in the Black Sea to merchants not only in London but also to continental ports like Rouen, Antwerp, or Hamburg. The system of sending samples of grain to the buyer was the usual method.[42]

The Vaglianos mediated for insurance in foreign insurance companies or insured vessels and cargoes themselves after the 1870s. Until 1869, the cargoes of the business associates of Mari Vagliano were insured via their relatives in Marseilles, and the Melas Brothers in the French insurance market of Marseilles (and, after 1869, by Andrea Vagliano).[43] Insurance at the time of sailing usually covered only the cargo, not the vessel. This was confirmed in a letter George Coutsis wrote to Mari Vagliano, "Note that I leave the ships always uninsured in the hands of Holy Providence."[44]

At times of crisis, the Vagliano Brothers' firm hand over the entire network was pivotal as they acted as a "mega agency."[45] Chartering hundreds of Greek sailing

---

[40] Private Archive of Coutsis family, Spetses, Letter of Panagi Vagliano (London) to G. I. Coutsis (Spetses).

[41] Private Archive of Coutsis family, Spetses, Letter of Mari Vagliano (Taganrog) to G. I. Coutsis (Spetses), 47/18, August 24, 1868.

[42] Vagliano Brothers to G. Vucina, June 30, 1887 in "Minutes of Evidence and Proceedings at the Trial. In the High Court of Justice," appendix 8 in "In the House of Lords. Appeal Case, the Governor and Company of the Bank of England vs Vagliano Bros," Freshfields Papers: Records of Civil Court Actions, 1798–1903, F13.38, Archives of the Bank of England, 234. This letter is signed by Alcibiades.

[43] Private Archive of Coutsis family, Spetses, Letter of Mari Vagliano (Taganrog) to G. I. Coutsis (Spetses), 47/18, August 24, 1868.

[44] Private Archive of Coutsis family, Spetses, Letter of G. I. Coutsis (Spetses) to Andrea Vagliano (Marseilles), 46/5, January 12, 1869.

[45] The concept of the "mega agency" was coined by Alexandra Papadopoulou in Gelina Harlaftis and Alexandra Papadopoulou, "The 'Mega' Agent and the 'Micro' Principal: The Evolution of Greek Shipping Firm in the Nineteenth Century," paper presented at the European Conference on Shipping, Intermodalism & Ports – ECONSHIP 2011

vessels was a major part of their business, but was risky, so the centrally controlled network helped to minimize this entrepreneurial risk by adopting a timely, unified response to crises.[46] This was evident in 1878, when the Vaglianos saved a large number of Greek sailing shipowners from bankruptcy. Greek ships were particularly active in British ports from 1871 to 1877; in 1877 alone, about 250 Greek sailing ships of about 65,000 net registered tons entered these ports each year, with cargoes insured in the London market.[47] The Russo-Ottoman War of 1877–1878 inflicted a major blow on Greek shipowners when London insurers excluded them from the London market, stating that their policies "warranted no Greek or Turkish flag."[48] In response, the Vaglianos chartered immobilized Greek-owned vessels in the Azov – probably at much lower freight rates – and undertook the insurance of cargoes and vessels. Their personal acquaintance and long-term collaboration with the Greek sailing shipowners helped them determine whom to trust.[49] Once the crisis had passed, the Vaglianos profited from this experience by increasing their insurance business: in their London Office Insurance Book of 1898–1903, they listed several hundred vessels.[50]

Trust within the network was generated by economic interest and by the social-control system of the Greek communities either on the islands or abroad. Any member of the community who breached this trust was cast out. An interesting example of this is Captain Metaxas-Laskaratos who in 1860 was given a sum of money in Constantinople by Andrea Vagliano to carry to Mari Vagliano in Tangarog. Mari Vagliano found out that the money the captain had given him was forged. The captain soon discovered that after deceiving Mari Vagliano he was no longer able to find work, not only in Tangarog but also in the other ports of the Azov.[51] Trustworthy captains and seamen were a valuable asset, not only within the Vagliano network but also within the broader "Ionian network." Letters of recommendation were an important tool to retain business within a trusted circle.[52]

"Maritime Transport: Opportunities and Threats in the Post-crises World," June 22–24, 2011, University of the Aegean, Chios, Greece. For more analysis, see Chapter 5.

[46] Harlaftis, *A History of Greek-Owned Shipping*, 152–154, 165; charter parties found in the Arvanitis Archive and the Archive of Captain Anastassios Syrmas, Private Collection of Admiral Anastassios Zografos Hellenic Literary and Historical Archives Society (ELIA).

[47] Harlaftis, *A History of Greek-Owned Shipping*, Appendix 1.33, 311.

[48] Andreas Lemos, *Το ναυτικόν του γένους των Ελλήνων: Η ιστορία του* [*The Shipping of the Greeks: Its History*], vol. A (Athens: Tsikopoulos, 1968), 153–154.

[49] Andreas Lemos, *Νεοέλληνες αειναύται* [*Modern Greek Eternal Seamen*] (Athens: Kostas Tsikopoulos, 1971), 380–382.

[50] General State Archives, Archive of the Prefecture of Cephalonia, Vagliano Archive, Insurance Book, 1898–1903.

[51] Metaxas-Laskaratos, *Commercial-Consular Prosecutions*, 10.

[52] Private Archive of Coutsis family, Spetses, Letter of Mari Vagliano (Taganrog) to G. I. Coutsis, Spetses, 47/6, October 11, 1869.

Trust was also safeguarded by meticulous and trustworthy bookkeeping. Each member of the Vagliano House sent current accounts in double-entry form on chartering, insurance, loading, unloading, wharfage, telegraphic expenditure, and bills of exchange to their collaborating shipowners. Accounts with Mari Vagliano were calculated in silver rubles. Every season, usually from April to October, the current account of every client was made up by Mari Vagliano's office in Taganrog and sent out (see Appendix 1.C). They made payments in French francs, pounds sterling, or more rarely in Ottoman lire. Every letter contained the exchange rate and the final negotiated rate at which the Coutsis or Vucina money was exchanged for the Vagliano cargo payments. Furthermore, the Vaglianos always double-checked the current accounts they sent (See Appendix 1.C).[53] According to the jurist Dalloz, there was a current account between two *négociants* as soon as there was credit or debit between them for commercial affairs.[54] The role played by the current account was that of trust between partners. It was indispensable in the construction of long-lasting commercial relations.[55]

The letter books in the Vagliano Brothers' London office indicate an annual flow of five to six thousand letters.[56] According to the company books, in the 1890s there were about 170 business associates with whom they had transactions and kept accounts. These included two in Belgium; two in Bulgaria; twenty-four in the British Empire (including Gibraltar and Malta, Cyprus, and Egypt); sixteen in France; three in Germany; seventy-six in Greece; six in the Netherlands; seventeen in the Ottoman Empire; four in Romania; eleven in Russia; one in Spain; and two in the United States (Appendix 1.E).

Trade

The Vaglianos continued the tradition of the big *négociants* of continental Europe and the British trading companies of the eighteenth and nineteenth centuries, which were the essential links in the commercial chain connecting the European colonies with Europe. Similarly, they fulfilled a multiplicity of functions and activities that linked the Russian colonies and frontier lands with western European markets.

---

[53] G. Vucina to Vagliano Brothers, June 17, 1887 in "Minutes of Evidence and Proceedings at the Trial. In the High Court of Justice," appendix 8 in "In the House of Lords. Appeal Case, the Governor and Company of the Bank of England vs Vagliano Bros," Freshfields Papers: Records of Civil Court Actions, 1798–1903, F13.38, Archives of the Bank of England, 232.

[54] Yannick Lemarchand, Cheryl McWatters, and Laure Pineau-Defois, "The Current Account as Cognitive Artefact: Stories and Accounts of La Maison Chaurand," in Pierre Gervais, Yannick Lemarchand, and Dominique Margairaz, eds., *Merchants and Profit in the Age of Commerce, 1680–1830* (London: Pickering and Chatto, 2014), 13–31, 33–52.

[55] Ibid., 30–31.

[56] General State Archives, Archive of the Prefecture of Cephalonia, Vagliano Archive, Foreign Letter Book, November 13, 1901–April 4, 1902, Ledger Book, 1901–1904.

At the peak of the Vagliano trading company business, between the 1860s and 1880s, Mari Vagliano became the biggest exporter of grain from the Azov, followed by other Greek, German, and Italian firms. Comparing Tables 3.1 and 3.2 confirms that within less than ten years, he replaced the primary merchants of the previous era, the Chiot Ralli and Chiot Scaramanga families. Both Chiot families, with almost ten million golden rubles-worth of imports and exports, constituted one of the top commercial groups of the whole Russian Empire (see Table 2.2). Mari Vagliano in 1860 followed with almost three million rubles-worth of imports and exports; this placed him as the second largest merchant of the Azov and sixth in all southern Russian ports. The German Karl Lander and Franz Bone followed, then the Russian Nikolai Toskov, the Greek Anton Avierino, and the Italian Stefan Mimbelli. By 1869, Mari Vagliano came top of the list and conducted 14 percent of the total grain exports of the Azov (Table 3.2). He kept close commercial relations with the Cuppa and the Ambanopoulo, with whom he developed family relations in the 1870s by the marriage of two of the daughters of Andrea Vagliano into these families. The ten biggest Azov exporters controlled more than half its exports, and Vagliano with Cuppa and Ambanopoulo controlled a quarter. In 1886, the Vaglianos retained their dominant position in the Azov according to the annual report of the British Consul Wagstaff in Taganrog,[57] as well as in 1899 in Novorossiysk.[58]

At the other end of the trade, the great leap forward happened after the establishment of Andrea Vagliano in Marseilles in 1869. Only one year after Andrea Vagliano arrived, he received 139 ships in Marseilles of about 35,000 tons; this remained at about the same level until the 1880s (Table 3.3). It was reported in an Athenian newspaper that 300 to 400 ships were chartered by the Vaglianos.[59] Considering all destinations, 300 vessels per year is not an exaggeration. If one counts as an average cargo 2,000 chetwerts per vessel, that would make it 600,000 chetwerts in total. Indeed, in 1869 Mari Vagliano exported about 600,000 chetwerts (Table 3.2).

The decline in Marseilles after the death of Andrea in 1887 is evident in the decrease by tonnage of ships handled in the French port in the 1890s. Arrivals of ships chartered by the Vaglianos in the port of London were about 15–20 ships during the same period.[60] Although their importance in these two ports

---

[57] Report by Consul Wagstaff on the Navigation and Trade at the Ports of the Sea of Azov for the Year 1886, *British Parliamentary Papers* 85–86 (Russia, 1886), 53.

[58] Information supplied by Mr. Thomas Sterne at Novorossiysk included in the Report of Consul-General T. Sandwith on the trade and shipping of Odessa and the rest of the South Russian ports for the year 1888, *British Parliamentary Papers* 80–81 (Russia, 1889), 294.

[59] Newspaper Ακρόπολις [*Akropolis*], January 26, 1896.

[60] Processed data from the *London Customs Bills of Entry*, 1880, 1890.

Table 3.1 *Main merchants (by value) of the Azov, 1860*

Exporter	Exports from	Imports	Exports	Imports and exports in rubles	Imports and exports in £
Scaramanga Ivan	Mariupol, Taganrog and Rostov	114,976	7,380,027	7,495,003	1,199,200
Ralli Konstantin	Rostov and Odessa	3,890	997,179	1,001,069	160,171
Ralli Alexandr	Taganrog, Rostov, and Odessa	134,809	1,117,486	1,252,295	200,367
Vagliano Mark (Mari)	Taganrog and Rostov	753,948	1,833,464	2,726,413	436,226
Lander Karl	Taganrog, Rostov, Mariupol and Yeisk	79,010	2,121,227	2,200,237	352,038
Bone Franz	Berdyansk and Taganrog	11,644	1,788,948	1,800,592	288,095
Toskov Nikolai	Rostov and Odessa	307,786	1,271,516	1,579,302	252,688
Avierino Anton	Taganrog	825,632	702,426	1,528,058	244,489
Mimbeli Stefan	Mariupol	2,183	1,155,026	1,157,209	185,153

• £1 sterling = 6.25 rubles.

Source: Государственная внешняя торговля в разных ея видах за 1859 год, [State Overview of the External Trade and Its Different Types], Department of External Trade, St. Petersburg, 1860.

Table 3.2 *Main grain exporters (by quantity) of the Azov, 1869*

Exporter	Exports from	Grain (wheat, rye, barley, oats) In chetwerts*	% of total
Vagliano Marko	Taganrog and Rostov	603,284	14%
Scaramanga & Co	Taganrog and Rostov	425,708	10%
Cuppa	Berdyansk	253,087	6%
Rokka	Taganrog and Rostov	206,758	5%
Kovachevich Brothers	Mariupol	152,200	3%
Mimbeli Brothers	Mariupol	147,000	3%
Yeames James	Taganrog and Rostov	144,355	3%
Ambanopoulo	Berdyansk	142,980	3%
Petrokokkino Dimitri	Taganrog and Rostov	119,569	3%
Sougdouri Pericles	Rostov	91,539	2%
Total of ten biggest exporters		**2,286,480**	**52%**
Total exports from the Azov		4,572,960	100%

* 1 chetwert = 5.77 British imperial bushels. 1 chetwert of wheat = 162.13 kg.
Source: Alexander K. Geyns, *О торговле по Азовскому прибрежью* [*For the Trade of the Azov*] (St. Petersburg: n.p., 1871), 26–29, 79–80, table 19.

Table 3.3 *Exports of the House of Vagliano Bros. to Marseilles*

Year	Arrivals of ships chartered by Vaglianos (number of ships)	Arrivals of ships chartered by Vaglianos (net registered tons)
1865	–	–
1870	139	34,404
1876	93	24,210
1881	92	32,097
1885	24	24,138
1890	24	10,182
1895	14	12,639

Source: Processed data from *Semaphore de Marseilles*, 1865, 1870, 1875, 1880, 1885, 1890; Harlaftis, *A History of Greek-owned Shipping*, Table 3.7.

diminished during the 1880s and 1890s, the Vagliano Brothers' activities had shifted to the continental ports of Rotterdam, Le Havre, and elsewhere. The usual route for ships carrying grain was to northern European ports, then in ballast to British ports, where they loaded coal for the return voyage.[61]

Banking and Finance

The Vagliano Brothers were also successful merchant bankers in four empires: the Russian, Ottoman, French, and British.[62] Europe's merchant bankers who controlled network firms established in many countries kept offices in at least one of Europe's financial capitals: London, Paris, Vienna, Frankfurt, and Geneva. The booming European economy, and the unprecedented expansion of world trade, made the growth of financial institutions indispensable during the nineteenth century, which witnessed a banking revolution in Britain, France, and Germany.[63] Among these centers, Constantinople developed as the financial center of the East, with close links to all the western European financial capitals.

In all nodes of their network, the Vagliano Brothers acted as financial institutions via which their clients carried out their business. They became an integral part of Europe's banking system, collaborating with other merchant banking houses from Taganrog or Odessa all the way to St. Petersburg, Constantinople, Paris, and London. Their laundry list of banking services included: cashing bills of exchange for a commission; transferring money on commission; providing mercantile and shipping loans with interest; depositing clients' money in banks; lending money for the purchase of ships, cargoes, or other investments to its members; buying and selling currency on commission; and buying and selling state bonds on commission.

The Vagliano House internalized the market within the firm and was able to secure credit via bills of exchange, thus coordinating the flow of payments within the network. It provided transfers of money that were made in three ways. The first was in the traditional way of "bundles" of money transferred by the Masters of their ships or other Masters they trusted. Second, they sent bills of exchange by letter, carried by trusted men, always taking into consideration

---

[61] Harlaftis, *A History of Greek-Owned Shipping*, 24–38.

[62] Richard Roberts, *Schroders: Merchants and Bankers* (London: Macmillan, 1992); Richard Roberts, "What's in a Name? Merchants, Merchant Bankers, Accepting Houses, Issuing Houses, Industrial Bankers and Investment Bankers," *Business History* 35, no. 3 (July 1993): 22–38; Stanley Chapman, *The Rise of Merchant Banking* (London: Allen & Unwin, 1984).

[63] Youssef Cassis, "Private Banks and the Onset of the Corporate Economy," in Y. Cassis and P. Cottrell, eds., *The World of Private Banking* (Aldershot: Ashgate, 2009), 43.

the interests of the client.[64] Third, they made bank transfers, usually via the Bank of England, the Azov Bank, or the Russian Imperial Bank.[65] The Mavros in Odessa acted as the main financial agents of the Vaglianos, since they were situated in the city with the biggest port and the best foreign exchange market in the area.[66]

Apart from their daily merchant banking business, the Vaglianos also got involved in dealing in Greek state loans – particularly Andrea Vagliano in Constantinople, who was referred to as "Agent of the National Bank of Greece" and dealt with state bonds from 1865 to 1890.[67] The connection with the National Bank started in August 1865, when the good reputation of the Vagliano Brothers, already established in London, encouraged Georgios Stavrou, the first Director of the National Bank of Greece, to ask the Vaglianos to open credit with them of £20,000.[68] Georgios P. Skouzes (1811–1884), a prominent Greek merchant banker, mediated the deal. Skouzes collaborated with the merchant bankers Charles Erlanger and Joseph Hambro, who were also close collaborators of the Vaglianos.[69] What the Vagliano Agency did was to provide on behalf of the National Bank sale and purchase of state bonds, repayment of coupons, and distribution of interest rates with all the top resident big merchants, traders, and bankers of Constantinople, like the Jewish I. Camondo and the Greek Dimitriades, Zographos, E. Baltazzi Syngros & Coronios, Zarifi & Zafiropoulo, A. P. Mavrogordato, Galatis and Psiachis, Z. Stephanovik Schilizzi, and Z. Chrysoveloni, Greek banker in Romania; other prominent merchants were the Rallis, Sechiaris, Vouros, Eugenides, and Trochanis.[70]

Mari Vagliano was one of the founders of the Azov-Don Bank along with other top merchants, both Greek and Jewish: Ivan Scaramanga, Mark Varvazzi, Theodor Rodocanachi, Jacob Polyakov, Samuel Wager, and Leon

---

[64] Private Archive of Coutsis family, Spetses, Letter of Mari Vagliano (Taganrog) to G. I. Coutsis, 47/21, September 20, 1868.

[65] Private Archive of Coutsis family, Spetses, Letter of Mari Vagliano (Taganrog) to G. I. Coutsis, 47/14, March 1, 1869.

[66] Private Archive of Coutsis family, Spetses, Letter of Mari Vagliano (Taganrog) to G. I. Coutsis, Spetses, 47/33, August 1, 1869.

[67] A1. 21.102, "Andreas Vagliano, Constantinople, 1869–1873," Foreign Correspondence, series A, Historical Archive, National Bank of Greece.

[68] Letter of Vagliano Bros. in London to the Director of the National Bank of Greece in Athens, August 17, 1865, A1.S21.Y17.103, "Vagliano Bros. London (1865–1890). Foreign Correspondence, series A," Historical Archive, National Bank of Greece.

[69] "Georgios P. Skouzes" and "Pavlos G. Skouzes," in Constantinos Vovolinis, Μέγα Ελληνικόν Βιογραφικόν Λεξικόν [Grand Greek Biographical Dictionary] vol. 1 (Athens: Publication of Industrial Review, 1958], 351–357. Ledger "Bills Payable," 1898–1902, Vagliano Archive, GSA, Cephalonia Archive. For the Hambros see Appendix 2.G.

[70] Processed data from A1.21.102.3 (1871), Historical Archive, National Bank of Greece.

90   AN INTERNATIONAL TRADING HOUSE

Rosenthal.[71] Apart from Taganrog, the commercial Azov-Don Bank opened branch offices in Rostov, Mariupol, and Berdyansk. It was the only bank in the southeastern port of the Russian Empire that accepted foreign bills of exchange. The bank, which collaborated with Italian, French, and English banks, acquired a very good reputation in the foreign exchange market and towards the end of the nineteenth century was regarded, by central economic authorities, as one of the most successful in the empire.[72] In participating in the formation of banks, Mari Vagliano was following in the footsteps of other Greek merchants, particularly the Chiots.[73] After all, Mari Vagliano had acted for years as a powerful merchant banker in Russia, providing large loans to the amount of 20 million rubles per year.[74]

But the best-known banker of the three was Panagi Vagliano. He opened his account with the Bank of England on August 5, 1858 and held it until November 1887, when his account was closed; it had been his firm's bank for twenty-nine years. The office of Panagi Vagliano was just around the corner from the Bank. He firstly held offices in 142 Gresham House before moving for good to 19 Old Broad St., where he stayed to the end of his life.[75] In his analysis of merchant banking, Stanley Chapman considers the Greeks as one of the groups that formed the core of the City's merchant banking, especially from the 1820s to the 1870s, building up the "unsullied business

[71] Memorandum of the Ministry of Economy in State Secretary, March 4, 1871.1152.8.214.2–3 in V. V. Morozan, "Деятельность Азовско-Донского коммерческого банка на Юге России в конце XIX в.", Исторический факультет МГУ, 31 января 2007 г." ["The Activities of the Commercial Bank of Azov-Don in South Russia at the End of the Nineteenth Century"], *III Научные чтения памяти профессора В.И.Бовыкина* [*III Scientific Readings Dedicated to the Memory of Professor B. I. Bovikina*], Department of History of the State University of Moscow, January 31, 2007], www.hist.msu.ru/Science/Conf/01_2007/Morozan.pdf (accessed February 15, 2009).
[72] Morozan, "The Activities of the Commercial Bank of Azov-Don."
[73] Chapman, *The Rise of Merchant Banking*, 166. See also Katerina Galani, "The Galata Bankers and the International Banking of the Greek Business Group in the Nineteenth Century," in Edhem Eldem, Vangelis Kechriotis, and Sophia Laiou, eds., *The Economic and Social Development of the Port-Cities of the Southern Black Sea Coast, Late 18th–Beginning of the 20th Century*, Black Sea History Project Working Papers, vol. 5 (Corfu: Ionian University, 2016), www.blacksea.gr (accessed November 10, 2016).
[74] Testimony at the Court of Kharkov of the ex-employee (he worked for Vagliano for eleven years), S. Simonovich, *Кіевлянинъ* [*Kievlianin*] (daily Kiev newspaper), February 21, 1885; see also Newspaper *Московскіе вѣдомости* [*Moskovie Vendomostii*], February 22, 1885.
[75] Vagliano Brothers' account in "Drawing Office: Customer Account Ledger," C98/3618, 1858, Archives of the Bank of England. For the Vagliano Brothers valuable information was drawn from the Customer Account Ledgers of the Drawing office where one can find all the daily transactions of the firm from 1858 to 1887; there is also a series of files including the famous Court case *Vagliano Bros.* v. *the Governor and Co. and the Bank of England.*

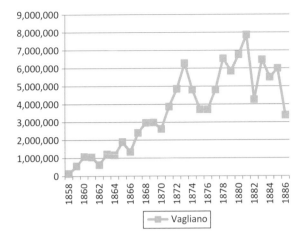

Figure 3.5 Vagliano Bros. transactions* at the Bank of England, 1858–1887
(aggregate value in pounds sterling)
* By "transactions" is meant the aggregate transactions including commercial bills,
cash, securities, advances, etc. along with customers' liabilities for acceptances.
Source: Appendix 2.F.

in acceptances."[76] Among the foreign big merchant bankers of the City that
developed its large international financial market were, for example, the
German Schröders and Barings, the Jewish Rothschilds and Cohens, and the
Greek Rallis or Vaglianos.

Figure 3.5 reveals the aggregate movements of the account of Vagliano
Brothers in the Bank of England, which involves their total assets (including
commercial bills, cash, securities, and advances) along with customers' liabilities for acceptances from 1858 to 1887. The transactions were of great
magnitude. From 835 payments of £554,363 in 1859, the firm reached 8,931
payments of £7,865,769 in 1881. In Figure 3.5 we observe a continuous
increase up to 1881, when they reached their peak with almost £8 million.
The rise of their transactions was not affected by the economic crisis of the
1860s, the American Civil War, or the Overend Gurney & Co. insolvency,
which shook the City in 1866. Furthermore, their business peaked during the
Russo-Ottoman war of 1877–1878, during which Mari Vagliano was able to
bypass trade embargoes in the Black Sea and send grain via the railways and
waterways to the Baltic Sea instead of the usual sea transport via the Black Sea.

[76] Chapman, *The Rise of Merchant Banking*, 127, 173.

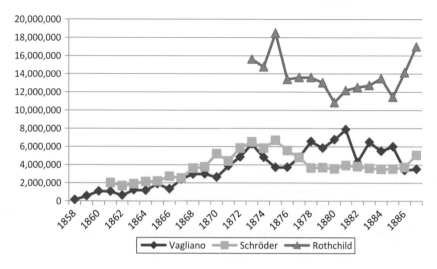

Figure 3.6   Comparison of Vagliano Bros., Schröder, and Rothschild transactions, 1858–1887 (in pounds sterling)
Source: Appendix 2.F.

The abrupt decreases in 1881 and 1886 were brought about mainly by internal problems (see Figure 3.5).

Comparing the size of their business to that of the Schröders and the Rothschilds of London (see Figure 3.6) underscores the importance of the Vagliano Brothers as bankers. Although the Rothschilds, involved as they were in government lending, carried out two or three times more transactions than the Vaglianos, in 1881 they were very close, with the Rothschilds transacting £10 million and the Vaglianos £8 million. That same year the Schröders were at £4 million. The Vagliano merchant banking activities were entirely comparable with the Schröders; in fact, it seems that Vagliano Brother dealt much better with the post-1876 economic crisis.

When Panagi Vagliano arrived in London, an important community of Greek merchant bankers, established in the 1820s, was already there, and it gradually became an integral part of the developing cluster of the City's merchant bankers.[77] Centered in Finsbury Circus in the City, the families of

---

[77] Katerina Galani, "Έλληνες έμποροι-τραπεζίτες στο City του Λονδίνου: η πρώ-τη εγκατάσ-ταση (αρχές 19ου αιώνα) [Greek merchant and bankers in the City of London: the first settlement (early 19th century)]", in *British-Greek Relations. Aspects of their Recent History* (Hellenic Parliament Foundation for Parliamentarism and Democracy: Athens, 2016), 237–256. For the earlier connection of Greek merchants with the Levant Company see Galani, *British Shipping and Trade in the Mediterranean in the Age of War*.

Ralli, Argenti, Petrokockino, Rodocanachi, Schilizzi, Scaramanga, Ionidis, and more connected the Russian and Ottoman financial market of Constantinople with the City of London.[78] The Bank of England became, for a large number of Greeks who opened accounts in the 1840s and 1850s, the Bank with which they collaborated the most. It is interesting to note that the Bank of England tracked the activity of the whole group closely, in a volume titled "Greek Accounts, 1848–1852."[79] By 1881, Panagi Vagliano in London collaborated with more than eighty Greek families from the Chiot and Ionian network and an equivalent number of City merchant bankers (see Appendix 1.E).

The London branch's foreign banking business consisted to a large extent of consignment and commission business on accepting bills of exchange.[80] The Archives from the Bank of England give us a superb view from the inside, revealing in detail the organization of the office and the daily course of business of Panagi Vagliano as a City merchant banker.[81] In the 1880s, the Vaglianos' office had eleven employees apart from Panagi himself and his nephew Alcibiades (compared to the Schröder office in the City of London, which in the 1870s kept twenty-five clerks).[82] Out of those eleven, only three were English and most of them had worked with the Vaglianos more than twenty years. The office was organized around correspondence and the acceptances and payments of bills of exchange. Figure 3.7 reveals the organization of the office in 1887; there were two managers – the outdoor manager and the indoor manager (a deputy manager – while the correspondence from abroad, the mainstay of the office, was handled by two clerks who were allotted different geographical areas. There were also two cashiers and four bookkeepers.[83]

The Vagliano Brothers acted as merchant bankers and agents for hundreds of small, medium, and large Greek trading and shipping businesses in the eastern Mediterranean and Black Sea. Although their network provided trust and control over fraud, the London office encountered the biggest fraud from inside: from one of their own clerks. The event made the Vaglianos the talk of

---

[78] Maria Christina Chatziioannou and Gelina Harlaftis, "From the Levant to the City of London: Mercantile Credit in the Greek International Commercial Networks of the Eighteenth and Nineteenth Centuries," in Philip L. Cottrell, Even Lange, and Ulf Olsson, eds., *Centres and Peripheries in Banking: The Historical Development of Financial Markets* (Aldershot: Ashgate, 2007), 13–40.

[79] "Discount Office Analyses and Summaries: Greek Accounts 1848–1852," C30/4, Archives of the Bank of England. To my knowledge, no other ethnocultural group was followed in this way.

[80] Roberts, *Schroders*, 48; "Minutes of Evidence and Proceedings at the Trial. In the High Court of Justice," appendix 8 in "In the House of Lords. Appeal Case, the Governor and Company of the Bank of England vs Vagliano Bros," Freshfields papers: records of Civil Court Actions, 1798–1903, F13.38, Archives of the Bank of England, 138–140.

[81] Ibid., 82–103.   [82] Roberts, *Schroders*, 76.   [83] Ibid., 75–82.

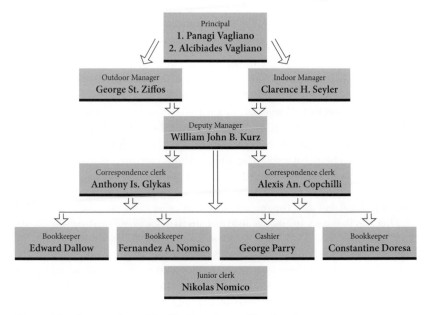

Figure 3.7   Organization of the Vagliano Bros. office, London

the City and brought them to the forefront of all the main English newspapers. The case touched the bread and butter of the City – the bill of exchange.

On October 12, 1887, seventy-three-year-old Panagi Vagliano, after taking his breakfast, left his house in the fashionable district of Bayswater, got into his carriage and was driven to his office at 19 Broad Street, in the City, as had been his everyday habit (excepting Sundays) for the past thirty years. Recent developments had left him depressed. His younger brother Andrea, established in Marseilles, had died at the age of sixty a few months before, while just a year ago, his older brother Mari was finally able to get out of the five-year legal confrontation with the Russian government and had decided to retire. Since May 14, 1887, the firm, led by the three brothers for decades, had only one partner. Arriving at his office did not change his mood. To his amazement, he found that between February 18, 1887 and October 12, 1887, there were forty-three forged bills of exchange purporting to have been drawn by George Vucina in Odessa to the order of the firm of C. Petridi and Co., carrying on business at Constantinople, and accepted by him. These bills were fabricated by his trusted correspondence clerk Anthony I. Glyka.

Panagi discovered further that Glyka had been engaged in enormous speculations on the Stock Exchange, and that in order to meet his engagements he forged the abovementioned bills and had received payments for them from the Vaglianos' account at the Bank of England in the amount of £71,500.[84] (This is about £8,937,500 in 2018 purchasing power.[85]) Glyka had carried out a careful, elaborate, and ingenious forgery; he printed excellent imitations of the bills of exchange of Vucina, forged the letters of advice, and manipulated the office's ledgers. He was arrested, pled guilty to the forgery of bills, and was sentenced to ten years' penal servitude.

The stolen amount, however, was enormous and the knowledge of the banking market led Panagi Vagliano on November 21, 1887 to sue the Bank of England to recover the sum of £71,500 and interest. He alleged that the amount had been improperly debited to him by the Bank of England and that the payment of the bills was wholly due to the negligence of the Bank of England, as they should have notified him before paying large sums over the counter.[86]

This fraud, which hit at the heart of the trade's primary financial instrument, the bill of exchange, was no usual case. It shook the community of the City merchant bankers, whose livelihood relied on this instrument of commercial credit, the Parliament, which had passed the Bill of Exchange Act only a few years previously (in 1882), and the City's commercial lawyers. The case was judged three times: in the High Court of Justice, in the Court of Appeal and in the House of Lords. Eighteen judges in all heard evidence.[87] The English legal corpus was divided in their opinion; the case not only involved major legal issues, it was also without precedent.

The case came up in the High Court of Justice before the Honorable Justice Charles on June 27, 1888, and was further heard by him on June 28 and July 4 to 7, 1888. The clerks of the Vagliano Brothers firm were examined by the lawyers of both sides. The whole procedure of the course of business was examined in detail: the way the ledgers of the company were held, the daily business of the firm, and so on. In addition, from the Bank's correspondence, it is evident the Bank of England carried out a thorough investigation of Panagi Vagliano and his correspondents George Vucina of Odessa and Petridis of Constantinople. The firm's ledgers were read in Court, along with the letter books, letters of advice, and bills of exchange. The organization and bookkeeping system of the office was impressive, and no fault or negligence on his part was really found. But the examination of Panagi Vagliano disclosed an

---

[84] Ibid., 1–15.

[85] Conversion from historical UK inflation rates and calculator, http://inflation.iamkate.com (accessed January 28, 2018).

[86] "In the House of Lords. Appeal Case, the Governor and Company of the Bank of England vs Vagliano Bros," Freshfields Papers: Records of Civil Court Actions, 1798–1903, F13.38, Archives of the Bank of England, 2.

[87] In the House of Lords, "Governor and Company of the Bank of England vs Vagliano Bros," Freshfields Papers: Records of Civil Court Actions, 1798–1903, F13.39–40, Archives of the Bank of England.

interesting and revealing detail: Panagi Vagliano, a millionaire and leading member of the City of London merchant bankers, could run a perfectly organized office with all the ledgers and documents required for his business – but could not really read or write in English.[88]

A.T. Can you read Greek letters yourself?
P.V. Vucina's? Oh, yes.
A.T. Can you translate them?
P.V. How do you mean, into English?
A.T. Yes.
P.V. No.
A.T. Can you read English writing?
P.V. I read it, but very little; I do not understand it well. Very indifferently I understand.
A.T. You cannot read the writing of the English language in English character?
P.V. I never write it at all. I copy it.
A.T. You cannot write it yourself, though you may copy it?
P.V. There may be a few words, and if I write it, it is not writing.
A.T. Any writing of English writing you leave to your clerks?
P.V. Yes, I read it myself, but anything I do not understand I ask my nephew or my clerks.

The Honorary Mr. Justice Charles took four months to decide upon the case. The correspondence of the lawyers of the Bank of England reveals their agony throughout the case. H. Greene, one of the lawyers of the Bank of England wrote to the Governor of the Bank hoping for the final decision to be reached soon, "that we must not continue our sleepless nights of anxiety."[89] He was right to be anxious.

The decision was in favor of Vagliano.[90] The Judge ordered the Bank of England to return to Vagliano the full sum adding the interest and trial expenses. He was to postpone the execution of his decision if the Bank appealed in two weeks. According to the decision, this followed both English Common Law and a precedent case in *Robarts* v. *Tucker* (1851), where the Bank was not entitled to debit his account with such payments. The decision brought turmoil in the City. How could a foreigner insult the Bank of England

[88] "In the House of Lords. Appeal Case, the Governor and Company of the Bank of England vs Vagliano Bros," Freshfields Papers: Records of Civil Court Actions, 1798–1903, F13.38, Archives of the Bank of England, 138–140.
[89] Correspondence on the *Vaglianos vs Bank of England*, F13.35, Archives of the Bank of England.
[90] "Minutes of Evidence and Proceedings at the Trial. In the High Court of Justice," appendix 8 in "In the House of Lords," Appeal Case, "the Governor and Company of the Bank of England vs Vagliano Bros," Freshfields Papers: Records of Civil Court Actions, 1798–1903, F13.38, Archives of the Bank of England, 173.

and win such a case? Reactions were condescending: "I do not like this Levantine being allowed to shuffle the loss resulting from his negligence, or misplaced confidence, onto the Bank," wrote Roger de Q. Quiency to the Governor of the Bank of England on November 5, 1888.[91]

The Bank took the case to the Court of Appeal, which again found for Vagliano (five Judges agreed with Lord Justice Charles and one was against the verdict).[92] However, it was the third trial that decided the case. The Bank appealed again, this time to the House of Lords. The final decision by eight Judges from the House of Lords was five against Vagliano and two for him. In the end, Vagliano lost his money.

The importance of *Vagliano v. Bank of England* lay in the fact that it involved the wider rules of the law, whether the Judges followed the previously existing law, the Common Law, or the new code, the Bill of Exchange Act.[93] Furthermore, behind this lay the liability of the Bank on the matter of the bill of exchange. The rule of the Common Law was harder on the Bank; it regarded the Bank, the payer, as an insurer. Consequently, it is no wonder that the Vagliano case has become a classic case for bills of exchange and merchant banking in general, highlighted in textbooks and legal studies to the present day.[94] But it also reveals the importance of the Vaglianos as merchant bankers in the City of London.

Conclusions

During the 1850s–1880s, the Vaglianos established an international trading house that expanded from Russia to the United Kingdom, excelled in trade, shipping, and finance, and developed a chain of agencies in the main European

---

[91] Correspondence on the *Vaglianos v. Bank of England*, F13.35, Archives of the Bank of England.

[92] In the House of Lords, "Governor and Company of the Bank of England v. Vagliano Bros," Freshfields Papers: Records of Civil Court Actions, 1798–1903, F13.40, Archives of the Bank of England.

[93] Mackenzie D. Chalmers, "Vagliano's Case," *The Law Quarterly Review* 2 (1891): 216–223; William Johnson Roberts, *The Bills of Exchange Act, 1882, with a Copious Index* (Dublin: John Falconer, 1882).

[94] A sample of books and articles referring to the Vagliano case against the Bank of England: Arthur Butterworth, "The Vagliano Case in Australia," *Law Quarterly Review* (January 1894); B. Kasunmu and S. A. Omabegho, "Provocation as a Defence Under the Nigerian Criminal Code," *International and Comparative Law Quarterly* 14 (1965): 1399–1410; David Kobrin and Vanessa Stotto, *Negotiable Instruments* (London: Anderson Keenan, 1980); Nicholas Kouladis, *Principles of Law Relating to International Trade*, 3rd edn (London: Butterworths, 1997); D. J. Gifford and John Salter, *How to Understand an Act of Parliament* (London: Cavendish, 1996); Peter Mirfield, *Silence, Confessions and Improperly Obtained Evidence*, Oxford Monographs on Criminal Law and Justice (Oxford: Clarendon, 1997); Michael Zander, *The Law-Making Process*, 6th edn (Cambridge: Cambridge University Press, 2004).

port cities trading between eastern and western Europe. It became the leading international trading house of the Greek entrepreneurial network, replacing the mighty Ralli Brothers in their prime role in European waters. In 1858, following the tremendous profits the House enjoyed after the Crimean War, Panagi Vagliano went to London, a move that proved to be decisive as it put the Vagliano House on its international western European course. As the previous chapter dealt with the first period of the Vaglianos' business that witnessed their path from merchant captains to a major trading house of the Black Sea and the eastern Mediterranean, this chapter examined the second period of the Vagliano business, which functioned as an international trading house (see Figure 1.1).

The Vaglianos developed their banking and financial activities in four empires: the Russian Empire (Taganrog), the Ottoman Empire (Constantinople), in the French Empire (Marseilles), and in the British Empire (London). In all four nodes they were involved in merchant banking, as well as in the banking institutions of their host countries. In Russia, they participated in the formation of the Azov-Don Bank. In Constantinople, they were involved in the Greek state loans by becoming one of the main intermediaries of the National Bank of Greece. But it was in the City of London that they became a truly powerful merchant banking institution.

An analysis of the internal organization of their business revealed its flexible structure and functioning; externally, its business network developed to connect the hinterland and the foreland of its various nodes. Finally, their activities in banking and particularly the legal confrontation in *Vagliano v. the Bank of England* illustrates the importance of the Vagliano Brothers in the City of London and its institutions, and investigates the dynamic interrelationship between the foreign City merchant bankers and the development of financial institutions like the bill of exchange.

If in November 1887, Panagi Vagliano shook the City of London by suing the Bank of England for negligence, on the Russian front Mari Vagliano had to face a much more important trial: he was sued for fraud by the Russian government in 1881. The trial took place in 1885–1886 and the final decision left Mari Vagliano untouched, with only a fine to be paid. Russian exports were taken over by the nephews Michael S. Vagliano in Rostov and Spyridon S. Vagliano in Novorossiysk and Mari Vagliano retired from the business in May 1887.

It was the blow that came from the French front, however, that led to the restructuring of the business. On May 14, 1887, the younger brother Andrea died at the age of sixty. The partnership of the Vagliano Brothers was dissolved and Panagi Vagliano remained the sole owner of the firm. On May 23, 1887, the London office sent a circular letter to all associates confirming this fact:[95]

---

[95] Archives of the National Bank of Greece, Series XXI Correspondence IA', Foreign Correspondence, file 103, "Vagliano Bros, London."

Vagliano Bros
  19 Old Broad Street,
  London, 23rd May 1887

Gentlemen,
  We beg to inform you that consequent on the death on the 14th inst. of
Mr. Andrea A. Vagliano, the partnership heretofore subsisting between
Messieurs Mari Vagliano, Andrea A. Vagliano and Panagi Athanase
Vagliano under the firm of Vagliano Brothers has been dissolved.
  We are Gentlemen,

Your most obedient Servants
Vagliano Brothers

From the 1880s to his death in 1902, Panagi Vagliano, with his nephews, continued in trade and banking, but mainly concentrated on operating the largest private steamship fleet of the eastern Mediterranean and the Black Sea. The growth of the shipping services of the Vagliano London office transformed it to a basic channel for the transition from sail to steam for the entire Greek-owned fleet.

4

The Russian Government *v.* Mari Vagliano, 1881–1887

In the 1880s, the Vagliano brothers faced major troubles with the Russian government that were beyond their control. For sixty years and under two Tsars, Nicholas I (1825–1855) and Alexander II (1855–1881), Mari Vagliano had developed his own business empire in Russia. Nine months after the new Tsar Alexander III succeeded his murdered father in May 1881, the seventy-seven-year-old magnate was imprisoned on charges of tax evasion, contraband, and forgery.[1] According to a contemporary:

> A committee sent from Petersburg went to the house of Mr. Vagliano from seven o'clock in the morning to six o'clock in the afternoon, and as they informed me they searched his house and they went through everything, they tore his chairs, armchairs, elastic sofas, made holes in the walls, stripped out his floors and at 9 in the evening in front of my eyes put him in the carriage in the most abusive way with police guards and took him to prison ... When they put him in the carriage there were, maybe, ten thousand men and women ... yelling to the Greeks, look your king is going like a common criminal to jail ... He paid a guarantee to the Imperial Bank [of] a million rubles ... and so came out of prison until he was going to be tried.[2]

Mari Vagliano was tried five years later. His case, like that of Aristotle Onassis in the United States seventy years later, is part of the long history of powerful governments accusing foreign entrepreneurial elites of fraud and corruption. It revealed the ability and flexibility of global businesses to by-pass laws and national interests that restrict their global activities, and demonstrated their ability to confront governments in their host countries.

---

[1] Parts of this chapter have been published in Greek in Harlaftis, "The 'Multimillionaire Mr. Marakis' Vagliano"; the case was also partly presented in Gelina Harlaftis, "Russian Port Customs, Anton Chekhov and Maris Vagliano, the 'Emperor' of Azov Sea: Confronting Institutions in the Russian Empire, 1880s," paper presented at the Annual Conference of the Economic History Society, March 26–28, 2010, Durham University, UK.

[2] Personal testimony of Spyridon Metaxas-Laskaratos on the arrest of Mari Vagliano in December 1881. See Metaxas-Laskaratos, *Commercial-Consular Prosecutions*, 92–93.

Vagliano's trial, which shook all of Russia for several months, has been described as the biggest in the legal history of Russia. This chapter investigates the confrontations between nations and rich foreign entrepreneurs involved in international business, and examines the relationship of Mari Vagliano with the commercial status quo of the era, the Russian government, and the Russian intelligentsia. As with Aristotle Onassis's legal battle with US authorities decades later, Mari Vagliano faced down highly public accusations of fraud and tax evasion, emerging from the confrontation unscathed.

Vagliano and Onassis were prime paradigms for the survival of Greek firms involved in the international shipping business. Throughout history powerful governments have attacked entrepreneurial elites of foreign origin during periods of increasing nationalism and xenophobia. But the same story upside down is the core of this chapter: the ability and flexibility of global shipping businesses to legally by-pass governments and national interests that seek to restrict their global activities. What strategies did shipowners employ to confront governments in host countries?

In a way international trading companies were a kind of proto-multinationals. A multinational business organization is characterized by the dispersal of its managerial centers among several nations "for the purpose of overcoming barriers of political instabilities."[3] Entrepreneurs like Vagliano and Onassis paved the way to the multinational by confronting the states through official and unofficial institutions they relied on and/or had created, including local, national, and international networks. After all, shipping is an international economic activity par excellence, and has institutionalized defense mechanisms vital for its survival.[4] Both cases reveal the ability and flexibility of cosmopolitan shipowners to survive powerful opponents such as national states.

The Trial of the Taganrog Customs

On December 25, 1881, the Muscovite newspaper *Moscovskii Listok* reported the arrest of the "multi-millionaire smuggler Vagliano." A few days later, the British Consul reported to the Foreign Office in London that the wealthiest merchant in town and head of the well-known firm of Vagliano Brothers of London, who "holds the trade of South Russia in his hand," had been arrested and thrown in jail.[5] Mari Vagliano, after about a month, bailed himself out

---

[3] Christos Carvounis, *Efficiency and Contradictions of Multinational Activity: The Case of Greek Shipping* (PhD thesis, New School of Social Research, New York, 1979).

[4] Harlaftis, Tenold, and Valdaliso, *World's Key Industry*, introduction.

[5] National Archives, London, FO 65/1146, January 26, 1882, "Letter from Consul Wooldridge to Her Majesty's Principal Secretary of State for Foreign Affairs."

with the unheard-of, for the time, amount of one million rubles.[6] The case made headlines, even in the country's main newspapers that usually regarded cases of corruption and the misuse of public money as a common phenomenon that went unpunished, particularly for the rich of the country.

In a country where class determined life and the meagre bourgeoisie was still being defined and delimited, self-made multi-millionaires like Mari Vagliano were the exception, not the rule. Vagliano held the highest rank an urban dweller and merchant could achieve, the position of a "hereditary honorary citizen," a title that gave him privileges similar to those of the nobility. Like the other first guild merchants and honorary citizens, his status gave him high rank in the administration of the city of Taganrog.[7] He was, among other things, a member of Taganrog's Chamber of Commerce (which had the jurisdiction of a Commercial Court), as well as of the Building Committee, which supervised all construction activity in Taganrog, Rostov, Nakhchivan, and Mariupol, including all state and public buildings, roads, bridges, passages, and lighthouses.[8]

Taganrog had a population of 50,000 people during the second half of the nineteenth century (today its fame lies in the fact that Anton Chekhov was born there in 1860).[9] Situated on an elevated peninsula, it descended to the Azov by way of the "Depaldo" stairs, named for the Cephalonian merchant Gerassimo Typaldo (1788–1825), who donated a sum of money to construct the stone stairs that would connect the so-called Greek street (*ulicha Grecheskaya*) with the waterfront.[10] The city planning of Taganrog, like that of all the new port cities of the Russian south, was beautifully done. It included wide, paved roads, a splendid Russian cathedral, a dozen other churches, schools for boys and girls, a hospital, a public library, an opera house, and a theater. Notwithstanding its small size, it was cosmopolitan: its population was composed largely of foreigners and its economic development was based on

---

[6] This deposit is confirmed from the documents located in the judicial case of the customs house in Taganrog from the courts of Kharkov in the Central State Historical Archives of Ukraine in Kiev (TsDIAK) 1072.3.1504, 207–208, 216–219, 278. There the lawyer who represented Mari Vagliano's son, Alcibiades Vagliano, requests the return of the bail. There is also a telegraph from Maris Vaglianos to the President of the Kharkov Court: "The delay of the acceptance of the deposit of 1,000,000 rubles from my son creates extended losses. I honourably ask the order of immediate payment. Vagliano." See, TsDIAK 1072.3.1504, 64–66, 278.

[7] For the importance of merchants in the governance of the Russian cities see Rieber, *Merchants*, 13–14.

[8] E. Gorobets, "Введение каталога архитектурных чертежей," ["Introduction of Catalogue of Architectural Plans"], GARO 577.1.

[9] The population of the city in 1830 was only 10,000; in 1856 it had increased to 18,500, and in 1897 it was 48,000. See P. Filevskii, *История города Таганрога* [*History of the City of Taganrog*] (Taganrog: K. F. Alexandrova, 1898).

[10] Sifneos and Harlaftis, "Entrepreneurship at the Russian Frontier."

hundreds of international and local merchant houses. According to Alexander Chekhov, brother of Anton, half of the population of the city were foreigners: mainly Greeks but also Italians, Germans, and English.[11] For that reason Taganrog had consulates representing almost all European countries, including Great Britain, France, Germany, Austro-Hungary, Spain, and Greece. It also had banks, insurance companies, a courthouse, and an active port where ships arrived from all parts of the Mediterranean and northern European seas.

In this city, the Greeks were the "lords of the town," wrote Irene Nemirovsky in the 1930s. "The grain trade was in their hands, [and] any brilliance or prosperity that Taganrog possessed was Greek."[12] According to Alexander Chekhov, the Greeks were the wealthiest ethnic group in Taganrog, concentrated in particular aristocratic neighborhoods. Purebred horses carried their carriages and their wives wore exquisite gowns and jewelry, while the Italian opera, accompanied by a municipal orchestra manned by first-class musicians, was subsidized by their husbands. All this, Chekhov wrote, was the result of "Greek money." Their wealth drew famous theatrical and opera troupes to this small frontier city. Liszt's student Laura Carrere, the great operatic singer Pauline Lucca and the famous actor Tomasso Salvini, and other internationally distinguished artists, played and sang in the rickety little theater on Petrovskaya Street.[13]

The legend of Mari Vagliano was made in Taganrog: the story of a poor, illiterate, immigrant seaman who came to Russia and became extremely wealthy. "Mr. Marakis," as he was called by the Greeks of the city, was the "Emperor," the "Tsar," the "God" of wealth. "The real emperor in Taganrog was Mari Vagliano," wrote a contemporary merchant captain.[14] "Vagliano is the 'God' for the commercial world ... there is no merchant that does not deal with him or does not owe him," S. Simonovich, a former Vagliano employee, testified in the Russian court.[15] Another contemporary, Simon Katakouzinos, called him the "Napoleon of Greek Commerce."[16] His huge fortune was estimated in the late 1860s at 10 million rubles;[17] in the 1880s, according to

---

[11] Irene Nemirovsky, *A Life of Chekhov* (London: The Grey Walls Press, 1950), 33. This study was first published in France as *La Vie de Tchekhov* (Paris: Éditions Albin Michel, 1946) after the death of the writer (1903–1942), 34.

[12] Ibid., 35.

[13] Sophie Laffitte, *Chekhov: 1860–1904* (London: Angus and Robertson, 1974), 35; Alexander Chudakov, "Dr Chekhov: A Biographical Essay (29 January 1860–15 July 1904)," in Vera Gottlieb and Paul Allain, eds., *The Cambridge Companion to Chekhov* (Cambridge: Cambridge University Press, 2000), 5.

[14] Metaxas-Laskaratos, *Commercial-Consular Prosecutions*, 15, 51.

[15] Newspaper *Moscovskie Vedomosti*, February 22, 1885.

[16] Katakouzinos, *Trade, Shipping and the Immigration of the Greeks*, 15.

[17] Morozan, "The Activities of the Commercial Bank of Azov-Don."

some, it exceeded 100 million rubles.[18] After his death in 1896, his estate was calculated at 148 million rubles,[19] more than a billion pounds sterling (in 2018 purchasing power, see Table 10.1).[20]

In 1881, the burgeoning economic power and cultural visibility of foreign merchants in Taganrog and other ports throughout the Black Sea region prompted what amounted to a political attack: a reminder to rich merchants of the authority of the new Tsar, and a new conservative, xenophobic, and protectionist economic policy. Taganrog, a small city, and its entrepreneurs, the majority of them foreigners, was apparently chosen as a scapegoat, an example for reformation. The attack started with an investigation of Taganrog's Customs House.

At the end of November 1881, a three-member Committee arrived in Taganrog on the order of the Ministry of Finance. The English Consul reported "on their arrival and the subsequent discovery and publication of a series of frauds which, it is said, has been going on for several years at the Custom House of this Port."[21] In addition, according to the Consul, "the Custom Houses of the neighbouring Ports of Rostov, Kertch and Odessa, are not above suspicion; and, that the inquiry is to extend to those places." This threat, however, was never realized, and the striking down of abuses was limited in the end to the Customs of Taganrog. Although the rumors talked of fraud amounting to millions of rubles, the English Consul commented that he regarded such rumors as exaggeration, and he stated that he was sure that the frauds would not ultimately prove more than the "usual" tax frauds of a few thousand rubles. The result of the court case four years later proved him right.

In the meantime, however, the city of Taganrog was paralyzed. After a month of interrogations, at the end of December the Committee gave orders

---

[18] Ibid. More conservative estimates put the figure at 50 million rubles. Newspaper *Московский листок* [*Moskovskii Listok*], February 8, 1882.

[19] The amount of 148–150 million rubles is mentioned in the following three Russian sources: the first is *Альманах-справочник по Городу Таганрог Ищу эго округи* [*Guide-Catalogue for the City of Taganrog and Its Region*] (Taganrog, 1912), 145–148. The second is found in the Archives of Rostov, GARO, P-2557.2.20. In this file there are notes on Mari Vagliano and the size of his fortune for the unpublished study by V. Anensky, *The History of Rostov, 1749–1944*. In the same file it is reported that V. Anensky worked for the Archive and the Secret Services of the Russian Empire that was merged with the State Archives of Rostov. The third source is the recent study by Oleg Pavlovich Gabrioushkin, *"Мари Вальяно и другие"* ["Mari Vagliano and the Others"], *Хроника обывательской жизни* [*Annals of the Local Society*] (Taganrog: AI MIKM, 2001), 272.

[20] E. I. Kapsabelis, *Τι οφείλει η Ρωσία εις την Ελλάδα* [*What Russia Owes to Greece*] (Athens: n.p., 2003), 105. According to the Greek newspaper *Επιθεώρησις* [*Epitheorisis*], January 27, 1896, he left "a legendary wealth of 200,000,000 drachmas."

[21] National Archives (London), FO 65/1146.

for massive arrests and imprisonments, and just before Christmas 1881, the port and Customs House were closed. The police and the administration of the city came under state control. Most of the officers and employees of the port and the Customs were arrested, put under detention, or fired, including the Director of the Port Nikitenko, the Inspector of the Ships Kuzovlev, the Inspector of the Warehouses Aykanov and another fifteen employees. The Chief of the Police Kuzovlev, brother of the Inspector of the Ships, was fired. The Governor of the city of Taganrog, Admiral Prince Makshoutov, was accused of receiving bribes, and of allowing shipmasters to throw ballast over the side of the ship in the bay instead of having it conveyed to shore, and left urgently for St. Petersburg.[22]

Although "Mark Athanasievich Vagliano" made banner headlines in Russian newspapers from St. Petersburg and Moscow to Kiev, Odessa, and Kharkov, he was not the only one jailed, although he was the first target of the police. Apart from Mari Vagliano, twenty-one individuals were arrested from the commercial world of Taganrog, most of them distinguished and substantial merchants of the city. These included the Greeks Anton Sfaello, Andrea Mussuri, Socrates Gyzi, Theodor Kumba (consul of Germany), Michael Vouraki, Stavro Karayanni, Panayoti Sakellaridi, and Michelangelo Darzenta, the Germans Gotfried Goiland and Michael Wechler, the Spanish consul Ivan Pissani, and the Russian Ivan Globin. Along with them were the merchant employees Constantine Sfaello, Pavel Kondo, Sava Grigoriev, Michael Nikolaev, Nikolai Papandopoulo, and Otto Kilbach.[23]

The trial took place four years later.[24] It started on February 13, 1885, at the Court (*Subednaya Palata*) of Kharkov, and lasted more than a month.

---

[22] "The Governor returned from St. Petersburg quiescent, as he was not received by the Tsar, and due to the anxiety of continuing interrogations died from apoplexy four months later, evidently due to the great pressures," reports the British Consul to the Foreign Office, adding that "the funeral was a very splendid." See FO 65/1146, January 26, 1882, "Letter from Consul Wooldridge to Her Majesty's Principal Secretary of State for Foreign Affairs." See also FO 65/1146, May 18, 1882, "Letter from Consul Wooldridge to Her Majesty's Principal Secretary of State for Foreign Affairs."

[23] Newspaper Южный Край [*Southern Region*], Kharkov, February 6/18, 1885 and March 7/19, 1885; Newspaper, Одесский листок [Odessa Paper], February 12/24, 1885.

[24] Unique and valuable archival material from this trial exists in the TsDIAK in the archival series "Харьковская судебная палата" ["Kharkov Court"], 1072.3, "О беспошлинном пропуске заграничных товаров Таганрогской таможней. Январь 1885–1 июня 1887" ["On the Imports of Foreign Goods Exempt from Taxes from the Custom House of Taganrog. January 1885–1 June 1887"], folders 1504–1508. The folders contain the reports of the interrogations of the witnesses and defendants, estimations of the tax evasion, reports of the experts after the examination of the ledgers, the commercial correspondence and documents (bills of lading, charter parties, etc.) of the merchant houses and their cross-examination with those of the Custom House, court orders, executive decisions, and various legal applications. More specifically, folder 1072.3.1504

According to Anatolii Feodorovich Koni, the Attorney General in St. Petersburg, the case of the Taganrog Customs was one of the largest ever adjudged in the annals of the Russian Courts.[25] Four judges, three Attorneys General, and a twelve-member jury composed the Court that had to examine 1,315 accusations. Twenty-one merchants and merchant employees were accused and put on trial alongside eighteen public servants from the Taganrog Customs House.[26] The thirty-seven defendants were represented by eighteen advocates, including some of the most famous lawyers in the Russian Empire.[27] The trial attracted enormous publicity and its image was described vividly by reporters.[28]

The judges' preliminary examination of the employees of the Customs, the Inspector of the Ships, and the Inspector of the Warehouses revealed a series of frauds prior to 1881, including many cases of untaxed imported goods found in Customs Office documents from 1878 to 1880, From the testimonies of more than twenty witnesses, they detected a general method of tax evasion:[29] To begin with, goods were smuggled illegally from the port without ever reaching the warehouse to go through customs control. These goods were then transferred via forged documents or documents that had already been used, without being checked by an inspector and usually at night (with the excuse of night work in warehouses to explain the derogation of rules). Finally,

contains documents that concern the merchants Andreas, Ilias, Grigori and Nikolai Mousouri, Anton Sfaellos, Mari Vagliano, Michail Vexler, Socratis Gyzi, Anton Lupi, Pavel Konto, Nikolai Papadopoulo, Semen Synodi-Popov, Gotfried Goiland, Panayioti Sakellaridi, and the employees of the Custom House, Nikolai Kuzovlev, K. Tsule, I. Zubkov, and M. Lipski. Folder 1072.2.1505 contains documents on the merchants Simon Sinodi-Popov (brother in law of Ivan Delaportas), Michael Angelo Darzenta and Theodoro Koumba (Feodor Borisov Koumbas), Mari (Mark) Vagliano, Ivan Delaporta, and Ivan Globin. Folder 1072.3.1506 contains documents on the merchants Emmanouel Koumani, employee at the Vagliano office, Ivan Globin, Andrei Mousouri, Ivan Delaporta, and the clerks of the Custom House, Porfyri Aikanov, Nikolai Kouzovlev, Vasilii Novikov (Inspector of the Custom Houses). Folder 1072.3.1507 on the cases of Michael Bouraki and Michael Nikolaiev. Folder 1072.3.1508 contains the decisions, the first on February 12 and March 13, 1885 and the second after the Repeal on April 23, 1886 of Mari Vagliano and the employees of the Custom House (Nikolai Kouzovlev, Piotr Petrov, Sigaev, Lipski, Zuvkov, and Tsoule).

[25] "Анатолий Федорович Кони" ["Anatolii Feodorovic Koni"], available at www.pravoteka.ru/lib/raznoe/0002 (accessed December 18, 2008).

[26] Two of the merchants, Koumba and Darzenta, escaped abroad, so nineteen merchants were tried.

[27] Newspaper *Moscovskie Vedomosti*, February 17, 1885, "Legal Chronicles: The Case of Embezzlement in the Custom House of Taganrog." This conservative newspaper had the largest circulation in nineteenth-century Russia. Newspaper *Одесский вестник* [*Odessa Herald*], February 16, 1885. Defense attorneys included the famous Plevako, Passover, Alexandrov, Andrievsky, and Korabchevsky.

[28] Ibid.   [29] Ibid.

during the control of the goods, smaller quantities than the actual ones were being registered and thus forged documents were being issued.

From the testimonies, it was evident that during the period 1878–1881 the Director of the Customs, together with his employees, was responsible for the inspection of cargoes, warehouses, and ships, and all were collaborating closely with at least twenty merchants and merchant employees of the city in these fraudulent transactions. What is more, Inspector of Ships Kuzovlev had instituted a secret ledger of imports of goods. The other members of the Customs who did not collaborate concealed this practice, and to that end, they received remuneration from those that collaborated. The Customs officials and employees facilitated tax evasion and received from the merchants between 10 and 40 percent of the amount of the successful tax avoidance, which they divided in equal shares.[30] During 1881, the Customs officials had divided 10,000 rubles among themselves.[31]

The Committee of the Experts, composed of members of the Customs Houses of Sebastopol and Odessa, checked all the documents and Registers of cargo imports of the Taganrog Customs and double-checked them with the evidence they received from the Ministry of Foreign Affairs for the cargoes that had been sent to Taganrog from various foreign ports, in order to detect the quantities of untaxed imports and the equivalent Taganrog Customs employee that dealt with the case. They compared bills of lading documents that certified quantities and weights with the entries in the Warehouse Register Books, according to the packaging of each cargo (in sacks, barrels, boxes, with the size) and the method of transport (sea or land). Cargoes included diverse goods such as olive oil, wine, dried figs, currants, or macaroni, tabulated according to their country of origin (for example, Greece, France, or Italy). This effort was particularly taxing and complex, as the weight of each cargo was never the same at the point of loading as it was when unloaded; it usually varied by 4–5 percent due to the change of climate and the length of stay on the ship.

Table 4.1 indicates the amount of the deliberate reduction of cargoes that Vagliano imported, according to the Committee of Experts. The Experts detected fraud in his cargoes, albeit on a much lesser scale than expected. The "Tsar of the Azov," in collaboration with the officials and employees of the Customs, did reduce by various methods the imported quantity of cargoes (for example by constructing smaller barrels or sacks).[32] It seems, however, that there were tacit rules between merchants and Customs officials as to what should be an acceptable amount of theft and tax evasion. Fraud, as shown in Table 4.1, varied at a fixed, predetermined 4–5 percent. Furthermore, despite

---

[30] Newspaper *Киевлянинъ* [*Kievlianin*], Thursday, February 14, 1885, "Judicial Chronicles: The Case of Embezzlement in the Custom House of Taganrog."

[31] Ibid.   [32] TsDIAK 1072.2.1505, 140.

Table 4.1 *The difference between the declared and actual amount of cargoes imported by Mari Vagliano, as determined by the Committee of Experts based on a sample of cases*

Date	Cargo	Difference of declared weight	Percentage of duty evasion
1872	With the ship *Konstantin* 168 barrels of olive oil of mixed weight of 6,963 pud	349 pud	4
1872	With the ship *Cephalonia* 286 barrels of olive oil of mixed weight of 12,046 pud	549 pud	4
1873	With the ship *Hydra* 10,443 pud of macaroni	510 pud	5

Source: KIAO, Kiev, 1072.3.1506, "Specialists Reports," 228–229.
1 pud [пуд] = 16.38 kg.

the much advertised defalcation of thousands of tons of cargoes, and the announcement of the enormous magnitude of smuggling by what they considered to be "the big shark" of southern Russia, the truth was that for the period of ten years, 1872–1881, that the Committee investigated, the Mari Vagliano's fraud was limited to the import of a few dozen barrels of olive oil and sacks of macaroni. The tax evasion of which he was finally accused was 65,573[33] rubles, a paltry sum for an entrepreneur who dealt with exports of hundreds of thousands of tons of grain.[34]

Although fraud was not found to be more than 4–5 percent of the total weight, the District Attorney A. A. Bashkirev was apparently certain that Vagliano was behind "most of the fraud that took place" and that "he must be held the main responsible not only for Taganrog Customs House but also in other cities."[35] As the Committee of Experts could not trace large sums of tax evasion in Vagliano's case, the main indictment against him was complicity in forgery of a Customs document. A criminal offense, Vagliano's knowledge of the forgery was punishable by exile, confiscation of fortune and disenfranchisement.

[33] TsDIAK 1072.3.1508, 19.
[34] Newspaper *Moscovskie Vedomosti*, February 17, 1885, "Judicial Chronicles: The Case of Embezzlement in the Custom House of Taganrog."
[35] Newspaper *Южный Край* [*Southern Region*], March 1, 1885.

The verdict by the Court of Kharkov came out on March 10, 1885. Of the thirty-seven defendants, twenty-five (eleven employees of the Customs and fourteen merchants and merchant employees) were found innocent. The rest, twelve defendants, out of which six were employees of the Customs, were found guilty of bribery and forgery. They were fired, disenfranchised, and sent to exile in Siberia, Tobolsk, or Tomsk. Six merchants were found guilty: Mari Vagliano, Anton Sfaello, Andrea Mussuri, Ivan Goblin, Michael Wechsler, and Stavro Karayanni. The heaviest sentence was imposed on Mari Vagliano. He was found guilty of receiving cargoes without the payment of duties and was fined 724,344 rubles (which was the value of smuggled goods and fivefold value of lost profit from the customs duties).[36] More serious, he was found guilty of criminal offense due to complicity in the forgery of a state document, and for this was sentenced to disenfranchisement, exile in Tobolsk, Siberia, and confiscation of his property.

A month later, on April 11, 1885, Mari Vagliano appealed the Kharkov ruling to the Supreme Court of St. Petersburg for the annulment of his penalty. On October 17, 1885, the Supreme Court of St. Petersburg annulled the sentence of the Court of Kharkov and referred the case back to the Court. The Court of Kharkov reexamined the case and announced its final judgment in April 1886, finding Vagliano innocent on the criminal side and repealing the sentence for exile, confiscation of his property, and disenfranchisement.[37] The fine was reduced from 724,344 rubles to 327,866, which was exclusively the fivefold value of the duty; along with various other Court expenses, the final calculation was 396,478 rubles.[38]

The final sentence was a triumph for the Vaglianos' illustrious advocate Alexander Yakovlevich Passover (1837–1910), based in Odessa. Passover, son of a pair of doctors of Jewish origin, had graduated from the Law School of the University of Moscow in 1867 and continued his studies abroad. After his return, he had worked at the Ministry of Justice and as a secretary in the Chamber of Justice in Moscow. Later he resigned and in 1871 moved to Odessa, where he worked as a private lawyer, specializing in civil law, and

[36] On the first decision of the Kharkov court on Mari Vagliano and the second after the repeal, April 23, 1886, see TsDIAK, Kharkov courts, 1072.3.1504, executive decision, May 25, 1885, 151, 153. Also in the 1072.3.1508 (pp. 18–19), it is mentioned that according to the court decision of February–March 1885 he had to pay 724,344 rubles, whereas on April 23, 1886 the fine was 327,866 rubles (with extra expenses it reached 396,478 rubles).
[37] On the annulment of the confiscation of his property see TsDIAK 1072.3.1504, 328–332, 346.
[38] Ibid., 19. For an opinion in relation to the reduction of the fine see "Анатолий Федорович Кони" ["Anatolii Feodorovich Koni"], part 6, available at www.pravoteka .ru/lib/raznoe/0002 (accessed December 17, 2008). Anatolii Feodorovich Koni, a famous law practitioner, was the judge; he had consulted on the case in the Court Appeal of Saint Petersburg.

eventually became one of the leading legal authorities.[39] He belonged to the group of lawyers who were able to develop their abilities and talents after the reformation of the Russian judicial system in 1864 that modernized Russian justice according to European standards, particularly the French legal system. The new system involved a new penal code and a simplified system of civil and penal legislation processes, where a public process replaced the secret one.[40]

The basis of the new system was an institutional framework with permanent judges, and district courts in every region dealing in both civil and penal cases as well as a normal system of Courts of Appeal. The new judicial system created the famed *advokatura* or corps of lawyers, the first essentially truly independent, non-hereditary, and self-governing professional association in Russia.[41] The law practice flourished as the new, popular profession attracted many of the brightest minds of the Russian intelligentsia. Before long, the first generation of lawyers developed its capabilities to such an extent that they were on a par with their western European counterparts. The modernization of the judicial system after 1864 designated the Court as the space for the expression of justice and defense of individual rights, and lawyers as the defenders of modern society. The most talented of the lawyers elaborated the eloquence of their orations and became famous for their rhetoric. The trials drew great publicity from the Russian press, which reproduced the details without much censorship.[42]

Passover belonged to this new generation of famous lawyers who rewrote the history of Russian jurisprudence. His stance during the trial of Taganrog Customs and his eloquent defense of Vagliano became legendary among Russian lawyers.[43] In a concise and luminous oration, Passover, based on his deep knowledge of the civil and penal legislation of Russia, crushed the indictment, proving that Mari Vagliano could not be prosecuted for a criminal offense. During his oration Passover, referring to the Attorney General sarcastically, calculated the exact cost of his words according to his monthly

---

[39] S. I. Emets, "Мемориал одесских присяжных поверенных" [Records of Lawyers in Odessa], *Вестник Одесской адвокатуры* [*Herald of Odessa Lawyers*] 2 (2008). The abilities of Passover are also mentioned in Samuel Kucherov, *Courts, Lawyers and Trials under the Last Three Tsars* (New York: Frederick A. Praeger, 1953), 141–145.

[40] On the reforms see W. Bruce Lincoln, *The Great Reforms: Autocracy, Bureaucracy, and the Politics of Change in Imperial Russia* (DeKalb: Northern Illinois University Press, 1990).

[41] William Pomeranz, "'Profession or Estate'? The Case of the Russian Pre-Revolutionary 'Advokatura'," *The Slavonic and East European Review* 77, no. 2 (April 1999): 240–268.

[42] Samuel Kucherov, *Courts, Lawyers and Trials under the Last Three Tsars* (New York: Frederick A. Praeger, 1953), chapter 5; Hugh Seton-Watson, *The Decline of Imperial Russia* (London: Methuen, 1952), 51–52; William Pomeranz, "Profession or Estate? The Case of the Russian Pre-Revolutionary 'Advokatura'," *The Slavonic and East European Review* 77, no. 2 (April 1999): 240–268.

[43] Emets, "Records of Lawyers."

salary and presented a famous phrase that ever since has been commonly used in the circles of lawyers, "the words of the Attorney General are not worth a penny!"[44] Although the Court of Kharkov followed the words of the Attorney, the Court of Appeal, as we have seen, seven months later vindicated the views of Passover and ultimately annulled the decision on the criminal and civil guilt of Vagliano, and forced the Court of Kharkov to reexamine it.

The final result was also a triumph of "Mr. Maraki," who had impressed the public by the composure with which he faced the whole trial, from which he emerged unscathed, and was able to return home.[45] On March 23, 1885 the Russian newspaper *Ruskiye Vedomosti* reported his return to Taganrog and how people demonstrated both love and hate when welcoming him at the railway station. Mari Vagliano spent the rest of his life, another ten years, in his city, Taganrog, but did not leave a penny to the town. Instead, he left all his fortune to his sons, who were established in London and Paris. From the time of his arrest, it seems that the administration of the Vagliano Brothers passed to Panagi in London. The Vaglianos' able nephews Michael S. Vagliano (son of their brother Spyridon), who had been working with Mari since 1878 in Rostov, and Athanasse S. Vagliano (also Spyridon's son), established in Novorossyisk, took over the Russian business.[46]

The Russian Press and Public Opinion

Russian newspapers were suspicious of the foreign merchants entangled in this sprawling fraud case. Who were these jumped-up capitalists with their international connections, connections that threatened "good old mother Russia?" Coverage of the case can be divided into two categories. The first category emphasized the importance of the trial in combating corruption and abuse of public funds by individuals; merchants in these publications were considered a priori fraudsters. Throughout the nineteenth century, relations between merchants and the intelligentsia were characterized by suspicion.[47] The second category of publications brewed Russian nationalism. An important, widely circulating part of the conservative press was heavily nationalistic. It was one venue for the debate between two intellectual movements, the Slavophiles and the Westernizers, which developed partly through periodicals and newspapers beginning in the 1830s and revolved around the historical legacy of Russia – whether it was unique or belonged to the West. The Slavophiles idealized early modern Russian history, when, they argued, the Tsar and the people collaborated harmoniously – an idyll destroyed by Peter the Great when he sought to follow foreign, Western ideals. According to this line of thought, "Europe was immoral, while Russia was virtuous."

[44] Ibid.   [45] GARO 301.8. 1558.   [46] Ibid.   [47] Rieber, *Merchants*, xxv.

Conversely, the Westernizers believed that Russia should follow a Western way of development, despite the fact that the country did not belong either to the West or to the East. The Slavophiles believed in the Russian Church, whereas the Westernizers believed that the Orthodox Church would lead the country to paralysis.[48]

Needless to say, Vagliano – a cosmopolitan businessman who led an enterprise headquartered in the City of London that was seen as both "British" and international – represented Europe. It is interesting to note that in no publication was the ethnic origin of the merchants mentioned. The judicial expulsion of such a local celebrity sparked a great debate about the negative impact this could have on the trade relations with western Europe.[49] Moreover, the conflict would not arise because, according to the journalists, there were many examples of such "international swindlers." One journalist wrote: "Remember my friend the European Vaglianos: remember the Rothschilds, remember the Pereira . . . remember whomever else you want – remember all those Vaglianos."[50] Mari Vagliano became the model of a western European capitalist, the wealthy who could not be anything other than an "international robber." Because, according to the Russian reporter, Europe, contrary to the yet uncorrupted Russia, rewarded and deified "robbers" like Vagliano. Because "Vagliano and his like" pulled the strings.[51] The Russian reporter used as an example some of Shakespeare's verses in order to indicate the decadence of "those" Europeans (mainly the British) who led the world to destruction through businessmen such as Vagliano: "there [in Europe] Vagliano is the Tsar and the God that sets the tone in life . . . This is why 'Till Birnam wood remove to Dunsinane, he cannot taint with fear. . .' And even if Birnam wood moves from this Vagliano, there will be nothing left."[52]

Beyond the explosions of Slavophile rhetoric, the common people expected momentous and spicy revelations about incredible corruption; they wanted all these multimillionaires like Vagliano, not to mention corrupt state officials, to be exposed.[53] The public waited anxiously and with anticipation, since through the courts and juries the Russian people were able to punish the rich and the powerful. If Mari Vagliano was able to bail himself out with the fabulous amount of one million rubles and 500,000 rubles were confiscated from his house, how many millions more could Russian justice reveal? The answer was: a few tons of macaroni, some barrels of oil, and some parcels of figs. Ultimately, the outcome of the case brought great disappointment, and

---

[48] Lincoln, *The Great Reforms*, 13.
[49] Newspaper *Южный Край* [*Southern Region*], "In Between," March 1/13, 1885. This was a local newspaper of Kharkov and the larger regional newspaper of Russia.
[50] Ibid.   [51] Ibid.   [52] Newspaper *Южный Край* [*Southern Region*], March 1, 1885.
[53] Ibid., March 3, 1885.

interest in the trial gradually deflated. "And the mountain labored and brought forth a mouse," went the report from a Kharkov newspaper.[54] The whole mission of justice, according to the newspaper *Iuzhnyi Krai*,[55] was to reveal "organized rapacity ... I hope that the case of Taganrog," it continued, "is the last echo of this 'rykovschina' that has lately almost flooded Russian life." The term "Rykovschina" appeared in the contemporary Russian press. It came from Rykov, a bank director in the city Skopin, who ended up in court when it was revealed that the bank went bankrupt because of his and his collaborators' abuses. These actions were interpreted by society as a typical expression of capitalistic predatory behavior.[56] Based on these public cases of fraud, young Anton Chekhov wrote his short story the "Mystery of 144 Catastrophes or the Russian Rocambol," in which one of the main protagonists is called M. Vagliano. In the novel the Knight Rykov receives a telegram from the town Skopin from his collaborator M. Vagliano in Taganrog: "Skopin. To the Knight Rykov of the Order of Lion and Sun. The case is lost. He confessed. I am imprisoned. In the Customs House there are arrests. It is terrible! There has been no payment. M. Vagliano."

Chekhov wrote this detective story in 1882 at the age of twenty-two; it was not published until after his death, in 1932. The story, which is full of intrigue, betrayal, and crooks, unfolds swiftly in settings of trains and high society gatherings. Chekhov's protagonists in this short story are all real people involved in major scandals that made newspaper headlines and captured the attention of the public in 1881. When Anton Chekhov was born in Taganrog in 1860, Mari Vagliano was the millionaire of the town. Chekhov, in this story, and in others where he uses the name "Vagliano," does not mention that Vagliano was Greek. His ethnicity was not a concern to him; he was just interested in characters involved in public scandals of Russian economic and political life.[57] It seems that economic fraud was embedded in Russia's

---

[54] Ibid., February 27, March 11, 1885.   [55] Ibid.

[56] Рыковшие. For the commendation on the specific play see Mikhail Gromov, А. П. Чехов, *Полное собрание сочинений и писем в 30-ти томах. Сочинения* [*A. P. Chekhov, His Works and Letters in 30 Volumes*] (Moscow: Editions Nauka, 1974–1982).

[57] In the title of this short story there is a note: "translation from French." This is a satirical note linking the novel with the detective stories of the French nineteenth-century writer Pierre Alexis Ponson du Terrail. This short story, as far as I know, has not been translated into English. See Anton Chekhov, "Тайны ста сорока четырех катастроф, или русский Рокамболь (огромнейший роман в сжатом виде, перевод с французского)" ["Mystery of 144 Catastrophes or the Russian Rocambol" (a huge novel in a short form, translation from the French]. For the commentary on this work see Gromov, *A. P. Chekhov, His Works and Letters in 30 Volumes*, vol. 1. Chekhov uses the name "M. Vagliano" in another short story titled "Находчивость г. Родона" ["The Resourcefulness of Mr. Rondon"], ibid., vol. 18.

capitalist development and was an issue very much talked about by journalists and intellectuals of the time.

The Importance of Foreign Capitalists for the Russian Economy

On a local and national basis, there were multiple problems the Russian government had to overcome before it was able to convict Mari Vagliano and the other Greek entrepreneurs. There are a number of questions that touch upon the main issues.

First, why were international foreign capitalists such as Vagliano useful to the Russian government? Greek businessmen like Vagliano engaged in the external trade of the country served their interests by providing low-cost trading and transport services. In the case of nineteenth-century Russia, the area was at the frontier of an expanding Empire and Greeks proved pivotal for the internationalization and integration of the area into the global market.[58] Since the time of Catherine the Great's acquisition of the northern coast of the Black Sea to the time of Tsar Alexander II, Imperial policy aimed to attract Christian populations of the Ottoman Empire to settle in the lands of New Russia, where new port cities were springing up and cultivation of the steppes was transforming the landscape. Russia was even willing to concede a certain amount of self-government in the form of taxless regimes for decades (into the mid-nineteenth century). Governmental reports clearly show concessions given to the ethnic minorities of the south, and particularly the Greeks, for the promotion of sea trade in the area. The aim was to promote the development of south Russia by providing the right proportion of "social alchemy" in the Russian port cities of the Black Sea.[59] Within this hoped-for framework of social relations among different ethnocultural groups in the region, the Greeks were needed for their shipping and trading expertise, in an effort to activate a new economic zone linked to international trade. Indeed, with regard to the particularities of the Azov Sea, the Greek entrepreneurs possessed both trading and seafaring skills, and therefore offered an important advantage over merchants of other nationalities. They made up for the lack of a Russian merchant fleet, and ensured international links with European ports. The Greeks, residing in the stretch of coast from Odessa to Taganrog, managed to compete successfully with all the western European merchants (especially the British) due to their family-oriented business organizations. These dense networks of relatives and fellow countrymen provided them with reduced costs. In addition to enjoying links with the local producers, they also had international bonds for transporting and supplying Russian grain. Their coastal and

---

[58] Harlaftis, *A History of Greek-Owned Shipping*, chapters 1–3.

[59] Dana Sherry, "Social Alchemy on the Black Sea Coast, 1860–65," *Kritika: Explorations in Russian and Eurasian History* 10, no. 1 (Winter 2009): 7–30.

seagoing fleet afforded them a practical monopoly on the transportation of agricultural produce from the shores and rivers of the region towards the roadstead of Taganrog, and thence onward to Mediterranean ports of destination.

Greeks in the coastal areas of south Russia had another important advantage: geographical proximity to the Greek state and the Ottoman Empire. They had a strong presence in the strategic location of Constantinople prior to the opening of the Black Sea to international trade, and indeed throughout the nineteenth to the beginning of the twentieth century. Constantinople was the springboard for expansion to the Azov Sea as well as a safe retreat when navigation out of the Black Sea was prohibited by the Ottoman government. In this way, the Azov entrepreneurs involved in the grain exports of the area, headed by Mari Vagliano since the 1850s, made a significant contribution to the creation of a new economic zone in the south of Russia and its linkages to international markets, thanks to their import-export activities.

The result was that by the last third of the nineteenth century the external trade of the Russian Empire was in the hands of either foreigners or ethnic minorities: Greeks, Armenians, and Jews.[60] The latter collaborated or coexisted harmoniously despite their competition. Mari Vagliano collaborated with the large Jewish international grain houses in the Black Sea: the Dreyfus, the Neufeld, and the Mendhl, among others. From grain in the Azov to the oil of Baku, Russian exports were in the hands of foreigners. In 1884, the largest oil industrialists and exporters were the Swedish Nobel, the Jewish Rothschilds, and the Armenian Mantashev (Mantashian).[61] The strategic plan of the Russian government for drawing businessmen from ethnic minorities to develop the south had been successful.

The second question surrounding the trial is, why was Vagliano taken to court at that particular moment? If the Greeks served the interests of Russia well, why were leading members of the prominent Greek business community of Taganrog tried – in the Imperial Court and in the court of public opinion – for what were, in the end, minor offenses? The causes were both political and economic: the Russian state felt that these foreign businessmen no longer served their host country, but insulted it with their actions.

The accusations also took place at a time of political change to a more conservative government. Despite his Russian citizenship, Mari Vagliano was not regarded as Russian; he belonged to the foreign capitalists of the Russian Empire. The policy of the new Tsar was national purification, Russification, protectionism, and state control. The pogroms against the Jews in 1881 at the beginning of the reign of Alexander III, although not instigated by him,

---

[60] Rieber, *Merchants*, 68–70.
[61] Seton-Watson, *The Decline of Imperial Russia*, 117–118.

heralded the xenophobic and conservative policy of the new Tsar.[62] This policy contradicted that of his father, the liberal Tsar Alexander II. The trial of Mari Vagliano, still seen in Russia as an international entrepreneur who led a British multinational trading company established in England and France and representing Europe as a whole, triggered the polemical national question of Westernizers versus Slavophiles. Mari Vagliano became the archetype of the western European capitalist, an incredibly rich person who could not but be an "international robber." The protest was against the continuation of the policy of the Russian government to attract the Christian populations of the Ottoman Empire during the reign of Alexander II.

The economic reasons behind this attack were probably equally important. In the case of Russia the attack against the Greeks, who were central to the external grain trade and shipping of the country, came at a time of deep economic crisis, not to mention the competition of the Moscow Russian merchants against foreign merchants. The aggrieved discourse surrounding the affluent foreign merchants of the south was expressed by one of the big Russian merchants of the Muscovite group, N. K. Krestovnikov, in a report to Alexander II: "most of Russia's export trade was handled by brokerage offices in the hands of Jews and Greeks who are not regulated by Russian law and [consequently] can victimize Russian traders."[63]

However, despite the competitiveness of the Old Believer merchants of Moscow and their ambition to become the center of the Russian bourgeoisie, in opposition to the "foreigners" of the south, they should not be seen as entirely responsible for exposing the scandal of the Customs of Taganrog.[64] The Russian merchants had been appealing for government protection against their more enterprising ethnic and foreign rivals since the time of Alexander II. Erecting tariff walls and abolishing free ports and transit rights remained the merchantry's first and main line of defense.[65] Appeal for protection was not only a demand of the Russian merchants but also of industrialists; we have

---

[62] Steven J. Zipperstein, *The Jews of Odessa: A Cultural History, 1794–1881* (Stanford, CA: Stanford University Press, 1986); Evrydiki Sifneos, "The Dark Side of the Moon: Rivalry and Riots for Shelter and Occupation between the Greek and Jewish Populations in Multi-Ethnic Nineteenth Century," *The Historical Review/La Revue Historique* 3 (2006): 189–204.

[63] Rieber, *Merchants*, 113.

[64] The old-believers, known as Раскольники [Schismatics] or old-ritualists, were those orthodox Christians who rejected the reforms of Patriarch Nikon in the middle of the seventeenth century in Moscow and preserved the old ways of worship. In the eighteenth century the rich old-believers merchants in Moscow created one of the most dense and powerful commercial communities in Russia, See S. K. Batalden, *Catherine II's Greek Prelate: Eugenios Voulgaris in Russia, 1771–1806* (Boulder: East European Monographs, 1982); and Rieber, *Merchants*.

[65] Rieber, *Merchants*, 115–116.

to take into consideration that this was the time of the industrialization of Russia, which affected local production as well.[66] The case of the trial of the Taganrog port Customs with Vagliano as protagonist might have been a convenient case of punishment for emulation, a pillar to absorb the dissatisfaction of all those that did not wish to see the profits of the external trade of the country in the hands of foreigners.

Third, why was Mari able to avoid actual conviction, the destruction of his business, and imprisonment? The answer here is found on multiple levels and has to do with the linkages of these powerful entrepreneurs with official and unofficial institutions on a national and international level. On a first level, entrepreneurs like Vagliano carried out their business guided by excellent local legal expertise. They were well advised on the legal proceedings of their businesses; hence, they knew how to deal with the accusations. Knowledge of local legal institutions is vital for survival in different countries, and Vagliano and his fellow Greeks were able to hire top-class lawyers, like Alexander Pavlovich Passover, Vagliano's lawyer, who belonged to the group of Russian lawyers that wrote history in the Russian courts before the Russian Revolution, as already mentioned.

On a second level, they had access to political power not only in the country where they were accused but also in the other countries where they carried out business. We cannot know what other political connections Vagliano had in St. Petersburg that he might have used, but what we do know is that there were close connections to the royal, political, and church milieu in both Russia and Greece. The King and Queen of Greece were close relatives to the Russian Tsar Alexander III; the Tsar had married the Greek King George's sister and Greek Queen Olga was the first cousin of Alexander III. There are clues that let us suppose that the Greek government most probably intervened on Vagliano's behalf. V. Anensky, who worked for the Archive of Secret Services of the Russian Empire, confirms, without further evidence, that the outcome of the final judgment was influenced by the intervention of the Greek government.[67]

The Vaglianos also had powerful connections in the Greek political establishment. They were relatives by marriage to most of the important families of the Greek diaspora – the Ralli, Mela, Petrokockino, Negreponte, Zarifi, Couppa, Ambanopoulo, and Romanos – family members of which either had close connections with the Greek government of the time or were

---

[66] For industrialization in Russia see Theodore H. Von Laue, *Sergei Witte and the Industrialization of Russia* (New York: Atheneum, 1969).

[67] GARO, P-2557.2.20. In this folder there are notes on Mari Vagliano and the amount of his fortune which come from the unpublished study by V. Anensky, "История Ростова, 1749–1944" ["The History of Rostov, 1749–1944"]. In the same folder it is evident that Anensky was employed in the Archive for the Secret Services of the Russian Empire, which was merged with the State Archive of the region of Rostov.

politicians themselves. They had close connections with leading figures of the Greek Church; Germanos (Kalligas) from Cephalonia who was bishop in Marseilles in 1880, in Cephalonia in 1884, and later the Archbishop, head of the Church of Greece in 1889, was a personal friend of Andrea Vagliano. Whatever the connections and wherever they came from, what we know is that Panagi Vagliano, on May 27, 1884, traveled from London to Athens and met the Greek Prime Minister Harilaos Trikoupis to make a donation of a million golden francs as a philanthropic gift to the Greek state.[68] Harilaos Trikoupis accepted the gift and chose to direct it to the construction of the National Library in Athens.[69] Four months before the trial in Russia, in September 1884, the Vagliano Brothers deposited one million golden francs for the construction of the Greek National Library, which bears the Vagliano name to the present day.

On a third level, the Vaglianos had access to economic power. Whatever they did affected other elite businessmen and the environment they worked in. Mari Vagliano's activities were identified with the area's economic life. He had developed close connections to the local government, local landowners, and the rich Cossack families that provided him with grain. He had developed the international connections of the region with western Europe, and the whole economic system of the external trade of the Azov was partially constructed by him. One must not forget that from the 1780s to 1840s the Greeks were allowed to retain their own self-governance.[70] All the of the port's banking, shipping, insurance, chartering, warehouses, trading, and employment were under their control, with Mari Vagliano being the de facto Tsar. To destroy him completely might have meant the collapse of the export-import system and might have led the rest of the Greeks to flee the country.

Finally, what were the effects of the conviction of Vagliano to the business environment where they operated? During the period 1881–1886, the time that Vagliano was under conviction, the external trade of Taganrog went through a severe crisis (which didn't abate until the 1890s). As is evident from Figure 4.1, the effect of the scandal of Taganrog Customs was detrimental to the city's commerce. During 1881–1886, the value of exports plummeted to one-third of their pretrial value. Mari was the employer of thousands, and the prosperity of the town depended partly on him and the other merchants brought to trial. The blow to the top businessmen brought a great crisis to

[68] See also Aikaterini Flerianou, ed., Χαρίλαος Τρικούπης: Η ζωή και το έργο του [Harilaos Trikoupis: His Life and Work] (Athens: Foundation of the Greek Parliament, 1999), 77.
[69] Letter of Panagi Vagliano to Harilaos Trikoupis, September 15/27, 1884, that refers to the grant of one million golden francs. Archive of Harilaos Trikoupis, 7.7.166. I would like to thank Dimitri Kontogeorgi for bringing this letter to my attention.
[70] Sifneos and Harlaftis, "Entrepreneurship at the Russian Frontier."

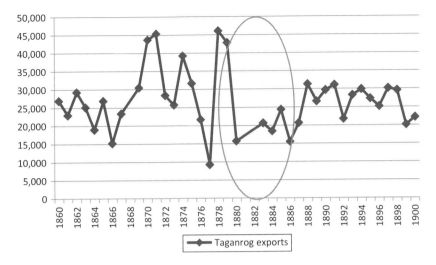

Figure 4.1   The impact of the Taganrog Customs trial on Taganrog's exports (in thousands of French francs)
Source: Socrates Petmezas and Alexandra Papadopoulou (eds.), *Black Sea Historical Statistics, 1812–1914*, www.blacksea.gr.

the town and also triggered the development of the neighboring port city Rostov-on-Don.

Mari Vagliano developed his leadership and entrepreneurial skills within the environment of the Russian Empire and was able to take advantage of the opportunities presented to him. As his contemporaries witnessed, he didn't show off his wealth; instead, they characterized him as hardworking, principled, and dedicated to "his people." His business was based on relations of trust with his business associates in Russia and abroad. Within the Greek entrepreneurial network, Mari Vagliano was highly respected and trustworthy, and his business in Taganrog totally relied on trust. During the trial, no witness gave evidence that Vagliano cheated any merchants. His practices were within the accepted rules of business in Russia. Thomas Owen, in his analysis of Russian merchants, mentions that the traditional Russian merchant could very well use fraud, forgery, and false weights and measures but would be extremely honest in his transactions within his own entrepreneurial network.[71] Mari Vagliano had created a multinational family company whose activities were entirely based on trust. His business was built

---

[71] Thomas C. Owen, "Entrepreneurship and the Structure of the Enterprise in Russia, 1800–1880," in Gregory Guroff and Fred Carstensen, eds., *Entrepreneurship in Imperial Russia and the Soviet Union* (Princeton, NJ: Princeton University Press, 1983), 60.

on collaboration and good relations with hundreds of business associates, and consequently it had become the most important trading, shipping, and financial business of the time.

Both Vagliano and Onassis became legends because of their enormous wealth, which dazzled their contemporaries. Suspicion against big money was prevalent in late-nineteenth-century Russia and the United States: this included businessmen, bankers, and industrialists who made colossal fortunes, which defined the economic development of their countries. Some well-known examples from America's old money are J. P. Morgan (banking and steel), John D. Rockefeller (oil), Cornelius Vanderbilt (railways), and Andrew Carnegie (steel).[72] Mari Vagliano, loved and hated at the same time, can be considered the Russian version of the classical US Horatio Alger rags-to-riches myth.

Conclusions

This chapter indicates the problems the Vagliano Brothers encountered as a foreign trading company in an unstable political environment. Their businesses could be described as a kind of proto-multinational that carried out international accounting beyond the interests of the host country. Their cosmopolitanism affected the hinterland of Imperial Russia's south, and the story of the confrontation of Mari Vagliano with the Russian Empire indicates the populist and nationalist reaction to perceived foreign economic influence during this first era of globalization.

Mari Vagliano confronted the commercial status quo of the era, the Russian government, and the Russian intelligentsia, and emerged unscathed. His case is a paradigm for the survival of Greek firms involved in the international shipping business. During his trial the Vaglianos mobilized all their powerful local, national, and international networks, and showed the ability of global shipping businesses to find legal ways around and through the laws and national interests that would otherwise restrict their global activities. Onassis, seventy years later, did the same. The fact is that shipping is an international economic activity par excellence and develops mechanisms vital for its survival.

In both cases, our heroes, such as they were, became legends. They both incarnated the capitalist dream of every immigrant to Russia or the United States: to emulate the classic rags-to-riches story. Mari Vagliano became a legend of south Russia. The mythical riches of the poor and illiterate seaman who started from nothing in the Imperial Russia of the second half of the

---

[72] For the robber-barons of the United Sates see Charles R. Morris, *The Tycoons* (New York: Times Books, 2005), and David S. Landes, *Dynasties: Fortunes and Misfortunes of the World's Great Family Businesses* (London: Penguin Books, 2006). See also Alfred D. Chandler, *The Visible Hand: The Managerial Revolution in American Business* (Cambridge, MA: Harvard University Press, 1999), who was of course against this term.

nineteenth century did not become the paradigm to imitate but the type of man to avoid. He became one of the symbols of south Russia's magnates and since his death, to the present day, novelists, journalists, and historians have written novels, theatrical plays, satirical articles, and books mentioning him as the stereotype of the miser millionaire who is ruthless, uneducated, and heartless.[73] I need not mention here the legend of Onassis. It seems that all Greek mythology has been recruited to describe the man as a "Minotaur" or the man "who had the Midas touch" – a modern Croesus. Contrary to Mari Vagliano, who was always described in a derogatory manner in the press, Aristotle Onassis became the friendly and popular mogul.

Mari Vagliano and Aristotle Onassis belong to a group of entrepreneurs who remained always aliens in their host countries, where their entrepreneurial leadership was also evident. They were instead international businessmen working for profit beyond national boundaries and interests; and both came under attack at specific times, by the state, for corruption and abuse. In both cases they survived. This happened because of their knowledge of the formal and informal institutional framework of the business they were involved in, and because of their ability to activate the national and international political and economic networks they had so carefully built.

---

[73] For a sample see D. Proskurnin, "Хищники (Изъ воспоминаній)" ["The 'Voulchers' (From Memories)"], Istoricheskiy Vestnik 110 (1907): 137–150; Sergei Zvantsev, Дело Вальяно [Vagliano Case] (Rostov-on-Don: Rostidzat editions, 1959); Gabrioushkin, Мари Вальяно и другие.

5

The Vagliano Fleet and Innovation in Ship Management

A landmark in the Vagliano's shipping business, and in the evolution of Greek shipping businesses in an era of globalization, was the creation of a hybrid ship management office in London. The Vaglianos' business went through the third stage of specialization in shipping, when trading companies began to transform into steamship companies, during the last third of the nineteenth century. The multinational dimension of their managing-agency operations made their London office a national bureau of sorts – a conduit enabling Greek shipowners to engage in international business.

It was Christmas Eve 1901. An aged Panagi Vagliano, eighty-seven, was in his office at 19 Old Broad Street in the City. On that day, in his characteristic, now shaky hand, he signed the letters of the usual daily shipping business as he had done for decades. They were addressed to his collaborators in the eastern Mediterranean and the Black Sea, like P. Margaroni in Chios, A. L. Negreponti, in Syros, P. Veja in Cephalonia, Retsinas Bros. and K. N. Lykiardopulo in Piraeus, T. Theophanis in Rostov-on-Don, O. A. Stathatos in Athens, and others. The office remained closed on Christmas Day and Boxing Day. Panagi Vagliano returned there on December 27, when he signed his last business letters.[1] He died twenty-five days later. After his death, almost twenty Greek London offices sprang up during the following decades, modelling themselves on the Vagliano London office. London has remained one of the main bases of Greek-owned shipping to the present day.

At the beginning of the twenty-first century, the largest group of foreign agents for overseas shipowners in London were the Greeks, with 120 agencies employing more than 1,500 people.[2] There are around 14,000 people employed in maritime services in the United Kingdom, mostly in London, generating £1.1 billion in net exports, a remarkable contribution to the UK's balance of payments for such a small group of people.[3] Despite the fact that

---

[1] General State Archives, Archives of Cephalonia Prefecture, Vagliano Archive, *Foreign Letter Book*, November 13, 1901–April 4, 1902.
[2] Richard Roberts, *The City: A Guide to London's Global Financial Centre* (London: The Economist, 2004), 206–220.
[3] Ibid.

the British fleet lost its primacy a few decades previously, London has remained the world's main maritime center, and the base of global maritime institutions like the Baltic Exchange, Lloyd's List, and Lloyd's Insurance, not to mention the many banks providing shipping finance. As Michael Miller has written, "when I interviewed leading figures at the Baltic Exchange at the end of the 1990s, I found that they could tolerate the decline of British shipowners because they still had the Greeks."[4]

The great competitive advantage held by the Vagliano Brothers was their shipping operation, which was the source of their starting capital and the place where they introduced important innovations. The firm was a trailblazer in this particular sector, pioneering in the operation of a large number of sailing vessels with timely investments, and adopting new technology on time, along with the development of new business methods in ship-management finance.

Vagliano's innovations and contribution to the evolution of Greek shipping can be identified on three levels. The first was the formation and operation of a large fleet and timely investment in the new technology of steamships, and the second was in ship finance. Third, Vagliano created, in effect, a mega-shipping agency that, during the third phase of the Vagliano business from 1887 to 1902, became a hybrid kind of shipping firm/shipping agency/ship-management office – what the Greeks called the "London office." In this way, the Vagliano Brothers pioneered the transition of Greek-owned shipping from sail to steam; and at the same time their shipping office in London operated as a clearinghouse for existing or aspiring Greek shipowners and, more significantly, provided a model for the Greek London offices of the twentieth century. Later, it was from one of these offices that Onassis started his shipping business.

The Vagliano Fleet

The Vaglianos started their business as Masters and shipowners and they maintained a large fleet throughout, the largest in the Greek-owned fleet at all times. They owned fleets in two distinct periods. The first one was the sailing ship era, which lasted until the early 1890s, although it diminished quickly, beginning in the 1880s. The new technology of steamships was introduced during the 1820s on commercial routes. However, it took nearly sixty years to overcome technological difficulties like the replacement of wood by iron and of iron by steel, the invention of the triple-expansion engine that reduced the amount of coal needed to produce steam, and the transition from the paddle wheel to the rudder. Furthermore, it took a long time for the new technology of engines to

---

[4] Michael Miller, "Review of *Leadership in World Shipping: Greek Family Firms in International Business*. By Ioannis Theotokas and Gelina Harlaftis," *Business History Review* 86, no. 1 (2012): 173–175.

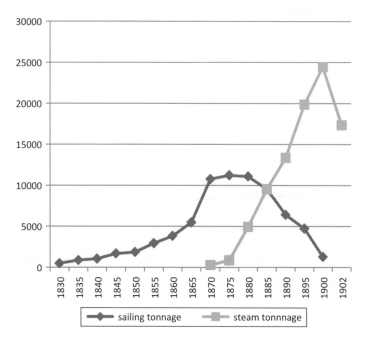

sailing tonnage steam tonnnage

Figure 5.1 The fleet of the Vagliano Bros., 1830–1900 (net registered tons)
Source: Table 5.1.

be established and, until the 1890s, steamships carried sails.[5] Steamships were very expensive floating capital. It was mainly the state-subsidized liner companies that were able to introduce them from the 1820s for short and then longer distances. The sailing ship reached a technological peak in the 1870s, and it took that long for technological advancements and shipbuilding to come to a point where it was economically viable to invest in steamships. In tramp shipping, the transition from sail to steam took place in the fleet of the world's main shipping nation, Great Britain, in the 1880s. The second period of steamships in the Vagliano business lasted from the late 1870s to 1902 (Figure 5.1).

The Vaglianos were pivotal in the internationalization of the Greek island shipping fleets. With a sailing ship fleet of sixty vessels in 1875, and a few dozen under their control as they were financing Greek shipmasters, the Vaglianos reigned in the shipping world of the eastern Mediterranean and the Black Sea (Figure 5.1 and Table 5.1). No other firm in the area owned and

5 Delis, *Mediterranean Wooden Shipbuilding*; C. Knick Harley, "The Shift from Sailing Ships to Steam Ships, 1850–1890," in D. N. McCloskey, ed., *Essays on a Mature Economy: Britain after 1840* (Princeton, NJ: Princeton University Press, 1971), 215–234; Gerald S. Graham, "The Ascendancy of the Sailing Ship, 1850–85," *The Economic History Review* 9, no. 1 (1956): 74–88; Palmer, "The British Shipping Industry, 1850–1914," 101.

Table 5.1 *The fleet of the Vagliano Bros., 1830–1902 (net registered tons)*

Year	Sailing ships	Sailing tons	Steamships	Steam tons	Total ships	Total tonnage
1830	2	484			2	484
1835	4	870			4	870
1840	7	1,045			7	1,045
1845	10	1,679			10	1,679
1850	10	1,850			10	1,850
1855	16	2,928			16	2,928
1860	24	3,819			24	3,819
1865	32	5,482			32	5,482
1870	58	10,773			58	10,773
1875	60	11,229	2	869	62	12,098
1880	53	11,092	7	4,935	60	16,027
1885	45	9,536	12	9,548	57	19,084
1890	25	6,409	17	13,369	42	19,778
1895	15	4,744	22	19,865	37	24,609
1900	3	1,294	27	24,420	30	25,714
1902			18	17,300	18	17,330

Source: Appendix 1.D.
Note: Much wider research in many sources needed to be done to identify the fleet of the Vagliano Brothers. Note the difference of the fleet of the Vaglianos as presented in Harlaftis, *A History of Greek-Owned Shipping*, table 3.16, 96, and in Gelina Harlaftis, "Μεγιστάνες του Ιονίου: Ο οίκος των Αδελφών Βαλλιάνου" ["The Tycoons of the Ionian Sea: The House of the Vagliano Brothers"], *Ιόνιος Λόγος* [*Ionios Logos*] (2007): 303–346, table 3.

controlled so many vessels. The novelty here was that this was not an island shipping group consisting of vessels owned by many shipping families, as was usually the case during the first and second stage of this evolution. This was a single shipping firm that had originated on one of the islands and operated a large fleet – but not from the island, from abroad. It was an international firm. However, more than half of its fleet was registered in Greece and most particularly at their home island, Cephalonia. Most important, Greek crews ran the fleet. The Vaglianos employed exclusively Greek captains and seamen, not only from the Ionian islands but also from the Aegean islands: a highly experienced workforce whom they could trust and control. The close connection to the maritime business milieu of the Greek state provided low-cost sailing ships and seamen, while the use of the Greek flag provided low-cost operations. In fact, all international Greek shipping firms would follow this system for the next hundred years.

Therefore, the Vaglianos pioneered in consolidating a form of ship management that other smaller or medium Greek diaspora shipping firms practiced, particularly in the last third of the nineteenth century. During its formative period (1820s to 1860s), their fleet increased from two vessels (in 1830) to twenty-four vessels with a total tonnage of about 4,000 tons in 1860 (Table 5.1). At its apogee in 1875, the Vagliano sailing ship fleet had almost tripled to sixty sailing vessels with a total tonnage of about 11,200 tons; it was an amazing fleet for the day and unique in the eastern Mediterranean and the Black Sea (Figure 5.1). After the mid-1880s, the sailing ship fleet shrank dramatically to only three vessels (in 1900). However, by this time the Vaglianos were well invested in steamship technology; they had started investing in steamships at the highest peak of their sailing ship fleet. They were opening the way to a new technological era for the Greek fleet.

It was mainly Mari and Andrea Vagliano that appeared as the shipowners of sailing vessels (Appendix 1.D); out of the eighty sailing ships that the Vaglianos purchased throughout their business life, Mari owned 60 percent and Andrea 40 percent. More than a third of the total number of sailing vessels was purchased in the 1860s, while Andrea Vagliano was in Constantinople. These timely purchases of ships took place after the Crimean War, which was a financial windfall for the Vagliano firm, and the low freight rates of the 1860s – ship prices tended to fall with the decrease of freight rates (Figure 5.2).[6]

The sailing ships were registered half in Greece and half in Russia. They were registered in Greece mostly in the Ionian islands, and particularly in Cephalonia, and in Russia in the Azov, mainly in Rostov and Taganrog. In this way, the Vagliano sailing ships flew the Ionian (up to 1864), Greek, and Russian flag. All sailing vessels purchased by Andrea Vagliano were built and registered in the Greek islands and carried the Greek flag; Mari Vagliano, on the other hand, owned a fleet of medium to small vessels mainly registered in Russia, carrying the Russian flag (Appendix 1.D).

They used brigs and schooners, of various sizes, in order to be able to reach all ports and deal with the shallow and difficult conditions of the Black Sea. From 1830 to 1900, twelve vessels were of a small size, below 100 tons each, all in the Azov serving the local and coastal trade; fifty-five were sailing ships of medium size between 100 and 300 tons each; and about ten vessels were between 300 and 600 tons each. A smaller number after the 1880s reached larger sizes; ten vessels were between 300 and 700 tons each.[7]

---

[6] Delis, *Mediterranean Wooden Shipbuilding*, Figure 3.5.
[7] There are tantalizing hints that the Vaglianos owned a large fleet of coastal vessels, the so-called *lotkas*, in the Azov, but specific evidence for them is not extant.

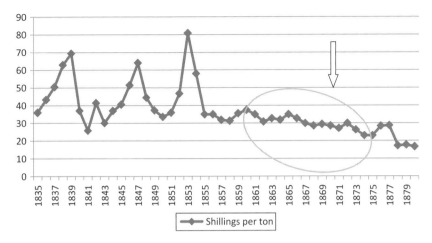

Figure 5.2   Timely purchases of sailing ships (freight rates from Odessa to England/ northern Europe, shillings per ton)
Source: Gelina Harlaftis and George Kostelenos, "International Shipping and national Economic Growth: Shipping Earnings and the Greek Economy in the Nineteenth Century," *The Economic History Review* 65, no. 4 (2012): 1403–1427, based C. Knick Harley, "Coal Exports and British Shipping, 1850–1913," *Explorations in Economic History* 26 (1989): 311–338; E. A. V. Angier, *Fifty Years' Freights, 1869–1919* (London: Fairplay, 1920); The National Archives, Washington, DC, "Dispatches from United States Consuls in Odessa," vols. 1–2, May 1831–January 1858.

The choice of shipyards was also important. The brothers procured a large number of their vessels by order from the various shipyards of the Greek islands, and particularly in the largest eastern Mediterranean shipyards, especially on the island of Syros (almost half of their ships were built on Syros, see Figure 5.3). Mari Vagliano had turned to the Syros shipyards from the very beginning in the 1820s. Historian Apostolos Delis has recently indicated that the Syros shipyards were the most productive in the Mediterranean by the middle of the century; more productive than the French in Provence or the Italians in Liguria, while they were equally competitive in terms of production with the major shipbuilding regions of the North Atlantic. They were also 30–50 percent cheaper than those of the French and between 40 and 160 percent cheaper than British yards.[8] About a third of the Vaglianos' vessels were built in the Azov (in Rostov and Taganrog) in Russia, most probably by Greek shipwrights. The rest were purchased either from other Greek shipbuilding centers (like those of Galaxidi, Kassos or Mount Athos), or secondhand from the Adriatic and other Italian ports, and England.

[8] Delis, *Mediterranean Wooden Shipbuilding*, 79–80.

Figure 5.3   The brig *Keramies*, 206 nrt, built in 1869 on Syros, owned by Andrea
Vagliano, registered in Cephalonia
Source: private collection Athanassios Akrivos, Athens.

If Mari and Andrea were absorbed with their dozens of sailing vessels,
Panagi Vagliano, following the trend in Britain, the first industrial nation,
made the groundbreaking move of investing in new technology, in
steamships. He bought his first steamship named *Vagliano* in 1869 from
the shipyards of North Shields (Appendix, Table A1.4).[9] For the next decade,
he proceeded to order on a massive scale: more than thirty small and large
steamships for himself and his clients from the shipyards of North Shields,
Glasgow, and Sunderland. As we are informed by the Glasgow newspaper
Herald on January 11, 1880:

> On Saturday forenoon Messrs B. Seath and Co. launched from Rutherglen
> Shipbuilding Yard an iron twin screw steamer of 280 tons. . . . She was
> named "Vagliano A." by Miss Jane Seath . . . The steamer, which has a
> very graceful appearance, is intended for the grain trade on the Danube,
> Don and Black Sea, and is the sixth which Messrs Seath have constructed
> for the same firm. A companion steamer, also for Messrs Vagliano Bros.,
> is on the stocks and will be launched in a week or two.

Between 1878 and 1883, Panagi launched an impressive shipbuilding
program: he received 12 new ships, the cargo steamers *Vagliano, Vagliano Bros,
Vagliano, A, Vagliano, B, Adelphi Cuppa, Mari Vagliano, P. A. Vagliano,
Vagliano Brothers, Andrea Vagliano, Adelphi Vagliano, Nicholas Vagliano*, and
Spyridon Vagliano (Figure 5.4) of about 1,000 nrt each from the shipyards in
Sunderland and North Shields. All vessels were registered in Cephalonia, and

---

[9] Harlaftis, "From Diaspora Traders to Shipping Tycoons." For the family of Theofilatos,
     see Harlaftis, Beneki, and Haritatos, *Ploto,* and for the ships, Harlaftis and Vlassopoulos,
     Pontoporeia.

Figure 5.4   Steamship *Spyridon Vagliano*, 1,111 nrt, 1,708 dwt, built at Bartram
shipyards for the Vaglianos in 1883, registered in Cephalonia
Source: House of Spyridon Vagliano family, Keramies, Cephalonia.

sailed under the Greek flag. Their operations remained in the London office, run
by Panagi Vagliano. It is interesting to compare this large shipbuilding program
with that of Onassis seventy years later.

After 1887, Panagi Vagliano remained alone, the "Pope" of the business,
as Andrea died the same year and Mari Vagliano retired from the business
at the age of eighty-three, after the lengthy and exhausting trial in Russia.
It seems that after his own adventure with the Bank of England in
1887–1889, Panagi, himself aged seventy-five, and his nephews turned even
more to shipping. The steamship fleet kept expanding, this time with
secondhand steamships. From 1886 to 1900 Panagi acquired twenty-one
secondhand and three newbuilt vessels, medium-size and large cargo ships,
either alone under Vagliano Brothers or with his nephews, sons of his
brothers Andrea, Metaxas, and Spyridon. Particularly the sons of his
brother Spyridon, his nephews Michael S. Vagliano and Athanasse
S. Vagliano, appear as owners of steamships. The fleet reached its peak in
1900 (Figure 5.1).

Panagi Vagliano was adept at buying and selling ships at the right time. He
was able to take advantage of the low prices of the 1880s; this was a time of
crisis and abrupt decreases in freight rates, and thus in prices of ships
(Figure 5.5). He also took advantage of low prices from 1890 to 1896 and
purchased 17 secondhand vessels. Then, just before his death, Panagi sold
high, during the Boer War (see Figure 5.5). Between 1899 and 1901 he and
his nephews sold seven steamships, some of which he had built almost
twenty years before, at high prices; namely the *Adelphi Vagliano*, *Andrea
Vagliano*, *Mari Vagliano*, *Nicholas Vagliano*, and *Panagi Vagliano*, along
with the ships *Aghios Ioannis* and *Eleni Milas* (Appendix 1.D). He planned
to go through a renewal of the fleet and the year he died his nephews
received three new vessels.

During his lifetime, Panagi Vagliano purchased forty-one steamships for his
own firm and for his clients. More than 60 percent of the steamships he

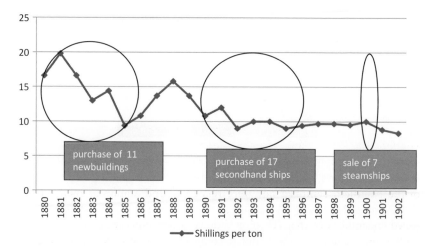

Figure 5.5 Freight rate index and timely purchases and sales of steamships by Panagi Vagliano
Source: L. Isserlis, "Tramp Shipping Cargoes and Freights," *Journal of the Royal Statistical Society* 101 (1938): 53–146.

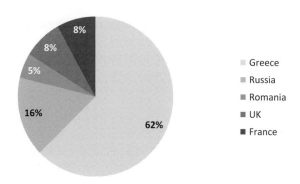

Figure 5.6 Registration of the Vagliano steamships
Source: Appendix 1.D.

operated were registered in Greece (mostly in Cephalonia but also in Piraeus) and they flew the Greek flag (Figure 5.6). Piraeus was the new emerging maritime center of Greece, an insignificant small town and port until the 1880s, which became the center of the fast-growing steamship fleet of the Greeks (replacing Syros and the other small sailing ship centers). Sixteen percent of the Vagliano steamships were registered in Russia, mostly in Rostov and Taganrog, 5 percent in Romania, and 16 percent in France (Marseilles) and the United Kingdom (London).

The early adoption of the new steam technology made the Vagliano Brothers prime movers and leaders for the Greek-owned steamship fleet. In the mid-1880s, steamships accounted for more than 50 percent of the tonnage of the Vagliano fleet, placing them some twenty years ahead of the rest of the Greeks. Apart from the Vaglianos, the main investors in steamships at this early stage were the Stathatos, the Theofilatos, and the Embiricos, who were based in the Danubian port of Braila.[10] Panagi collaborated with all three, as he had represented their businesses in London since his establishment there; these families purchased their steamships through him.[11] The Embiricos family from the island of Andros proved to be the main shipowning Greek family of the first half of the twentieth century; they were related to and employed members of the Goulandris family, which came to be among the leading Greek shipowning families of the second half of the twentieth century.

Therefore, the importance of the Vaglianos went beyond the activities of their own fleet. They also became the main financiers, brokers, and agents of the Greek island shipping firms as a whole. And, in the second half of the nineteenth century, they were the largest tramp-shipping firm of the eastern Mediterranean and Black Sea. However, their fleet cannot be compared with Britain's top tramp operators, like the Furness Withy of Hartlepool, which ranked first in 1910, with ninety-five vessels of 178,837 nrt, or the Hain of Cardiff, which ranked fourth with thirty-six ships of 93,169 nrt, or the Turnbulls of Whitby, which ranked eighth with twenty-nine ships of 65,150 nrt, and the Runcimans from Newcastle, which ranked ninth, with twenty-nine vessels of 64,436 nrt.[12] The last two were family firms that had been involved in shipping for several generations; they were established in northeast England and operated in the Black Sea grain trade. The Vaglianos, however, who by British standards could be characterized as large tramp operators, compared favorably with their Mediterranean counterparts: the top Spanish fleet Sota & Aznar in 1900 owned twenty-four vessels of 49,630 grt, compared well the thirty ships of 42,857 grt (25,714 nrt) that the Vaglianos owned in 1900 (see Table 5.1).[13]

[10] Harlaftis, *A History of Greek-Owned Shipping*, 102–104.
[11] Lemos, *Modern Greek Eternal Seamen*, 380–382.
[12] Harlaftis and Theotokas, "European Family Firms in International Business," tables 3 and 5.
[13] A net registered ton is about 60 percent of a gross registered ton. For Spanish shipping see Jesùs M. Valdaliso, "The Rise of Specialist Firms in Spanish Shipping and their Strategies of Growth, 1860 to 1930," *Business History Review* 74 (Summer 2000): 268–300, appendix 2. See also Valdaliso's *La familia Aznar y sus negocios (1830–1983): Cuatro generaciones de empresarios en la España contemporánea* (Madrid: Marcial Ponts Historia, 2006).

Ship Finance

The Vaglianos mobilized resources from their trading company and channeled them to finance their own ships and, more important, to other Greek
shipping firms. If Aristotle Onassis later opened a path to the US banks (whose
financing of Onassis's tankers opened the way to other Greek shipowners), the
mighty Vaglianos became themselves the bank that provided finance to other
Greek shipping firms, in three ways. First, they invented a method to overcome the lack of a ship mortgage law in both the Ionian and Greek legal
systems. Second, they provided finance not only to their co-islanders and the
Ionians, as was usually the case, but also to shipping firms from the Aegean
islands; they were the first to do this in a shipping world characterized by
island networks. Third, they provided finance through their offices for both
sailing ships and steamships.

The only type of maritime finance permitted under Ionian and Greek law
was the shipping loan, which, after 1850, was written on a special ledger of the
ship, the so-called libretto. These were short-term loans with high interest. In
fact, shipping loans at the beginning of the journey were almost an integral
part of shipping. The Master needed money to prepare the ship for the next
journey and in most cases had to borrow to supplement the cash available: the
ship always needed small repairs, new equipment, and foodstuffs. These loans
were usually contracted for a few months, with interest rates (in the 1840s)
varying between 2 and 2.5 percent per month (24–30 percent per year).[14] The
high interest rates were justified by the high-risk nature of shipping. The loans
were not guaranteed by mortgages and the loss of the ship took with it all
contracted loans. The mortgage, as a security for the repayment of a loan,
could lower the credit, as large sums of maritime loans were impossible with
such high interest rates.[15]

In the nineteenth century, Greek shipping firms purchased sailing ships
through joint partnerships, usually of related families.[16] Such partnerships
were necessary in Greece for three reasons: insufficient capital to build a ship;
the necessity to spread the risk involved: and the need for an outlet for residual
capital where several vessels are controlled. The Vaglianos broke this mold.
They financed Masters and aspiring sailing shipowners of the Ionian and
Aegean islands and put the sailing vessel under their name until repayment
was made. For example, just about the time Andrea Vagliano was established

---

[14] Demetrios Polemis, *Τα ιστιοφόρα της Άνδρου* [*Sailing Ships of Andros*] (Ανδρος: Kaireios
Library, 1991), 51, presents equivalent data for the same period from the notarial archives
from Andros.
[15] Harlaftis, *A History of Greek-Owned Shipping*, 143–144.
[16] Ibid.; Papadopoulou, "Maritime Businesses."

in Constantinople, he granted a loan of 30,000 piasters[17] (or 6,900 French francs) to the Cephalonian shipowner Spyridon Metaxas-Laskaratos on 0.5 percent monthly interest (an annual 6 percent) to supplement his capital and be able to purchase a ship. As a guarantee to the loan, the Cephalonian shipowner "was obliged to sign a document which put the ownership of the ship on his [Andrea's] name in good faith, and this is what happened."[18] The brig was thus purchased for the amount of 90,000 piasters (or 20,700 French francs) and it changed to the name of the shipowner when he ultimately repaid the debt.

Using this method, apart from their own vessels, the Vaglianos always had a large fleet under their name, one that they partly owned and controlled. This proved handy, as they were able to monopolize and indirectly control this fleet, as one angry captain and shipowner revealed. Captain Spyridon Metaxas-Laskaratos wrote that:

> They [the Vaglianos] hold them for 5–6 months during the whole winter at anchor in Taganrog whereas other ships were loading from the same company and from others [other merchants] because the ships "addressed" to M. Vagliano were not loaded by anybody else, and none of our agents came nearby, as this was their system and particularly if the ownership of one of our ships seemed to be of Vagliano.[19]

This became the usual practice of finance among merchants-financiers, particularly on Syros, and ultimately financed a large part of the transition to steamships before 1910, when the mortgage on ships was finally legally institutionalized in Greece.[20] Because of this practice, the identification of the sailing ship fleet of the Vagliano Brothers has been a complex and painstaking procedure. Many a time sailing ships bore the name of Andrea Vagliano or Mari or Panagi Vagliano but belonged to other shipowners. Appendix 1.D indicates the vessels they actually owned, which they usually kept for more than twenty years. Information on any one ship has been derived from many sources and hence identifies the span of the each of the Vagliano vessels.

We have been able to trace a sample of shipowners that the Vaglianos financed (Table 5.2). Two-thirds of the sailing shipowners financed between 1870s and 1890s had their ships named after Mari Vagliano. It is interesting to note that in the Vagliano fleet (Table 5.1), only one ship was named after Mari Vagliano. It seems then that the Vaglianos followed a system of naming the financed vessels after one of the brothers, Mari Vagliano, or it might be that

---

[17] 1 piaster = 0.23 francs in the 1850s.
[18] Metaxas-Laskaratos, *Commercial-Consular Prosecutions*, 5.   [19] Ibid., 7.
[20] Harlaftis, *History of Greek-Owned Shipping*, 144–146.

Table 5.2 *A sample of sailing ships financed by the Vaglianos, 1870s–1890s*

Name of ship	Master	Year of registration	NRT	Type of ship	Flag	Where registered
Athanassios Vagliano	Tsatsaronis and Tsolas	1880	616	Gabara		Chios
Alcibiades Vagliano	Kammenos-Geroussi	1875	293	Brig	Gr	Galaxidi
Andrea Vagliano	Revidis A. N.	1875	230	Brig	Gr	Hydra
Mari Vagliano	Tsatsaronis D.	1870	307	Gabara	Gr	Melos
Marino Vagliano	Kambitsis D.	1870	214	Brig	Gr	Cephalonia
Mari Vagliano	Comnas L.	1875	174	Gabara	Gr	Syros
Marinos Vagliano	Cuppa N. B.	1880	455	Gabara	Gr	Cephalonia
Mari Vagliano	Mazlum Mahmud	1890	260	Bombarda		Crete
Mari Vagliano	Clonis K.	1900	226	Brig		Crete
Panagi Vagliano	Lykiardopoulo F.	1890	261	Bombarda	Gr	Cephalonia

Source: Gelina Harlaftis and Nikos Vlassopoulos, Ιστορικός νηογνώμονας, Ποντοπόρεια: Ποντοπόρα Ιστιοφόρα και Ατμόπλοια 1830–1939 [*Pontoporeia: Historical Registry Book of Greek Cargo Sailing Ships and Steamships, 1830–1939*] (Athens: ELIA/Niarchos Foundation, 2002).

Mari Vagliano was the main sailing ship financier in collaboration with Andrea. The Vagliano ship finance included a spectrum of sailing shipowners originating from a number of Aegean islands, like Chios, Hydra, Melos, Syros, and Crete, making them the first to transcend the island and/or regional boundaries. Similar systems of ship finance eventually sprang up on other islands, and mainly from the merchants in Chios and in Syros.[21]

Providing ship finance to an aspiring shipowner by becoming a temporary owner of the vessel to guarantee the repayment of the loan was a system based on trust. As this kind of loan – using collateral – was illegal under Greek legislation, loans from Greek or foreign banks for such purchases were ruled out; this allowed the Vagliano Brothers, who granted loans at 7–8 percent interest for the purchase of steamships, to accumulate a great deal of power. Syros merchants and other diaspora traders followed this method, which allowed the transition to steam to take place in the Greek fleet. In these transactions, the Vaglianos secured in cash half the sum they demanded and mortgaged the ship by becoming the ship's owners. As the loans from the Vagliano office were 1 percent higher than the official interest rate of the Bank of England, it has been estimated that the office's profit from each came to 14 percent of the sum lent.[22] They financed at least thirteen prominent Greek shipowners in the twentieth century: Ambatielo, Foca, Lykiardopulo, and Kambitsi from Cephalonia, Goulandris, Moraitis, Polemis, and A. Embiricos from Andros, Margaronis, Nikolakis, and Michalinos from Chios, Vatis from Syros, and Roussos from Leros.[23]

Moreover, the Vaglianos influenced the transition to steam of the Greek shipowners on the Danube, most of whom also originated from Cephalonia and Ithaca and collaborated closely with the Vaglianos. The largest Danube riverboat owners, deep-seagoing vessels owners and merchants were the Theofilatos, Stathatos, and Embiricos, who eventually transferred their activities to Piraeus and London at the turn of the century and continued their entrepreneurial activities as shipowners. Dracoulis Bros. initially worked at the Theofilatos and Stathatos enterprises before starting their own business in partnership with their relatives, the Gratsos, before 1914, and in the interwar period opened a London office. It was from the Dracoulis office that Onassis purchased his first steamships in the early 1930s, and it was Costas Gratsos

---

[21] Notably by M. Zygomalas in Chios or Calvocoressis in Syros, see Harlaftis, *A History of Greek-Owned Shipping*, 145–146.

[22] This has been estimated by the shipowner Nikolas B. Metaxas (the father of the maritime economist Basil Metaxas). Cited in Andreas Lemos, *The Greeks and the Sea: A People's Seafaring Achievements from Ancient Times to the Present Day* (London: Cassell, 1970), 157.

[23] Harlaftis, *A History of Greek-Owned Shipping*, chapter 3.

who became the right-hand man who introduced him to the Greek shipowning world.

Ultimately, two-thirds of all Greek steamships bought from 1890 to 1914 were financed either by the Vaglianos themselves or by members of the Ionian network headed by the Vaglianos.[24] The largest amount of capital for the transition came from the members of the Ionian network, especially during the first stages in the 1880s and 1890s. A significant number of the Masters employed on these ships were part owners; frequently when the steamers became too old they bought them and became shipowners themselves. In the 1890s, the Vaglianos London office collaborated with more than a hundred Greek shipowners/captains from the Aegean and Ionian islands, some of whom became prominent twentieth-century Greek shipowners.[25] Moreover, their operation was not confined to their compatriots from Cephalonia; it encompassed owners of the whole of Greek shipping enclave from Andros, Chios, Syros, Mykonos, Spetses, and Ithaca.

On their own vessels, the Vaglianos used Cephalonian Masters almost exclusively (Appendix 1.D). All of these belonged to sailing shipowning families, so it could be that some, who initially worked for the Vaglianos, were financed by them and eventually were able to buy their vessels. They used Masters from other islands too, since Masters usually hired crews from their home island. For example, the Master and crew of the steamship *Nikolaos Vagliano*, belonging to the Vaglianos, were all from the island of Andros (see Table 5.3). But it also might be that Captain Georgios L. Goulandris had borrowed from the Vaglianos to gradually buy the steamship run by the Vagliano Brothers.

The Vagliano London Office

The shipping industry developed its own unique institutions in London, the world's maritime capital.[26] These were consolidated in the 1830s and were predicated on a distinctive culture of trust and the reputation of its members, not only on a regional but also on an international basis. The services sector, like transport or banking, has always been characterized by the interplay between risk and security. The shipping sector in the nineteenth century established mechanisms to control what has been vital to the business: information and trust. In fact, the motto of London's prime shipping charter market, the Baltic Exchange, is "my word is my bond." Shipping institutions, in order to provide an unfettered flow of information, had taken their official

---

[24] Ibid., table 3.19.

[25] Theotokas and Harlaftis, *Leadership in World Shipping*; Harlaftis, Beneki, and Haritatos, *Ploto*.

[26] Boyce, "The Development of Commercial Infrastructure for World Shipping," 106–123.

Table 5.3 *Monthly wages for the crew of the ship* Nikolaos Vagliano, *under Captain G. L. Goulandris, March 10, 1898*

Specialty	Name	Monthly wages in French francs
Master	Georgios L. Goulandris	400
First Mate	Leonidas A. Polemis	200
Second Mate	Alkiviadis L. Goulandris	150
Bosun	Nikolaos Axiotis	100
Steward	Ioannis Palaiokrassas	90
Carpenter	Ioannis Perlourentzos	90
Cook	Ioannis Lykouriotis	85
Seamen	Valmas, Polemis, Hatzapis, Harharas (70 each)	280
First Engineer	Alexandros Kairis	400
Second Engineer	Spyros Polemis	250
Third Engineer	Nikolaos Dapontes	150
Bosun-Engineer	Constantinos Kokkinos	100
Donkeymen	Zannis Koutsoukos, Egglezos (80 each)	240
Trimmers	Kourtesis, Kokkinos (60 each)	120
Steward	Andrea Hazapis	50

Source: General State Archives, Archives of Cephalonia Perfecture, Vagliano Archive, f. 20.

modern form by the second third of the nineteenth century. Since what a shipping company does is sell space in the holds of its ships to those who want to have cargoes transported from one port to another, a geographical space was needed for the shipowners, who provided the ships, to meet the shippers, who provided the cargoes: this became the Baltic Exchange, formed as a limited club in 1823 at the Baltic Coffee House.[27] This is still the place where the price of the sea transport for a cargo is fixed – the freight rate, documented in the "charter-party." The deals in the Baltic are still closed by "gentlemen's agreement," and it is days after that when the charter parties are signed. Panagi Vagliano was a member of the Baltic Exchange from 1858.

However, for a ship to be chartered at the Baltic Exchange it had to be insured. Thus, Lloyd's of London, the world's leading marine insurance market in its modern phase, emerged in 1834. The insurance brokers keep files of shipping companies and their performance over the last decades. The Vaglianos acted as insurers at least from the 1870s for their own and other

---

[27] Barty-King, *Baltic Exchange.*

Greek sailing shipowners and steamship owners, as the Vagliano Archive indicates. It was difficult, and in many cases impossible, for Greek sailing shipowners to be insured at Lloyds, as they did not meet the prerequisites set. The Vaglianos filled the gap.

To be insured, a ship needs to have a certificate from a Classification Society that it is fit to sail; the Classification Societies are nonprofit organizations with specialized surveyors in all ports of the world, who can survey ships constantly for quality-control purposes. Lloyd's Register of Shipping, as distinct from Lloyd's the Insurers, became an independent organization in 1834; at about the same time Bureau Veritas (the French Classification Society), Lloyd Austriaco (the Austrian Classification Society), and American Bureau of Shipping (the American Classification Society) emerged, among others. The Classification Society follows a ship from its birth through the rest of its life, no matter how many hands it passes through. Both Panagi and Mari Vagliano were subscribers at Lloyd's Register of Shipping since 1866.[28] The Greek sailing ship and steamship vessels, apart from those registered in Russia, are to be found in all or some of the books of the above classification societies.

Additionally, of course, the building of a ship is not carried out without the collaboration of a banker. In order to be performed, the product of shipping depends on the assessment of a chain of shipping institutions that developed mechanisms to safeguard trust in business and secured the minimization of risk. Throughout the nineteenth and twentieth centuries, this has been an almost self-regulated business between principals and agents. The Vaglianos acted as the bankers in some cases and as brokers or agents in others, between the shipyards and Greek shipowners that wanted to invest in newly built steamships.

The Vagliano Brothers functioned for almost fifty years in London, providing services for dozens of small shipping firms with the London shipping market and its maritime institutions. This function, however, was more evident in the last third of the nineteenth century. The Vaglianos all carried out shipping, trading, and financial services either on their own account or for their clients. Moreover, this brings out what has been one of their innovations: that of the "mega" agent, meaning an extraordinarily large shipping agency.[29] Thus, the Vaglianos, apart from operating their own fleet, acted as agents and brokers practically for the whole Greek-owned fleet. Their innovation here is that they became a "mega agency," which served a large number of "micro principals." In general, the principal-agent theory presupposes that the principal is the most powerful party in the relationship, defining and controlling the

---

[28] Lloyd's Register of Shipping, List of subscribers.
[29] Gelina Harlaftis and Alexandra Papadopoulou, "The Mega Agent and the Micro Principal: The Evolution of Greek Shipping Firm in the Nineteenth Century," paper presented in Econ-Ship 2011, University of the Aegean, Chios.

transactions of the agent. The interesting point in the Greek case of the Vaglianos is the reverse: we are talking of a mega-agent that dealt mostly with micro-principals. Apart from an international trading company, the Vagliano Brothers as a mega-agent and broker provided services for the few hundred Ionian and Aegean shipping companies. This was another innovation that proved fundamental for the rise of Greek shipping. First, the Cephalonian Vaglianos, in contrast with their predecessors, the Chiots, dealt not only mainly with trade and with finance, but also at an equal scale with shipping. Second, at least half of their collaborators were not other merchants, but small-scale shipowners (Appendix 1.E). Therefore, the Vaglianos were the first firm that transcended island boundaries, serving not just Ionians (Cephalonians, Ithacans, or Zakynthians), but also the Aegean shipping firms (from Syros, Andros, Santorini, Mykonos, Melos, and Chios). Through them, the island shipping firms acquired access to the international markets, and thus they internationalized the small Greek island shipping firms.

As a mega agent/broker, the Vaglianos achieved significant financial and managerial economies of scale. They also controlled the competition, and there were economies of agglomeration due to incoming information flows from many principals. Their micro-principals would choose the Vaglianos due to the managerial efficiency of their operations. The Vagliano trading company and mega-agency provided liquidity and access to their own financial resources, low-cost supply of credit, lower transaction costs through the direct access to central markets, and informational efficiency. There was a constant flow of updated information through access to an extended network in which the Vaglianos held a central position that provided them expertise on all fronts of shipping: technical information on logistics of sea transport in the difficult conditions of the Azov Sea, information on commodities, and financial facilities. Services were of course given on commission.

The other Greek international trading houses, like the Chiots, also acted as agents of other clients but their clients/collaborators were usually among their own trading group, also coming from Chios. They were primarily merchants and certainly did not act as agents to the shipping firms of Greek islanders. The Vagliano Brothers' position as mega-agent/broker of a few hundred small shipping companies was unique during the sailing ship era. In the new steamship era their agency proved groundbreaking and remained known as the first Greek London Office, an arrangement that proved fundamental for the global evolution of the Greek island shipping groups.

The Vaglianos' London office had a large network that covered a wide range of countries. According to the Office's books of 1901–1902, they had collaborators/clients in twelve countries and forty-five ports (see Appendix 1.E). The great majority were Greeks: 136 out of the 170 collaborators and clients in the twelve countries with which it did business. Economic transactions within this network were based on relations of trust and reduction of business risk, while the dense communication network, borne out by thousands of letters, guaranteed the flow of information and systematic and reliable service. By 1902, the specialization into the shipping business is evident. More than half (98 out of the 170) were Greek shipowners or shipping agents based in Greece, Russia, Romania, the Ottoman Empire, and France (Appendix 1.E).

The London Office particularly became known during the last fifteen years of the business, when Panagi Vagliano was left with his eight nephews to run the business. After the death of Andrea and of Mari, the entire power of the business evidently passed into the hands of Panagi in London, which he maintained until his death in 1902. It was characteristic of his patriarchal management that he did not make any of his nephews members of the firm in London. After the death of Andrea in May 1887 and the retirement of Mari the same year, the Vagliano Brothers had just one major shareholder left, Panagi Vagliano, who remained in control of the business and directed it until his death in 1902.

During the final fifteen years of Panagi's entrepreneurial activity, the main agents running the branches of the company throughout the Mediterranean and the Black Sea were exclusively his nephews. In Rostov-on-Don there was Michael (son of his brother Spyridon); in Novorossiysk Athanasios (son of his brother Spyridon); in Constantinople there was Gerasimos Michael Kambitsis (son of his sister Maria), and Athanasios Lazaros Rosolymos (son of his sister Santina); in Marseilles, Athanasse (son of his brother Metaxas) and Marinos (son of his brother Andrea); in Paris, Athanasse (son of his brother Mari); while in London there were Basil (son of his brother Metaxas) and Alcibiades (son of his brother Mari) (see Figures 5.7–5.8, 10.4, 10.6).[30]

The London office was the on one hand a shipowning firm operating its own large fleet. In 1895, it operated thirty-seven ships of 22,960 nrt, twenty-two steamships and fifteen sailing ships (Table 5.1). On the other hand, and parallel to their shipowning activity, the London office acted as shipbroker, ship agent, ship manager, and ship insurer. In other words, it became a new kind of hybrid office: both large shipowner and ship management/agent/broker firm. All of these functions were becoming more clearly defined as separate from the shipowner and from each other in the last third of the nineteenth century. The Vagliano London office during the 1890s–1900s was different: a new institution that both specialized in the operation of steamships and included all shipping activities.

The shipbroker brings together two parties and acts for one principal. He does not usually have the authority to conclude an agreement for the

---

[30] "Will of Panagi Athanasios Vagliano," Management Committee of the Panagi A. Vagliano Bequest, *Panagi A. Vagliano Bequest for Philanthropic Purposes in Cephalonia* (Athens, 1932).

Figure 5.7 Basil Vagliano (son of Metaxas) worked in the Constantinople office until the mid-1890s. He then moved to London, where he worked with Panagi Vagliano, eventually becoming his right-hand man
Source: Collection of Stephan and Frances Vagliano, Korgialeneio Historical and Folklore Museum of Cephalonia.

Figure 5.8 Athanasse S. Vagliano worked in Novorossiysk. After the death of Panagi he continued his activities in shipowning until he settled with his young wife in Cote d'Azur, around 1920
Source: Private Collection Athanassios Akrivos, Athens.

principal – he can only negotiate.[31] Therefore, the shipbrokers are specialist
intermediaries that negotiate the chartering and the purchase and sale of ships
between interested parties. The shipbroker has to have access to the main
international shipping centers and direct contact and knowledge of the shipping markets. The Vaglianos acted as shipbrokers for their own vessels but
also for the ships that they represented or managed for others.

Of course, apart from shipbrokers, the Vaglianos were major grain traders
in their own right, so their company chartered their own vessels but also a
large number of Greek-owned sailing ships, thereby guaranteeing reliable, low-
cost sailing ships and seamen. In the 1890s, however, despite the importance
of Michael S. Vagliano as a major grain exporter in Rostov-on-Don, the
Vagliano steamships, and those of their clients, indicate that they more often
sold transport services to others instead of trading for themselves. Evidence
indicates that they collaborated with the major Jewish grain merchants established in Russia and the Danube, like the Dreyfus, the Mendhl, or the Neufeld,
chartering their ships or ships of their clients.[32]

Apart from chartering, the Vaglianos were shipbrokers for the sale and
purchase of vessels. Their early adoption of the new technology of steam
enabled network members to adopt it as well. The Vaglianos linked the
members of their network with British shipyards, brokering vessel purchases
for the rest of the Greek shipowners. *The Northern Echo* reports, on March 10,
1879:

> The screw steamer *Cephallonia* was completed in Raylton Dixon and Co
> of Middlesborough on the order of Messrs Vagliano Brothers of London
> for Signor Stathopoulo of Naples, 1,650 tons, gross register 1,200 tons. She
> has been built under the inspection of Captain Paspalas who along with
> the company on board expressed their extreme satisfaction with the
> construction of the ship and the successful trial ship.

The Vaglianos were also the agents of the Nicolopulo House, established in
Galatz by Demetrius Nicolopulo, and in Marseilles by his son Ioannis. The
Nicolopulos ordered a new steamship at the British yard of Bartram Haswell in
Sunderland through the Vaglianos in June 1880. For the order and building of
the ship, the Vaglianos were the Nicolopulos' formal bankers and agents,
handling payments and supervising construction. Half of the payment for
the ship was given on its completion, and the other half was paid in London
(in pounds sterling) during the next six months without interest, based on a
guarantee by the Vaglianos. The steamship *Calliope Nicolopulo*, 1,004 nrt, took

---

[31] Lars Gorton, Patrick Hillennius, Rolf Ihre, and Arne Sandevärn, *Shipbroking and Chartering Practice*, 7th edn (London: Informa, 2009), 40.
[32] Harlaftis, *A History of Greek-Owned Shipping*, 95–98.

five months to finish.[33] However, it was not only the Stathopulos or Nicolo-pulos who profited from the investment in the new steam technology. Information on the steamship market was disseminated to the shipowners of the Aegean and the Ionian islands. Greek merchants or shipowners inquired about the cost of steamships, methods of payment, and the time required to build a ship.[34]

As ship managers, the London office introduced partial or total ship management, by which they provided finance to the shipowners, found chartering, insurance, provided for its bunkers, and financed ship repair and supplies, while the owner/captain provided crewing and operation. As ship and port agents, the Vagliano office kept a wide network of connections in all ports where the company's ships were trading, ensuring berths for incoming ships, the pilots if necessary, and all the bureaucratic functions for the customs and port authorities. They dealt with ship provisions, cash, and whatever else the Master, the crew, and the vessel needed to continue the journey or load and unload the cargo; they also collected the freights and communicated with the shippers. Finally the Vagliano London office also acted as insurers. The insurance book of the London office indicates that just for the year 1898, there were 1,269 acts of insurance contracts. These covered both the Vagliano fleet and the vessels of their clients who were shipowners. Insurance contracts insured the hull or machinery of the vessel, or the cargo, and they were issued for each individual trip or for a whole year.[35]

In this way, the London office provided a channel to the world's maritime and economic center and had multiple effects on the transition from sail to steam in the Greek fleet. Other Greek shipowners imitated the structure and business methods of the Vagliano London office in the first half of the twentieth century. When Panagi Vagliano died, another two London offices already existed. Zorzis Michalinos from Chios established one of them in 1892; Michalinos was a close friend and protégé of Panagi Vagliano. The other was established by S. G. Embiricos in 1896. After Panagi Vagliano's death, another eleven London offices sprang up, all close collaborators of the Vaglianos.[36] The most important of this group was those from the Ionian islands of Cephalonia and Ithaca: the Ambatielos brothers, the Lykiardopoulos, the Vergottis, the Frangopoulos, and the Theofilatos. From Andros, there was also the Embiricos and from Chios the Michalinos, the Scaramanga and Sechiari, the last two remnants of the once-mighty Chiot network.

---

[33] "Professional Correspondence of Captain A. Syrmas with Nicolopulos, 1880–1881," Sunderland, August 17, 1880, *Syrmas Archive*, ELIA.
[34] Harlaftis, *A History of Greek-Owned Shipping*, 165.
[35] Insurance Book, 1898–1903, Vagliano Archive, General State Archives, Archive of the Prefecture of Cephalonia.
[36] Harlaftis, *A History of Greek-Owned Shipping*, appendix 4.19.

In 1938, the number had grown to seventeen London offices. While by the eve of World War I the London offices represented and managed one-third of Greek-owned tonnage, by 1938 they managed half of it. The Ionians were still prominent, with new offices like the Dracoulis and Vlassopoulos replacing some of the older ones. However, the major new force was from the island of Kassos and Chios. The Kulukundis, the leading family on the island of Kassos, were repeatedly chartered by the Vaglianos; the Rethymnis and Kulukundis London office (known as R&K), which Manolis Kulukundis established with his four brothers and his compatriots Rethymnis in 1921 is the office that one can say continued the Vagliano tradition. R&K not only managed the ships of their co-islanders as the other London offices did, they also managed ships from shipowners coming from many islands.[37] These were new shipping businessmen from the northern part of the island of Chios: from Vrontados, Kardamyla, and the small island of Oinousses. These became an important "force" of Greek shipowning in the second half of the twentieth century and were not related to the Chiot merchants from the center of the island like the Ralli, Rodocanachi, Scaramanga, etc.

The London offices operated along exactly the same lines as the Vaglianos': they managed their own fleets and acted as ship managers, brokers, and agents for Greek shipping firms, the largest numbers of which were single shipping firms. In most cases, the London offices and the companies they represented had shares in each other's ships. The purchase of a ship for a client usually required the latter to advance half the amount, with the other half secured by the London office or other collaborating British companies. Moreover, the London offices handled sales and purchases of used ships, provided chartering through the Baltic Exchange, and took care of insurance and fuel. A number of shipowners, by handing over half the purchase price of a ship, thereby had their ship chartered, insured, and fueled, leaving them to only provide crews, operation, and maintenance. This system apparently reduced overheads sufficiently to cover the payments on borrowed capital and commissions. The Greek Committee for the Merchant Marine reported that "these commissions surpassed £1,000 per ship annually. In this way, a cargo ship worth £10,000, with a mortgage on half of its value, gave to the lender-administrator £1,500 annually."[38] It was a lucrative but also painstaking business. Half of the London offices that existed in 1938, after World War II, abandoned ship management for others and became large global shipowning groups working in their own right: Vlassopulo, Vergottis, Lusi,

---

[37] Ibid., chapter 6 and appendix 6.9–6.10.

[38] Cited in Costas Chlomoudis, *The Greek Merchant Marine, 1910–1939: The Co-existence of Different Modes of Production* (Unpublished PhD thesis, University of Macedonia, Thessaloniki, 1991), 131.

Lykiardopoulo, Goulandris, Embiricos, Livanos, and Kulukundis. Most of those they represented were able to do the same after World War II.

Conclusions

The great contribution of the Vagliano Brothers' trading house was their shipping operation, which was the source of their starting capital. It is in this sphere that they introduced important innovations. Their firm was certainly the only one in the Greek-owned fleet in the entire eastern Mediterranean basin and in the Black Sea that operated such a large number of sailing vessels. It was also the only independent shipping firm in the area that was a prime mover in adopting the new technology on time, launching an unprecedented program of new shipbuilding in British yards in the late 1870s to early 1880s. The order of eleven new steamships in the British shipyards dazzled their contemporaries the same way that Onassis's massive orders of new ships did in the German yards a few decades later. More important, the Vaglianos Brothers' greatest contribution to the evolution of Greek-owned shipping was their innovation of a megashipping agency: a hybrid form comprising shipping firm, shipping agency, shipbroking and ship-management office – what the Greeks called their London office.

They created the first shipping office in London in 1858, which became the model for the creation of other Greek London offices after the death of Panagi Vagliano. Essentially, this was a shipping company and agency for the national Greek fleet. The Vaglianos worked on commission, administering the vessels of other Greek shipowners, providing services in chartering, cargo, ship insurance, bunkering, sale and purchase of secondhand steamships, shipbuilding, and loans. Two-thirds of all Greek-owned steamships bought between 1890 and 1914 were owned or financed by members of the Ionian network, headed by the Vaglianos. A noteworthy structural feature of their London office was that, unlike their British counterparts, they did not run branch offices (and their constituent departments, such as stevedoring, outward and inward freight, and wharfage) as separate profit centers. All the various activities were the responsibility of this one office, which ran all the management of the ships and agency work as an undivided whole.

The Vagliano Brothers had an unusual business organization that was both vertically integrated to a degree and yet highly networked, with the London office becoming the center of their business during the last third of the nineteenth century. The Vagliano London shipping office introduced a new form of organization and set the precedent for maritime business administration in tramp shipping. In a way, it was the predecessor of the modern ship-management company, which became the new organizational form in international shipping after the 1950s. The Vagliano office proved to be the catalyst of the Greek entrepreneurial network, marking the transition from the nineteenth-century form of an international trading firm to a modern shipping/ship-management firm.

The Vagliano business which covers the first part of this book indicates the evolution of the Greek shipping company in the first three stages of the evolution of the European and Greek shipping company. Their actions capture all the aspects of nineteenth-century Greek shipping that precipitated its rise to international competitiveness. Their London office provided the first model of a modern ship-management firm and became the driving force behind the globalization of both Greek-owned shipping and bulk shipping all over the world. The career of Aristotle Onassis was one of the results of the Vaglianos' innovations. Onassis started his business from one of the seventeen London offices that were formed after the death of Panagi Vagliano. It is from one of those that he learned the shipping business and purchased his first two ships and started a tramp-steamship company. He therefore started his business from what has been described as the third stage of the development of Greek shipping, and from there he led the way to the fourth stage, the great leap forward to becoming a global tramp/bulk-shipping group.

6

Merchant to Shipowner

Aristotle Onassis from Buenos Aires to London and New York, 1923–1946

Aristotle Onassis was born two years after the last of the Vagliano brothers, Panagi, died. Although they never met, Onassis inherited much of the legacy of the Vaglianos, and the Ionian maritime tradition as a whole, when he entered the shipping business. However, Onassis did not start in shipping; he started from a business where he already had a competitive advantage – the tobacco trade. As is so often the case, behind his innate entrepreneurial talent there were significant societal and entrepreneurial factors. Aristotle (Aristotelis in Greek'; "Aristo" or "Ari," as his family and friends called him) was the son of a prosperous middle-class tobacco merchant in Smyrna. Smyrna, at the beginning of the twentieth century, was the prime export city port of the Ottoman Empire, a cosmopolitan entrepôt where Greeks, British, Italians, French, Americans, and others coexisted and collaborated.

The professional career of Aristotle Onassis covers fifty years, from 1924 to 1975. Two distinct periods in his career coincided with the third and fourth stage of the evolution of Greek and European shipping (see Figure 1.1). From 1924 to 1946, he first established his trading business and entered shipping in Buenos Aires; then, after 1933, consolidated his business as a medium-sized shipowner of dry-cargo and tanker vessels and moved his base from Buenos Aires to New York. This period was characterized by his conflicts with the Greeks in Argentina and the Greek international shipping milieu established in New York, London, and Piraeus. The second period, between 1946 and 1975, witnessed the apogee of his career. Between 1946 and 1958 he specialized in tanker shipping and was embroiled in conflicts with the US government and US oil and shipping interests. At the end of this period he had already become famous worldwide, and had moved his headquarters to Monte Carlo. From 1958 to 1974, a world celebrity, he spent most of his time in the Mediterranean, between Monte Carlo, France, and Greece, and at sea on his yacht. He was one of the undisputed global kings of tankers.

This chapter will cover his business during the first period of his entrepreneurial activity, from 1924 to 1946, when he set up his trading and tramp-shipping company. During these first twenty-two years, he was unknown to the public. The aim is to investigate Onassis's activities in America as well as in Europe and to reveal the significance of the beginnings of his business. From the very beginning of his career Onassis was a restless businessman who followed a cosmopolitan path, traveling constantly between America and Europe, making no special commitments to the local communities of the countries where he was established. In a striking contrast with the Vagliano Brothers, he built the new model of the global shipowner. In all places he was able to employ multiple entrepreneurial networks and develop conjectural strategic alliances with both the Greek and the Argentinian authorities and entrepreneurial elites. He was able to penetrate and become established in the latter, although not without conflicts.

During this period Onassis advanced his career within the Greek maritime tradition established by the Vaglianos, but also led the way to break this tradition, reinvent it, and advance it further. The Vaglianos fundamentally modernized the technology and organization of the Greek-owned fleet which had claimed a position in the top ten European and world fleets by the last third of the nineteenth century. In the same way, Aristotle Onassis proved fundamental for the technological and organizational advancement of Greek shipping, and its establishment as a leader in European and world shipping, by the last third of the twentieth century.

In Buenos Aires: From Immigrant to Tobacco Merchant, 1923–1932

The arrival of Aristotle Onassis in Argentina in 1923 with a Nansen passport – an identity document issued by the League of Nations to stateless refugees – valid only one way, passed unnoticed by the gradually expanding Greek community in Buenos Aires. Later, dozens of immigrants would claim that they had shared a room with Onassis in the hotel La Voladora at Michael Sofronas, in Boca, a working class neighborhood, which had become the temporary abode for many a Greek immigrant to Buenos Aires at the beginning of the twentieth century.[1] Everybody wanted to say they had had contact with the legendary Onassis, a myth for the Greek community of Argentina – among others.

According to most of these testimonies, he arrived in Buenos Aires in 1923 on the Italian transatlantic steamer *Tomaso di Savoia*. Most of his biographers describe him as a penniless refugee stacked alongside thousands of other immigrants in the third class of a passenger ship (in actuality, he had support from his family, who had retained some of its capital, as we shall see). Two years after his arrival, Onassis started to travel to Europe for business. He is found in the catalogs of the passengers arriving with transoceanic vessels at

---

[1] See also Maria Damilakou, *Η ελληνική μετανάστευση στην Αργεντινή: διαδικασίες συγκρότησης και μετασχηματισμοί μιας μεταναστευτικής κοινότητας, 1900–1970* [*Greek Immigration in Argentina: Formation Procedures and Transformations of an Immigrant Community, 1900–1970*] (Athens: Historical Archive of the Commercial Bank of Greece, 2004).

the port of Buenos Aires; it appears he arrived back in Buenos Aires on November 10, 1925 via New York on the vessel *American Legion*, traveling first class. To shipboard authorities, he declared he was a merchant, twenty-five years old, born in Salonica.[2]

The mythology surrounding Onassis starts from the date of his birth, variously claimed as 1900, 1903, or 1906 – Onassis himself never resolved the mystery. It seems that the odyssey of his life made him invent various birth dates. In order to be able to leave safely from Smyrna in 1922, as a refugee with a temporary pass from the US Embassy, he had to be a minor; hence, it was written in papers that he was born in 1906. But to open up business in Buenos Aires in 1924, he had to be an adult, so he gave a birthdate of 1900. In order to avoid being registered in Argentina as a "Turk" he declared that he was born in Salonica. When the FBI was spying on him during the 1940s, they reported that he was born in Salonica in 1906. Twenty-eight years later, the FBI thought it had found his real date and place of birth on his children's passports: "Onassis was born in Smyrna on 20 January 1900."[3] Today, the Onassis Foundation website gives Onassis's birth year as 1906; this is also the date inscribed on his grave on the island of Skorpios. Likely none of these dates are true: evidence points to 1904 as Onassis's actual year of birth.[4]

Onassis was the son of a well-off middle-class family of Smyrna. He graduated from the best Greek school of the city, the Evangelical School. But soon after finishing his education, the Onassis family, along with hundreds of thousands of other Greek refugees from Ottoman territories, were forced to flee to Greece as a result of the Greco-Turkish war (1919–1922). Aristotle

---

[2] Database of the Foundation CEMLA (Centro de Estudios Migratorios Latinoamericanos), Buenos Aires, Argentina.

[3] "As you might have noticed recent news stories, concerning the marriage of Aristotle Onassis and Mrs. Jacqueline Kennedy have reported his age as 62. I thought you might be interested in knowing that information furnished to the Department of State by Onassis's daughter and son Christina and Alexander show he was born in 1900. Files of the Passport Office disclose that Christina Onassis born on 12/11/1950 at New York City was last issued passport Z-762056 at the Embassy in London on 10/27/67. In her application she listed her father as Aristotle Onassis, born at Smyrna, Turkey, on January 20, 1900." FBI Archives 100–125834-19, "Aristotle Onassis" (October 4, 1968).

[4] His sister Artemis, born in 1902, was two years older than Aristotle Onassis. What is more, in the letter from Aristotle (Aristo) Onassis to his sister Artemis (Arta) from Buenos Aires on June 18, 1924, it is evident that in 1924 Onassis is twenty years old – hence the date 1904 seems the most probable. For the published letters of Socrates and Aristotle Onassis see the book by Yannis Mantidis, Όταν ο Ωνάσης συγγένευε με το Πήλιο: Οι δυο ζωές της άγνωστης ανηψιάς του [*When Onassis Was Related to Pelion: The Two Lives of His Unknown Niece*] (Thessaloniki: Adelfoi Kyriakides Publishers, 2009), 171–172, 177–178, 183–184. Yannis Mantidis uses a previously unknown source: the correspondence of Socrates and Aristotle Onassis with Artemis Onassis and her first husband, Pantelis Papanikolaou. For Onassis Foundation see www.onassis.gr/ (accessed November 25, 2015).

stayed barely a year in Athens before migrating to Argentina in 1923.[5] His
initial destination was London; he had had the idea to go to England to study.
He was accompanied on the journey by a family cousin who was to continue
on to Buenos Aires. Eventually, Onassis decided to follow his cousin to South
America.[6]

When Onassis arrived in Argentina, along with a large number of refugees
from Asia Minor who had also decided to immigrate in Latin America, there
were already 6,000 Greek immigrants established in Buenos Aires and its
environs.[7] The Greek community was fragmented and disorganized; no stable
social hierarchies had formed. Although the majority of immigrants were
workers, officials, or petty merchants, there were some Greeks whose education and entrepreneurial abilities made them stand out from the crowd.
Among this elite were those engaged with industry (mainly winemaking,
carpets, and tobacco) and external trade. Some of them had been established
in Argentina since the end of the nineteenth century.[8]

The Greek community showed great interest in promoting imports of Greek
products in Argentina, such as tobacco, carpets, silk textiles, marble from
Mount Pendeli, olive oil, grapes, figs, and nuts.[9] They gave particular emphasis
to tobacco, which in the interwar period was about 60 percent of Greece's
exports. In 1926, the newspaper *Patris* published articles detailing how to
promote Greek tobacco to Argentina and highlighting the need to establish
direct trade links between the two countries, in order to concentrate capital
and establish a bank, which would facilitate financial transactions without
intermediaries. One of the articles spoke of the two most well-known Greek
cigarette manufacture companies in Argentina: the merchant House of the
Xoudi Brothers, and that of the Mavridi Brothers. Both had come from Asia

[5] The research on Onassis in Argentina was performed by Maria Damilakou. It was first
     presented by Maria Damilakou and Gelina Harlaftis, "The Beginning of an 'Empire':
     Aristotle Onassis between Argentina and Europe, 1924–1940," 16th Annual Conference
     EBHA Paris, August 30–September 1, 2012.
[6] Written testimony by his half-sister Meropi Konialidi. It was given to me during the
     interview with Ritsa Konialidi, December 22, 2016.
[7] According to the national census of 1914, 5,907 Greeks lived in Argentina (2,921 in
     Buenos Aires). In 1936, according to the municipal census of the city of Buenos Aires, the
     number in that city had grown to 3,408. See *III Censo Nacional*, 1914, vol. II; *IV Censo
     Municipal de la ciudad de Buenos Aires*, 1936, vol. II. It should be noted that the
     Argentinian census only records immigrants as different nationalities (that is, people
     born outside Argentina); immigrants' offspring born in Argentina are registered as
     Argentinians.
[8] Maria Damilakou, "Μικρασιάτες πρόσφυγες στην Αργεντινή: μεταναστευτικές διαδρομές
     και στοιχεία ταυτότητας" ["Refugees from Asia Minor to Argentina: Immigration Routes
     and Identity Clues"], *Ιστορικά [Istorika]*, 42 (July 2005): 177–202.
[9] "Μελέτη περί εμπορίας των ελληνικών ταπήτων εν Αργεντινή" ["Study of the Carpet Trade
     in Argentina"], newspaper *Πατρίς [Patris]*, December 25, 1926, 7.

Minor and had lived in Egypt before establishing themselves in Argentina. Periklis Mavridis, in 1914, had founded the manufacture "of high quality Egyptian cigarettes" with the brand name *The Adamas*, which was later bought by Romanian entrepreneurs.[10] In this climate, and with a father whose business had been in the tobacco trade, it was only natural that Onassis decided to deal in tobacco.

It took him two years to start his own business. For a year after arriving in Argentina in 1923, he worked in the British United River Plate Telephone Co. Evidently disappointed by what he thought of as a dead-end job, he wrote from Buenos Aires to his sister Artemis in Greece:

> You know of my mania and passion to become a merchant . . . However, this now changed and I am very different . . . For these reasons, I have decided to study, so after six years I can have an intellectual property that nobody can take from me. When I will become 25–26 years old, I will be an engineer in society . . . After three months I will leave for London.[11]

It seems that one year in the telephone company in Argentina saw none of his dreams fulfilled and he decided to change his life and go to England to study as initially planned. However, the arrival of his cousin Nikos (Nicolas) Konialidis in August or September 1924 probably changed his mood and the possibilities of professional development.[12] Nikos started working to the same telephone company, where he remained for some time before the cousins launched into trading activities.[13] They were further reinforced by the arrival of a younger cousin, Costas (Constantino) Konialidis, in 1927.

In late 1924, Onassis opened an import-export office to expand the family business; in 1927, it appears as Aristotelis Onassis, Import-Export, 25 de Mayo Street, number 340, in Buenos Aires.[14] Having a trusted man employed back in Buenos Aires, Onassis began traveling back and forth to Europe to establish contacts, making his first overseas trip in 1925. His father also traveled to Buenos Aires to check on his son and the new business. A photo of Socrates Onassis, the Konialidis brothers, and Aristotle in Buenos Aires with a handwritten inscription in the right-hand bottom of the photo "Buenos Aires, 29 December 1929" confirms this visit (see Figure 6.1). Aristotle, twenty-five years old, sits proudly next to his father, Socrates, with his two cousins, Nikos and Costas Konialidis, standing behind. Socrates sits in an armchair, looking

[10] Ibid., November 17, 1926.
[11] Mantidis, *When Onassis Was Related to Pelion*, 171–172.
[12] For the date that Nikos Konialidis left for Argentina see the letter of Socrates Onassis in ibid., 177–178.
[13] Platon Filippidis, *Εμπορικός και Κοινωνικός Οδηγός των Ελλήνων της Νοτίου Αμερικής* [*Commercial and Social Guide of the Greeks in South America*] (Buenos Aires: n.p., 1938), 42.
[14] Mantidis, *When Onassis Was Related to Pelion*, 192.

Figure 6.1   The Onassis-Konialidis family business, Buenos Aires, 1929. From left to right: Socrates Onassis, Nicolas Konialidis, Aristotle Onassis, and Constantino Konialidis
Source: Courtesy of the Onassis Archive. © 2018 Onassis Archive/Onassis Foundation.

calm and serious, maybe with a hint of worry on his face. Aristotle, with folded arms, looking intensely straight into the camera, is clearly the leader of the group; he appears calm and sure of himself, with an almost hidden smile.

The Onassis family (initially named Onassoglou) hailed from the area of Cesareia (the present Kayseri in Turkey) in Cappadocia. Socrates Onassoglou (Aristotle's father) and his brothers immigrated to Smyrna, the largest port city and economic center of the area after Constantinople, and changed their names to Onassis. In Smyrna, Socrates Onassis collaborated with his brother Omiros (Homer) and formed the company S. & O. Onassis. They developed a prosperous trading house involved in the tobacco, currant, and colonial goods trade. After being expelled from their city in September 1922, the brothers fled to Athens, where they immediately formed a new S. & O. Onassis in Piraeus.[15] In Greece they were able to bring bills of exchange on cargoes they had sold a

---

[15] Notarial contract 5784 on the extension of the duration of the company S. & O. Onassis, October 2, 1929, to the notary of Athens Petros Nikolaou Kavadias, Onassis Business Archive, Alexander S. Onassis. Foundation Mantidis, *When Onassis Was Related to Pelion*, 143–144, 177–178, 183–184.

few months ago from their company in Smyrna.[16] They used these bills as starting capital when, utilizing their commercial network, they turned to the tobacco trade. They were quickly able to expand their business in collaboration with Aristotle in Buenos Aires, forwarding cargoes of tobacco from Greece to Argentina.

This traditional family business network, rooted in the tobacco trade of the northeastern Mediterranean, was Onassis's great asset; he extended it into the south Atlantic and relied on it to develop his entrepreneurial activities, beginning with the importation of oriental tobacco to Argentina. Business flourished during the next decade. In 1947, before he had become a multimillionaire and world celebrity, he responded to the gossip surrounding his name in Greek shipowning circles:

> There is no mystery, and I stress this because dozens of my malignant and miserable colleagues accuse me of everything. What did he do before entering our business? How did he get his first money? In what secret profession was he employed? Ah, well, I answer: My father was an important merchant. Despite the Asia Minor catastrophe, he carried with him his credibility and some capital. Then they started sending me tobacco. From 15 parcels annually in 1924, I reached hopefully 15,000 parcels annual import from the Near East and elsewhere. I got connected with leading members of the Argentinian tobacco industry. Anybody that understands anything about tobacco would understand the importance of what I say.[17]

Contrary to the gossip, Onassis had seized his entrepreneurial opportunity in 1924 with both hands. He took advantage of information from his family network in Greece and recognized the possibilities of tobacco imports to Argentina. Tobacco, at the beginning of the 1920s, was a new agricultural export in Greece that had replaced currants; its cultivation and rising production was connected with the influx of hundreds of thousands of refugees to Greece from Asia Minor. What is more, however, he correctly diagnosed the economic crisis that started in 1929 and left the tobacco trade to enter

---

[16] Notarial documents on S. & O. Onassis business, Onassis Business Archive, Alexander S. Onassis Foundation.

[17] Aristotle Onassis, "Η ναυτιλία μας μετά τον πόλεμον και η δράσις των Ελλήνων εφοπλιστών" ["Our Postwar Shipping After the War and the Activities of the Greek Shipowners"], Memorandum to the President of the Greek Shipowners in New York, M. Kulukundis in 1947, published in *Ethnikos Kyrex* (*National Herald*), March 8, 1953. The memorandum was published in thirteen parts on March 8, 10, 11, 12, 13, 15, 17, 18, 19, 20, 22, 24, 25. 1953. It has been republished with an introduction in Gelina Harlaftis, "Το 'κατηγορώ' του Αριστοτέλη Ωνάση προς τους εφοπλιστές και την ελληνική κυβέρνηση το 1947" ["The 'J'accuse' of Aristotle Onassis to the Shipowners and the Greek Government in 1947"], *Ionios Logos* (2013): 325-400.

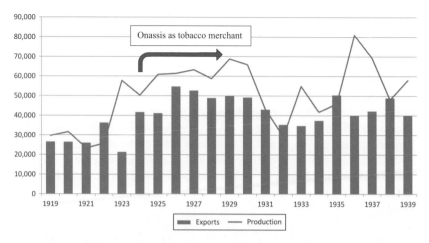

Figure 6.2   The development of Greek tobacco exports, 1919–1939

Source: Socratis Petmezas, *Προλεγόμενα για την Ελληνική αγροτική Οικονομία στο Μεσοπόλεμο*
[*Prolegomena for the Greek Agricultural Economy in the Interwar Years*] (Athens: Alexandreia
Publishing House, 2012); Βασ. Τ. Δρούγκα, *Εξαγωγές ελληνικού καπνού* [*Greek Tobacco Exports*]
(Athens: Agricultural Bank of Greece, 1984).

shipping. Figure 6.2 reveals that he remained a tobacco merchant during the
heyday of Greek tobacco production and exports, from 1924 to 1931.

An entrepreneur is also a market maker.[18] Recognizing this, Onassis realized that just trading in tobacco was not enough. From the beginning of his
engagement in the tobacco trade, he focused on promoting oriental tobacco; it
was lighter than the more commonly used Cuban tobacco, making it possible
to target women. As part of worldwide social changes at the time, women were
a new and increasingly important consumer group for the tobacco industry.
Due to the difficulties encountered in the promotion of Oriental tobacco
within the existing tobacco industry, and despite the good relations that he
developed with the important tobacco industrialist Juan Gaona, who owned
the large company Piccardo, Onassis decided to shift to the manufacture of
cigarettes. The first brands he made, the Primeros ("the best") and Osman
(referring to the Sultan and founder of the Ottoman Empire), with a golden
filter he thought would attract women, were quite successful in Argentinian
high society. He also produced more economical cigarettes under the name Bis
(an exclamation meaning "Bravo!"), which were advertised widely in the
Greco-Argentinian press in the 1920s. In the meantime, along with investment

[18] Ibid.

in cigarette production and the imports of oriental tobacco, he became involved in exports to Greece of unprocessed hides and tannin.

Identifying the importance of the rising market of female smokers, and taking the risk to invest to the production of cigarettes for this target group, was the first sign of Onassis's understanding of current trends in new markets. The second characteristic of his way of doing business that is identifiable at this early stage was his constant mobility. With trusted associates in Buenos Aires, the Konialidis Brothers, and having established his business in Buenos Aires, Onassis started to travel extensively between Europe and Argentina from the very first year he established his business. Continuous mobility helped him build international networks that he maintained throughout his life. Onassis's third characteristic throughout his career was his skill in cultivating relations with political elites in order to both expand and defend his business. During the worldwide economic crisis in 1929, the export-import business faced a slump as world trade contracted. States were launching protectionist measures, in particular increasing tariff walls to protect national industries. High import duties were going to be established by the Greek authorities on imports from countries where they had no bilateral agreements, and Argentina was one of these.

Penetrating the Greek and Argentinian Political and Economic Milieu

In order to surpass the hurdles that might affect his business, Aristotle Onassis took the transoceanic sea route to Piraeus and then to Athens in late summer 1929, in another of his frequent trips to Europe for his business. Following the path of many a diaspora Greek merchant, he knew that relations with the political authorities in both their host country and country of origin were vital. There Onassis met with Andrea Michalakopoulos, a gifted politician who was just being appointed Minister of Foreign Affairs in the newly formed liberal government with Prime Minister Eleftherios Venizelos. It seems that he was successful in persuading Michalakopoulos to postpone the imposition of high tariffs on imports from Argentina. He acted on his own accord and initiative on this front, something that produced negative reactions from the well-established elite of Greek-Argentinian industrialists, as we shall see later. Eventually, in 1931, Onassis was appointed to the Greek consulate in Buenos Aires with the responsibility for the study of a bilateral commercial agreement between Greece and Argentina, carrying the title "Special Attaché for the study and construction of a trade agreement between Greece and Argentina."[19]

Following the death in 1931 of Constantinos Xanthopoulos, the first paid Consul General of Greece in Argentina (1926–1931), Onassis was appointed

[19] Filippidis, *Commercial and Social Guide of Greeks in South America*, 96.

Deputy Consul General, thanks to the influence of the Greek Minister of Foreign Affairs. However, as he was continually traveling, Onassis appointed Nikos Konialidis as his substitute. Onassis remained in the position of Deputy Consul until 1936 and Nikos Konialidis took his position until 1938. Unlike Onassis, who followed a cosmopolitan way of life, Nikos Konialidis had settled permanently in Buenos Aires and eventually became President of the Greek community there during the years 1933–1935. He married Onassis's half-sister Merope Onassis in 1938.[20] In 1934 Costas Konialidis was sent on business to Montevideo to purchase a ship, which was eventually named *Maria Onassi* (his mother's maiden name). He remained there until 1956 and periodically after that running the Montevideo office of the Onassis business in the post-World War II period.

As a Deputy Consul, Onassis dealt almost exclusively with shipping affairs and met with many Greek shipowners. The abundance of Greek ships meant a plethora of shipowners, seamen, ships' chandlers, and agents in the port of Buenos Aires. Onassis had a wide range of jurisdictions, since all commercial and immigration traffic had to be cleared by the consuls. The Consul certified all quantities of imports and exports of goods from and to Greece, oversaw the composition of crew lists, and solved problems facing Greek captains and shipowners. He was also in charge of all the comings and goings of immigrants, and signed lists of immigrants. He thus had close connections with the local port authorities and customs.

During that era there were two types of consuls: businessmen and officials from the diplomatic service. The businessmen were unpaid. They were well-off entrepreneurs who would benefit for social and economic reasons by retaining this position, and this was probably the case with Onassis. We know that Konialidis later received a wage, and "his consular remuneration he donated to the Greek community."[21] It is true that the Consulate offered opportunities for profits but we have no way of knowing to what extent; there were too many competitors in Argentina watching every step by both of them not to reveal a scandal if they could. According to FBI reports, the appointment became extremely lucrative, since, "as consul, Onassis was able to obtain substantial sums of currency at official rates and sold the same in the Black Market, which at that time was flourishing."[22] On the one hand, the FBI reports relied on informants whose quality of information was highly questionable, as the FBI officials themselves reported repeatedly to Hoover. On the other hand, foreign exchange currency restrictions were a hot topic for the Greek commercial community in Argentina in the 1930s.

---

[20] The couple had two sons, Marios (b. 1940) and Christopher (b. 1942). Theotokas and Harlaftis, *Leadership in World Shipping*.

[21] Filippidis, *Commercial and Social Guide of Greeks in South America*, 45.

[22] FBI, "Aristotle Onassis," part 1, Bufile 100-125834-5.

As Deputy Consuls and successful entrepreneurs, Onassis and Konialidis became important members of the Greek community in Argentina with direct access to the Greek and Argentinian political and economic elites. They were both very young and ambitious and they were certainly regarded as intruders by the old guard, the group of long-established distinguished Greco-Argentinian entrepreneurs. Harsh accusations against Aristotle Onassis were published in the newspaper *Patris*, issued by a group of wealthy entrepreneurs from Asia Minor. They claimed that he had converted the Consulate into an immigration agency facilitating the entrance of "talented" Bulgarians, Czechoslovaks, and Poles, who satisfied the appetites "of the consular agency and the profiteering masters of cargo ships."[23]

It is quite possible that the elite of the old establishment was organized the year Onassis became Deputy General. They created the Hellenic Chamber of Commerce in 1933 in Buenos Aires, with the principal aim of lifting restrictions on currency exports in Greece and the signing of a Greco-Argentinian Convention for the promotion of commercial relations between the two countries. When the Chamber of Commerce was created, Greek importers had a total debt of about 360,000 pesos to their exporting counterparts in Greece because of the foreign currency restrictions imposed by the Argentinian government.[24]

It is quite probable that the Hellenic Chamber of Commerce was formed as a counterattack to the two young cousins. After all, Onassis had been appointed by the Greek government as a special envoy for this particular issue. The prosperous community of Greeks in Argentina deployed their own networks with the Greek political establishment back in Greece and were able to attack Onassis with the support of the influential Greek diplomat Vasilios Dendramis. In 1938, the Greek diplomatic representation in Argentina was upgraded to Embassy status, and Vasilios Dendramis was appointed the first Greek Ambassador to the country; he promptly signed the long-awaited Treaty of Commerce and Navigation between Greece and Argentina,[25] sparking a lifelong enmity with Onassis. Dendramis, apparently representing his own interests and the interests of the other side of the Greek community in Argentina, refused to let Konialidis act as a Consul in Buenos Aires. Dendramis also probably caused the letter to be sent to the FBI suggesting they spy on Onassis while he was traveling in the United States in 1942, as we shall see later.

---

[23] Newspaper Πατρίς [*Homeland*], October 29, 1932.
[24] Andreas Melas, *Los griegos en la Argentina* [*The Greeks in Argentina*] (Buenos Aires: Pellegrini Editions, 1954), 39.
[25] See Vassilios Katsomalos, Αργεντινή, Χιλή, Ουρουγουάη, Βραζιλία και οι Έλληνες [*Argentina, Chile, Uruguay, Brazil and the Greeks*] (Buenos Aires: n.p., 1972), 67. According to the author this treaty was never used.

Onassis was not very interested in achieving a central role in the public affairs of the Greek community, unlike other Greeks from Constantinople or Asia Minor, who established cultural associations and local newspapers. He does not appear to have undertaken any relevant community activity. During his time in Buenos Aires, he simply attempted to strengthen his social position through direct contacts with important members of Argentinian high society and the Greek political elite.

Onassis developed close friendships not only with Argentinian tobacco industrialists like Juan Gaona but also with the largest Argentinian shipowner, Alberto Dodero. One of the main priorities of the Argentinian government in the 1930s was the creation of a strong national merchant fleet independent of foreign interests. The man who played a decisive role in the formation of a national Argentinian merchant fleet was Alberto Dodero. In 1930 Alberto Dodero, assisted by his brothers Louis and Joseph, became head of the biggest Latin American shipping company – formed by the Croatian Michanovich family established in Buenos Aires in the nineteenth century – the Argentina Navigation Company Limited Michanovich,[26] which included the region's main shipyards. The company, which had been taken over by a large Royal Mail consortium under Lord Kylsant, after the bankruptcy of the latter, was operated by Alberto Dodero together with Nicolas Michanovich – a difficult coexistence. Committed to the nationalist economic policy of the Argentinian government and the "Argentinization" of the company, Dodero helped the Argentine state to become a shareholder in the company, replacing British capital; this was against the will of Nicolas Michanovich, who took a tough stance towards any kind of state intervention. Dodero was a close friend of the Perón couple and it was he who brought Onassis into contact with Perón himself, but also with other partners of the Peronist regime. It was these contacts that would later lead the FBI to denounce Onassis as an entrepreneur with "fascist" sympathies, something that in the end was found to be untrue.

Buenos Aires and Greek Shipping

Buenos Aires had become very important for Greek shipping in the 1920s as Argentina experienced a spectacular growth in grain exports in the interwar period.[27] Greek shipping served as the transport of primary products for the commodity markets that were instrumental for globalization. By the eve of World War I, the Greek fleet's activities were still centered within European waters, carrying grain from the Black Sea and coal from Great Britain as a return cargo (echoing the mainstay of the Vagliano business). The outbreak of

---

[26] "La era Mihanovich," in www.histarmar.com.ar/BuquesMercantes/HistMarinaMercArg/04Mihanovich.htm (accessed September 15, 2015).
[27] Harlaftis, *A History of Greek-Owned Shipping*.

the war closed the Dardanelles Strait, and excluded Greek ships from Black Sea grain cargoes, and after 1917 the October Revolution closed down Russian exports. As a result, Greek ships were forced to leave the Mediterranean market and carry cargoes mainly on Atlantic routes; they eventually turned to the Argentinian grain trade – the so-called La Plata-Continent route – to northern Europe with return coal cargoes. Although Russia and the Black Sea remained the main granary of Europe, this trade was challenged by the United States at the turn of the twentieth century and later by Canada and Argentina. The closing down of exports from the Black Sea gave a great push to Argentinian grain exports during the interwar period.[28] Greek shipowners collaborated closely with the major Argentinian grain export trading company Bunge y Born, carrying millions of tons of grain in the Atlantic routes.

One of the most frequented new itineraries for Greek ships in the interwar period developed between Britain and Argentina. Table 6.1 indicates the arrivals of British and Greek ships at the River Plate. In the 1920s, the involvement of the Greek fleet increased from nothing to 1 million net tons and, after coming to a complete standstill in 1930, it then rose to 12 percent of total arrivals in Argentinian ports. This accounted for a presence of 300–400 vessels of 1–1.5 million tons annually when Aristotle Onassis was Deputy Consul of Greece, making the Greek flag the second biggest visitor to the River Plate after the British.[29] In that period Greeks along with the British and the Norwegians were the three main world tramp operators. All the rest entering and leaving Buenos Aires were mainly liner or passenger vessels.[30]

Furthermore, the interwar period was characterized by intense conflicts on the part of seamen worldwide. World War I had a dramatic effect on the organization of seamen into trade unions all over the world. The reduction in the number of vessels due to war losses resulted in unemployment for thousands of seamen for a number of years, and a remarkable level of rank-and-file militancy. The long maritime crisis in the early 1920s, combined with the

---

[28] María Inés Barbero, "Business Groups in Nineteenth and Twentieth Century Argentina," in Geoffrey Jones and Andrea Lluch, eds., *The Impact of Globalization on Argentina and Chile: Business Enterprises and Entrepreneurship* (Cheltenham: Edward Elgar, 2015), 6–44. For United States-United Kingdom grain trade see Kevin H. O'Rourke, "The European Grain Invasion, 1870–1913," *Journal of Economic History* 57, no. 4 (1997): 775–801. See also Kevin H. O'Rourke and Jeffrey G. Williamson, *Globalization and History: The Evolution of a Nineteenth-Century Atlantic Economy* (Cambridge, MA: MIT Press, 1999). For Russian and Black Sea trade see Alexandra Papadopoulou and Gelina Harlaftis, "The Development of Trade and Shipping of Black Sea Port-Cities and Their Integration to the Western European Economy, 1830–1910s" (Kyoto: XVIIth World Economic History Congress "Diversity in Development," August 2015).

[29] See *Report on the Financial, Commercial and Industrial Situation of Argentina, Department of Overseas Trade* (London: His Majesty's Stationary Office, 1932), 133.

[30] Ibid.

Table 6.1 *Arrivals of ships at the port of La Plata, 1920–1938*

Year	British		%	Greek		%	Total	
	Ships	Nrt 000		Ships	Nrt 000		Ships	Nrt 000
1920	164	541	61	2	5	1	273	888
1921	91	249	44	84			232	561
1922	925	3,117	45		211	3	2,075	6,895
1923								
1924	1,343	4,690	47				2,949	10,011
1925								
1926	1,242	4,419	45				2,784	9,723
1927	1,563	5,620	47				3,376	11,863
1928	1,410	5,110	44	292	746	6	3,323	11,716
1929	1,375	5,086	43	333	886	8	3,325	11,702
1930	1,064	4,289	43	94	260	3	2,557	9,887
1931	1,402	5,116	44	282	770	7	3,216	11,548
1932	1,164	4,395	43	239	651	6	2,744	10,128
1933	844	3,441	37	300	822	9	2,511	9,254
1934	933	3,706	37	414	1,158	11	2,751	10,076
1935	1,069	4,155	40	394	1,132	11	2,852	10,389
1936	934	3,778	38	394	1,075	11	2,766	10,047
1937	1,064	4,214	37	519	1,426	12	3,245	11,409
1938	661	3,041	34	169	468	5	2,349	9,021

Source: Data compiled from the "Reports on the Financial, Commercial and Industrial Situation of Argentina," Department of Overseas Trade (London: His Majesty's Stationary Office, 1920–1938).

lengthy shipping crisis of 1929–1934, led to successive strikes and widespread radical leadership, often from communists. Militancy among seamen extended from the aged British tramp ships to the giant luxury liners of the Hamburg-America line.[31] Greek seamen proved no exception to the rule, and the Greek seamen's movement bears many similarities to the rest of the world. The principal reasons for continual daily frictions were working time, victualling and wages. These issues were also the cause of disputes between captain and crew. The Panhellenic Seamen's Federation (PNO) was created in 1920 and an alternative communist-led federation called the Seamen's Union of Greece

[31] Harlaftis, *A History of Greek-Owned Shipping*, 214.

(NEE) a few years later, appointing representatives of the seamen's union in all major ports where Greek vessels traded.[32]

In the performance of their duties at the Greek Consulate, Onassis and Konialidis took an active role in the port of Buenos Aires and not only cooperated with the Argentine port authorities but also with the so-called consular port officials appointed by the Greek government in Buenos Aires to suppress strike movements of Greek seafarers in Argentinian ports. It was back in 1919 during the modernizing administrative reforms of the Venizelos liberal government that the new body, called the Port Authority Body (the equivalent of a Coastguard), was formed. The idea was to create an autonomous administrative unit for shipping affairs. The Port Authority Body was manned by port officials who had a military hierarchy and acted not only as guards of ports, coasts, and ships in Greece but also as a kind of police force for Greek ships abroad. To that end, the institution of the consular port official was created in 1921. A network of these officials was appointed during the interwar period in all major ports where Greek ships were trading: in the Mediterranean, northern seas, and the Atlantic. Due to the importance of Buenos Aires for Greek shipping, Greek consular port officers were appointed there with the particular mission to "file" all unionist seamen that were prone to strike.

During the period 1936–1941, Prime Minister Ioannis Metaxas imposed a dictatorship in Greece on August 4, 1936, governing until his death in January 1941. With the communist-led seamen's unions banned as illegal during the Metaxas regime, consul port officials had orders to be very strict in the implementation of Greek laws and to persecute unionist seafarers instigating strikes. As representatives of the Greek state, Onassis and Konialidis probably collaborated with the consular port officials in handling repeated problems with strikes of Greek ships in Argentina.

At the same time, relations between Deputy Consul Onassis and the Greek consular port officers were probably not very good, as he would not have tolerated their intervention. Onassis cultivated an intense dislike of the whole concept of the consular port officials, of which he wrote: "no country has such a luxury, this is an exclusively Greek invention ... Simplification [is needed] and if possible abolition ... No other countries have their port authorities policing [their ships] in the various ports."[33] Onassis had a famous conflict with a Greek consular port officer in 1938 in Rotterdam when the officer refused to let his Greek flag ship sail without a Greek cook on the crew list.

[32] Gelina Harlaftis, "Η ακμή του ναυτεργατικού κινήματος της 'Ελευθέρας Ελλάδος'" ["The Rise of the Seafaring Labor Movement during World War II"], in Christos Hadjiiosif and Prokopis Papastratis, eds., Ιστορία της Ελλάδος του 20ού αι [History of Twentieth-Century Greece] vol. 3 (Athens: Vivliorama, 2007), 261–283.
[33] Onassis, "Our Postwar Shipping."

Onassis hoisted the Panamanian flag on both of his Greek flag vessels the following year.[34]

As a representative of the Greek government in Argentina, Onassis acquired sufficient political strength to negotiate with the local political authorities. He was not concerned about politics but about facilitating his commercial and shipping business. He claims that in 1933 he dissuaded the Argentinian government from imposing a tenfold increase in the port and custom dues for Greek ships:

> They were ready to make this tenfold increase as a retaliation to a thoughtless and unjust measure by the Greek government. From 500 sterling pounds, the port dues were going to become 5,000 sterling pounds, and we had about 100 Greek vessels on the way to Argentina there, whose average cost was not more than 5,000 sterling pounds. It was this kind of agreement [that I had made] that Dendramis came three years later to confirm and sign. Nobody of our profession ever felt the need to express not his thanks but not even his acknowledgment of what had been achieved.[35]

From Tobacco Merchant to Shipowner, 1932–1939

It is not clear whether the death of his father on March 21, 1932 was central to the final decision by Onassis to abandon the tobacco trade and invest in shipping a few months later, or if it was just a combination of minimal Greek tobacco exports and continually falling ship prices that led him to this decision. To combine trade with shipping was a natural course for a Greek businessman and his involvement in the Greek consulate brought Onassis very close to the shipping affairs and shipowners. Onassis was certainly not worth a million dollars in 1931, as most of his biographers claim, but he probably had capital of £50,000 (about $227,000) ready to invest in shipping.[36] Indeed, in 1932 ship prices had plummeted to unprecedented lows. Ships that were worth £200,000 in 1919 were worth only £4,500 in 1932 (see Figure 6.3).

It seems that the initial idea to invest in shipping came via his tobacco business. According to contemporary testimonies, he wanted to purchase warehouses for his tobacco trade and he was given the idea by Costas Gratsos

---

[34] Ibid.   [35] Onassis, "Our Postwar Shipping," March 20, 1953.

[36] Costas Vlassopoulos, Σελίδες μιας ζωής [Pages of a Life] (Athens: Zaharopoulos Editions, 1994), 86, 197. Costas Vlassopoulos, a close collaborator of Onassis, has written a valuable testimony on Onassis and his business in his memoirs. Vlassopoulos, who sprang from a shipowning family from the island of Ithaca, was educated as an economist and trained in the family shipping business. He was one of the managers of Olympic Maritime in Monte Carlo for thirty-one years. He served as member of the Alexander Onassis Foundation until 1992.

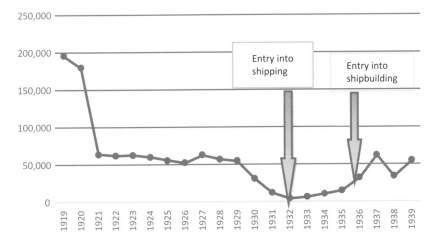

Figure 6.3 Prices of newly built cargo steamships of 7,500 dwt, 1919–1939, indicating the timely entry of Onassis into shipping and shipbuilding
Source: Harlaftis, *A History of Greek-Owned Shipping*, appendix 6.4.

to purchase ships that could be used as warehouses if freight rates were so low that it was not worth operating. It took him at least one and a half years of apprenticeship in the Greek London shipowning milieu before he entered shipping. In 1931, Aristotle Onassis spent at least six months in London staying in the Savoy hotel, spending almost every day at the crammed quarters of the Dracoulis London shipping office deciding about investments in shipping. For this purpose he went to Halifax with the experienced ship engineer from the Dracoulis office, George Kallinicos, to inspect laid-up Canadian cargo vessels; Kallinicos became Onassis's close associate and teacher in ship technology.[37]

Onassis's incursion into the shipowning business produced negative reactions from some leading members of the established London offices like Manuel Kulukundis. Kulukundis, a fifth-generation shipowner from the Aegean island of Kasos, almost the same age as Aristotle Onassis, had formed the Rethymnis & Kulukundis London shipping office in 1921. He was known to have the most comprehensive knowledge of the ship sales and purchase market in Europe and North America and became the largest Greek shipping

---

[37] Dimitris Paizis-Danias, Θαλάσσης Μνήμες [*Memories of the Sea*] (Athens: Syllogos Filomiron Ithakis "Efhin Odyssei," 2008), 45–46.

office in London, operating about sixty ships of about 145,000 grt.[38] Recall that London offices, apart from shipowning, also acted as agents and mediators on commission; they made negotiations on sales and purchases of ships representing their clients. Onassis, although he found his ships through the Dracoulis office, did not let Dracoulis make all the negotiations; he instead negotiated with the Canadian sellers himself to purchase his ships at £11,000 each. This enraged Kulukundis, who wrote to Michael Pneumaticos, another top shipowner of his time in Syros, Greece, that "a silly Greek has spoilt our market with the Canadian ships by buying two of them at the price of £11,000 each."[39]

It is no wonder that within about a decade, Onassis, "that silly Greek," and Kulukundis would have a direct and highly publicized conflict. Patience, however, was a characteristic of Onassis, who finally did not proceed with the purchase, proving Manuel Kulukundis wrong. He listened to the advice of more experienced shipowners, but also watched the prices of ships falling every month for a couple of years. He finally bought two Canadian ships in late 1932, built in 1919 and owned by the Canadian government, at the price of £3,750 each ($13,100), and a third two years later in Uruguay.[40] He named the first two ships after his parents, *Socratis Onassi* and *Pinelopi Onassi*, and the third *Maria Onassi*, after the mother of the Konialidis Brothers, who was also his aunt, his father's sister. The latter vessel, built in 1915 in Britain, was considered a total loss after foundering off the Uruguayan coast, and had become property of the Montevideo port authorities. Costas Konialidis was sent there, and bought it for Onassis for 33,100 pesos ($9,735 or £1,930) in September 1934; he repaired it and it started to travel between Argentina and the Mediterranean. The first two ships started sailing in April/May 1933, bringing profits to Onassis until 1939, when they were sold. *Maria Onassi* lasted only one year, as on its way to Genoa it was stranded off Corsica and was classified as a total loss. Onassis received the sum of £19,000 ($94,430) from insurance in 1936, as prices of ships were skyrocketing at the time.[41]

The establishment of powerful shipping offices in London that represented a large number of Greek shipowners was pivotal for the operation, survival, and growth of the Greek-owned fleet during the great 1930s crisis. In fact, Greeks, along with Norwegians in the 1930s were the only European fleets that

---

[38] Harlaftis, *A History of Greek-Owned Shipping.*
[39] Letter of Manuel Kulukundis from London to Michael Pneumaticos in Syros, April 6, 1932, published in George Foustanos, *Onassis: Pioneer in Shipping* (Athens: Argo, 2009), 35.
[40] Foustanos, *Onassis*, 34–35. Conversion of pounds sterling to dollars in www.measuring worth.com/calculators/exchange/result_exchange.php (accessed June 5, 2015).
[41] Onassis, "Our Postwar Shipping," March 15, 1953.

expanded their business instead of contracting.[42] Western European ship-owners, particularly the British, sold ships at extremely low prices and the Greeks via their London offices bought them.[43] In this way, during the worst years of the slump, between 1932 and 1935, the Greek fleet grew rapidly in all but one year. This response to the world shipping crisis is a phenomenon that a Greek maritime economist has called "anticyclical investment behaviour," by which Greek shipowners made purchases when the freight market was at its nadir and ships were cheap.[44] While this anticyclical behavior is not a Greek invention, what is unique about the Greeks is that they practiced it far more effectively than did any of their competitors.[45] This habit, which continues to the present day, made the Greeks dominant in the London sale-and-purchase shipping market and contributed to the expansion of the fleet since the beginning of this century. However, it was first identified as a strategic maritime policy of Greek companies during the shipping crisis of the 1930s.[46]

Onassis followed the anticyclical method of his contemporaries, who pur-chased dry-cargo tramp ships in the secondhand market at the worst possible time for freight rates and the best possible time to achieve purchases at the lowest possible prices. However, purchasing a vessel is one thing – having the experience and know-how to run it is another. Penetration into the Greek shipping milieu came before investing in shipping. The fact that Onassis picked the right time to purchase reveals his insightfulness in following the leading London Greek offices, who advised their clients when to purchase. In 1932, he formed his first shipping company, A. S. Onassis, based in Greece, with an agency in Buenos Aires.[47]

Onassis bought his first ships following the advice of Costas Gratsos, a traditional Greek shipowner who opened the door for him to the information and knowledge of the business of shipowning and who remained his right-hand man and lifelong friend. Under the guidance of Gratsos, he manned the ships with Gratsos' compatriots, the experienced seamen from the island of Ithaca.

[42] Stig Tenold, "Crisis? What Crisis? – The Expansion of Norwegian Shipping in the Interwar Period," in Lars U. Scholl and David M. Williams, eds., Crisis and Transition – Maritime Sectors in the North Sea Region – 1790–1940 (Bremen: Verlag H. M. Hauschild, GmbH, 2008), 117–134, Table 1.
[43] Gelina Harlaftis, "The Greek Shipping Enterprise: Investment Strategies, 1900–1939," in M. Dritsas and T. Gourvish, eds., European Enterprise: Strategies of Adaptation (Athens: Trochalia Publications, 1997), 139–159.
[44] Helen A. Thanopoulou, "Anticyclical Investment Strategies in Shipping: The Greek Case," World Transport Research, Proceedings of the 7th World Conference on Transport Research, Transport Management, vol. 4 (Sydney: Pergamon, 1995).
[45] It was of course the English that first had an identifiable shipping policy, particularly Burrel in Glasgow. See Argyros, Burrel and Son of Glasgow.
[46] Harlaftis, A History of Greek-Owned Shipping, 187–194.
[47] Lloyd's Register of Shipping, "List of Owners and Shipowners," 1932–1933.

He ran his thirteen-year-old tramp ships under the Greek flag on the lucrative sea routes of La Plata-Continent, transporting Argentinian grain to Europe and returning with coal. Freight rates, which in 1932 were at a nadir, were steadily growing. Running these two ships for five years provided him with high profits; as we see in Figure 6.3, freight rates saw a continuous rise after 1933. In 1935–1936, leading Greek shipowners like the Livanos and Kulukundis started ordering new ships, investing their profits from the lucrative freight rates in dry-cargo vessels. Onassis did the same, but he entered a new market; he was the first Greek shipowner to build a tanker and get involved in the oil market.

The main independent tanker owners of the interwar period were the Norwegians. After the Norwegians bought a few dozen tankers from Anglo-Saxon Oil on time-charters in the late 1920s the Norwegian tanker fleet flourished; in the 1930s, it became the largest independent tanker fleet, leading up to World War II.[48] The interwar years were a transitional period in the international shipping market. One of the main characteristics of these years was the distinct decline in British hegemony. A significant portion of the tramp trades were absorbed by the Norwegians and the Greeks, who were able to dominate a number of bulk cargo routes, the Greeks in the dry cargoes, the Norwegians in both dry and liquid cargoes. In Buenos Aires, Onassis had the opportunity of observing the practices not only of Greek shipowners but also those of their Norwegian counterparts, who, together with the British, were the most important shipowners visiting Buenos Aires. With an eye on opening up to new trades and new ideas, it is most probable that he perceived the potential for the development of crude oil as a basic global energy source. Onassis met a number of leading Norwegian shipowners during the 1930s with whom he kept in close contact during the following decades: Anders Jahre, Erling Dekke Naess, and Lars Christensen, just to name a few.[49] All of them, apart from being engaged in the carriage of crude oil, were primarily owners of whalers and whale-oil carriers. This is when Onassis's interest in whaling started; he was to make an important investment in whaling a decade later.

In the mid-1930s, Onassis decided to enter the oil business and ordered new ships – tankers – from the Swedish yards. He did this with the guidance, advice, and eventual partnership of the Norwegian shipowner Anders Jahres, another lifelong friend and advisor.[50] In Onassis's, own words:

---

[48] Sturmey, *British Shipping and World Competition*, 61–97. See also Tenold, "Crisis? What Crisis?"

[49] Alf R. Jacobsen, *Eventyret Anders Jahre* (Oslo: Forlaget, Oktober A/S, 1982). Erling D. Naess, *Autobiography of a Shipping Man* (Colchester: Seatrade Publications, 1977), 103. For a recent account of the "new breed" of Norwegian shipowners see the new book of Stig Tenold who provides the first full and comprehensive account of Norwegian shipping in the twentieth century. For the interwar period see Tenold, *Norwegian Shipping in the 20th Century*, 119–121.

[50] Jacobsen, *Eventyret Anders Jahre*, 60.

I went to meet [the Scandinavians] before I started a relation with a Scandinavian woman.[51] Just my physical appearance was enough to make them suspicious of me. I was able to change their bad opinion about the Greeks and a few weeks were enough to like, respect and trust us as to give me credit.[52]

Although he was not the first Greek shipowner to buy a tanker, Onassis was certainly the first Greek shipowner to order new tankers to be built.[53] Between 1936 and 1942 he built three tankers – *Ariston* (10,227 grt) launched in 1938, *Aristophanes* (10,224 grt) launched in 1940 and *Buenos Aires* (11,106 grt), launched in 1942 – in the shipyards of Götaverken, Göthenburg, Sweden.[54] The ships, which sailed under the Swedish flag, cost around £100,000 ($497,000) each.[55]

In 1936, he ordered the building of *Ariston*. It seems that Onassis's contact with the Director of the Swedish shipyards Götaverken in Göthenburg, Hug Hammar, and Ernst Heden, who owned the shipyards in 1938, was made through Anders Jahres.[56] It was the Swedish shipyards that financed the shipbuilding with long-term loans at a low interest rate, the right of first mortgage, and the obligation by the owners to put them under the Swedish flag.[57] The company A. S. Onassis Göthenbureg A/S was formed with the Swedish partners Gustav Sandström and Gunnar Carlsson.[58] *Ariston*, which was launched in June 1938, was chartered immediately for nine consecutive years by the Tidewater Oil Company of John Paul Getty for the carriage of oil between the United States and Japan.[59] It gave good profits for a year until the war broke out in September 1939.

The war brought opportunities but also great problems. Onassis was able to sell his ships *Socratis Onassi* and *Pinelopi Onassi* to the Japanese in 1940 for $100,000; that is eight times more than the price he paid for them.[60] However, he encountered great problems with the Swedish-built vessels. *Aristophanes* was almost ready when the war broke out in September 1939. Sweden

---

[51] In 1934, while traveling from Buenos Aires to Europe, he met Ingeborg Dedichen, the daughter of the Norwegian shipowner Ingeval Martin Byde. Their affair lasted for more than a decade and Ingebord brought him into further contact with the Scandinavian shipping circles. Ingeborg Dedichen, *Onassis mon amour* (Paris: Éditions Pygmalion, 1975).
[52] Onassis, "Our Postwar Shipping."
[53] The Coutsis brothers from Spetses bought the first Greek tanker in the 1890s. They were not successful with the vessel, however, and no other Greek shipowner followed their lead until Onassis. See Harlaftis, Beneki, and Haritatos, *Ploto*, 441.
[54] Jacobsen, *Eventyret Anders Jahre*, 191.   [55] Vlassopoulos, *Pages of a Life*, 82–83.
[56] Jacobsen, *Eventyret Anders Jahre*, 191.   [57] Vlassopoulos, *Pages of a Life*, 86.
[58] Atle Thowsen, *Handelsflåten i krig 1939–1945: Nortraship: Profit tog patriotism*, vol. 1 (Oslo: Grøndahl, Dreyer, 1992), 97.
[59] See Appendix. For the chartering see Foustanos, *Onassis*, 40–42.
[60] Vlassopoulos, *Pages of a Life*, 86.

prohibited the export of ships, including non-Scandinavian-owned ships built at Swedish shipyards. In order to be able to receive his vessel, Onassis formed, with Anders Jahre, a Norwegian company named Jaris (from the beginning and end of their two names), which took over the ship. In January 1940, *Aristophanes* was placed under the Norwegian flag, but Onassis was its real owner, as he owned the bonds.[61] After the outbreak of the war in Norway in April 1940, the entire Norwegian merchant fleet was requisitioned to sail for the Allies' cause and was operated by the Norwegian Shipping and Trade Mission (known as Nortraship). Nortraship faced a problem with Onassis, who was the real owner.

Apparently, Onassis had already chartered the ship at much higher freight rates and he was not going to give up his vessel easily; when the vessel reached Rio de Janeiro on one of its trips, he had the ship "arrested" and demanded its restitution or compensation of $800,000. In the end, he managed to negotiate with Nortraship to have the total of the money paid ($800,000) plus his legal expenses and a certain amount of compensation for the profits the vessels would have made. The deal was signed on August 15, 1940.[62] Onassis was thus able, in collaboration with the Konialidis brothers, to purchase two tankers, the nineteen-year-old *Calliroy* for $1,050,000 and the twenty-seven-year-old *Antiope* for $500,000, registered under the Panamanian flag, and thus was able to profit from the high freight rates.[63] He chartered these tankers to the US War Shipping Administration in July 1942 and the vessels were engaged in the US foreign trade mainly in the Pacific Ocean.[64] He was not as lucky with the other two vessels registered under the Swedish flag. *Ariston* was not able to sail due to Swedish prohibitions and equally the *Buenos Aires*, after being launched in 1942, was also held up; both vessels were laid up in the Baltic throughout the war.[65] After the war, the vessels were returned to Onassis.[66]

During this first period, Onassis expanded his business in Europe. He had established shipowning companies in Greece, Sweden, Norway, Argentina,

---

[61] Thowsen, *Handelsflåten i krig 1939–1945*, 97. See also "Norwegian Merchant Fleet 1939–1945," http://warsailors.com/singleships/aristophanes.html (accessed March 5, 2014). See also Jacobsen, *Eventyret Anders Jahre*, 183.

[62] Thowsen, *Handelsflåten i krig 1939–1945*, 180. Thowsen based this information on FO archives: "Telegram from Sir R. Craigie, Tokyo, to the Foreign Office," April 15, 1940, FO 371/25180, National Archives, UK.

[63] See Onassis, "Our Postwar Shipping," March 19, 1953.

[64] FBI, "Aristotle Onassis," Bufile 100-125834, Document 100-125834-5, September 14, 1942.

[65] Onassis, "Our Postwar Shipping."

[66] *Ariston* and *Aristophanes*, under the Norwegian flag, were chartered on October 24, 1947 by Socony-Vacuum for a period of five years from Sociedad Maritima Miraflores at rates of $4.10 and $4.20 per deadweight ton per month. FBI, "Aristotle Onassis," part 2, Bufile 46-17783, "Fraud against the government," New York office 46-2507 report, May 10, 1952, 50.

Table 6.2 *Structure of Aristotle Onassis's shipping business, 1932–1940*

Shipowning company	Managing company
Greece – A. S. Onassis (1932–1938) **Sweden** – Onassis A. S. Gothenburg, (1939) **Norway** – Skibs A/S Jaris, 1940 **Panama** – Sociedad Maritima Miraflores, (1939)	**Argentina** – A. S. Onassis, Calle Reconquista 336, Buenos Aires N. Konialidis **Uruguay** – Constantino Konialidis **Sweden** – Gustav E. Sandström (Hamngattan 6, Gothenburg, Sweden **Norway** –Anders Jahre

Source: Lloyd's Register of Shipping, 1932–1939.

Uruguay and Panama and held his managing offices in Argentina and Uru-guay, from where he collaborated with his Scandinavian agents (Table 6.2). In the 1930s, for his dry cargo vessels, he collaborated with the London charter-ing offices of Lambert Bros. and Simpson & Young, and for his oil tankers with the US oil companies Tidewater Oil Company and Socony-Vacuum. Apart from investing in tankers, another move proved extremely important for the future of his business, as we shall discuss in a later chapter, namely the creation of his first Panamanian company and the choice of the Panama-nian flag. In 1939, Onassis abandoned the use of the Greek flag and Greek companies, which had restricted his movements, and changed the flag on his two vessels. Again, he followed the tactic of the leading Greek and Norwegian shipowners of the time, who had being doing the same since the early 1930s.[67]

Onassis arrived in New York for the first time in July 1940 on the *Samaria* of Cunard, but it was not until 1942 that he settled in the United States, when he declared to the US authorities that his business was shipping.[68] It is interesting to note that, following the recommendation of J. Edgar Hoover, founder and Director of the FBI, Onassis was spied on by FBI agents from 1942 to 1944, while he was resident in the United States.[69] Although Hoover

---

[67] Rodney Carlisle, *Sovereignty for Sale: The Origins and Evolution of the Panamanian and Liberian Flags of Convenience* (Annapolis, MD: Naval Institute Press, 1981), Tables 6 and 7, 60–61. See also Onassis, "Our Postwar Shipping."

[68] He stated in his application at Ellis Island that he had previously visited the United States on July 10, 1940 and on April 17, 1942.

[69] FBI, "Aristotle Onassis," Bufile 100-125834, Document 100-125834-1, July 27, 1942.

was known to have a long history of concern about foreign subversives,[70] not to mention that this was wartime, it was probably not entirely his own doing to initiate the surveillance on Onassis. The FBI records report that Onassis was suspected of "sentiments inimical to the war efforts"; the information was released by the Greek Embassy of Buenos Aires, by Ambassador Vasilios Dendramis, a few days after Onassis had traveled on Panair to the United States on June 18, 1942.[71]

The confidential FBI reports for this period are highly interesting, as they seem to include a great deal of malignant gossip and fallacies provided by various informants about this "playboy," who lived between New York, Long Island, San Francisco, and Los Angeles. FBI reports, however, also indicate that some of their informants provided wrong and malicious evidence against him.[72] The FBI stopped its inquiries on Onassis in 1944 "as investigation to date has not reflected any activity of a subversive nature on the part of the subject, no further investigation is deemed warranted and the case is hereby closed."[73]

Conclusions

This chapter followed the creation of the Onassis tramp-shipping company, which coincided with the third stage of the evolution of Greek shipping business (Figure 1.1). It is highly interesting to see how he set up the basis for the fourth stage: the creation of the global shipping business in which he led the way not only for Greeks but globally.

During the first twenty years of his business career Onassis created the foundations of his empire, with Buenos Aires as the basis of his entrepreneurial activities. Buenos Aires, then a booming port city, the largest in the South Atlantic routes, proved an excellent choice for the ambitious young Greek. He arrived in 1923 in a familiar environment, as a significant Greek community already existed in the city. Based on his family business know-how and

---

[70] Athan G. Theoharis and John Stuart Cox, *The Boss: J. Edgar Hoover and the Great American Inquisition* (New York: Bantam Books; Philadelphia: Temple University Press, 1990), 49–53. On the Hoover-McCarthy attitude to the "red menace" and their attempts to reveal communist penetration in US society under the Roosevelt and Truman administrations, see Athan Theoharis, *Chasing Spies: How the FBI Failed in Counterintelligence but Promoted the Politics of McCarthyism in the Cold War Years* (Chicago: Ivan R. Dee, 2002), chapters 6 and 7.

[71] FBI, "Aristotle Onassis," Bufile 100-125834, Document 100-125834-1, July 18, 1942. See also Gelina Harlaftis, "Aristotle Onassis and FBI Archives in the 1940s," *Entreprises et Histoire* 2 (2011): 80–85.

[72] Harlaftis, "Aristotle Onassis and FBI Archives in the 1940s," 80–85.

[73] FBI, "Aristotle Onassis," Bufile 100-125834, Espionage on "Aristotelis Onassis," Los Angeles Bureau, March 22, 1944.

network, he collaborated with his father and uncle in Greece, and with his first cousins in Argentina, to found a sound business of tobacco imports, which he further expanded in the niche and rising market of the manufacture of cigarettes for women. From the beginning of his career, Onassis demonstrated what characterized him for the rest of his life: a constant mobility between the Americas and Europe, and a global attitude in business. Right away, he showed his lifelong ability to penetrate established political and economic networks of power, by which means which he managed to survive.

In Buenos Aires, an important international port for tramp shipping and a center of grain exports, he realized the importance of Greek and Norwegian shipping and the centrality of London to the shipping economy. He was able to penetrate all these centers by traveling constantly between Greece, the United Kingdom, and Norway. In Greece, he penetrated the political establishment by promoting Greco-Argentinian relations, and was able to become a Deputy Consul for five years. Representing his country of origin to his host country gave him further political and economic strength, which made it possible for him to manipulate and surpass the old-established elite Greeks in Argentina. The indirect conflict with the latter was fought via the newly appointed Ambassador in Buenos Aires in 1938, who remained in the post until 1945 and proved to be one of his fiercest enemies. However, most important of all, Onassis was able to realize the importance of shipping, a mobile industry that suited his character, and enter it at the best possible time for investment, in 1932. He became acquainted with the London office of the Dracoulis Brothers, who originated from the island of Ithaca in the Ionian Sea, and it was from them that he bought his first two steamships. During the 1930s, he acquired experience in the sale and purchase of secondhand vessels of both dry-cargo vessels and tankers, in shipbuilding, and in the operation of shipping companies.

During this decade, Onassis devoted himself to learning about Greek and Norwegian shipping methods and techniques and was able to expand and reinvent them. By 1940, he had made the choices that marked his path to global shipping: specialization in tanker shipping, use of offshore companies, and adoption of flags of convenience. Good timing in investing proved to be one of his strengths, which he revealed during the time of his great expansion after 1946. By the second year of World War II, Aristotle Onassis was a medium-sized shipowner of five tankers: his two Panamanian tankers were chartered to the US government; of the other three, one had been requisitioned by the Norwegian government and the other two under the Swedish flag were laid up in Sweden. However, after twenty years of doing business he had much more: a cosmopolitan concept of how to run a global shipping business from five countries.

7

The Onassis Fleet, 1946–1975

From 1946 to 1975, Aristotle Onassis consolidated his position as a charismatic shipping tycoon and international businessman. During this period (the fourth stage in the evolution of the shipping company), he pioneered what would become the basic structure of the global tramp/bulk-shipping group. Between 1946 and 1975, he purchased 140 vessels of about 3.7 million grt and received more than $250 million of finance (in current prices) for these purchases from US banks. Half of the vessels, representing 74 percent of all purchased tonnage, were tankers. Two-thirds of his tankers were newly built in US, European, and Japanese shipyards. His fleet in terms of numbers of ships and tonnage grew exponentially from 1946 to 1955, then slowed down its rate of growth between 1957 and 1960, only to take off again up to 1970, continuing to grow at a slightly slower rate until 1975 (see Figure 7.1). By the time of Onassis's death, in 1975, the fleet had reached its peak of 2.5 million grt or 5.1 million dwt. Aristotle Onassis was an undisputed world-class shipowner, described by the press as the "King of Tankers." He kept surprising the world with his forward-thinking shipbuilding programs and massive purchases of ships. After 1951, he never purchased a secondhand vessel again, but kept building new ships and tankers – each time a larger one. How did he do it?

This chapter analyzes how Aristotle Onassis built his shipping business empire, examining his sale and purchase (S&P) methods and showing how he constructed his fleet by gathering capital resources, and how he managed his resources and exploited the choices given. Onassis confronted both opportunity and crisis as he built his fleet: he successfully navigated the great opportunities given him by the US government, which sold en masse war-built vessels, Liberty ships, and tankers of the so-called T2 type; but he also faced conflict with the traditional Greek shipping milieu – including his father-in-law.

Onassis built his fleet starting with the S&P of a Liberty ship fleet, which furnished the necessary capital to proceed to further investments. He formed a fleet of US-built wartime T2 tankers and cargo vessels, putting them under the US flag; this fleet brought him into direct conflict with the US government. He also launched massive shipbuilding programs in US, German, and French shipyards in the 1940s and 1950s, and in Japanese and French shipyards in the

172

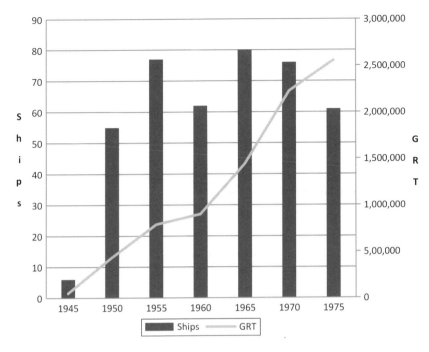

Figure 7.1   The Onassis Fleet, 1946–1975
Source: Appendix 1.B.

1960s and 1970s. He found success through trial and error, making attempts to enter all kinds of shipping that were not always successful.

In the end, expanding his business empire within and beyond shipping was not easy; it involved a number of unsuccessful ventures that consumed Onassis's entrepreneurial talents. The main one was his oil business. His most notorious venture in oil was through an agreement with Saudi Arabia that brought him into direct confrontation with the oil majors, the US government and the European and US shipping world.

Onassis, US Shipping, and the Greek State in the Postwar Era

At the time Onassis was settling in the United States, the United States Maritime Commission (MARCOM) under Admiral Emory Scott Land launched the largest and most successful shipbuilding project in history. MARCOM was established under the Merchant Marine Act of 1936 to determine US maritime trade policy. The huge losses of Allied merchant cargo vessels in the war of the Atlantic meant that new ships were urgently needed. The MARCOM program eventually built 4,694 ships of all kinds, both commercial and military.[1] At the end of 1946, the US possessed the largest fleet of merchant ships in the world, with 60 percent of world tonnage, up from 14.5 percent in 1939.[2]

American officials were faced with the huge problem of what to do with the enormous and costly fleet, which was six times larger than needed and too costly to be operated by US shipowners. They estimated in 1946 that about a thousand vessels were enough to cover the shipping requirements of the four types of US sea trade: coastal, intercoastal, contiguous (Alaska, Hawaii, and Puerto Rico), and foreign. The first three could only be undertaken by vessels built, owned, and operated in America; only the fourth, foreign trade, was open to foreign competition.[3] MARCOM's merchant fleet proved to have an additional problem. Although it included various types, dry-cargo merchant vessels (Liberty, Victory, C1, C2, C3) of about 10,000 dwt and tankers (T2) of about 16,500 dwt, 60 percent of the fleet consisted of dry-cargo vessels of the Liberty type.[4] The latter, although built using the new welding technique, were obsolescent steamships converted to operate with oil, and were slow as well as comparatively small. No US shipowners had shown any intention of buying them and it was obvious that unless foreign shipowners showed some interest most of the Liberty ships would be mothballed.[5]

In the end, US policymakers decided to sell two-thirds of the fleet and form a reserve fleet with the rest. In March 1946, President Truman signed the Merchant Ship Sales Act, which authorized MARCOM to sell government-owned vessels to domestic and foreign shipowners.[6] The Act was based on a report by the Graduate School of Business Administration at Harvard, which proposed rapid sales of ships at fixed prices for short periods of time, at a price formula of 50 percent of prewar domestic cost for each class of ships (87.5 percent for tankers), adjusted for depreciation and allowances. There were, however, a number of restrictions on the types of vessels available to foreigners. For example, tankers were not available for sale to foreigners except in

---

[1] Rebecca Achee-Thornton and Peter Thomson, "Learning from Experience and Learning from Others: An Exploration of Learning and Spillovers in Wartime Shipbuilding," *The American Economic Review* 91, no. 5 (December 2001): 1350–1368.

[2] Hobart S. Perry, "The Wartime Merchant Fleet and Post War Shipping Requirements," *The American Economic Review* 36, no. 2 (May 1946): 520–546.

[3] Ibid.

[4] L. S. Sawyer and W. H. Mitchell, *The Liberty Ships: The History of the Emergency Type Cargoships Constructed in the United States during the Second World War*, 2nd edn (London: Lloyd's of London Press, 1985); Frederic C. Lane, *Ships for Victory: A History of Shipbuilding Under the U.S. Maritime Commission* (Baltimore: Johns Hopkins University Press, 2001, reprint); Achee-Thornton and Thomson, "Learning from Experience."

[5] Perry, "The Wartime Merchant Fleet."

[6] More on the review in John G. B. Hutchins, "United Merchant Marine Policy and Surplus Ships," *Journal of Political Economy* 59, no. 2 (April 1951): 117–125.

specific cases and limited numbers.[7] Moreover, MARCOM was authorized by Congress to offer even better prices if there was a government guarantee on vessels purchased by independent foreign owners; indeed, foreign owners could obtain a ten-year loan on 75 percent of the original price.[8]

The Greeks were among the first to purchase Liberty ships. As the Norwegian shipping tycoon, Erling Dekke Naess, stated, "For their price they turned out to be the finest workhorse ships ever produced on maritime history. Once their worth was generally recognised they were snapped up by Greeks and Norwegians in astonishing numbers and the rest of the maritime world followed suit."[9] In 1939, the Greek merchant fleet consisted of 1.8 million grt but by 1946 only 500,000 grt remained. The sale of Liberty ships was a great opportunity for Greek shipowners to acquire new ships on highly favorable terms. On April 9, 1946, the Greek government guaranteed the purchase of 100 Liberties on behalf of its shipowners, their only obligation being to hoist the Greek flag. Greek shipowners paid about $485,000 for each ship, a third of their original price. Only 34 percent was paid in cash (that is, $165,000); the remainder was financed through a long-term loan from the US, guaranteed by the state. Another 300 vessels of the MARCOM fleet were purchased by Greek shipowners at higher prices, in cash, supplemented by US bank loans, and under the condition that they would hoist so-called flags of convenience.[10]

US maritime policy had been torn between the political need to show the flag across the world's oceans as a demonstration of US sea power, and an economic imperative to maintain a profitable fleet or use low-cost sea transport. It was able to do the first through a highly protectionist and costly official maritime policy that pleased US Congressmen, shipowners, seamen's unions, state officials, and the US Navy, but had obvious and deleterious effects on the reasonable development of the US flag merchant fleet. It also pursued a shadow maritime policy that effectively outsourced sea transport by supporting the use of flags of convenience by US and foreign shipowners. US flag ships were at the same time saddled with high wages and high operating costs. According to Erling Dekke Naess, the operation of a vessel under the

---

[7] Daniel Marx Jr, "The Merchant Ship Sales Act," *The Journal of Business of the University of Chicago* 21, no. 1 (January 1948): 12–28.
[8] Ibid.; Kaare Petersen, *The Saga of Norwegian Shipping* (Oslo: Dreyers Forlag, 1955), 190.
[9] Naess, *Autobiography of a Shipping Man*, 109.
[10] Ναυτικά Χρονικά [*Nautika Chronika*] (April 1 and 15, 1946); Onassis, "Our Postwar Shipping"; Harlaftis, *History of Greek-Owned Shipping*, 235–240; A. I. Tzamtzis, Τα Λίμπερτυ και οι Έλληνες: Το χρονικό μιας ειρηνικής αρμάδας [*The Liberties and the Greeks: The Chronicle of a Peaceful Fleet*] (Athens: Hestia, 1984).

Panamanian flag cost less than half of what a US ship would cost.[11] Even worse, in 1957 US officials admitted that "runaway wage bills [of ships with flags of convenience] would be anywhere from one-third to one-fifth the American cost."[12]

Flags of convenience, as they came to be called in the 1950s, became a key tool in the formation of global shipping in the second half of the twentieth century, and were encouraged by the shift of political power and influence from Britain to the United States after 1945, which ushered in a new era in world shipping. "Flagging out" from traditional registers to flags of convenience was fully supported by US policymakers and economic interests, such as oil companies. The United States had been a weak shipping power in the first half of the twentieth century. Its subsequent "hegemonic ascendancy" was built, according to political economist Alan Cafruny, "not through supplanting the European powers and filling the oceans with American flag vessels but rather through constructing a system in which the European merchant fleets could flourish but in which core American interests were safeguarded."[13] The flags of convenience of Panama, Honduras, and Liberia, known as the PanHoLib fleet, were part of a trend to turn to offshore companies, which not only provided an economic shelter and low taxes that offered cheap sea transport for large US corporations like United Fruit or the oil companies, but also flexibility beyond state control in a global environment.[14] When a sealift was needed, the PanHoLib would immediately become the United States' allies, and the US Navy could forcibly requisition this fleet. Thus, in the second half of the twentieth century, the United States was able to rule the waves through a tacit policy that started in the interwar period and culminated in the 1940s and 1950s.[15]

The US government informally encouraged US oil companies and independent owners to adopt flags of convenience, and powerful lobbies were established to ensure their continued existence. Encouraged by the US credit institutions that financed them, the Greeks were able to take advantage of the situation, simultaneously serving both US and their own interests. The late

---

[11] Naess, *Autobiography*, 94.
[12] "Growth of Runaway Fleets," *Current Merchant Marine Problems, Hearings before the Committee on Merchant Marine and Fisheries, House of Representatives, Eighty-fifth Congress, first session, February 6 and 7, 1957* (Washington, DC: United States Government Printing Office, 1957), 694–700.
[13] Cafruny, *Ruling the Waves*, 87.
[14] See ibid. For a classic on flags of convenience, see Metaxas, *Flags of Convenience*. For the resort of the Greeks to flags of convenience see Harlaftis, "Greek Shipowners and State Intervention."
[15] For the use of flags of convenience by American shipowners see René de la Pedraja's, *Rise and Decline of US Merchant Shipping in the Twentieth Century* (New York: Maxwell Macmillan International, 1992).

1940s marked a decisive shift away from operation under the Greek flag to operation under flags of convenience. From 1949 to 1959, Greeks owned on average 45 percent of the Panamanian fleet and 80 percent of the Liberian fleet.[16]

So, Greek shipowners were able to buy US-built ships with US credit, put them under US-backed flags of convenience, and carry US cargoes at a low cost. They were thus much more competitive than US ships and took away US business in foreign trade. It was to be expected that there was great opposition from the US seamen's unions to flags of convenience, and they launched a worldwide boycott in collaboration with the ITF (International Transport Federation) and ILO (International Labor Organization). There was also widespread opposition from both shipowners and union leaders to the sale of US ships by the MARCOM to foreign shipowners; they wanted to keep the protectionist prewar regime alive, retaining "American cargoes for American ships," as they knew that foreign shipowners operated at half the cost of Americans.[17] Articles from the *American Journal* and the *Journal of Commerce* calling for the decision to be reversed were published in the Greek shipping journal, *Nautika Chronika*, in December 1946. Almon E. Roth, the president of the National Federation of American Shipping, objected that British and Greek shipowners were able to buy and run US ships at much lower prices than the US shipowners, causing unfair competition.[18]

Under pressure on multiple fronts, Congress passed an amendment to the Act on February 27, 1948 stipulating that MARCOM could continue to sell ships until March 1, 1949, but only to US citizens.[19] The opportunities for foreign shipowners, therefore, lasted for less than two years, and mainly excluded tankers. It was during precisely this period that Aristotle Onassis and other prominent Greek shipowners, including Stavros Livanos, Stavros Niarchos, and Manuel Kulukundis, bought most of their MARCOM ships, bypassing the amendment by forming dummy US companies. They were able to do so with the help of US politicians, the advice of top US law firms, the tacit consent of top US financial institutions, and the support of US oil companies, as we shall see.

Meanwhile Onassis, immediately after the war, tried to seize the opportunity to purchase ships from the US wartime fleet and to network with the postwar Greek governments. He purchased ten small frigates from Canada to be converted into passenger ships to be used in Greek coastal shipping, which

---

[16] Harlaftis, *Greek Shipowners and Greece*, 53–55.
[17] Almon E. Roth, "Sea Transportation," *Proceedings of the Academy of Political Science* 21, no. 2 (January 1945): 4–16.
[18] Newspaper Ναυτικά Χρονικά [*Nautica Chronika*], January 15, 1947.
[19] "Under Two Flags: Foreign Registry of American Merchantmen," *Stanford Law Review* 5, no. 4 (July 1953): 797–813.

had been completely destroyed under German occupation. In 1946, he offered to put these ships in service in Greece in return for a monopoly on their operation in Greek waters, but the proposal was rejected.[20] Onassis sold this fleet but kept one of the frigates for himself, converting it a few years later into his famous yacht *Christina*.

Apart from coastal shipping, Onassis tried other types of shipping, like liner shipping. In 1946, in collaboration with Costas Gratsos, Stavros Niarchos, and Manolis Kulukundis, he started a liner company named Pacific Mediterranean Line. Its headquarters would be in New York and each of the shipowners would contribute two Liberty ships. The line would operate monthly from Pacific ports and would be in joint service with the American Pacific line.[21] It operated for just one year, in 1947 with the Onassis ships *Merope* and *Socrates*, and the Kulukundis ship *Master Elias Kulukundis*. For various internal reasons, and primarily because of the high freight rates in the tramp-shipping market, Onassis withdrew his ships from the line.[22]

His main plan was investing in tramp shipping by acquiring ships from the available MARCOM merchant fleet via the Greek state, which would ensure the best possible price. Despite having been an early advocate of the purchase of Liberty ships, and having asked for ten Liberties and two T2 tankers through the guarantee of the Greek state, he did not receive any of the 100 Liberties delivered to Greek shipowners in April 1946; the official justification that he was an Argentinean citizen. The purchase of the 100 Liberties was followed by the sale of seven T2 tankers (16,500 dwt) by the US Maritime Commission to Greek shipowners, guaranteed by the state and on the same favorable terms, in September 1947. In order to secure these much wanted vessels, and be able to compete with other shipowners, Onassis made an unusual proposal to the Greek Ministry of Shipping: he would purchase the seven T2 tankers with cash and dispose a large part of the profits to the Seamen's Pension Fund.[23] His offer brought an immediate reaction from the rest of the shipowners: the seven tankers were bought in cash by the traditional shipowners, Nikolaos Lykiardopoulos, Stratis Andreadis, Stavros Livanos, George Nikolaou, Petros Goulandris's sons, Markos Nomikos, and the Chandris brothers. Onassis was completely excluded: not only no tankers, but no Liberty ships either. He was enraged.

He channeled his anger against the shipowning status quo into a long memorandum written after that purchase, which Costas Gratsos is said to

---

[20] Ναυτικά Χρονικά [*Nautica Chronika*], July 1, 1946; Onassis, "Our Postwar Shipping," March 8, 1953.
[21] Ναυτικά Χρονικά [*Nautica Chronika*], October 1, 1947.
[22] Foustanos, *Onassis: Pioneer in Shipping*, 56.
[23] Ναυτικά Χρονικά [*Nautica Chronika*], September 1, 1947.

have called the "Onassiad."[24] He submitted the memorandum in September 1947 as an open letter to the President of the Greek shipowners association in New York, Manolis Kulukundis. It circulated in the form of various typed copies in the shipping circles of New York, London, and Piraeus. The "Onassiad," an invaluable source of Onassis's thinking about the shipping industry (it was probably written with the encouragement and help of his friend Costas Gratsos), is a denunciation of his treatment at the hands of the traditional Greek shipowning elite (which included his own father-in-law), in the context of harsh postwar competition. In it, he accuses Manuel Kulukundis, the leading Greek shipowner in New York, of manipulating Greek government officials against him. He accuses various government officials (including the Greek Ambassador in Buenos Aires) and shipowners of slandering him unjustly. He reveals various tricks and illegal business practices of some of these top Greek shipowners during World War I and the interwar period, and accuses all shipowners of tax evasion and of not giving anything to the Greek state (Greece was in a state of civil war from 1945 to 1949). He calculates that in 1947 the 100 Liberty ships generated sufficient net profits to repay most of the loans, hence they were "given as a gift" by the Greek state and "the ragged Greek women and children."[25] His denunciatory writing bears a remarkable resemblance to the contemporary rhetoric of leftist Greek newspapers against Greek shipowners. Onassis used nicknames to accuse particular individuals of certain acts, circulating the manuscript in the tight-knit shipowning community and then threatening to publish it, disclosing the real names. Publicity has always been an Achilles' heel for traditional Greek shipowners. The manuscript was eventually published in its original form in the Greek newspaper *Εθνικός Κήρυξ* (*National Herald*) six years later, in 1953.

Why was Onassis unable to get sufficient support from the leaders of the Greek shipowning community at that time? Why was he excluded from this lucrative state-supported deal, unable to buy a single Liberty ship or tanker? After all, in December 1946 he had taken the ultimate step towards gaining access to traditional Greek ship-owning circles by marrying seventeen-year-old Tina Livanos, daughter of Stavros Livanos, the leading shipowner from the island of Chios. Stavros Niarchos shortly after married Eugenia, the older sister of Tina. In this way Aristotle Onassis became the son-in-law of one of the most powerful Greek shipowners and the brother-in-law to his future most powerful competitor, Stavros Niarchos. Niarchos proved another emblematic Greek shipowner. His rivalry with Onassis became notorious and was beloved by the press. It is a fact that they led very similar business lives, with fleets and investments of the same magnitude. It seems that they discussed business

---

[24] Nicholas Fraser, Philip Jacobson, Mark Ottaway, and Lewis Chester, *Aristotle Onassis* (New York: Ballantine Books, 1977), 75.
[25] Onassis, "Our Postwar Shipping," March 17, 1953.

closely at a critical stage of their career, since they were related by marriage. Niarchos built his fleet, entered tanker shipping, obtained loans from US finance, and organized his business globally exactly like Onassis. There is still a controversy as to who led and who was the follower. Archival evidence and testimonies, among which are Niarchos's own people, indicate that Niarchos followed Onassis and not the reverse.[26]

Both, despite their marriages to Greek shipping old money, were regarded as newcomers. Although Niarchos managed to collaborate with the inner circle of traditional Greek shipowners, Onassis was excluded and encountered great animosity. Prior to 1946, he was an ambitious and provocative upstart shipowner, and it was clear that he was not going to be given an easy ride. Moreover, he probably also represented a section of the shipowning circle that was excluded by the elite of Greek shipowners based in New York, the smaller shipowners. What the "Onassiad" proved was that someone considered to be an outsider was in fact a full member of the group. After fifteen years in the shipping business, Onassis had all the inside information on Greek shipping and its actors.

Building Fleets

The Liberty Fleet, 1946–1951

As of spring 1946, Onassis, who was not included in the list of Greek shipowners that purchased Liberty ships with the Greek state guarantee, acted alone. In the winter of 1946 he was able to raise finance and he purchased ten Liberty ships from the United States Maritime Commission, which he put under the Honduras flag, giving them names prefixed with "Ari-" or Aristo-." Therefore, *Aris, Aristarchos, Aristocratis, Aristogiton, Aristomenis, Aristopais, Aristotelis,* and *Aristidis,* along with *Chrysostomos* (the name of the father of the Konialidis brothers) and *Mario II* (name of the son of Nikos Konialidis), were all cargo ships of the Liberty type built between 1943 and 1944 in the US shipyards (see Table 7.1).

The ships were purchased by the Sociedad Armadora Aristomenis Panama, SA, a new Panamanian company created in 1946; under the laws of Panama, the ships owned by Panamanian companies could hoist non-Panamanian

---

[26] For Stavros Niarchos's shipping company see Theotokas and Harlaftis, *Leadership*. For testimonies from his employees see Yannis Frangoulis, *Ο Σταύρος Νιάρχος όπως τον έζησα* [*Stavros Niarchos as I Lived with Him*] (Athens: Fereniki, 2001); Parina Douzina Stiakaki, *Σταύρος Νιάρχος – Ο αρχηγός του Στόλου* [*Stavros Niarchos – Chief of Fleet*] (Athens: Mikres Ekdoseis 2017).

Table 7.1 *The Liberty fleet*

Name of ship	Flag	Type	GRT	DWT	Year built	Year of purchase
Aris	Panama	CSH	7,248	10,837	1943	1947
Aristarchos	Honduras	CSH	7,248	10,837	1942	1947
Chrysostomos	Panama	CSH	7,247	10,870	1943	1947
Mario II	Panama	CSH	7,278	10,800	1944	1947
Aristocratis	Honduras	CSH	7,260	10,920	1943	1946
Aristogiton	Honduras	CSH	7,217	10,890	1943	1946
Aristomenis	Honduras	CSH	7,210	10,950	1943	1946
Aristopais	Honduras	CSH	7,217	10,890	1943	1946
Aristotelis	Honduras	CSH	7,217	10,890	1943	1946
Aristidis	Honduras	CSH	7,247	10,870	1943	1947

CSH = cargo ship.
Source: Onassis Archive, Alexander S. Onassis Foundation, Minutes of Sociedad Armadora Aristomenis Panama SA, 1946–1947; Lloyd's Register of Shipping, 1946–1948.

flags. The directors of the owning company were "Aristoteles [sic] Socrates Onassis (Chairman), Nicolas Konialidis as co-director and Constantino Konialidis (Secretary)."[27] The capital of the company was $10,000 and, according to the Minutes, the stock (1,999 shares) was owned by another Panamanian company, the Sociedad Armadora Miraflores Panama, Ltd. This was the point at which Onassis introduced his model of multiple holding companies (see Chapter 9).

Onassis started his postwar empire in 1946 with an investment of his own capital of about $3 million, which went towards this initial purchase of Liberty ships. The first post-World War II meeting of the Board of Directors of the Sociedad Armadora Miraflores Panama, Ltd took place in Manhattan, New York on November 20, 1946. The meeting took place in order to enable the directors of the company to acquire ten Liberty ships for the price of $600,000 each. This meant that $6 million had to be found. Onassis had already secured a loan from National City Bank of New York

---

[27] The spelling of the names is according to the original. See "Minutes of the First Meeting of the Board of the Sociedad Armadora Aristomenis Panama, S.A.," Corporate books of Sociedad Armadora Aristomenis Panama SA, vol. 1, Onassis Archive, Alexander S. Onassis Foundation.

(NCBNY) for half the amount; the other $3 million was his own capital.[28] This was Onassis's first agreement with the National City Bank of New York. Up to 1959, the Bank would lend him $90.4 million (see below Table 7.6). For the rest of his career he had unlimited credit, as his collaborators later indicated.[29] The most important part of this first agreement with NCBNY, however, was not only the loan per se, but what it involved.[30] What Onassis did was to secure five charter parties from the French government for one year. In order to get the loan, he offered the income of five of the ten ships that would come from the secured time charter parties to the bank as guarantee, apart from the first mortgage. The income of the five ships would go directly to the bank for the repayment of the $3 million loan. Aristotle Onassis made his fortune on the back of this type of loan and contract with NCBNY.

Under the agreement with NCBNY, from the charter with the French government, and the earnings of the five vessels, the loan would be mostly repaid in one year. According to Aristotle Onassis's own calculations, the income from a one-year time charter of a Liberty ship carrying coal would earn $420,000; so the Bank could receive $2.1 million in just one year ($420,000 × five ships).[31] The purchase of these ten Liberty ships thus proved fundamental for his subsequent moves. By using the strategy of asset play, when freight rates rocketed in 1948–1949 and the price of ships shot up, he sold seven of them for more than $1 million dollars each, between 1948 and 1951. The Minutes of Sociedad Armadora Aristomenis Panama, SA reported the level of the prices: "The Chairman stated that it was desirable to confirm and approve the sale of the s/s *Aristocratis* to the Phoenix Compania de Navegacion on the basis of about $1,100,000."[32] He had purchased *Aristocratis* for $600,000, out of which $300,000 was provided by a loan from the City Bank, a sum repaid by the time charter of the vessel.

---

[28] Ibid.

[29] Stelios A. Papadimitriou, "Ο άλλος Ωνάσης" ["The Other Onassis"], Lecture at the Museum of Cycladic Art, November 27, 1995, published at Αργώ [*Argo*] (January 1996).

[30] Ibid.

[31] For Liberty ships, he calculated $1,400 daily income for a one-year charter for carriage of coal, minus $200 daily expenses, which would leave $1,200. Calculating 350 days of work for the ship, $1,200 × 350 = $420,000 net income. See Onassis, "Our Postwar Shipping," March 17, 1953.

[32] "Minutes the Sociedad Armadora Aristomenis Panama, SA, 7 June 1951," Corporate books of Sociedad Armadora Aristomenis Panama SA, vol. 1, Onassis Archive, Alexander S. Onassis Foundation.

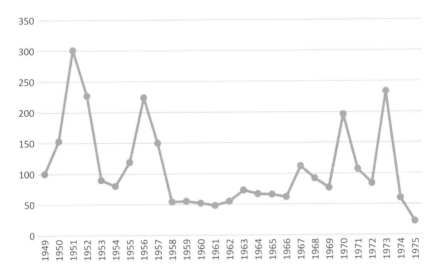

Figure 7.2   Tanker freight index on the spot market, 1949–1975

Source: Table 201, *Norwegian Shipping News* freight indices. Average, Central Bureau of Statistics of Norway, *Historical Statistics 1978* (Oslo: Central Bureau of Statistics of Norway, 1978), 405.

Tanker freight rates reached the highest point between 1949 and 1951 (Figure 7.2). The asset play with the dry-cargo ships of the Liberty type during this period provided Aristotle Onassis with adequate capital for a great leap forward: the purchase of US T2 tankers built during the war and multiple orders of newly built tankers in US shipyards (see Table 7.2). Within 2–3 years not only did he repay the Bank for the loan for the Liberties and amass millions but further opened the way to abundant US credit by gaining the NCBNY's trust. With a capital of at least $10 million from the timely sale and the earnings of his Liberty fleet and more from the earnings of his other ships, Onassis launched into an expansion of his tanker fleet, grabbing the opportunities available in the United States at that time. One should not forget that in 1946 Onassis, apart from his newly purchased Liberty fleet, had another six vessels: two "Empire"-type cargo ships, *Meropi* and *Socrates* (also called "Canadian Liberties"), which he put on the aforementioned Pacific-Mediterranean line; and four other operating tankers, the *Antiope, Calliroy, Ariston,* and *Aristophanes.* He had sold the tanker *Buenos Aires* to the Argentinean government in 1945.

Table 7.2 The American flag fleet, 1948–1957

Owning company/agency	Name of ship	Type of ship	grt	dwt	Year built	Year of purchase
United States Petroleum Carriers, US	1. Arickaree	TSH	10,532	16,460	1943	1948
	2. Battle Rock	TSH	10,448	16,640	1944	1948
	3. Camas Meadows	TSH	10,172	16,460	1943	1948
	4. Camp Namanu	TSH	10,511	16,460	1944	1948
	5. Fort Bridger	TSH	10,172	16,460	1944	1948
	6. Lake George	TSH	10,582	16,460	1943	1948
	7. Stony Point	TSH	10,506	16,460	1943	1948
Trafalgar Steamship company, US	8. Republic	TSH	10,581	16,748	1944	
	9. Federal	TSH	10,599	16,460	1944	1948
Pacific tankers/Olympic Whaling SA	10. Olympic Challenger	TSH	10,448	16,576	1943	1948
Pacific Tankers/Western Tankers Inc., US	11. Mckittrick Hills	TSH	10,521	16,539	1944	1948
	12. Montebello Hills	TSH	10,521	16,539	1944	1948
	13. William A.M. Burden	TSH	10,642	16,656	1943	1949
Victory Carriers Inc., US	14. Ames Victory	CSH-VICTORY	7,644	10,757	1945	1949
	15. Coe Victory	CSH-VICTORY	7,643	10,757	1945	1949
	16. Coeur D' Alene Victory	CSH-VICTORY	7,645	10,745	1945	1949
	17. Heywood Broun		7,643	10,767	1945	1949

18. Jefferson City Victory	CSH-LIBERTY	7,643	10,767	1945	1949
19. Lewis Emery Jr	CSH-VICTORY	7,238	10,920	1943	1949
20. Longview Victory	CSH-LIBERTY	7,639	10,745	1945	1949
21. Mankato Victory	CSH-VICTORY	7,645	10,745	1945	1949
22. Northwestern Victory	CSH-VICTORY	7,628	10,733	1945	1949

TSH = tanker ship; CSH = cargo ship.

Sources: Lloyd's Register of Shipping, 1946–1975; Onassis Archive, Alexander S. Onassis Foundation, SA, Corporate Books and Minutes of Meeting of the Board of Directors of owned companies.

The US Flag Fleet

Onassis's aim was tankers. He wanted to purchase the much-sought-after T2 tankers from the United States Maritime Commission. These vessels brought a lot of money and cost about $1.7 million each in 1946. According to his calculations, the T2 tankers on a three-year time charter on $4 per ton would yield profits of $1.44 million, which meant rapid repayment of the loans.[33] After not receiving a single vessel out of the seven T2 tankers granted to Greek shipowners on state guarantee, he proceeded to apply through Costas Konialidis for the purchase of eighteen tankers directly to the Maritime Commission; on September 12, 1947, the Maritime Commission declined this application.[34] MARCOM disposed of very few T2 tankers to foreign shipowners, as it wanted to direct this fleet to US subjects. Thus, by February 1948, sales of ships to foreigners by MARCOM was prohibited.

As only US citizens could purchase T2 tankers, this presented a great problem to Greek shipowners. Prominent US lawyers found a solution to their citizenship problem.[35] Onassis, following legal advice, formed five US companies with stockholders (so-called quiet Americans) who would appear to own the majority, 51 percent, of the stocks of the company, when in fact Onassis was the real owner. Through the US Congressman Joseph E. Casey, who was involved in tanker purchases from MARCOM, he used the prominent Washington Attorney Office of Goodwin, Rosenbaum, and Meacham to create his companies; his lawyer Robert W. Dudley, Joseph E. Casey's brother-in-law, worked there, so Onassis was able to plan everything in accordance with US law.

[33] He calculated that a monthly income of $66,400 minus expenses of $26,400 would yield profit of $40,000 per month. Calculating $40,000 × 36 months = $1,440,000, See Onassis, "Our Postwar Shipping," March 10, 1953.

[34] Evidence from FBI, "Aristotle Onassis," part 2, Bufile 46-17783, from Director FBI to Assistant Attorney General James M. McInerney, "North American Shipping and Trading Company; United Tanker Corporation; United States Petroleum Carriers Inc.; American Overseas Tanker Corporation; Simpson, Spence and Young. Fraud against the Government" (January 9, 1952) and Allen J. Krouse to Fred E. Strine, Administrative Regulations Section, "U.S. Petroleum Carriers, Inc." (October 31, 1951).

[35] "Testimony of Aristoteles S. Onassis," *Study of the Trade-Out and Build Activities of Onassis Companies, Hearing before the Special Subcommittee of the Committee on Merchant Marine and Fisheries House of Representatives, Eighty-Fifth Congress, Second Edition, June 17, 18, 19, 24, July 8, 15, 22, August 13 and 15, 1958* (Washington, DC: United States Government Printing Office, 1958), 175–176.

The first US company he formed was the United States Petroleum Carriers Corporation on September 27, 1947 with stockholders Admiral N. I. Bowen, Robert W. Dudley, and Robert L. Berenson. Onassis made Admiral Bowen, who was introduced to him by Casey, President of the company. This was a clever move, as the Chairman of the United States Maritime Commission was also a Navy man (Vice Admiral W. W. Smith). The group of stockholders selected by Onassis also formed Boards of Directors of his companies.[36] The day United States Petroleum Carriers Co. was formed, it applied for ten tankers and, on December 30, 1947, the Maritime Commission approved the purchase of four tankers. The second US company he formed was Pacific Tankers Inc. on May 10, 1948, followed by Victory Carriers Inc., formed on December 11, 1948. Onassis purchased twenty-three vessels through his US companies from MAR-COM, of which fourteen were tankers, seven were cargo Victory vessels and two were Liberties (see Table 7.2). Other Greek shipowners, like Stavros Niarchos, Manuel Kulukundis, Gregory Kallimanopoulos, and Los-Pezas, were making similar purchases at this time.

In order to form his US flag fleet, comprising the ships purchased from the United States Maritime Commission between 1948 and 1949, Onassis was able to raise loans from the NCBNY, Chase Manhattan, and Metropolitan Life to the amount of $20 million on first preferred mortgages of the vessels, and other vessels of the Onassis fleet.[37] The loans were further supported by assignments of charter earnings directly to the bank for the security of loans. He was able to do this on three-year time charter guarantees from the US oil company Socony Vacuum Oil Company.[38] For example, the purchase of the ships *Battle Rock, Camp Namanu,* and *Stony Point* took place through a $4.3 million loan agreement with Chase National Bank on March 23, 1948 on the first preferred mortgage of the vessels. This loan was refinanced through the Metropolitan Life Insurance Company by a bond issue of $4.5 million to mature on March 20, 1953, with the earnings of these tankers also assigned as security on the bond issue. For the purchase of the seven Victory vessels by Victory Carriers a

[36] FBI, "Aristotle Onassis," part 2, Bufile 46-17783, "Fraud against the government". New York office 46-2507 report (May 10, 1952). For details of the stockholders of his companies see appendix II.
[37] FBI, "Aristotle Onassis," part 2, Bufile 46-17783, Allen J. Krouse, Special Assistant to the Attorney General, to Fred E. Strine, Administrative Regulations Section, "U.S. Petroleum Carriers, Inc." (October 31, 1951).
[38] FBI, "Aristotle Onassis," part 2, Bufile 46-17783, Allen J. Krouse, Special Assistant to the Attorney General, to Fred E. Strine, Administrative Regulations Section, "U.S. Petroleum Carriers, Inc." (October 31, 1951).

loan of $2.8 million from the National City Bank of New York was obtained.[39] All loans were supported by the personal guarantee of Aristotle Onassis. All agreements with the banks featured, at the end of the documents, as a last exhibit, the "Guaranty Agreement" signed by Aristotle Onassis.[40]

The Whaling Fleet, 1950–1956

Onassis was interested in any kind of oil: not only crude oil, but also whale oil. His interest in whaling had been piqued by the Norwegians in the 1930s, and his friendship with top Norwegian shipowners with interests in whaling, like Anders Jahre and Erling Dekke Naess, gave Onassis abundant information and the initiative to enter the business. From 1950 to 1956, Onassis constructed in the German shipyards a whaling fleet of sixteen vessels that fished for five seasons in the Antarctic, bringing high profits. The whaling expeditions were headed by two experts, a Norwegian and a German, and were manned up to 99 percent by German crews. It was really an Onassis-German collaboration based on German and Norwegian know-how. Any kind of challenge was worth it for Onassis, and penetrating the Norwegian quasi-monopoly on whaling oil must have been a great challenge. The great demand for animal fats throughout war-stricken Europe had increased the market for whale oil and tripled its price since the eve of World War II. The market was highly oligopolistic and oligopsonistic: on the supply side, the Norwegians dominated the scene, followed by the British, with the Germans and the Japanese having lost their fleets in the immediate postwar era; on the demand side, the Unilever Group was the best customer and determined the price of whale oil.[41]

Onassis's first venture into whaling occurred in the United States during World War II in collaboration with Costas Gratsos, then a Greek consul in San Francisco. With the price of whale oil escalating during the war, the two of them purchased an old small Californian whaling station for the processing of whale oil from whales caught off the Californian coast, a business that lasted for a couple of years.[42] They both studied the postwar whaling market and, in

[39] FBI, "Aristotle Onassis," part 2, Bufile 46-17783, "Fraud against the Government," New York Office 46-2507 report (October 5, 1952).

[40] Onassis Archive, Alexander S. Onassis Foundation, Minutes of Board of Directors of Montserrado Panama SA, "Credit Agreement between Olympic Trading Corporation, a Delaware Corporation and the National City Bank of New York, a National Banking Association" (May 20, 1957), "Indenture of Trust" (June 1, 1948), "Guaranty Agreement," Exhibit 11.

[41] Fraser et al., *Aristotle Onassis*, 116.   [42] Vlassopoulos, *Pages of a Life*, 97.

1949, Onassis decided to enter the business. As mentioned, to do so he used mainly German know-how and crews.

With a small but sound tradition in the whaling business, the German whaling fleet reached its apogee in the interwar period. Due to the great economic depression, Germany suffered a shortage of fats and oils, and after the Nazis took over in 1933, German whaling figured prominently in the economic plan of the Third Reich. The plan was to promote the creation of a whaling fleet, which would provide the raw material needed for the margarine industry, formed as an import-substitution productive unit that would help the autarchic economic policy of Nazi Germany. Unilever's German margarine sales branch also collaborated with German production in Hamburg, and Norwegian whalers were also acting under the German flag. The most important business became the Erste Deutsche Walfang Gesellschaft m.b.H, based in Hamburg. The German fleet in the last prewar season of 1938–1939 comprised fifty-six whale catchers, turning Germany into the third largest whaling nation after Norway and Britain.[43]

Onassis revived the German whaling fleet and used its know-how and its jobless German crews. Only three months after the restrictions set by the Potsdam Agreement of 1945, which outlawed building of ships over 1,500 grt in Germany and German crews working on foreign ships, were lifted by the Allies in November 1949, Onassis entered into a contract with the Erste Deutsche Walfang Gesellschaft m.b.H based in Hamburg. As head of his whaling fleet he hired Wilhelm Reichert, and as chief engineer Johaness Doorenz. Kurt Reiter became head of the Olympic Maritime agency in Hamburg. He was the perfect choice, as he had been the first postwar director of AG Weser, in Bremen. Reiter and the Hamburg German team undertook the recruitment of 500 German seamen and Norwegian gunners, the latter of which were instrumental for the success of whaling expeditions.

The Erste Deutsche Walfang Gesellschaft Company, under this contract, undertook the conversion, outfitting, and crewing of his whaling fleet. A T2 tanker, *Olympic Challenger*, of 16,000 dwt, was converted to a whale factory (owned by the Panamanian Olympic Whaling company) and sixteen Canadian and English corvettes were converted to whale catchers (owned by Balleneros Ltd, a Panama corporation) that hoisted the Honduran flag

---

[43] Lars U. Scholl, "German Whaling in the 1930s," in Lewis R. Fischer, Helge W. Nordvik, and Walter E. Minchinton, eds., *Shipping and Trade in the Northern Seas 1600–1939* (Bergen: Association for the History of the Northern Seas, 1988), 103–121; Klaus Barthelmess, "A Century of German Interests in Modern Whaling, 1860s–1960s," in Bjørn L. Basberg, Jan Erik Ringstad, and Einar Wexeilsen, *Whaling and History: Perspectives on the Evolution of the Industry* (Sandefjord: Sandefjordmuseene, 1993), 121–138.

Table 7.3 *The Onassis whaling fleet*

Name of ship	Flag	Type of vessel	Grt	Year built	Year of purchase
Olympic Arrow	Honduras	whaling	702	1944	1950
Olympic Conqueror	Honduras	whaling	714	1940	1950
Olympic Chaser	Honduras	whaling	708	1941	1950
Olympic Cruiser	Panamanian	whaling	699	1943	1950
Olympic Champion	Honduras	whaling			
Olympic Explorer	Honduras	whaling	699	1942	1950
Olympic Fighter	Honduras	whaling	712		1950
Olympic Hunter	Honduras	whaling	715	1941	1951
Olympic Lightning	Honduras	whaling	702		
Olympic Rider	Honduras	whaling	717	1940	1951
Olympic Promoter	Honduras	whaling	699	1942	1950
Olympic runner	Honduras	whaling	715	1940	1950
OlympicTracer	Honduras	whaling	406	1949	1951
Olympic Victor	Honduras	whaling	702	1944	1950
Olympic Winner	Honduras	whaling	744	1942	1951

Sources: Lloyd's Register of Shipping, 1950-1956; Onassis Business Archive, Alexander S. Onassis Foundation, Minutes of Balleneros Ltd SA, 1949-1951.

(see Table 7.3). Finance came from the usual source, the National City Bank of New York. In the Onassis Business Archives, there is the financial agreement between Olympic Whaling and the US bank covering the cost of eight of the ships and of *Olympic Challenger*, "on aggregate amount of $3,750,000 currency to cover the cost price for the conversion, outfitting, stores, equipment, bunker fuel, wages and repairs and any other disbursements relative." Onassis well knew that he had penetrated new business territory and he expected the negative reactions he would get from both the Norwegians and the British. At the time, Norwegians owned half of the floating factories and whaling catchers in the world, and had a restrictive policy regarding the entry of new whaling companies and ships. What is more, according to a Norwegian law passed in 1934 in an effort to keep their monopoly, it was forbidden for

Norwegian gunners to work on foreign vessels; those who did would be deprived of their citizenship.[44]

Whale fisheries operated under restrictive conventions imposed by the International Whaling Commission (ITW): there were annual catching quotas, opening and closing catching seasons, minimum catching sizes for various species, and bans on killing certain types of whales. Furthermore, starting a new fleet meant sharing the annual catching quotas that, for the most part, supported the Norwegian whaling interests. A further source of worry for the Norwegian Whaling Association and for ITW was that the new fleet sailed under Honduran and Panamanian flags, meaning that the restrictions would not be properly controlled. Onassis's fleet fished successfully in two consecutive seasons in 1951–1952 and 1952–1953; because of low whale oil prices he did not undertake an expedition in the season 1953–1954. Ultimately, the attack on his whaling fleet, orchestrated by Norwegians, followed by the British, and tacitly supported by the US, took place in his final whaling expedition in 1954–1955, as we shall see in the next chapter.

The Olympic Fleet, 1948–1958

Ensuring a large tanker fleet under the US flag with secondhand vessels, Aristotle Onassis proceeded at the same time into the massive shipbuilding programs with which he created his famous Olympic fleet. It was this fleet that turned him into the "king of tankers." In fact, after 1951 he never purchased a secondhand vessel again. During his lifetime, he built eighty-four brand-new tankers, all with the prefix "Olympic," apart from *Tina Onassis* and *Al-Malik Saud Al Awal*, in US, German, French, Belgian, British, and Japanese shipyards. For his new ships, he turned first to US shipyards, which desperately needed clients after an intensive period of extraordinary shipbuilding during the war. The first tanker Onassis built after the war was in the American Sparrow Point Shipyards in Bethlehem, Pennsylvania. It was of 11,298 grt and 18,151 dwt, about 3,000 dwt bigger than his Swedish-built tankers from a decade before. *Olympic Games*, delivered in 1949, launched his Olympic fleet (the circles on the ship's chimney became his brand image, see Figure 10.1). The same shipyard delivered another five tankers in 1949 and 1950; these were much bigger, at 28,000 dwt.

In 1951, Onassis turned to the German shipyards, for two reasons. First, he had developed close contacts with Hamburg thanks to his whaling fleet. He saw the war-devastated shipyards, and the wasted know-how of thousands of workers and shipping engineers, and grabbed the opportunity. The second reason was that he saw the possibility of an upcoming conflict with the US

---

[44] Fraser et al., *Aristotle Onassis*, 116.

government, which was no longer hospitable. In 1951, the FBI had started investigations into his shipping business in New York and his purchases of US tankers from the United States Maritime Commission. This culminated in February 1954, when the US government sued him for "illegal purchases" of tankers from United States Maritime Commission.

Thus, turning his back on America, he launched massive shipbuilding programs in the war-torn European shipyards. He brought back to life the Howaldtswerke shipyards of Kiel and Hamburg and the A. G. Weser shipyard in Bremen by launching an amazing shipbuilding program (still financed by the NCBNY). In three years, the German shipyards built eighteen tankers for him, mostly of 21–22,000 dwt. However, the great technological achievement of the Onassis/German partnership, which received worldwide attention, was the launching of *Tina Onassis*, the largest tanker in the world and the first to be called a "supertanker." It was only superseded by Onassis's *Al-Malik Saud Al Awal*, of his ill-fated Saudi Arabian Tankers Co.; the supertanker that hoisted the Saudi Arabian flag for a few years was of 47,130 dwt (Figures 7.3–7.4).

All German- and French-built ships flew the Liberian flag (Table 7.4), as did his ships built in America after 1959 (Table 7.5). After the international boycott of 1958 against flags of convenience, particularly Panamanian and

Figure 7.3 The launching of the tanker *Al-Malik Saud Al Awal*, 29,440 grt, 47,130 dwt, in 1954 in Howaldtswerke, Hamburg, Germany
Source: Courtesy of the Onassis Archive. © 2018 Onassis Archive/Onassis Foundation.

Figure 7.4 The launching of the tanker *l-Malik Saud Al Awal*. Second from left, Tina Onassis, fourth from the left Aristotle Onassis with his two children, Christina and Alexander
Source: Courtesy of the Onassis Archive. © 2018 Onassis Archive/Onassis Foundation.

Honduran flags, Onassis mainly used the Liberian flag in his Olympic fleet. Apart from the German shipyards, Onassis also turned to France. In the shipyards of St. Nazaire, he ordered three tankers of about 32–34,000 dwt. From 1948 to 1954, he had built thirty tankers of the largest size, using the latest technology. His fleet was noted everywhere for its quality. The ships not only were built to the highest specifications, they also showed off their difference, inside and out. Besides, the Olympic tankers were distinguishable from afar because he kept them painted a brilliant white, at substantial expense.

As Tables 7.1–7.5 indicate, in three years, from 1946 to 1951, Onassis had purchased fifty-six secondhand vessels, of which thirteen were tankers, for which he took loans from the US banks (see Table 7.6). In 1951, he purchased his last secondhand vessel. He launched a gigantic shipbuilding program from 1948 to 1954, of thirty brand-new tankers in US, German, and French ship-yards, financed by loans of $46 million from the same banks. From 1957 to 1959, he proceeded to order another seven tankers, two from US shipyards, three from German yards, and two from Japanese yards for the first time, with loans from NYCBNY for $17 million. Overall, from 1946 to 1959 he purchased ninety-two ships and received loans from US banks of about $90 million.

Apart from gigantic tanker shipbuilding programs, this was decidedly the era of tanker gigantism. The 1960s witnessed the largest-ever increase in sizes of tankers. Onassis, of course, was in the frontline. Already by late 1957 Onas-sis had planned the world's first 100,000 dwt tanker but canceled the contract due to the fall in freight rates. This allowed Niarchos, a few years later, to step in with an order for his own 106,500 dwt vessel, the *Manhattan* (delivered in January 1962), the biggest tanker afloat at that time. Onassis was a careful planner, and freight rates were depressed in the 1960s. He ordered a pair of

Table 7.4 *German and French shipyards, 1951–1955*

Name of ship	Flag	Type of ship	GRT	DWT	Year built	Shipyards
Olympic Light	Liberian	TSH	14,009	21,441	1952	Germany
Olympic Mountain	Liberian	TSH	13,660	21,441	1953	Germany
Olympic Dale	Liberian	TSH	13,713	21,298	1954	Germany
Olympic Hill	Liberian	TSH	13,580	21,513	1954	Germany
Olympic Ice	Liberian	TSH	13,665	21,337	1954	Germany
Olympic Lake	Liberian	TSH	17,999	30,558	1954	Germany
Olympic Rock	Liberian	TSH	13,665	21,268	1954	Germany
Olympic Snow	Liberian	TSH	13,665	21,337	1954	Germany
Olympic Valley	Liberian	TSH	13,652	21,279	1954	Germany
Olympic Brook	Liberian	TSH	13,709	21,382	1955	Germany
Tina Onassis	Liberian	TSH	27,853	46,080	1953	Germany
Al-Malik Saud Al Awal	Saudi Arabian	TSH	29,440	47,130	1954	Germany
Olympic Breeze	Liberian	TSH	13,934	21,995	1954	Germany
Olympic Storm	Liberian	TSH	14,047	22,034	1954	Germany
Olympic Wind	Liberian	TSH	14,047	22,204	1954	Germany
Olympic Rainbow	Liberian	TSH	13,934	22,017	1955	Germany
Olympic Cloud	Liberian	TSH	14,221	21,955	1953	Germany
Olympic Sky	Liberian	TSH	14,000	21,850	1955	Germany
Olympic Honour	Liberian	TSH	20,611	31,712	1954	France
Olympic Valour	Liberian	TSH	20,453	31,761	1954	France
Olympic Splendour	Liberian	TSH	20,595	34,333	1954	France

Sources: Lloyd's Register of Shipping, 1946–1975; Onassis Archive, Alexander S. Onassis Foundation, SA, Corporate Books and Minutes of Meeting of the Board of Directors of owned companies.

tankers of 65,000 dwt, which were very economical, from Howaldtswerke in Germany, delivered in 1963 and 1964. From 1964 onwards, he turned to the Japanese shipyards, which were offering generous credit to establish a foothold in world shipping. The bulk carrier emerged as a new type of cargo ship, and low freight rates and the new type of vessel prompted Onassis to order ten bulk carriers from Japan's Nippon Kokan KK, of 27,000 dwt each. In 1964, three more 62,000 dwt tankers were commissioned from Mitsubishi and a

Table 7.5 *New tankers built in US shipyards, 1948–1954*

Name of ship	Flag	Type of ship	GRT	DWT	Year built
Olympic Games	Honduran	TSH	11,298	18,151	1948
Olympic Flame	Honduran	TSH	17,723	28,385	1949
Olympic Laurel	Honduran	TSH	17,723	28,380	1949
Olympic Star	Honduran	TSH	17,722	28,358	1949
Olympic Torch	Honduran	TSH	17,794	28,385	1949
Olympic Thunder	Honduran	TSH	17,722	28,350	1950
Olympic Sun	Liberian	TSH	18,790	30,125	1955
Olympic Eagle	Liberian	TSH	27,602	46,191	1958
Olympic Falcon	Liberian	TSH	27,602	46,108	1958

Sources: Lloyd's Register of Shipping, 1946–1975; Onassis Archive, Alexander S. Onassis Foundation, SA, Corporate Books and Minutes of Meeting of the Board of Directors of owned companies.

Table 7.6 *Loans from US banks for the purchase of ships, 1946–1959*

Years of purchase	Type of ship	Type of purchase	Number of ships	Loans ($ million)
1946	Liberties	Secondhand	10	3
	Whaling	Secondhand	16	3.8
1948–1949	Tankers T2	Secondhand	13	20
	Liberties and Victories	Secondhand	9	
1949–1954	Tankers	New build	30	46.6
1958–1959	Tankers	New build	6	17
Total loans			**84**	**90.4**

Sources: Onassis Business Archive, Alexander S. Onassis Foundation, Minutes of Sociedad Armadora Aristomenis Panama SA, 1946–1947; Credit Agreement dated June 1957 between Olympic Trading Corporation and the National City Bank of New York"; "Supplemental Bond Purchase Agreement dated June 1957 between Olympic Trading Corporation and Metropolitan Life Insurance Company"; Credit Agreement dated June 1959 between Olympic Trading Corporation and the National City Bank of New York," attached to the Minutes of Meeting of the Board of Directors of Sociedad Maritime Miraflores Panama Ltd.

Table 7.7 *The Olympic fleet, 1959–1969*

Name of ship	Type of ship	GRT	DWT	Year built	Shipyards
Ondine	refrigerated	5,960	4,450	1960	Belgium
Olympic Challenger	TSH	37,958	64,750	1960	Germany
Olympic Champion	TSH	37,744	66,278	1960	Germany
Orpheus	refrigerated	5,972	4,450	1961	Belgium
Monticello Victory	TSH	27,414	47,700	1961	United States
Mount Vernon Victory	TSH	27,412	47,000	1961	United States
Montpellier Victory	TSH	27,797	47,000	1962	United States
Mount Washington	TSH	27,797	47,184	1963	United States
Olympic Chariot	TSH	30,320	55,939	1963	Germany
Olympic Chivalry	TSH	30,327	58,920	1964	Germany
Olympic Freedom	TSH	47,493	88,000	1964	France
Olympic Glory	TSH	38,598	65,300	1964	Japan
Olympic Games	TSH	32,380	61,362	1964	Japan
Olympic Fame	TSH	49,586	94,956	1965	France
Olympic Garland	TSH	38,607	73,986	1965	Japan
Olympic Goal	TSH	38,607	73,992	1965	Japan
Olympic Grace	TSH	32,407	61,316	1965	Japan
Olympic Palm	bulk carrier	15,577	26,774	1965	Japan
Olympic Pearl	bulk carrier	15,577	26,464	1965	Japan
Olympic Pegasus	bulk carrier	15,557	26,452	1965	Japan
Olympic Phaethon	bulk carrier	15,625	26,705	1965	Japan
Olympic Gate	TSH	32,478	61,162	1965	Japan
Olympic Pioneer	bulk carrier	15,625	26,425	1966	Japan
Olympic Pride	bulk carrier	15,697	26,771	1967	Japan
Olympic Power	bulk carrier	15,809	26,998	1968	Japan
Olympic Peace	bulk carrier	15,668	27,007	1969	Japan
Olympic Progress	bulk carrier	15,688	26,998	1969	Japan
Olympic Prestige	bulk carrier	15,808	26,958	1969	Japan

Sources: Lloyd's Register of Shipping, 1946–1975; Onassis Archive, Alexander S. Onassis Foundation, SA, Corporate Books and Minutes of Meeting of the Board of Directors of owned companies.

Figure 7.5   The launching of the VLCC *Olympic Aspiration* in 1972, 106,123 grt, 219,447 dwt, in Chantiers de l'Atlantique, St. Nazaire, France. On the left Christina Onassis (1950–1988), in the middle the "godmother" of the ship, and on the right Alexander Onassis (1948–1973)
Source: Courtesy of the Onassis Archive. © 2018 Onassis Archive/Onassis Foundation.

series of three 64,000–74,000 dwt tankers were ordered from the Ishikawajima Harima Shipyards. At the same time, Onassis built a pair of 90,000 dwt tankers at France's Chantiers de l' Atlantique (Table 7.7).

Freight rates shot up again between 1967 and 1974 bringing new opportunities. It was the second Suez crisis and the closure of the canal, the result of the Six Day War between Israel and Egypt in June 1967. As a result, by the end of 1967 shipowners were ordering gigantic tankers of more than 200,000 dwt, called Very Large Crude Carriers, or, as they later became known, VLCCs.

Taking advantage of the high freight rates and the opportunity to renew his tankers, many of which had reached the age of twenty, between 1970 and 1974 Onassis scrapped twenty-two tankers, mainly in Taiwan. To replace them, he ordered eighteen new vessels. Fourteen of these were VLCCs of more than 200,000 dwt; his first VLCC was the *Olympic Armour*, ordered from the Japanese Hitachi shipyards. Apart from the Hitachi shipyards, he built his other tankers in the Japanese Ishikawajima-Harima Heavy Industries Co. Ltd, the French Chantiers de l'Atlantique (Figure 7.5 and Table 7.8), and the British Harland & Wolf Ltd shipyards. In the last months of his life, Onassis encountered the worst tanker crisis the world had seen. In 1973, OPEC increased the price of a barrel of oil almost five times, which had detrimental consequences for tanker freight rates. Onassis's tankers had long-term time charters with major oil companies but he had another four tankers on order. Two of his

Table 7.8 *The Onassis VLCC tanker fleet, 1969–1975*

Name of ship	GRT	DWT	Year built	Shipyards
Olympic Armour	109,580	216,508	1969	Japan
Olympic Athlete	97,468	216,940	1969	Japan
Olympic Accord	98,726	215,895	1970	Japan
Olympic Adventure	97,466	216,287	1970	Japan
Olympic Alliance	97,206	216,441	1970	Japan
Olympic Ambition	97,206	216,430	1970	Japan
Olympic Anthem	98,566	219,274	1970	France
Olympic Archer	96,679	215,046	1970	Japan
Olympic Arrow	96,627	214,770	1970	Japan
Olympic Aspiration	106,123	219,447	1972	France
Olympic Avenger	106,123	219,447	1972	France
Olympic Banner	128,561	264,548	1972	United Kingdom
Olympic Bond	126,027	264,993	1972	Japan
Olympic Brilliance	128,561	264,820	1973	United Kingdom
Olympic Bravery	126,622	277,599	1976	France
Olympic Breeze	126,991	269,532	1976	Japan

Sources: Lloyd's Register of Shipping, 1946–1975; Onassis Archive, Alexander S. Onassis Foundation, SA, Corporate Books and Minutes of Meeting of the Board of Directors of owned companies.

orders, *Olympic Bravery* and *Olympic Breeze*, were received after his death (another two were canceled by his heirs).[45]

The Oil Business and the Saudi Arabian Fleet, 1954–1959

In January 1954, Onassis signed an agreement with Saudi Arabia, which shocked the oil and shipping industries by its global implications. The agreement authorized Onassis to form a company in Jeddah, named Saudi Arabian Maritime Tankers Co., which would develop a fleet registered in Saudi Arabia and flying the Saudi Arabian flag, with vessels having Saudi Arabian names. Onassis would further establish a maritime school, and its graduates would man the Saudi Arabian fleet. Onassis's Saudi Arabian Tankers Co. would pay the Saudi Arabian government a royalty on every ton of oil shipped abroad,

---

[45] On the high contracting of tanker tonnage for the period 1965 to 1973, the crisis that followed and the effect on tanker owners, see Stig Tenold, "Tankers in Trouble: Norwegian Shipping and the Crisis of the 1970s and 1980s," *Research in Maritime History* 32 (St. John's, Newfoundland: International Maritime History Association, 2006).

but the company would be exempt from income tax. The company would have priority in transport of oil for thirty years. The Onassis agreement was ratified by a Royal Decree on May 18, 1954, which had the force of law.[46]

To that end, an Onassis office was formed in Jeddah in 1954. Onassis sent his cousin Michael Dologlou to open an office there. He subsequently chose a young Greek lawyer, aged twenty-four, from the Greek community of Alexandria, Egypt, who knew Greek, Arabian, French, and English and had graduated from the University of Alexandria Law School. The young man, Stelio Papadimitriou, proved to be fundamental for the future of Onassis's business. His fluent Arabic, knowledge of Islamic and European law, and keen intelligence proved pivotal for the formation of statutes of the new Saudi Arabian Tankers Co., as it had to comply with Islamic law.

Papadimitriou and Dologlou stayed in Jeddah from 1954 to 1960. Jeddah was transformed during the 1950s into a thriving international city, on the margins of Saudi Arabian society and business. It was full of delegations and foreign embassies. The wife of Stelio Papadimitriou, Alexandra Papadimitriou, has written a consummate autobiographical narrative of their life in Jeddah, describing their common home with the Dologlou, which also housed the office of the Saudi Arabian Tankers Co., as the "Onassis Embassy."[47] As the offices were settled, Aristotle Onassis was baptizing his new supertanker, *Al-Malik Saud Al Awal* of 47,130 dwt, in a festive atmosphere in the Howaldts-werke shipyards at Hamburg, in the presence of the Saudi Arabian elite.

However, the Saudi connection led to problems. The Onassis-Saudi Arabian agreement shook the foundations of the US oil companies, which had secured a monopoly in Saudi Arabia since the 1930s. More particularly, in 1933 the Standard Oil Company of California had signed a concession agreement with the Saudi Arabian government by which

> The Government grants to the Standard Oil Company of California on the terms and conditions hereinafter mentioned, and with respect to the area defined below, the exclusive right, for a period of sixty years from the effective date hereof, to explore, prospect, drill for, extract, treat, manu-facture, transport, deal with, carry away and export petroleum, asphalt, naptha, natural greases, ozokertie, and other hydrocarbons and the derivatives of such products. It is understood, however, that such right does not include the exclusive right to sell crude or refined products within the area described below or within Saudi Arabia.[48]

[46] Stephen M. Schwebel, "The Kingdom of Saudi Arabia and Aramco Arbitrate the Onassis Agreement," *The Journal of World Energy Law and Business* 3, no. 3 (2010): 245–256.
[47] Alexandra Papadimitriou, *Τζέντα [Jeddah]* (Athens: Kastanioti Publications, 2008), 133.
[48] Alexander S. Onassis Foundation, Onassis Archive, Royal Government of Saudi Arabia. Memorial, "In the Name of God, the Merciful, the Compassionate. In the Matter of an Arbitration between the Government of Saudi Arabia and the Arabian American Oil Company," Geneva, September 10, 1955.

The area covered was vast, and included the Arabian Gulf waters as well. The risk of the company in the barren, desolate, and totally underdeveloped area was large, as it had to explore and then to produce and transport oil. After five years, the Saudi subsidiary of Standard Oil of California (Californian Arabian Standard Oil), set up to develop this virgin territory, found the world's largest oil reserves.[49] Meanwhile in 1936 Texas Company (later Texaco) acquired shares of the previous company to help with the finances. In 1944, Californian Arabian Standard Oil was renamed Arabian American Oil Company (Aramco); in 1948, Standard Oil Company of New Jersey (Exxon) and Socony-Vacuum Oil Company (Mobil) acquired shares in Aramco. Exports of oil increased exponentially after World War II, bringing unprecedented profits to the company and to Saudi Arabia.

Onassis had probably been thinking of challenging the US oil majors for years previously. Ownership and operation of tankers meant he had had a close involvement and knowledge of the oil business since the late 1930s. His collaboration and friendship with J. Paul Getty must have been fundamental for the concept of the plan to penetrate the oil business of Saudi Arabia and achieve the same enviable independence that Getty had. As Getty recalled, "Aristotle Onassis and I formed what grew to be a close friendship and association in several business ventures."[50] In fact, his first tanker charter, *Ariston*, was with J. Paul Getty's Tidewater Oil in 1938. Getty had made much of his fortune going against the US oil companies. He bought a medium-sized oil company, Tidewater Oil, previously owned by Rockefeller, and became one of the so-called American independents, meaning outside the cartel of the oil majors. His great success was breaking the monopoly held by Aramco and acquiring a concession for his Pacific-Western Oil Co. (later Getty Oil) to build a 12,000-barrel refinery in Saudi Arabia in an area not utilized by Aramco. Getty achieved this by offering a truly lucrative deal, a $5.5 per barrel royalty when Aramco was paying only $0.33, plus a $9.5 million initial and a $1 million annual payment.[51]

Aramco had been very worried about these developments and tried to renegotiate with the Saudis in order to exclude more independents. It was only natural that the Onassis agreement was perceived as an additional threat to its exclusive rights. The chance for Onassis to implement a shipping project in collaboration with Saudi Arabia appeared in 1953 in Cannes through Mohammed Ali Reza and his brother Ali Reza; these were members of the

[49] Schwebel, "The Kingdom of Saudi Arabia," 2-12.
[50] Jean Paul Getty, *As I See It: The Autobiography of J. Paul Getty*, revised edn (Los Angeles: The Paul Getty Museum, 2003), 71.
[51] Irvine H. Anderson Jr., *Aramco, the United States, and Saudi Arabia: A Study of the Dynamics of Foreign Oil Policy, 1933-1950* (Princeton: Princeton University Press, 1981), 188; Getty, *As I See it*, 201.

Saudi Arabian rich merchant-class families, entrepreneurs controlling the port of Jeddah and Saudi Arabian shipping. They were accompanying the Minister of Finance, Sheikh Abdullah bin Suleiman Al-Hamdan, on a political and financial mission in Europe.[52] The meeting and eventual negotiation ended up with an agreement between Onassis and the Saudi Arabian government. The agreement was regarded as unacceptable by Aramco.

Aramco refused to comply with the Onassis contract. Onassis refused to negotiate anything less. What was unacceptable was Article IV of the Onassis-Saudi Arabia agreement as it was amended in April 1954:

> The Company [Saudi Arabian Tankers Company Limited] will have the right of priority to ship and transport oil and its products exported from Saudi Arabia to foreign countries by way of the sea whether shipment is effected from Saudi Arabian ports or from the terminals of pipelines abroad and whether that shipment is effected by the concessionary companies themselves or their parent companies or the buyers (of oil and its products).[53]

What followed from 1954 to 1956 was a fierce espionage battle, a secret war that raged behind the scenes, with the united forces of the US government (including the CIA and FBI), the US and European oil majors, and US and European shipowners, including the Greeks (led by his brother-in-law Stavros Niarchos), all ranged against Onassis. What is more, the oil majors orchestrated a boycott of Onassis's tankers in US and European ports. His tankers were delayed at ports and new ships or those that had their time charters finished were not rechartered but were left idle. Onassis was losing millions of dollars.

After months of pressure from the US government and Aramco, the Saudi Arabian government, which did not want to annul its concession to Onassis, failed to settle the dispute, and in 1956 a proposed resolution was arbitrated in the International Court of Justice in The Hague. In the summer of 1956 in Geneva, there were "three rounds of extensive written memorials" and "eight weeks of oral argument, in 42 sittings."[54] These included 500 pages of the "Royal Government of Saudi Arabia Memorial," "The answering memorial and the Exhibits" in both English and Arabic in books bound in dark-green leather.[55]

Each side created powerful legal teams. Onassis's and Saudi Arabia's was led by Professor Myres McDougal of Yale Law School, a famous academic, and the

---

[52] Fraser et al., *Aristotle Onassis*, 135.
[53] "Royal Government of Saudi Arabia. Memorial," Exhibit 5, Onassis Archive, Alexander S. Onassis Foundation.
[54] Schwebel, "The Kingdom of Saudi Arabia," 2–12.
[55] "The Answering Memorial and the Exhibits," in "Royal Government of Saudi Arabia. Memorial," Onassis Archive, Alexander S. Onassis Foundation.

Aramco team by Lord McNair, a recently retired President of the International Court of Justice.[56] During the arbitration process, as the parties would not agree to the questions put in the Tribunal, each one crafted its own questions. The Saudi Arabian government asked about Aramco's right of transportation by sea of oil, and whether it had the right to refuse preferential treatment to tankers flying the Saudi Arabian flag (as requested by the Saudi Arabian government). Aramco asked whether the Onassis agreement was in conflict with the Aramco agreement.

In order to write the memorial for the arbitration for Onassis-Saudi Arabian government, the Onassis legal team met in the hotel Ambassadeur in Cairo, where they were joined by Onassis; this was a top-secret job and the meetings were to be entirely discreet. The difficulty of communication is vividly portrayed by Alexandra Papadimitriou's personal testimony. The posh English accent of the British lawyers and the Americans' rougher, flatter accents were not understood by the Egyptian lawyers, who tried desperately to follow. Equally, the Western lawyers could not understand the Egyptians' Anglo-Egyptian accent and just "moved their heads all the time mumbling 'hear, hear.'" Alexandra, along with her lawyer husband Stelio, acted as both interpreter and ad hoc secretary. Fortunately, she happened to have many skills. An English teacher by profession, she also knew Arabic and French, had a certificate in stenography, and knew how to type. An external secretary was out of the question; the meetings were far too secret and sensitive for that. During noon and evening breaks, Alexandra wrote the Anglo-Arabic dialogues in English to be distributed at the beginning of every meeting.[57]

According to Judge Stephen M. Schwebel, who took part in this arbitration, the Onassis case was "one of the most significant arbitrations of the 20th century."[58] The decision came out in 1958 in favor of Aramco, as expected. The crux of the matter for the Tribunal was whether Aramco could be forced to carry the oil it produced on tankers it could not choose. The Concession Agreement of Aramco had given it the exclusive right to sell oil, which excluded the competition of other persons. Certainly, in the agreement, land and sea transport was included. By replying to the legality of Onassis's contract, it said that, "when one party has granted certain rights to the other contracting party, it can no longer dispose of the same rights, totally or partially, in favour of another party."[59] It is interesting to note that in 1973, only twenty years after the concession was signed, the Saudi Arabian government asked Aramco to sell and transfer its interests to the government, which it did over a certain period. As Schwebel wrote, "the Onassis Award stands as one of the earliest, most searching and substantial – and uncompromising – of

[56] Lord McNair said this. Schwebel, "The Kingdom of Saudi Arabia."
[57] Papadimitriou, *Jeddah*, 55.   [58] Schwebel, "The Kingdom of Saudi Arabia."
[59] Ibid.

the arbitral awards passing upon the regime of oil concessions." It was all about oil and politics, the exercise of sovereignty, the rights granted by the government, and the regulatory powers of one weak and one powerful government.

Conclusions

In the immediate post–World War II era, Onassis was among the prime movers forming the global shipping business. He was able to exploit opportunities offered by the outcome of the massive US shipbuilding programs during World War II, and the spectacular rise of the oil trade. Greek shipowners were able to exploit these opportunities better than did their main competitors, the Norwegians, who were handicapped by their state's decision to prohibit purchase of foreign vessels. The Greeks engaged with the US, the world's new economic power, as their main trading partners, as they had done with Great Britain in an earlier period. This was the advantage of cross-traders and of tramp owners: by serving international trade rather than the needs of a particular nation, they were able to adjust to changes in the world environment.

The other reasons for Onassis's entrepreneurial success are endogenous. They include his ability to recognize opportunities and his ability to assemble resources to exploit these opportunities. He was thus able to grab the opportunities given by purchases of secondhand war-built vessels that belonged to the United States Maritime Commission. He was able to turn to the US shipyards that were left redundant after the end of the war. The German shipyards were completely destroyed and Onassis was the first to be able to revitalize them, along with those of France. He gathered financial resources from the National City Bank of New York, Chase Manhattan, and Metropolitan Life Insurance, which he persuaded to finance his shipping projects, while US and European oil companies provided him with charter parties for yet unbuilt ships. In the 1960s to the early 1970s, the fleet constructed in the previous couple of decades continued to operate with the same partners: US finance and oil companies. In the meantime, Onassis was building new tankers in the new Japanese shipyards, but he also remained faithful to French and British yards.

He exploited opportunities and experimented in every sector of shipping: dry cargo, tanker shipping, tramp shipping, liner shipping, coastal shipping, secondhand ships, newly built ships, and small, medium, and gigantic ships. Building his success took thirty years, from the 1920s to the 1950s, a period of trial and error and fierce competition in all the business and political environments in which he was active. Onassis did experience a number of failures, notably with a liner company in the Pacific and with whaling; most important, he ran into serious trouble with the oil industry via his provocative Saudi Arabian agreement, which brought him into direct confrontation with oil majors. He tried to invest in a huge oil refinery in Greece, known as Omega project, during the period of Greek dictatorship but he withdrew from the project, not having reached agreement with the Greek junta. He had also invested in the Harland and Wolff shipyards in Ireland, which he was not able to purchase as he wanted in the 1970s. On the other hand, he was terribly successful in building an international airline, Olympic Airways, and from 1956 to his death turned it into a major international airline that flew around the world. Building one of the largest tanker fleets in the world was not easy or always successful; it took him much trial and error, and constant confrontation with local elites, governments, and global interests.

8

The United States Government *v.* Aristotle Onassis, 1951–1958

Exactly seventy years after Mari Vagliano was accused of conspiracy to defraud the Imperial Russian state, Aristotle Onassis was accused of conspiracy to defraud the US government. It was Friday February 5, 1954. Aristotle Onassis was having lunch at the fashionable Colony Restaurant in New York when a marshal went to his offices with a warrant to arrest him. Three days later, Onassis flew with his lawyer Edward J. Ross and other legal advisors to Washington, where he "voluntarily appeared in the United States District Court for the District of Columbia, at which time he was arraigned and entered a plea of not guilty. He paid 10,000 US dollars and left the court-room."[1] The conflict was related to the purchases of US ships built during the war, particularly tankers that he was able to purchase by forming US shipping companies, which he controlled; such ships could only be bought by US citizens.

Like Vagliano, Onassis faced both civil and criminal charges, and like Vagliano he was able to win his case. In both cases, the litigation was not just personal; as in Russia, when a whole group of Greek merchants was accused, in the US version the government indicted a whole group of prominent Greek shipowners. In the mid-1880s, the legal case of the Taganrog Customs was one of the largest ever judged in the annals of the Russian courts.[2] In the mid-1950s, according to George Cochran Doub, Assistant Attorney General of the Civil Division of the United States Department of Justice, the Aristotle Onassis litigation "was one of the most extensive litigations ever conducted by the Department of Justice . . . in spite of many doubts as to the validity of the legal position of the Government."[3] Contrary to Mari Vagliano, however, Aristotle

---

[1] FBI, "Aristotle Onassis," part 3, Bufile 46-17783, From Warren Olney III, Assistant Attorney General, Criminal Division, to Director, FBI, "Victory Carriers Inc. et al." (March 1, 1954).

[2] According to Anatolii Feodorovich Koni, the Attorney General in the Russian Ministry of Justice, "Анатолий Федорович Кони" ["Anatolii Feodorovic Koni"], available at www.pravoteka.ru/lib/raznoe/0002 (accessed December 18, 2008).

[3] Statement of George Cochran Doub, Assistant Attorney General, Civil Division, Department of Justice, *Study of the Trade-Out and Build Activities of Onassis Companies*, 270.

Onassis was never taken to court, because, despite the extended and exhaustive investigation, the charges against him could not be proved. Therefore, the US government could not even take his case to court, let alone win it.

Both cases stemmed from political decisions. They are prime examples of powerful governments accusing foreign entrepreneurial elites of fraud and corruption in order to fulfill short-term political goals. Foreign entrepreneurs were useful as scapegoats to defuse internal political and economic problems – a recurring story in international business. Mari Vagliano in the 1880s became an improbably unpopular figure, making headlines in mainstream Russian newspapers because of a case that involved a much larger number of other powerful merchants and shipowners. In the same way, Onassis became the protagonist in the US media in a "conspiracy to defraud the United States," when a larger number of powerful Greek shipowners were equally involved.

The shipping business has always been an international business par excellence. The path to its globalization was opened by businessmen like the Vaglianos and Onassis, and was a dialectic path, a process through conflicts. The process of internationalization-globalization was both threatening and useful to the states it served.

Why Were Aristotle Onassis and Mari Vagliano Accused?

The stories of Aristotle Onassis and Mari Vagliano demonstrate the ability of foreign entrepreneurs to confront governments through official and unofficial institutions they relied on, or had created through local, national, and international networks. Comparing the two cases is enlightening: both of these international businessmen had to pass a variety of hurdles on their way to revolutionizing the global shipping business. The comparison reveals their ability to coordinate resources, identify opportunities, and overcome obstacles and conflicts on a national and international level.

The similarities between the two cases reveal important answers to some of the main questions raised in this book. First, why were these foreign capitalists so useful to the Russian and US governments? The answer is almost identical for both cases. In both nineteenth-century Imperial Russia and the twentieth-century United States, Greek businessmen engaged in the external trade of each country and served their interests by providing low-cost trading and transport services. In nineteenth-century Russia, these cosmopolitan businessmen operated on the frontier of an expanding empire and proved pivotal for the internationalization and integration of the area in the global market.[4] They had the ships and the contacts. Greek exporters were the largest in south Russian port cities, and were valuable for Russia's economy.

---

[4] Harlaftis, *A History of Greek-Owned Shipping*, chapters 1–3.

Greeks also served the United States well in the 1940s and 1950s. They were willing and able to become the main owners of fleets, under flags of convenience, that provided low-cost transport services for both dry cargoes and oil. In this way, the shift of political power and influence from Britain to the United States after 1945 ushered in a new era not only in Greek, but also in world shipping. Flags of convenience became the key manifestation of US postwar shipping policy; they guaranteed low-cost, US-controlled shipping in a new global era. In this way Greek shipowners who operated and owned such fleets served the interests of the United States very well. Not only did they purchase US ships of obsolete technology, and carried US cargoes in low-cost vessels, they were also ordering new ships from US shipyards that had been left redundant after the war.

Second, if Greeks served the interests of Russia and the United States well, why were leading members of their business communities sued? In both cases we find similar patterns; the causes were both political and economic. Both Vagliano and Onassis were accused in times when the national governments felt that these foreign businessmen no longer served their host country, but rather harmed it with their actions. In both cases, the accusations took place at a time of political change towards more conservative governments. Vagliano was accused a few months after Tsar Alexander III, a much more conservative autocrat than his liberal father Alexander II, came to power. In the case of Onassis, investigation into his business took place a few months before the Republicans took power from the Democrats in 1952, and accusations were presented to him two years later. It was also clear that the MARCOM ship sales to foreigners were used to embarrass the Truman administration in the presidential campaign of 1952. In Russia, the Vagliano case signaled a resurgent xenophobic nationalism, characterized by a desire for ethnic purification and the assimilation of minorities. The anticommunist hysteria of the McCarthy era, aided and abetted by a large number of Congressman and the "Tsar" of US espionage, J. Edgar Hoover, demonstrated perhaps a similar xenophobia and mistrust of aliens.

If Hoover and conservative Americans feared and hated the Russians in the 1950s, so were the Russians, seventy years before, deeply mistrustful of "Westerners." The trial of an international entrepreneur like Mari Vagliano, and his "British" multinational trading company, triggered polemical rhetoric on the national question and the division between Westernizers and Slavophiles. Mari Vagliano became the archetype of the western European capitalist: an incredibly rich person who could not but be corrupt.

Moreover, it is important to remember that in both cases the governments did not just attack specific individuals. They aimed at the business community that Vagliano and Onassis represented. In particular, they both targeted Greek businessmen involved in trade and shipping, and any punishment Vagliano and Onassis received was to be a lesson and warning for the rest, suspected as they were of various illegalities and general corruption. For Hoover, Onassis had to be taught a lesson: he and his extended Greek shipping family, as the FBI chief thought of it, were trading behind the "Iron Curtain" using US-built vessels.[5]

The economic reasons behind this attack were equally important. In both our cases, there had been pressures from national economic groups. In the case of Russia the attack against the Greeks, who were central in the external grain trade and shipping of the country, came during the deep economic crisis of the 1880s and burgeoning competition between Russian merchants in Moscow and foreign merchants. The Russian merchants had been appealing for government protection against their more enterprising ethnic and foreign rivals since the time of Alexander II. Erecting tariff walls and abolishing free ports and transit rights remained the merchantry's first and main line of defense.[6] Appeal for protection was not only a demand of the Russian merchants, but also of the industrialists; we have to take into consideration that this was the time of the industrialization of Russia and protectionism affected local production as well. The case of the trial of the Taganrog port Customs, with Vagliano as protagonist, might have been a case of making him a scapegoat, to absorb the dissatisfaction of all those who did not wish to see the profits of the external trade of the country in the hands of foreigners.

In the case of Onassis, it is true that US shipowners and seamen were not happy at all with the Greek penetration of their business. Between 1946 and 1949, the Greeks had acquired more than 400 Liberty ships from the Maritime Commission, apart from the tankers. There were protests and pressures against Greek shipowners in the US press:

> While the United States has poured several billion dollars into Greece to prevent that country from going communist a little group of Greek shipping men have put across the type of high finance that helps inspire communism . . . and now control a large part of the world's shipping.[7]

Most of the acquired ships were put under flags of convenience, particularly Panamanian flags, and there was a worldwide boycott against them by US and European seamen during 1947–1948.[8] In fact, US maritime unions had been in conflict with Greek shipowners, who seemed in their minds to be taking over external sea trade, going back to 1946.

[5] FBI, "Aristotle Onassis," part 1, Bufile 1100-125834, Department of Justice, Memorandum for Mr J. Edgar Hoover, Director FBI by Warren Burger, Assistant Attorney General (February 4, 1953).
[6] Rieber, *Merchants*, 115–116.
[7] Drew Pearson, "Greek Ship Empire Traced," *The Washington Post (1877–1954)*, May 16, 1951.
[8] Harlaftis, "Greek Shipowners and State Intervention."

The US Maritime Commission administrators with shipping backgrounds, like Clarence Morse, were allowing US ships to be transferred to flags of convenience during "times when there was no national emergency." In fact, they encouraged it: administrators admitted later that their approval of such transfers was largely a matter of profit. As Congressional testimony later revealed,

> it is obvious that since 1954 the Maritime Administration has been actually encouraging the transfer of American-flag ships to the runaway flags. In August 1954, they had initiated a new liberalized transfer foreign program, which in 4 months permitted 69 dry-cargo tramp Liberty ships to transfer to the runaway flag. This was ... to be a bargain-basement dealing which was indeed shameful.[9]

Powerful US shipowners like Daniel Ludwig, the so-called invisible billionaire, must have also played their part in the indictment of the top Greek entrepreneurs.[10] His company, National Bulk Carriers, the largest US shipping company, was a primary competitor to the Greeks, building new tankers in lockstep with them.[11] There was growing unrest and dissatisfaction from the US business community towards the Greeks, which reinforced the political decision to attack when the question of the "Red trade" came up. Ultimately, as Rodney Carlisle suggests, the Greeks were scapegoats. The government indicted them to satisfy various domestic maritime interests, particularly those devastated by low freight rates. The case provided an outlet for the anger of these constituencies during the turbulent political and economic climate following the Korean War.[12]

US Government versus Greek Shipowners

It all started in early 1950 when CIA agents, backed by photographic evidence, informed the Departments of Commerce and Justice (which in turn notified the FBI) that New York-based Greek shipping tycoons were carrying cargoes

---

[9] "Study of Vessel Transfer, Trade-In and Reserve Fleet Policies," *Study of the Trade-Out and Build Activities of Onassis Companies, Hearing before the Special Subcommittee of the Committee on Merchant Marine and Fisheries House of Representatives, Eighty-Fifth Congress, second edition, June 17, 18, 19, 24, July 8,15, 22, August 13 and 15, 1958* (Washington, DC: United States Government Printing Office, 1958), 700.

[10] Jerry Shields, *The Invisible Billionaire: Daniel Ludwig* (Boston: Houghton Mifflin, 1986). Ludwig was among the ten wealthiest American millionaires. See "List of 76 Said to Hold Above 75 Millions," *New York Times (1857–Current file)*, October 28, 1957. On the building of Ludwig's tankers, Arthur H. Richter, "Largest Tanker to Be Launched," *New York Times*, December 5, 1958.

[11] Drew Pearson, "Greeks Grow Rich with U.S. Ships," *The Washington Post*, March 27, 1953.

[12] Carlisle, *Sovereignty for Sale*.

on US-built ships not only for the United States and its allies, but also for its enemies, North Korea and China.[13] Four phases can be distinguished in all the cases of the US government versus Greek shipowners. The FBI launched its investigation during the first phase, in 1951–1952. During the second phase, from 1952 to 1954, aggressive government tactics resulted in ship forfeitures and arrest warrants. From 1954 to 1956, the third phase, Greek shipowners took part in lengthy negotiations, reaching final settlements with the government. In the fourth phase when the case of Onassis was raised again by the Justice Department, further investigations and hearings took place, but the whole thing petered out by 1959.

Investigation, 1951–1952

During the Korean War (1950–1953), freight rates skyrocketed as demand for supplies reached extraordinary heights. Wars are extremely profitable times for international shipping,[14] and Greek shipowners made their tonnage available to whomever gave the best freight rates. If it was the "Reds," then so be it. At the height of McCarthyism this was not to be tolerated.[15] What was worse was that attention was brought to the fact that Greeks had purchased US ships from the United States Maritime Commission using US companies that were not really American, but were controlled by Greeks. This potential fraud initiated investigations and hearings focusing on Aristotle Onassis, his father-in-law Stavros Livanos, his brother-in-law Stavros Niarchos, the President of the Greek Shipowners' New York Committee, Manuel Kulukundis, and the companies of the shipowners Pericles Kallimanopoulos and Los-Pezas.

The irony was that neither Onassis nor Niarchos had been trading with communist nations. Photographs of the ships taken by the Navy during the later part of 1952 indicated that it was Stavros Livanos, their father-in-law, that did so, as well as the Kulukundis group of companies. It might be worth noting that British ships were also trading with China but, of course, British shipowners were not residing in the United States as the abovementioned Greeks did.

The investigation into the surplus war vessels commenced in April 1951, and the General Accounting Office began an inquiry into the circumstances

---

[13] Ibid. In fact, it was not Onassis who was involved in the "red" trade but rather his father-in-law, Stavros Livanos. See Arthur H. Richter, "Livanos Predicts Shipping Revival," *New York Times*, March 21, 1954.

[14] Harlaftis, *Greek Shipowners and Greece*, Figure 7.2, 142.

[15] FBI, "Aristotle Onassis," part 1, Bufile 1100-125834, Department of Justice, Memorandum for Mr J. Edgar Hoover, Director FBI by Warren Burger, Assistant Attorney General (February 4, 1953).

relating to the sale, chartering, and resale of government-owned surplus tanker vessels.[16] During the period of investigations, Greek shipowners attracted significant negative publicity in the US press. Joseph McCarthy launched demagogic warnings, as described by a group of British journalists in Onassis's biography: "At least 96 ships which the US had sold to foreigners were engaged in a 'blood trade' carrying strategic material to the Iron Curtain, where it was being used to 'kill Yanks in Korea.'"[17] Stavros Livanos was trading with Communist China with Greek-flag Liberty ships purchased with the guarantee of the Greek state.[18] It was reported that Livanos met Hoover and promised to end this trade, and hence was left alone.[19]

The US companies controlled by Onassis were one of the immediate targets of the FBI. A team of FBI investigators thumbed through Onassis's records in the offices of his US companies looking for evidence of foreign control. The investigation was thorough: besides going through all the company books, they investigated and interviewed everyone who handled the purchases of the vessels, the stockholders and the Board of Directors of his US companies, the agencies with which they worked, the suppliers, the captains of the ships, the bankers, and the shipbrokers. In June 1951, the FBI forwarded reports on Onassis and the other Greeks stemming from this investigation to the Department of Justice; they detailed the activities of numerous companies which had purchased and chartered surplus tankers, for possible violations of various provisions of the shipping laws requiring US citizenship and other statutes relating to false statements. The investigation was so extensive that, as the eloquent Onassis put it later, when addressing a Congressional committee: "Excuse me for the parable, Mr. Chairman, I have even to go to state whether my grandmother knew how to swim or not."[20]

---

[16] FBI, "Aristotle Onassis," part 2, Bufile 46-17783, "Fraud against the Government," New York Office 46-2507 report (May 10, 1952).

[17] Fraser et al., *Aristotle Onassis*, 108.

[18] According to Drew Pearson, "At least 28 of Livanos' American-bought ships have been spotted entering or leaving Communist ports." "Greeks Grow Rich with U.S. Ships," *The Washington Post*, March 27, 1953. See also Drew Pearson, "McCarthy Charge Boomerangs," *The Washington Post and Times Herald*, July 18, 1954; "Red Cargoes Reported Few," *New York Times*, March 30, 1953. Stavros Livanos and Manuel Kulukundis reached an agreement with McCarthy to stop "trading with the Reds"; see "Greek Ship Owners to Stop Red Trade," special to *The New York Times*, March 29, 1953; Edward F. Ryan, "Greek Owners of 242 Ships Bar Red Trade," *The Washington Post*, March 29, 1953.

[19] For example, in a very eloquent article Stavros Livanos is described as "the antithesis of the popular conception of a multi-millionaire shipping tycoon": a man who was not glamorous at all and who "received the 'attention' of Joseph R. McCarthy and came through unscathed." See Richter, "Livanos Predicts Shipping Revival?" See also Drew Pearson, "McCarthy Urged to Push Probe," *The Washington Post*, April 7, 1953; "Five Are Indicted in Cargo Ship Sales," *The Washington Post*, December 23, 1953.

[20] *Study of the Trade-Out and Build Activities of Onassis Companies*, 175.

On April 17, 1952 James M. McInerney, Assistant Attorney General of the Criminal Division, sent a memorandum to Hoover requesting that further investigation be conducted into the activities of the United States Petroleum Carriers Inc. and subsidiary companies. It set forth seventy-seven different questions (so-called items in the FBI reports) to be covered. Within a month, an interim report of 190 pages was submitted recommending that the Department of Justice take prompt action.[21] It concluded that United States Petroleum Carriers Inc., Western Tankers Inc., and Trafalgar Steamship Corporation, although ostensibly US-citizen corporations, were in fact controlled by foreigners, particularly Aristotle S. Onassis, and therefore were not citizens within the meaning of the shipping laws. Their acquisition and operation of twenty-three US-flag vessels was deemed to be in violation of the shipping laws, thus subjecting the vessels to forfeiture by the United States (see Appendix 2.C).[22] Similar conclusions were drawn regarding the Niarchos group of companies, the Kulukundis group of companies, the Los-Pezas group of companies, the Kallimanopoulos group of companies, and the so-called Chinese group of companies.[23]

The report concluded that ships nominally owned by the companies North American Shipping & Trading Co. Inc., American Pacific Steamship Co. Inc., Ventura Steamships Corp., and Delaware Tanker Corp. were actually controlled by Stavros Niarchos (see Appendix 2.C). In fact, the latter company had purchased the stock of American Overseas Tanker Corp., which owned five Panamanian tankers purchased from the Maritime Commission and was headed by former Congressman Joseph Casey.[24] Equally, for the Kulukundis group, the US corporations that owned war-built ships were Seatrade Corp., Seatrade Corporation of Delaware, Aegean Marine Corp., Tramp Shipping & Oil Transportation Corp., Philadelphia Marine Corp., Potrero Corp., Cienega Tanker Corp., and Veritas Steamship Co. Inc. (Appendix 2.C). The report reached similar conclusions for the Los-Pezas and Kallimanopoulos group (Appendix 2.C).

The whole question of the surplus ship sales was formally opened on March 1952, when a Subcommittee of the Senate Committee on Government

---

[21] FBI, "Aristotle Onassis," part 2, Bufile 46-17783, 'Fraud against the Government'," New York Office 46-2507 report (May 10, 1952).

[22] See FBI, "Aristotle Onassis," part 3, Bufile 46-17783, Office Memorandum from Warren Olney III, Assistant Attorney General, Criminal Division to the Director of FBI, subject "United States v. Onassis et al." (December 28, 1955).

[23] Herbert Brownell Jr. in *Study of the Trade-Out and Build Activities of Onassis Companies*, 315.

[24] *Current Merchant Marine Problems, Hearings before the Committee on Merchant Marine and Fisheries, House of Representatives, Eighty-Fifth Congress, First Session, February 6 and 7, 1957* (Washington, DC: United States Government Printing Office, 1957), 204–205, 394.

Table 8.1 *Forfeitures of US flag ships suspected of being owned by non-US companies*

Shipowning group	Number of ships to be seized	Ships seized
Kulukundis	31	6
Onassis	23	17
Niarchos	20	20
Chinese	6	5
Los-Pezas	5	1
Kallimanopoulos (Drytrans Inc., and Transfuel Corp.	5	0
Total	90	49

Source: Appendix 2.C.

Operations (SSCGO) was formed, whose members included Senators Joseph McCarthy, Karl Mundt, and Richard Nixon. This was of course in part an inside political game, parallel to the Justice Department's investigation, which was part of broader efforts by the Republican majority in Congress to embarrass the Democratic Truman administration via a flood of Congressional investigations. Numerous Republican charges of corruption in Truman's administration were linked to certain members of Truman's cabinet and senior White House staff. It was also a central issue in the 1952 presidential campaign, which Republicans won after almost twenty years of Democratic dominance of the White House. Dwight D. Eisenhower succeeded Truman in January 1953, with a mandate to fight corruption.[25]

Aggression, 1953–1954

The new administration drew up plans to force Greek shipowners to comply with US policy. Ninety ships (T2 tankers and Liberties), eighty-six of which were Greek-owned under US flags, were targeted for forfeiture (see Table 8.1). Out of these, thirty-one ships belonged to the Kulukundis group of companies, twenty-three to Onassis's companies, twenty to the Niarchos group, five to the Los-Pezas group, and five to the Kallimanopoulos group (see Appendix 2.C).[26]

---

[25] Robert J. Donovan, *Conflict and Crisis: The Presidency of Harry Truman, 1945–1948* (Columbia: University of Missouri Press, 1996).

[26] For Pericles Callimanopoulos, owner of Hellenic Lines as owner of Drytrans and Transfuel see Georgios M. Foustanos, *Hellenic Lines, όραμα δίχως τέλος* (Syros: Argo Publishing, 2010), 56. For the "Chinese group" see *Current Merchant Marine Problems, Hearings before the Committee on Merchant Marine and Fisheries, House of Representatives,*

From February 1953 onwards the US government proceeded to forfeitures, before any civil litigation against any shipowner or shipping company took place. Ships were seized by US Customs officials each time they docked in a US port. The first forfeiture case was that of Niarchos's tanker *Monitor* on February 16, 1953, and the first Onassis tanker to be seized was *Lake George* on March 24, 1953. Over the course of the next two years, a total of forty-nine ships that approached US ports were actually forfeited. Out of these, twenty belonged to Niarchos, seventeen to Onassis, six to Kulukundis, five to the Chinese, and one to Los-Pezas (Table 8.1).

Forty-nine of these forfeitures were proved illegal by the US courts, but it was clear that the pretext for all of them was political. The justification for the forfeitures was that these ships were trading with the communist bloc, but most weren't; it was a smokescreen for xenophobic nationalism. The US government was really seizing the ships it suspected of belonging to non-citizens, but it had not really proved it; and, as was found out, it could not legally do it. And ultimately the forfeitures did not harm Onassis or the other shipowners. The ships when seized were not laid up; they continued to trade but the earnings went into a special account and were eventually returned to the shipowners. In effect, the government was operating the ships of those it sued.

The action against the shipowners was monitored by the Department of Justice. Herbert Brownell Jr. was the Attorney General responsible for both the Civil and Criminal Divisions, and signed all the forfeitures and indictments. He commenced litigations along two tracks. The first was a civil case that concerned the forfeitures of the US flag ships that belonged to US companies suspected of being controlled by aliens; shipowners would have to pay fines if taken to court. The second was a criminal case: "a conspiracy to defraud the American government," something much more serious as it involved arrest and imprisonment. The civil litigation against the Onassis's interests proceeded through the seizure of his vessels in US ports. By October 1953 a criminal indictment and a warrant for arrest was issued against Onassis, and was sealed by court order, in anticipation of his return to the United States.[27]

The sealed indictment against Onassis, eight other individuals, and six corporations, concerned violations of the False Statements Statute. It alleged fraudulent purchases of twenty-three surplus tankers from the US Maritime

---

Eighty-Fifth Congress, First Session, February 6 and 7, 1957 (Washington, DC: United States Government Printing Office, 1957), 186–187.

[27] FBI, "Aristotle Onassis," part 3, Bufile 46-17783, Office Memorandum from C. A. Evans to Rosen, "North American Shipping and Trading, Inc., et al., Fraud against the Government" (February 8, 1954).

Commission by the Onassis-controlled US corporations, financed by US funds.[28] Along with Onassis, the accused included the officers of his US shipping companies Robert Berenson, Nicolas Cokkinis, George Cokkinis, and Harold O. Becker; the US Congressman Joseph E. Casey; the lawyers Robert W. Dudley and Joseph H. Rosenbaum of the Washington Attorney Office of Goodwin, Rosenbaum and Meacham; Charles Aughenthaler of Simpson Spence Young, New York, the chartering and financial agent for Onassis. The above were charged individually with conspiracy to defraud the US government in the purchase of surplus government-owned vessels.[29] Along with them, some of his US corporations were accused, like United States Petroleum Carriers, Inc., and some of his Panamanian ones, like Sociedad Industrial Maritima Financiera Ariona Panama. It is interesting to note that among the accused were US politicians, lawyers, shipbrokers, and shipowners, but no US bankers or oil company men.[30]

On December 22, 1953, Manuel Kulukundis and his brothers were indicted on charges of conspiracy to defraud the US government.[31] Stavros Niarchos's indictment followed. Niarchos, knowing about his indictment in advance, avoided entering the United States; his close collaborator Walter H. Saunders Jr. handled his case with the US authorities and reached a settlement agreement. Onassis also knew about the indictment, but voluntarily went through the confrontation himself, flying to New York on February 1, 1954. However, before arriving in New York and turning himself in, he had prepared a game of global chess with the United States.

He carefully moved his pawns by proceeding with three strategic moves while being investigated. The first was aimed at US maritime policymakers, which needed not only US flag ships but also US shipyards to keep going. He gave them a blow by turning his back on the US shipyards where he had already built seven tankers between 1948 and 1950, providing work for the Bethlehem Sparrows Point Shipyard in Sparrows Point, an activity much advertised by US newspapers.[32] In April 1951, when US investigators were

---

[28] Ibid. (February 2, 1954).
[29] FBI, "Aristotle Onassis," part 3, Bufile 46-17783, United States District Court for the District of Columbia. Holding a Criminal Term (Grand Jury Impaneled on September 2, 1952), "The Grand Jury Charges."
[30] *United States v. Onassis*, 125 F. Supp. 190 (D.D.C. 1954), US District Court for the District of Columbia-125 F. Supp. 190 (D.D.C. 1954), September 9, 1954, http://law.justia.com/cases/federal/district-courts/FSupp/125/190/1410674/ (accessed March 2, 2016).
[31] See "Ship Sales Fraud Charged to Five," special to the *New York Times*, December 23, 1953; "Greek Shipowners Indicted for Fraud in Ship Purchases," *The Washington Post*, January 5, 1954.
[32] See repeated reports of American shipyards building tankers, "New Tanker Sails On Maiden Voyage," *New York Times*, November 21, 1948; "New Supertanker Set for

going through his companies' books, Onassis went to Germany and France and launched an unprecedented shipbuilding program (see Chapter 7).

He also physically turned his back on the United States, as it were. He moved his family from New York to Paris and Cannes and, by early 1953, he found his perfect European domicile, Monte Carlo in Monaco. In setting up his main business in Monaco, Onassis also achieved something else: "he also got himself catapulted overnight into being a world-renowned celebrity."[33] For the next twenty years, until his death, Monte Carlo became the center of his business affairs. In addition to glamor, great publicity provided him with a shield against US government actions and an alliance not only with a western European state but also with the European financial and political elite.

The third move was his entry into the Middle East, a strategic shot aimed at US oil business interests in the region. Indicted in October 1953, Onassis knew that US officials were waiting for him to return to present it to him officially. Cycling between Paris and Monte Carlo, he prepared the Saudi agreement during this uncertain time, with the help of Spyros Catopodis, an Ithacan and schoolmate of his close collaborator Costas Gratsos; it was signed on January 20, 1954, alongside the Saudi Minister of Finance Abdullah bin Suleiman Al-Hamdan and with the full consent of King Saud. According to the agreement, which would come into effect on April 9, 1954, Onassis obtained the right to carry all Aramco oil in excess of that carried by Aramco's own tankers (which carried about 10–20 percent of the total production). The agreement would prohibit the shipment of oil in chartered tankers of other nations.[34]

Although this was a business agreement first and foremost, Onassis also meant it to be perceived as a threat and a counterattack to the US government. It certainly succeeded in this. As already mentioned in the previous chapter, the agreement undermined the agreement of Aramco (Arabian-American Oil Company, the consortium of Standard Oil of New Jersey, Standard Oil of California, Texas Company, and Socony-Vacuum) with Saudi Arabia, which had promised the US consortium a monopoly on mining, refining, and distribution of oil until the end of the century.[35] Moreover, under the Cold War logic, things were perceived to be even worse. According to an FBI report

Launching," *New York Times*, February 23, 1950; "Last Supertanker in Group Launched," special to the *New York Times*, February 25, 1950.

[33] Maxwell Hamilton, "The Man who Bought the Bank at Monte Carlo," *True: The Man's Magazine* (December 1954): 17–20, 83–86.

[34] "Royal Government of Saudi Arabia. Memorial," Alexander S. Onassis Foundation, Onassis Archive, the Government of Saudi Arabia and the Arabian American Oil Company.

[35] FBI, "Aristotle Onassis," part 4, Bufile 46-17783, Office Memorandum from a. H. Belmont to L. V. Boardman, "Visit to Middle East and North Africa by Bureau's Army Liaison Representative" (June 16, 1954). The Court at The Hague finally passed an agreement in 1958 in favor of Aramco.

analyzing the situation, "diversion of such oil to Soviet bloc interests, either for their use or for resale with the ruble as the monetary unit, would completely offset world trade, as well as increase the possibility of precipitating a conflict."[36]

After Onassis carried out his three strategic moves, he decided to return to the United States and voluntarily submit himself to the US Justice Department in February 1954.

Negotiations and Settlement, 1955-1956

At this stage, however, the US government was ready to reach a settlement with the Greeks. For starters it was evident that if they took the case to court they could not win. The main case against individuals like Onassis was that they had defrauded the US government by forming US companies illegally controlled by foreigners. But here the Justice Department started encountering difficulties.

First, it was inherently difficult to define in legal terms what constituted "control" of a corporation, as the question of "controlling interest" by US citizens in the Merchant Ship Sales Act was quite problematic.[37] The issue of controlling interest, as described in law, was too vague, and thus presented government officials, and judges, with a problem right at the outset. As Onassis's US companies were formed according to all legal formalities, "alien control" became extremely difficult to prove, and there was no certainty what the outcome would be at trial.[38]

Secondly, the Maritime Administration had unloaded many of its surplus ships to foreign-controlled corporations or individual foreign owners. The case of Joseph Edward Casey was only one of those that raised questions. Casey was a lawyer and a Democratic Congressman from Massachusetts from 1935 to 1943. In 1947, he formed shipping companies and purchased eight tankers from the Maritime Commission; he eventually sold three of these to US companies that, as emerged later, were controlled by Chinese interests. He was also permitted by the Maritime Commission to transfer the other five to the Panamanian flag; he then sold them in 1950 to the Stavros Niarchos group of companies.[39]

---

[36] FBI, "Aristotle Onassis," part 4, Bufile 46-17783, Office Memorandum from A. H. Belmont to L. V. Boardman, "Visit to Middle East and North Africa by Bureau's Army Liaison Representative" (June 16, 1954).

[37] FBI, "Aristotle Onassis," part 2, Bufile 46-17783, Allen J. Krouse to Fred E. Strine, Administrative Regulations Section, "U.S. Petroleum Carriers, Inc." (October 31, 1951).

[38] *Study of the Trade-Out and Build Activities of Onassis Companies*, 321.

[39] "The Career of Stavros Niarchos", Ναυτικά Χρονικά [*Nautica Chronika*], April 15, 1952. This article was written after an article on Stavros Niarchos published in *Business Week*.

Furthermore, whether legally or illegally (depending on one's interpretation of the statute), MARCOM had sold more than 400 wartime ships to Greeks. The big Greek company Orion, led by Peter Goulandris's sons, had bought thirty-eight vessels (both cargo vessels and tankers). Orion was never indicted; it had, not coincidentally, chartered its vessels to the US Navy. After all, MARCOM administrators like its Chairman, Clarence G. Morse, came from shipping backgrounds, and wanted to sell as many ships as they could to replace the enormous number of obsolete US ships with new and modern vessels built in US shipyards. In the hearings of the eighty-fifth Congress in 1958, when Congressman Zelenko reopened the Onassis case, these clashes of interests between US maritime administrators and politicians became evident.[40]

Third, and most important, the Justice Department could not proceed without revealing the secrets of the US bankers and oil companies that had backed Onassis and the others. It was Aristotle Onassis in person who conducted all the negotiations, both with the National City Bank of New York and Metropolitan Life, and with the oil companies. The credit agreements for the twenty-three vessels in question, their first preferred mortgages, along with those of the Metropolitan Life Insurance Company, all had the signature of Aristotle Onassis and his personal guarantee at the end of the fat volume of about 200 pages of the loan agreement. It was stated clearly: "Agreement made by and between A. S. Onassis (hereinafter called the 'Guarantor') and The First National City Bank of New York as Trustee (hereinafter called the 'Trading Trustee') under an Indenture dated as of June 1948, as amended and supplemented." The five pages of the document called "Guaranty Agreement" were also signed and sealed by "A. S. Onassis" in person.[41] The credit agreements were amended and supplemented as Aristotle Onassis's group accumulated further finance from City Bank and Met Life throughout the early 1950s for purchases of ships (including newly built ships) in German and French shipyards. Remember, too, that loans from the US financial institutions were given on the guarantee of the time charters of the US oil companies. In the same loan agreement volume, alongside the Onassis documents, were the "tanker voyage charter parties" of the companies that purchased for Socony Vacuum Oil Company, Tidewater, and Gulf Oil Corporation. Bankers and CEOs of the oil companies knew very well what vessels they financed or chartered and who were the owners of these vessels.

[40] *Study of the Trade-Out and Build Activities of Onassis Companies*, 2–75, 516.
[41] Onassis Archive, Alexander S. Onassis Foundation, Minutes of Board of Directors of Montserrado Panama SA, "Credit Agreement between Olympic Trading Corporation, a Delaware Corporation and the First National City Bank of New York, a National Banking Association" (May 20, 1957), "Indenture of Trust" (June 1, 1948), "Guaranty Agreement," Exhibit 11.

All this financing was still going on while FBI agents and the Department of
Justice were trying to find out whether those companies were actually owned
by Onassis. It is extremely interesting to see that in the FBI archives, parts of
the interviews of all high officials of the First National City Bank or the
Metropolitan Life Insurance or Socony Oil were erased. The FBI officially
redacted them.

Finally, after Onassis was indicted, three court decisions portended trouble
for the government. The first decision concerned the civil cases, the forfeitures
of ships. After the first forfeiture of the tanker *Lake George* in March 1953,
Onassis, through his United States Petroleum Carriers, brought suit to have
the courts determine whether the US government had a legal right to seize the
vessels. He eventually won the case, and, in turn, when the US government
brought a suit against United States Petroleum Carriers' tanker *Lake George* to
have its forfeiture justified, it lost the case. In July 1954, Federal District Judge
Leahy decided that the case "should be dismissed for failure to state a cause of
forfeiture."[42] The cause of the forfeiture, according to the government, was
that the ship was "alien controlled." According to the Judge, however, the
government could not maintain the forfeiture proceeding as the Maritime
Commission had sold the vessel to a US corporation.

Two other decisions on the criminal cases, concerning the "alien control"
and the conspiracy to defraud, were in the case of *U.S. Government
v. Philadelphia Marine*, which was the Kulukundis group, and in that of *U.S.
Government v. United Tanker*, which was the Chinese group; both cases were
dismissed by the court.[43] Therefore, if Onassis's case went to trial, he had the
precedent of two similar criminal cases where no conviction was obtained. In
the end, the whole case was settled out of court, because it was clear that the
government would have lost.[44] According to Warren Olney, Assistant Attorney General, Criminal Division, "we had very good reason to believe that the
judge would not impose a jail sentence in this case, particularly Onassis."[45]

This outcome confirms that the pressure against Greek shipowners had to
be more political and it would only be through settlement agreements that the
US government could enforce fines and public humiliation. In order to force
Onassis to make the move for a settlement on the most favorable terms for the
US, the government took action on canceling the Onassis-Saudi agreement,

---

[42] 123 F.Supp. 216 (1954), *United States v. Tanker Lake George et al.*, United States District
Court D. Delaware, July 22, 1954 in www.leagle.com/decision/1954339123FSupp216_
1291.xml/ (accessed February 24, 2016); *Study of the Trade-Out and Build Activities of
Onassis Companies*, 268.

[43] *Current Merchant Marine Problems*, 186–190; *Study of the Trade-Out and Build Activities
of Onassis Companies*, 316.

[44] *Current Merchant Marine Problems*, 186–190.   [45] Ibid., 223.

attacking his whaling fleet, and boycotting his tankers. The issue of the agreement with Saudi Arabia was very sensitive. The US government proceeded in such a way as to jeopardize the agreement. On the US side, it used the FBI, CIA, and Aramco and on the Greek side, Onassis's brother-in-law Stavros Niarchos, who was under indictment himself, and Onassis's ex-collaborator Spyridon Catopodis.

Aramco was of course outraged and sent a strong protest to the Saudi government but had problems in dealing with King Saud. The agreement, according to Aramco officials, was a direct contravention of the terms of the Aramco-Arabian agreement. The US government sent a delegation to Saudi Arabia in April 1955 with the aim to gain an audience with the King and present their protest against the agreement. The Saudis were informed that they might expect substantial loss from the implementation of the Onassis agreement; they might lose markets and their financial benefits if they chose to follow it, as there was an increasing global resistance to this affair. After months of unrelenting pressure from the US government and Aramco, the Saudi government agreed that if Onassis did not agree a settlement with Aramco then the case would be resolved by arbitration. The Saudi government did not want to dishonor the agreement it had signed with Onassis and, as a settlement was not acceptable to Onassis, the case was sent to arbitration at the Court of The Hague, which decided in favor of Aramco in 1958.[46]

At the same time, Stavros Niarchos collaborated with the US government against the Saudi-Onassis agreement, as it hurt his own interests. His New York office found for him Robert Maheu, a former FBI agent who had the assignment of "mobilizing opposition to Onassis's deal." Funded by Niarchos, Maheu worked with other FBI agents to produce an analysis of the Onassis-Saudi Arabia contract.[47] In the meantime, it seems that Niarchos and Maheu got hold of Spyridon Catopodis. Apparently, there was a falling out between Catopodis and Onassis when Catopodis accused Onassis of a breach of their agreement. He prepared a lengthy deposition in the presence of the British Consul in Nice accusing Onassis of bribe payments of about $1 million to

---

[46] FBI, "Aristotle Onassis," part 4, Bufile 46-17783, Office Memorandum from a. H. Belmont to L. V. Boardman, "Visit to Middle East and North Africa by Bureau's Army Liaison Representative" (June 16, 1954). For taking the case to arbitration see "Aramco Hearing Opens," *New York Times*, June 16, 1955; Schwebel, "The Kingdom of Saudi Arabia."

[47] Ibid. Robert Maheu in a documentary about Onassis declared that he was hired to boycott the Saudi Arabian agreement between Onassis and the Saudi Arabian government; see *Aristotle Onassis, The Golden Greek*, TV movie, written and directed by William Cran, BBC, 1992.

various Saudi ministers and palace officials and other details of his agreement that exposed the Saudi Arabian government.[48]

It seems that Catopodis only had a photocopy of his most significant document, that of his written contract with Onassis. Catopodis submitted his case to Paris, where the French judge dismissed it due to the failure of Catopodis to present the original contract.[49] He also submitted his case to the United States in Washington and New York. However, as Onassis's lawyers argued, this was an agreement that happened in France between two Greeks; it should have been dismissed immediately in New York and should not be taken to court.[50] There it dragged on until December 1955, just before the final settlement with Onassis. In the hearings, Niarchos was called and questioned and it was revealed officially that he had employed Maheu in connection with the Saudi deal and that Maheu had shown him the Catopodis affidavit. Niarchos refused any other connection with Catopodis and four days later he dropped the case. Eventually, the Supreme Court dismissed it.[51]

The second action against Onassis was the one that hit him the hardest. It was a tacit worldwide boycott against his tankers; there was nothing official or written about it, but there was no doubt it was a "concerted boycott operation."[52] Most of his tankers were on 2–3 year time-charter agreements signed in the early 1950s with the oil companies. Every time a charter expired, Onassis found that it would not be renewed, and would instead be given to a competitor. By the end of 1955, Onassis had lost over $20 million from this boycott, and half of his fleet was idle.[53]

The third action against Onassis's businesses was an attack on his whaling fleet, backed by the US and British-Norwegian whaling interests. In November 1954, the Onassis whaling fleet was fishing off Peru. Peruvian naval and air forces attacked the fleet and forced it into Paita, a small port north of Lima, where it was seized. The Peruvian government blamed Onassis, stating that he had illegally fished 2,500 whales in their territorial waters. Peru's claim of territorial waters was rather shaky and not accepted by either the United States

[48] "Onassis Accused of Defrauding His Agent on Arabian Oil Deal," special to the *New York Times*, November 20, 1954.

[49] "Onassis Disputes Charges in Paris," special to the *New York Times*, March 27, 1955.

[50] *Spyridon Catapodis, Plaintiff* v. *Aristotle S. Onassis, Defendant*, Supreme Court, Special Term, New York County, April 4, 1956, https://casetext.com/case/catapodis-v-onassis (accessed February 5, 2016).

[51] ""Libel Suit Filed Against Onassis," *New York Times*, December 4, 1954; "Copy of Agreement Shown," *New York Times*, December 4, 1954; "Niarchos Disclaims Attack on Onassis," *New York Times*, January 22, 1955.

[52] Fraser et al., *Aristotle Onassis*, 155. For the boycott of Onassis's ships from Aramco see "Biggest Tanker Idle In Hamburg," *New York Times*, February 23, 1955; "Onassis in Cairo for Oil Case Talk," *New York Times*, January 20, 1955.

[53] Fraser et al., *Aristotle Onassis*, 155.

or the European countries. It was based on a decree in 1952 signed in Santiago by Chile, Peru, and Ecuador to create a distance of 200 nautical miles from the coast. The legality of the 200-mile zone was strongly opposed by Britain, Norway, and the United States, which claimed that Peru was in its zone of influence. However, the United States stood passive when the Peruvians attacked and demanded a fine of about $3 million. Onassis, however, had foreseen trouble and had included a clause providing for retention by foreign powers and losses when he insured the fleet and its cargo with Lloyd's of London, which ended up paying the fine.[54]

The Peruvian gambit failed, but the next, and final, attempt did not. It came in November 1955 from a meeting of the International Whaling Commission, an international convention for the regulation of whaling. The carefully prepared blow came from the Norwegian Whaling Association. It presented photographs from Japanese whalers, as well as "curiously detailed" photographic and written evidence from some of the German seamen of Onassis's fleet, to prove that at least half of the whales killed by Onassis's fleet since 1951 either were caught out of season or were below minimum size, and that Onassis had acquired at least $8.6 million from this illegal catch.[55]

It is clear that Onassis at this stage wanted to get out of this mess by finding a settlement. He was sure the US government also wanted to settle, since it had already done so with similar cases (see Table 8.2). The Niarchos group was the first to reach a settlement agreement with the United States on May 28, 1954. The Justice Department press release stated that Niarchos paid $4.5 million ($7.5 million less $3 million credit when the new construction was completed in US shipyards); in addition, six T-2 tankers, having a current market value of approximately $6 million, were returned to the Maritime Administration as government property, part of the reserved fleet.[56] Assistant Attorney General Doub claimed that the US government's gain from the Niarchos settlement was about $15 million.[57] Niarchos was allowed to transfer the other fourteen ships to foreign flags with a commitment to construct two 25,000 dwt tankers in US shipyards. His US corporations that would run those ships were put in a trust with directors approved by the US government. The "Chinese" case was settled on the same date as the Niarchos one; they paid the US government

---

[54] "Peru Frees 8 U.S. Ships," *New York Times*, February 22, 1955; "Peru Releases Crews," *New York Times*, February 21, 1955; "Onassis Pays $3,000,000 Fine," *New York Times*, December 14, 1954; "Onassis Fine Being Paid," *New York Times*, December 13, 1954; "Onassis in London; Protests Seizures," special to the *New York Times*, November 27, 1954; "Britain Acts On Whalers," special to the *New York Times*, November 20, 1954. On the Onassis whaling fleet see "Whalers To Sail Without Our Flag," *New York Times*, November 3, 1950. On the Onassis whaling fleet see Barthelmess, "A Century of German Interests in Modern Whaling, 1860s-1960s."

Fraser et al., *Aristotle Onassis*, 163.   [55] Ibid., 130.   [56] Ibid., 201.
[57] *Current Merchant Marine Problems*, 200, 207–208, 391.

Table 8.2 *Settlement agreements stemming from litigation by the Department of Justice's Civil Division, 1954–1955*

Case	US vessels	Fines payable to the United States (in US dollars)	Vessels returned	Settlement agreement on
Niarchos	15	15,579,500	6	May 28, 1954 modified on September 9, 1954
Chinese (United Tanker et al.)	5	2,000,000		May 28, 1954
Onassis	21	7,500,000		December 21, 1954
Kulukundis	18	1,500,000		June 20, 1955
Los-Pezas	5	110,000		July 8, 1955
Kallimanopoulos (Drytrans Inc., and Transfuel Corp.)	5	125,000		July 8, 1955
Total	69			

Source: Current Merchant Marine Problems, Hearings before the Committee on Merchant Marine and Fisheries, House of Representatives, Eighty-fifth Congress, first session, February 6 and 7, 1957 (Washington: United States Government Printing Office, 1957), 192, 200, 207–208, 391.

about $2 million. The Kulukundis case was settled a year later, on June 20, 1955, with a fine of $1.5 million. Any other charges were dismissed, since Manuel Kulukundis, a Greek citizen, had started the procedure of becoming a citizen of the United States some time before, and by the time of the settlement he eventually had become American.[58] The Kallimanopoulos case was settled on July 8, 1955, along with the Los-Pezas group.[59]

Onassis and the US government spent months in negotiations and reached a settlement in December 1954. The Onassis settlement received most of the press attention in comparison to the other Greek shipowners. The Attorney General Herbert Brownell Jr. led the negotiations. The agreement signed on December 21, 1955 between the United States of America on the one side and

[58] Ibid., 198–199.
[59] Ibid., 206; "Court Winds Up Ship Sale Case," *New York Times*, November 29, 1955.

the individuals and corporations on the other settled all pending issues in twenty-seven pages and stated clearly: "The Government hereby releases and forever discharges Aristoteles S. Onassis" and all his companies and collaborators.[60]

In order to reach this agreement, under which both civil and criminal charges were dropped, Onassis had to plead guilty on behalf of six corporations to defrauding the US government by illegally placing US ships under foreign registry. Although Onassis would, as we have seen, likely not have been convicted of any of the charges against him, his guilty plea was the price for avoiding lengthy and expensive trials – and it allowed the United States to save face.[61]

In this way, Onassis was forced to plead guilty in the US District Court to charges of conspiracy to defraud and making false statements, for which he paid a $7.5 million fine (a $1 million down-payment followed by annual installments).[62] Moreover, he had to reorganize his US corporations, which was little more than confirmation of the status quo, with the qualifications that the Justice Department rather than Onassis would choose his "quiet Americans." Therefore, he formed a trust in his children's names (Alexander and Christina), as they were both born in the United States and were US citizens. The American Grace National Bank of New York was appointed as Trustee of the Alexander S. Onassis Corporation, a Liberian corporation, owned by Alexander and Christina Onassis. Thus, under the 1958 trust agreement Grace National Bank became the corporate trustee and Onassis, the grantor, transferred to Grace National Bank the controlling stock interest of four owning corporations: United States Petroleum Carriers, Trafalgar Steamship Corporation, Western Tankers Inc., and Victory Carriers. Under that agreement the four owning corporations merged into one, the Victory Carriers, 75 percent of which was owned by the Grace National Bank trust, and 25 percent by Sociedad Industrial Maritima Financiera Ariona, SA.[63] All the directors of Victory Carriers and the trust were Onassis's choice, albeit subject to approval by the US government.

The guilty plea, fine, and reshuffled corporate structure allowed Onassis to keep the twenty-three US ships that he bought from the Maritime Commission, and which had been temporarily seized. The trust agreement included

---

[60] FBI, "Aristotle Onassis," part 3, Bufile 46-17783, "Fraud against the Government, Final Agreement" (December 21, 1955).

[61] *Study of the Trade-Out and Build Activities of Onassis Companies*, 218, 316.

[62] The report by the *New York Times* is accurate when compared with the original agreement with FBI. Luther A. Huston, "Ship Owner Pays 7 Million Penalty," special to the *New York Times*, December 22, 1955.

[63] *Study of the Trade-Out and Build Activities of Onassis Companies*, 268–269.

provisions that Victory carriers could apply for the "trade-out-and-build" contracts with the Maritime Administration to transfer ships to PanHoLib flags under the condition that it would build ships in US shipyards. An important detail was that this was not part of the settlement agreement as it was with the Niarchos one; it just gave him this possibility. Following this program, fourteen of the Victory Carriers vessels were transferred to PanHoLib flags after making three contracts with Bethlehem shipyards to build two tankers of 46,000 dwt and one tanker of 106,000 tons.

The *US Government* v. *Onassis* case, from beginning to end, required an extensive investigation handled by the FBI New York office with as many as forty agents assigned, in collaboration with the FBI's Washington and Los Angeles offices.[64] With the case closed, the Director of the FBI Edgar Hoover wrote to Warren Burger: "It is indeed gratifying to know that the investigative efforts of representatives of this Bureau were so material to the successful termination of this matter."[65] Although the result was a certain amount of negative publicity, Onassis's business edifice remained untouched. "It was all dressed up to look like a government victory," recalled Edward J. Ross, Onassis's lawyer, "but even they knew we had won."[66]

Reinvestigation, 1957–1958

The saga of the confrontation of Onassis with the US government continued for another two years, without any harm done, apart from more publicity that this time was in favor of Onassis. The case was reopened in 1958, again a time of low freight rates, because Onassis tried to cancel his orders to the US shipyards due to the international shipping crisis. The Justice Department responded immediately. On June 12, 1958, it instituted a suit on behalf of the US government against Victory Carriers and its parent companies, Alexander S. Onassis Corporation Inc. and Grace National Bank, for breach of agreement.[67]

The hearings took place before a special subcommittee of the House of Representatives during June, July, and August 1958. They were really headed by Herbert Zelenko a liberal Democrat from New York, and a tough, shrewd lawyer. Zelenko, who had little knowledge of shipping in general and almost none at all about international shipping, had a dislike of flags of convenience and foreign shipowners like Onassis who did not work, as he thought they

---

[64] FBI, "Aristotle Onassis," part 3, Bufile 46-17783, 'Fraud against the Government," Office Memorandum (September 1, 1956).
[65] Ibid.   [66] Fraser et al., *Aristotle Onassis*, 114.
[67] *Study of the Trade-Out and Build Activities of Onassis Companies*, 271–275.

should, for the good of America. His ultimate goal was to prove that the previously concluded settlement went against the interests of the United States.[68]

Zelenko examined all who were involved in the settlement agreement of 1955. These included the top officials of the Maritime Administration, the heads of the Civil and Criminal Divisions of the Department of Justice that negotiated the settlement agreement and the directors, officials of Victory Carriers, and its owners, the Trust of the Grace National Bank and Sociedad Industrial Maritima Financiera Ariona. The subcommittee wanted to prove three things: first, that the officials of the Maritime Administration were corrupt and had behind-the-scenes dealings with Victory Carriers and Onassis; second, that some of the heads of the Civil and Criminal Divisions of the Department of Justice had also been corrupted by personal interests, which prevented them from taking the foreign shipowners to court; and third, that Onassis had breached the settlement agreement by canceling the orders and that he, and not the Trust, was in control of Victory Carriers.

Zelenko examined George Cochran Doub, Assistant Attorney General of the Civil Division, Warren Olney III, Assistant Attorney of the Criminal Division, and Allen Krouse, Special Assistant to the Attorney General. He asked them repeatedly in various forms the same question: "you had a good solid criminal case against Onassis, in plain language?" They all answered "no"; if they had taken Onassis to court, the Justice Department officials said, he would have been found innocent, as happened with Kulukundis in the *U.S. v. Philadelphia Marine* case in December 1954. Edward Ross, Onassis's lawyer, also cited the criminal case of the United Tanker Corp., which was a Chinese group that was also dismissed by the court. Backed by these precedents, Doub and the other government officials insisted that settlement, as it had been in the Niarchos and Kulukundis cases, was the correct outcome. The government would have lost the case.[69]

The most interesting part of the hearings was the examination of Attorney General Brownell, who had been in charge of the indictments and the settlement agreements. Brownell had been a close collaborator of General Dwight D. Eisenhower, and was an effective surrogate during Eisenhower's 1952 presidential campaign. After his election, Eisenhower promptly appointed Brownell Attorney General. However, prior to his government service, Brownell had practiced law at Lord, Day & Lord, a law firm founded in 1845, and one that specialized in maritime law. One of its most prominent partners was George DeForest Lord, a third-generation lawyer and an authority on Admiralty Law who had published extensively on the subject.[70] From 1948 until his death in 1950, Lord was the lawyer for Aristotle Onassis, although Onassis eventually changed lawyers and went to Goodwin, Rosenbaum and Meacham. However, Manuel Kulukundis, also a client of Lord, Day & Lord, remained with them throughout the indictment and the settlement agreement. In fact, Herbert Brownell was Kulukundis's lawyer until his appointment as Attorney General in 1953. It so happened that when Manuel Kulukundis's *Philadelphia Marine* was taken to court for the criminal action "conspiracy to defraud the US government" on the cause of "alien control," Herbert Brownell was called as a witness. It was rather interesting that the lawyer of the very office that had advised both Kulukundis and Onassis how to cover up their citizenship and open up US companies was the Attorney General who signed the indictments against his clients, against the very advice he had given them![71]

As it happened, the office of Lord, Day & Lord had given solid advice to both Onassis and Kulukundis, advice that, in the end, made it possible for the Greek magnates to avoid prosecution. It was, in the last analysis, simple advice: an American corporation is American when 50 percent of the stock, plus 1 share, is held by an American, and this is what the Greeks followed. Despite his efforts to accuse Herbert Brownell of an inappropriate client-lawyer relationship, Zelenko could not do so. Brownell was never Onassis's lawyer; from June 1950 his law office had ceased to give legal advice, and that happened before any investigation began.[72]

Aristotle Onassis was telling Congress that he had done nothing wrong; he had simply followed the advice of US lawyers. It seems that he persuaded the Subcommittee that he was sincere.[73] Despite being at times on the borderline of the law, Onassis never crossed it. As his biographers have written, "Onassis believed he did everything legally."[74] Indeed, in 1947 he prided himself on the fact that he had never entered a legal conflict. He wrote: "From the beginning of my career until today, 24 whole years, and despite the fact that I worked in many countries, it never happened that I should turn to or being called by legal authorities."[75] He fought all his life against the stereotype of the "fraudulent nature of the Greeks." As he wrote in 1947, "Everyone knows the terrible bias of the northern people against us and particularly our profession ... Against

[70] George deForest Lord and George C. Sprague, *Cases on the Law of Admiralty* (American Case Book Series. St. Paul: West Publishing Company, 1926).
[71] *Study of the Trade-Out and Build Activities of Onassis Companies*, 315.   [72] Ibid.
[73] Fraser et al., *Aristotle Onassis*, 165–166.   [74] Ibid.
[75] Onassis, "Our Postwar Shipping."

this bias I fought, I won, and today I have not only friends but also business partners among the most prominent of their shipowners."[76]

Conclusions

Why were Aristotle Onassis and Mari Vagliano able to avoid real conviction, which would have meant destruction of their business and their own imprisonment? The answer has multiple levels, and has to do with the linkages of these powerful entrepreneurs with official and unofficial institutions on a national and international level. Both Vagliano and Onassis were acting as proto-multinationals. At one level of analysis, they both carried out their business guided by excellent local legal expertise. Both were very well advised on the legal proceedings of their businesses; hence, they knew how to deal with the accusations. Such knowledge of local legal institutions was vital for their survival in different countries. They were both able to hire top-class lawyers: Alexander Pavlovits Passover, Vagliano's lawyer, belonged to the group of Russian lawyers that wrote the history of the Tsarist courts before the Russian Revolution, while Onassis hired prominent lawyers from the maritime law firm Lord, Day & Lord (from 1948 to 1950) and the DC firm Goodwin, Rosenbaum and Meacham to ensure good legal advice from US lawyers in order to handle the US legal system.

On a second level, they both had access to political power, not only in the country where they were accused, but also in the other countries where they carried out business. By the 1950s Onassis, apart from having connections with US Congressmen, had developed relationships with Europe's gentility like Prince Rainier of Monaco, and political figures like Conrad Adenauer, Constantine Karamanlis, and King Saud of Saudi Arabia, as well as other respected figures in the political world of Germany, France, and England, like Winston Churchill.

We cannot know what other political connections Vagliano had in St. Petersburg that he might have used, but what we do know is that Queen Olga of Greece, wife to King George of Hellenes, was the beloved sister of Tsar Alexander III. Moreover, it is likely that the Greek government intervened on Vagliano's behalf.

On a third level, the two entrepreneurs also had access to economic power. Whatever they did affected a large milieu of top businessmen and affected the environment in which they worked. In the case of Onassis, it was America's financial institutions that would be damaged should Onassis, and the rest of the Greeks, be destroyed – namely US banks, insurance companies, and oil companies. As the main aim of the FBI was to reveal that Onassis had deceived

---

[76] Ibid.

the US government by hiding the fact that he controlled US corporations, it was certainly clear that US bankers and oil companies also deceived the US government by financing and chartering Onassis's US ships.

Equally, Mari Vagliano's activities were closely identified with the region's economic life. He had developed close connections to the local government, to the local landowners, and to the noble Cossack families that provided him with grain. He had developed the international connections of the region with western Europe, and the entire economic system of the external trade of the Azov was partially constructed by him. All the banking, shipping, insurance, chartering, warehouses, trading, and employment associated with the port's activities were under their control, with Mari Vagliano being the local "Tsar." To destroy him completely might have meant the collapse of the export-import system, and this might have caused the rest of the Greeks to flee the country.

On a fourth, global, level, the formation of the informal institutions of global business protected them both. Vagliano Brothers was the core company of the Greek entrepreneurial network. Their business was not limited to the Azov; it affected exports of the Black Sea in their entirety. Onassis, on the other hand, proved the ability and flexibility of global shipping businesses to bypass government laws and national interests when they affected their international activities. After all, shipping is an international economic activity par excellence, and institutionalized the defense mechanisms vital for its survival. These were: (a) the complex structure of shipping businesses, where is impossible to distinguish owner from manager and agent, (b) the institutions of shipping founded on trust and personal relations without written agreements, (c) flexibility and mobility through the use of flags of convenience registries geared towards tax avoidance and low-cost operating, and (d) cosmopolitanism, which is experience of working in many states and with many institutional environments. Put together, these form a formidable defense against any national government.

Finally what were the effects of the conviction of Vagliano and Onassis in the business environment where they operated? During 1881–1886, the time that Vagliano was under conviction, the external trade of Taganrog went through a severe crisis, from which it only began to recover in the 1890s. He was the employer of thousands, and the prosperity of the town depended largely on him and the other twenty merchants brought to trial. The blow to the top businessmen brought a great crisis to the town and the development of the neighboring port city of Rostov-on-Don (see Chapter 4).

In the case of Onassis the effects on New York were even worse regarding the shipping business. What the *U.S. Government* v. *Onassis* (not to mention the rest of the leading Greek shipowners) taught was that the persisting protectionist maritime policy of the United States was not friendly to international shipping operators. At the peak of shipping activities and their connections with the oil companies, as Greeks and other operators were turning New York into a new world shipping center, the euphoria disappeared. In order to keep shipping operators, a state had to tolerate the rules of global shipping: international mobility and a low-tax regime. After the mid-1950s Stavros Niarchos, Stavros Livanos, and most of the Kulukundis brothers, along with a large number of New York-based Greek firms, had moved back to London, while Onassis was established in Monaco. The death-blow to New York as an international shipping center was the 1963 Equalization Tax Law, under which the revenues of foreign companies established in the United States were taxed in the same way as revenues of domestic companies.[77]

Mari Vagliano and Aristotle Onassis were entrepreneurs who always remained aliens to their host countries, where their entrepreneurial leadership was evident. They were international businessmen working for profit beyond national boundaries and interests. Furthermore, they were also international capitalists: they lived in an era of a globalizing world and were part of an international business elite that was attacked at specific historical moments by the state mechanism of their host countries, usually with accusations of corruption and abuse. In both cases they survived their trials, judicial or otherwise. This happened because of their unique knowledge of the formal and informal institutional framework of the business they were involved in, and because of their ability to activate the national and international political-economic networks based on their expanded economic strength in various countries. It was through these kinds of conflicts that they were able to create the defense mechanisms of the global shipping business and to develop a model of an international business that was resilient to national constraints.

---

[77] See "The Interest Equalization Tax Act of 1963" (HR 8000): outline of provisions of HR 8000, as passed by the US House of Representatives, and amendments recommended by the Treasury Department (1964), www.archive.org/details/theinterestequal1064unit (accessed December 15, 2011).

9

Innovation in Global Shipping: The Onassis Business, 1946–1975

On January 1, 2000, *Lloyd's List* published a leading article titled "Giants who changed the face of shipping"; not surprisingly, the biggest picture, in the middle of the photo spread, featured Aristotle Onassis. He was among the first in the shipping business to take advantage of global sourcing, and was instrumental in creating the global shipping business that reinvented the European maritime tradition. His business was not attached to any nation; this was a business beyond borders that at the same retained its distinct Greek character. The choices he made were much talked about, and often harshly criticized. He chose to build his global shipping empire around offshore companies and flags of convenience. His choices in the 1940s and 1950s were new and unusual, but today they have become common practice in the global shipping business.

Onassis was a transitional figure in the newly globalized era of shipping practices. He was able to establish the new institution of the global shipping company, a kind of multinational company that was based in many countries and used Panamanian and Liberian companies and many different flags, all of which meant that it was taxed under the law of these countries. This went against the European maritime tradition of a genuine link between the ship-owner, the shipping company, the ship and its flag; a British shipowner would hoist a British flag on his ship, equally a German shipowner a German flag and so on. Global actors like Onassis were instead based in Europe, the Americas, and Asia, and drew on European expertise, American finance, and Latin American and African institutions – all at the same time. They were at the forefront of the changes in the global economy and their activities and the institutions they introduced remained the mainstay of European primacy in global shipping to the end of the twentieth century. Greeks were not the shipowners of Greece. They were Europe's shipowners and remain so to the present day.

The model of the global shipping business was very much first sketched out by Aristotle Onassis. "Onassis saw the future, not the present day, but the day after. He had great business intuition," said one of his close collaborators.[1] And perhaps it was no coincidence that Onassis was one of those who innovated the global shipping business. When he arrived in Buenos Aires, he had no country. He started his business career when he was still in effect a stateless refugee. It was in the third decade of his business career, only after he had become a world-renowned shipping tycoon, that the Greek government sought his support and collaboration. His global edifice was constructed among the many countries he traveled to and resided in. After his confrontation with the US government in the 1950s, his main concern became to construct a business that was not dependent on any nation, and to protect it from possible legal attacks by the various states he collaborated with.

Onassis's innovations and contributions in creating global shipping operated at four levels. First, he formed, developed, and consolidated the modern model of ownership and management of global shipping companies. Second, he was the first to open the US financial markets to ship finance and advanced ship finance methods. Third, by building tankers in US, European, and Asian shipyards, he contributed to the evolution of ship technology and gigantism. Fourth, he was able through his business philosophy to take advantage of traditional Greek shipping practices related to local island maritime culture and apply those practices to a globalized corporate culture.

The Model of Ownership and Management of Global Shipping Companies

Onassis's creation of the model of ownership and management of the global shipping company included three basic components. The first was his extensive use of the institution of the offshore company; multiple offshore holding companies became the key to rendering the owner of a ship practically invisible. Second, he chose to employ flags of convenience – the forerunner of today's open registries or international registries. Finally, he managed the business group from many locations around the globe.

Offshore Companies and the Multiple Holdings

Today, the use of offshore companies is a common practice engaged in by most businesses and businessmen. In the nation-centered postwar world of the 1940s and 1950s, on the other hand, offshore companies were a novelty, considered even an anomaly by many nation-states and state administrators. Offshore companies that sprang up during World War I started to be used on a small scale during the interwar period, grew on a larger scale on the eve of

---

[1] Interview with Pavlos Ioannidis, Athens, April 11, 2016.

World War II, and have attained unprecedented scale and influence since that time. They became a prime manifestation of globalization during the second half of the twentieth century. Ironically, however, the United States has consistently supported the growth and elaboration of offshore companies, as is characteristically the case of Panamanian and Liberian offshore companies.[2] Although often decried as "tax havens" and accused of unaccountability and illegal practices, offshore companies are today clearly an integral part of state systems and the global economy.[3]

In 1916, a provision in Panamanian law opened domestic corporations to foreign control; it was later supplemented by provisions in the Commercial and Fiscal codes approved by the Panamanian assembly and enacted in 1925.[4] These laws allowed for the formation of Panamanian incorporations by foreign companies through a system of Panamanian consuls abroad and under a special tax regime.[5] Shipping businesses were among the first to use the Panamanian registry, as according to its law any shipowner, irrespective of nationality or domicile, may register vessels under the Panamanian flag.[6] Large American steamship companies have used Panamanian companies and the Panamanian flag for their ships since the late 1920s, along with some European shipping and oil companies, long before Onassis formed any Panamanian company.[7] Furthermore, in order to circumvent the 1939 American Neutrality Act, American shipowners were allowed to transfer their vessels to Panamanian registry with the approval of the United States Maritime Commission.[8] Apart from shipping companies, other US companies also started to use Panamanian companies; the prospect of World War II resulted in a large number of Panamanian companies being European-owned,[9] including Nestlé and other Swiss-based companies.[10]

Aristotle Onassis did not invent the Panamanian companies or the Panamanian Maritime Registry; what he did invent, however, was the model of a global shipping company, which was imitated and expanded by other Greek

---

[2] Carlisle, *Sovereignty for Sale*.

[3] Béatrice Hibou, "Economic Crime and Neoliberal Modes of Government: The Example of the Mediterranean," in Renate Bridenthal, ed., *The Hidden History of Crime, Corruption, and States* (New York: Berghahn, 2013), 237–262. See also Ronen Palan, Richard Murphy, and Christian Chavagneux, *Tax Havens: How Globalization Really Works* (Ithaca, NY: Cornell University Press, 2010).

[4] Carlisle, *Sovereignty for Sale*, 21.   [5] Ibid., 2, 20.

[6] *Panama Ship Registry: Guide and Procedure*, Icaza, Gonzalez-Ruiz & Aleman, Abogado-Attorneys at Law, 2012, 5, www.icazalaw.com/practice_area.php?ID=13 (accessed July 20, 2016).

[7] Carlisle, *Sovereignty for Sale*, 38–73. See also Mira Wilkins, *The History of Foreign Investment in the United States, 1914–1945* (Cambridge, MA: Harvard Studies in Business History, 2009), 823–824.

[8] Wilkins, *The History of Foreign Investment*, 451.   [9] Ibid., 476, 841.   [10] Ibid., 476.

Table 9.1 *The Onassis model of company organization*

---

1. **Ownership**
   - **A-Company** – the A-company owns the shares of the B-company. This was the "**grandmother**"
   - **B-Company** – the B-company owns the stock of all the C-companies, it is the stockholding company of all the C-companies. This was the "**mother**"
   - **C-Company** – Every ship is owned by a different Panamanian or Liberian company. This was a C-company, otherwise called "**the daughter**"
2. **Operation:**
   - **D-Companies** – the D-companies were delegated by the C-companies to purchase, order the shipbuilding, charter or finance the ships owned by C-companies. These were the "**aunts**"
   - **E- Companies** – the E-companies were the window to the world. They were the agencies, delegated by the C-companies to carry out the business of the vessels. These were the "**cousins**"

---

shipowners. Onassis created 164 Panamanian and 19 Liberian companies through which he ran his business (see Tables 9.1–9.2). He actually started a new offshore shipowning company for each ship, and set up multiple holding companies for each of those new shipowning companies. The aim of this strategy was twofold: to give his companies invisibility, and, more important, to provide flexibility and speed of action. Invisibility meant "defense" in a global and risky economic environment. First, the multilayered defense secured each ship from the financial or legal problems of the others. The Onassis fleet was not consolidated under one shipowning company, or even under one representative agency. The eighty ships of the Onassis fleet in 1970, for example, in the books of *Lloyd's Register of Shipping*, the world's most complete ship register, are found under the eighty different names of their shipowning Panamanian or Liberian companies. The aim here, apart from defending the ships, was to insulate the shipowner through invisibility. If something happened to one ship, no harm would come to either the other ships or the owner.

To make the owner even more invisible, Onassis implemented two important codicils related to shipping in Panamanian and Liberian law. The first was the anonymity of the shares of the *Sociétés Anonymes* whether they are listed or not listed in the Stock Exchange. The anonymity of a share is the essence of the public incorporations or *Sociétés Anonymes* that are listed in the stock exchange. Shares of listed companies are anonymous – they belong to the bearer. Under most European states' legal systems during this period – and for most to the present day – the shares of unlisted companies have to carry the names of the owners; not so, however, under Panamanian or Liberian law. The anonymity of the shares of Onassis's Panamanian companies brought great

Table 9.2 *Nationalities of Onassis shipping companies formed between 1939 and 1975*

Type of company	Panamanian	Liberian	Other	Total
For shipping				
A-company	3			3
B-company	5	1		6
C-company	74	11	10	96
D-company	6			6
E-company	6			6
Total for shipping	*94*	*12*	*11*	*117*
For other business				
A-company	(3)			
B-company	2 (+3)			2
C-company	63	7	6	76
D-company	5			5
Total for other business	*70*	*7*	*6*	*83*
Grand total	**164**	**19**	**17**	**200**

"Other" includes nine American, one Saudi Arabian, two Swedish, and four Greek companies.
Sources: Onassis Archive, Alexander S. Onassis Foundation, Corporate books; Results of all companies as of December 31, 1975.

confusion to the US administrators in the 1950s and proved an important defense during the case of *U.S. v. Aristotle Onassis.*

The second important element in the shipping companies of Panama and Liberia is that the owner of the shipping company could exchange the flag of his ship with any other flag. A ship owned by a Panamanian company could hoist a Liberian, or Honduran, or any other flag that permitted this practice. A question that might arise here is: if the idea was to make himself invisible through offshore companies and many flags, why did then Onassis name his ships with the prefix "Olympic," which made them easily identifiable? Aristotle Onassis had no problem with visibility: from the early 1950s to his death his life was so exposed to the press that fame became a habit.

Why then did he choose the offshore companies and the flags of convenience for his ships? Shipowners that did this left themselves vulnerable at the time to accusations from the American and European Maritime Unions of tax evasion, running substandard old ships, and undermanning their vessels. Onassis's ships under the flags of Panama or Liberia paid the same taxes and fees as defined in Panama law as the fleets of respected US oil companies or shipowners; his ships were brand new, as indicated in Chapter 7,

Table 9.3 *The architecture of the Onassis shipping business in 1970*

1. Ownership

A-companies	B-companies	C-companies
Grandmothers	*Mothers*	*Daughters*
Sociedad Armadora Miraflores Panama Ltd (1939)	Sociedad Armadora Aristomenis Panama SA (1946)	62 shipowning companies
Sociedad Industrial Maritima Financiera Ariona Panama SA	Alexander S. Onassis Corp., Liberia	24 shipowning companies
	Benmore Panama SA	
	Oceanic Transport Co.	
	Silverton	

2. Operation

D-companies	Six shipping companies	
Aunts		
E-companies	Six agencies	
Cousins	Olympic Maritime SA (Monte Carlo, Paris, London)	
	Springfield (Piraeus)	
	Constantino Konialidis (Montevideo)	
	Central American Agency (New York)	

and his vessels were certainly not undermanned. Low-cost operation was not his first aim; his crews were among the best paid in the Greek-owned fleet, as the payrolls indicate.[11]

The answer is that it served the second leg of his strategy, flexibility. As a cosmopolitan businessman not attached to the interests of any country, acting in a global, highly competitive environment, having to deal with hostile host countries, offshore companies provided a secure refuge to defend his business through relative invisibility and flexibility of actions. In today's world of global business it is accepted that the emphasis of the benefits of offshoring are less on cost reduction and more on such benefits as flexibility and speed in delivering business solutions.[12]

Aristotle Onassis formed his first Panamanian offshore company in 1939. This was Sociedad Armadora Miraflores Panama Ltd, Miraflores for short. The

---

[11] Onassis Archive, Alexander S. Onassis Foundation, Payrolls of Tankers *Olympic Banner, Olympic Armour, Olympic Garland, Olympic Champion, Olympic Chivalry, Olympic Eagle, Tina Onassis,* and *Olympic Pearl.*

[12] Ramanathan, *The Role of Organisational Change,* 16.

formation of Miraflores was completed on April 14, 1939 at the Consulate General of the Republic of Panama in London. Costas Gratsos and Pericles Dracoulis, shipowners from the Greek London office, who had introduced Onassis to Greek shipping in the 1930s, assisted him. The members of the Board of Directors of Onassis's first Panamanian company and shareholders appear as Constantine George Gratsos, Demetre George Gratsos, Panos George Gratsos, Constantine Pericles Dracoulis, and Aristotle Onassis. The domicile of the corporation was located in Panama and its registered agent and representative remained Mr. Carlos Icaza Arosemena (1895–1979) until its closure.[13]

Aristotle Onassis collaborated closely with two law offices that specialized in offshore companies. The first was a Panamanian firm, Icaza, Gonzàlez-Ruiz & Alemán, where Onassis collaborated with Carlos Icaza Arosemena and Francisco Gonzalez Ruis.[14] Onassis, certainly among the firm's most valuable clients, developed with them the technique of the creation of offshore shipping companies. The Icaza law office formed all his Panamanian companies. The second one was the law firm of Dr. Eduardo Albanell Mac Coll based in Montevideo. The latter proved essential for the function of his firm, as will be indicated later.

On February 13, 1940, the new Panamanian company Miraflores opened its bank account with the National City Bank of New York. The first meeting of Miraflores after World War II took place in Manhattan, New York on December 20, 1946. It proved very important, as major issues were resolved as to the actual running of the companies (such as the Board of Directors, the proxies in the event of the absence of the Directors, and the location of Board meetings). In the meeting of the Board of Directors, as the "terms of office of the Directors of the Corporation elected in 1939 had expired," new Directors were to be elected: "a) Aristoteles [sic] S. Onassis (President), Constantine Konialidis (Vice President and Treasurer) and Nicolas Konialidis (Secretary)." The three of them were on the Board of Directors of all companies formed until 1954.[15] It was only after his conflict with the US government that Aristotle Onassis started to disappear from the Boards of Directors of all his companies.[16]

The Miraflores Board decided in 1946 that all future meetings of the Boards of Directors of all the Onassis companies would be held at the Misiones Str.,

---

[13] Onassis Archive, Alexander S. Onassis Foundation, Corporate Books, vol. 1, Sociedad Maritima Miraflores, Panama Ltd.

[14] *Panama Ship Registry: Guide and Procedure*, Icaza, Gonzalez-Ruiz & Aleman, Abogado-Attorneys at Law, 2012, 5, www.icazalaw.com/practice_area.php?ID=13 (accessed July 20, 2016); "Offshore Service Provider – Icaza Law," *Streber Weekly, Offshore, Banking, Incorporations, Payments*, www.streber.st/2014/09/offshore-service-provider-icaza-law/ (accessed July 20, 2016).

[15] Onassis Archive, Alexander S. Onassis Foundation, Corporate Books, Sociedad Maritima Miraflores, Ltd, 1946–1952.

[16] Onassis Archive, Alexander S. Onassis Foundation, Corporate Books Transatlantica Financiera Industrial, Panama, SA.

1481 in Montevideo, Uruguay. The Onassis offices were on two of the floors of the building; on the other floors were the Greek Consulate and later the law firm of Dr. Eduardo Albanell Mac Coll.[17] Eduardo Albanell Mac Coll was a Professor at the School of Law of the University of Uruguay and an expert on Commercial and Banking Law, with a rich publication record, and the founder of an important legal periodical that runs to the present day. Eduardo Albanell Mac Coll was trusted by Aristotle Onassis throughout his life. At the same address, the family legal office of the Albanells is run today by the third generation.[18] It was Eduardo Albanell Mac Coll who supervised the writing of all the Minutes of corporate books of the Onassis group of companies.

It was in that same meeting of the Miraflores Board in December 1946 that Onassis made his next move, one that proved to be the foundation of his business: the institution of multiple holding companies. In the December 1946 meeting, it was decided that Miraflores would become the holding company of Sociedad Armadora Aristomenis Panama, SA. Therefore, Miraflores became the holding company of Aristomenis, and Aristomenis became the holding company of almost all Panamanian and Liberian companies that owned the Onassis ships. All companies operated separately. They were separately incorporated, filed separate tax returns, maintained a separate payroll and bank accounts through which they paid their employees, and separately paid all their operating expenses.

The Onassis model of company organization is presented in Table 9.1. It has two parts, which reveal the structure of the multiple holding companies of his business. The first part concerns the ownership of vessels. Every vessel was owned by a C-company, called the "daughter" company. The C-company would be owned by a B-company, called the "mother." The B-company would be owned by an A-company, the "grandmother," which would be the main holding company. The naming of the companies – daughter, mother, and grandmother – was commonly used in the interoffice correspondence between Montevideo and Monte Carlo. The second part concerns the operating activities of the companies: shipbuilding, ship purchases, contracting of loan agreements with the banks, and chartering, all of which were carried out by a different set of companies. These were the D-companies, which I have named the "aunts." These were formed in order to receive loans from the banks or charter the ships. They were the intermediaries of the C-companies with institutions such as the banks or the shippers. The E-companies, which I have named the "cousins," were the main agencies, which carried out the daily operations.

Onassis's global operations, including shipping and his other investments (see Table 9.2), was composed of 200 separate companies, of which 82 percent (164 companies), were Panamanian, 10 percent Liberian, and the rest

---

[17] Interview with Ritsa Konialidis, December 22, 2016.
[18] www.estudioalbanell.com/en/historia.php (accessed August 25, 2016).

American, Greek, Swedish, and Saudi Arabian (there was just a single Saudi company). The companies that dealt with shipping are highlighted in the first part of Table 9.2 and totaled 117 companies, about 60 percent of the overall total. The rest were either companies that owned his other business, Olympic Airways, or other investments in banks, shipyards, refineries, and real estate.

The architecture of this vast, complex edifice is presented in Table 9.3, all managed by Onassis and his team. There were three A-companies or "grand-mothers." This was the aforementioned Miraflores, the Sociedad Industrial Maritima Financiera Ariona Panama SA (Ariona for short) and the Sociedad Armadora Aristotelis Panama SA (Aristotelis for short). The two A-companies that owned and controlled his shipping business were Miraflores and Ariona; all other business was undertaken by Aristotelis. Miraflores and Ariona were the two main "grandmothers" that owned about 90 percent of all the shipown-ing C-companies. Miraflores owned Aristomenis, the main stockholding B-company. Aristomenis owned the stock of sixty-two "daughters," the C-companies that owned the ships. The second most important A-company was Ariona. Ariona, was initially formed to be the minority owning company of 49 percent of Onassis's US companies. After 1957, it became the second most important "grandmother." It owned the stock of the four B-companies, the Alexander S. Onassis Corp., Liberia SA, Benmore Panama SA, Oceanic Transport Corp. and Silverton Panama SA, which in their turn were the "mothers" of twenty-four "daughter" companies.

The other A-company, Aristotelis, owned the rest of the non-shipping business of Onassis. More particularly, it became the main A-company, the "grandmother" of the companies of Olympic Airways and other investments in banks, shipyards, or refineries.[19] This meant that practically all the account-ancy and control took place through these three "grandmothers," Miraflores, Ariona, and Aristotelis. It might be noteworthy to mention that the private fortune and personal expenses of Onassis were also managed in the A-, B-, and C- company model. It was the "grandmother" Aristotelis that owned all companies, which in turn owned his apartments and houses all over the world, his island Skorpios and his yacht *Christina*.[20]

The other group, the D- and E-companies, operated the business and acted as windows to the world. The D-companies, the "aunts," were the companies that purchased, sold, chartered, took finance from the banks, or ordered ships

---

[19] But it was not only Aristotelis that dealt with his other business. Miraflores was also owner of aircraft.

[20] Results of all companies as of December 31, 1975; Onassis Business Archive, Alexander S. Onassis Foundation, Corporate Books A. S. Onassis Panama SA, Sociedad Armadora Aristidis Panama SA, Ashland Shipping Panama SA, Anonimos Ktimatiki kai Emboriki Etaireia Agamemnon, Anonimos Ktimatiki kai Emboriki Etaireia Mykinai, Rawson Panama SA Jancourt Marine Panama, SA.

from the shipyards. All the E-companies were agencies that operated the vessels from various locations. The main operating agency of Onassis, Olympic Maritime SA (OMSA), was founded in 1952 in Paris and moved in 1954 in Monte Carlo. It was Olympic Maritime SA and its subsidiaries that formed the main agency of the group.[21]

The Flags of Convenience

If the institution of the offshore companies provided invisibility and flexibility through multiple holdings, Onassis's flexibility and speed of action was further reinforced by the choice of the flags of these offshore companies. A ship owned by a Panamanian or Liberian company could change its flag at any time. For example, the Liberty *Aristotelis*, purchased in 1946 and owned by Columbia Marine SA (a C-company), which was owned by Aristomenis (a B-company), owned by Miraflores (an A-company), hoisted the Honduran flag from 1946 to 1958; it changed to the Greek flag from 1960 to 1965[22] and then again to the Liberian flag from 1965 until it was eventually scrapped in Japan in 1969. A change of flag could be due to the trades it served. Most of the Onassis ships were owned by Panamanian companies, but they also flew various other flags, mainly Liberian, Honduran, Panamanian, and Greek.

The choice of flag depended usually on the political situation around the world at the time. During the Cold War era, Liberian and Panamanian flags were identified with the United States, and were unwelcome in the socialist countries. Thus, if the Onassis tankers that served Western developed countries hoisted almost exclusively the Liberian flag, cargo vessels like the Liberty *Aristotelis*, if they were chartered by the Chinese or the Soviets (for example) had to change to the Greek flag. The procedure of changing flag took (and still takes) in total approximately one day and could be carried out in any consulate, and completed while the ship was afloat.[23]

[21] Onassis Business Archive, Alexander S. Onassis Foundation, Corporate books of Somerset Navigation Company, Panama SA.
[22] According to article 13 of the Greek Legislative Decree 2687 of 1953, "concerning the investment and protection of foreign capital," vessels belonging to foreign Greek-owned firms were allowed to sail under the Greek flag: if conditions in Greece were found to be unsatisfactory, the vessels could revert to a foreign flag without prior state permission. In order to prevent foreigners from registering their ships in Greece, a provision was made that foreign shipping firms had to be at least 50 percent owned by Greek citizens. This legislation, incorporated in the Constitution of Greece, institutionalized the absence of state intervention in the activities of Greek shipowners. See Harlaftis, *Greek Shipowners and Greece*, 130–131.
[23] *Panama Ship Registry: Guide and Procedure*, Icaza, Gonzalez-Ruiz & Aleman, Abogado-Attorneys at Law, 2012, 5, www.icazalaw.com/practice_area.php?ID=13 (accessed July 20, 2016); "Offshore Service Provider – Icaza Law," *Streber Weekly, Offshore, Banking, Incorporations, Payments*, www.streber.st/2014/09/offshore-service-provider-icaza-law/ (accessed July 20, 2016), 7–8.

Open registries, or international registries as they are called today, were called, in a derogatory manner, flags of convenience during the early postwar era. Flags of convenience were initially controversial, and the traditional maritime nations of northern Europe disputed their legitimacy from the 1940s all the way into the 1980s. However, the choices Aristotle Onassis made back in 1939 and followed in the decades after were, in hindsight, the correct ones – they turned him into perhaps the world's leading shipowner. In 2018, more than half the world's fleet sailed under open registries and the Panamanian and Liberian flags figure at the top of this fleet.[24] Greek shipowners are found at the top of beneficial ownership to the present day (see Table 9.4). As Table 9.4 indicates, among world's ten largest maritime nations, according to the ship registry, Panama, Marshall Islands and Liberia figure in the first three positions followed by Hong Kong, Singapore and Malta. Indeed, seven out of the fifteen largest fleets belong to flags of convenience or open registries.

Offshore companies and flags of convenience abolished the genuine link between ownership and operation, but they also created global shipping in a globalizing world. The problem that took several decades to get beyond – and is still not accepted fully by many countries with nationalistic (sometimes even xenophobic) political cultures that tend to see the world only as it is defined by national boundaries – is the various difficulties engendered by that linkage of citizenship, ownership, and operation of a vessel. Shipping, particularly cross-trading tramp shipping, cannot survive within the restrictive framework of a national economy. This was accepted by American businessmen, but not fully by American politicians and their voters. The official US merchant policy, for example, took for granted that a nation's fleet is the one under its own flag.[25] US businessmen and shipowners had a different view. However, the US fleet under flags of convenience accounted for more than three-quarters of the total US-owned fleet. For example, in 1984 there were ships about 20 million dwt hoisting the US flag. However, in the same year, there were ships of at least 50 million dwt owned by US citizens flying open-registry flags.[26] This continues to the present, as, according to Table 9.4, the US-owned fleet (meaning ships owned by US citizens under all flags) ranks eighth in the world fleet.

During the aftermath of World War II and on into the Cold War, offshore companies and flags of convenience were featured on the front pages of newspapers as "unpatriotic," with concerns raised concerning national defense and labor conflicts, intermingled with shadowy business practices like

---

[24] Jari Ojala and Stig Tenold, "Maritime Trade and Merchant Shipping: The Shipping/Trade Ratio since the 1870s," *The International Journal of Maritime History* 29, no. 4 (2017): 838–854.

[25] See Andrew Gibson and Arthur Donovan, *Abandoned Ocean: A History of United States Maritime Policy* (Columbia, SC: University of South Carolina Press, 2000).

[26] Harlaftis, *A History of Greek-Owned Shipping*, table 9.8, appendix 9.3.

Table 9.4 The top shipping fleets of the world according to registry and beneficial ownership, 2018 (in deadweight tonnage, above 1,000 dwt)

Registry	Number of vessels	Dead-weight tonnage (thousands of tons)	Share of world total dead-weight tonnage (percentage)	Beneficial ownerships	Number of vessels	Dead-weight tonnage (thousands of tons)	Share of world total dead-weight tonnage (percentage)
Panama	7 914	335 888	17.46	Greece	4 371	330 176	17
Marshall Islands	3 419	237 826	12.36	Japan	3 841	223 615	12
Liberia	3 321	223 668	11.63	China	5 512	183 094	10
Hong Kong (China)	2 615	181 488	9.43	Germany	2 869	107 119	6
Singapore	3 526	127 880	6.65	Singapore	2 629	103 583	5
Malta	2 205	108 759	5.65	Hong Kong (China)	1 592	97 806	5
China	4 608	84 184	4.38	Republic of Korea	1 626	77 277	4
Bahamas	1 418	76 659	3.98	United States	2 071	68 930	4
Greece	1 343	72 345	3.76	Norway	1 982	59 380	3
Japan	5 299	37 536	1.95	Bermuda	494	54 252	3
World Total	50 732					1 910 012	

Source: Review of Maritime Transport (New York and Geneva: UNCTAD, U.N., 2018), Tables 2.3 and 2.8.

money-laundering, smuggling, tax evasion, environmental pollution, and energy crises, all of which were inimical to the American public conscience. The system of the use of the flags of convenience, however, grew uninterrupted.

The Liberian system of offshore companies and maritime registry introduced in 1949 by American businessmen and political leaders was made to serve American shipping businesses.[27] Onassis was able to take advantage of the opportunities afforded by the new state of things. From 1946 to 1974, 90 percent of the Onassis fleet operated under open registries, using mainly the Liberian flag. He, and the other leading members of the international shipping community, like the Greek Stavros Niarchos, Manolis Kulukundis, and P. Goulandris's sons, the Norwegian Erling Dekke Naess and W. Wilhemsen, or the American Daniel Ludwig, set the pace for the rest. In the 1950s, in fact, the Liberian fleet was almost entirely Greek-owned: the percentage of Liberian-flag ships that were - Greek-owned fluctuated between 60 and 100 percent of the total Liberian fleet, although between the 1960s and 1970s it fell to just under 40 percent. The Greek-owned Panamanian fleet reached about 50 percent of the total Panamanian fleet in the 1950s and after the 1960s to mid-1970s never exceeded 20 percent.[28]

Ship Finance and Finances

It was Onassis's ability to gain access to American bankers and their vast resources that proved groundbreaking; he was the first foreign shipowner to involve American banks in international tanker finance. He pioneered obtaining loans from top American bankers to purchase and build tankers guaranteed by the time-charters he secured from oil companies. In this way, anticipated revenues were used as security for vessel mortgages, with the bank receiving its repayments directly from the chartering company. According to the maritime economist Martin Stopford, charter-backed finance was quite a novel method in ship finance in the 1940s, introduced by industrial shippers such as oil companies.[29] The "charter-backed" policy was first introduced into the tanker market during the interwar period by oil companies which, due to the crisis, decided to offer incentives to independent shipowners to purchase tankers, an offer that was taken up by Norwegian shipowners.[30] In the immediate postwar period, Onassis also established ship loans on time charters; furthermore, he developed and refined them into a common mechanism

---

[27] Carlisle, *Sovereignty for Sale*, xvi.
[28] The decrease in the years that followed concerned mainly the Panamanian fleet; strikes against the flags of convenience meant a large decrease between 1958 and 1961, followed by fluctuations of 30–50 percent up to the 1970s. See Harlaftis, *Greek Shipowners and Greece*, 52–57; Harlaftis, "Greek Shipowners and State Intervention," 37–63.
[29] Martin Stopford, *Maritime Economics* (London: Routledge, 1997), 197.
[30] Sturmey, *British Shipping*, 75–81.

in the US financial markets, and introduced them as a means of launching major large-vessel shipbuilding programs. According to Costas Vlassopoulos, one of Onassis's chief executive officers for thirty-one years, Onassis developed tanker-ship loans involving large US insurance companies such as Metropolitan Life.[31] Time charters of tankers were usually long term, fifteen to twenty years, whereas US bank regulations limited provision of ship loans to five years. However, Onassis introduced a method to extend the loans by involving, for example, Metropolitan Life to secure the repayment of the loan to the bank for another ten or fifteen years.

He also improved on the method by ordering a standard series of vessels at single shipyards, reducing costs and guaranteeing employment in the US, German, and French shipyards. With the registration of an initial mortgage and the assignment of a long-term charter-party in the borrowing banks that collected the monthly freights directly from the charterers, Onassis was able to achieve finance that frequently covered up to 95 percent of the total cost of the ship. Although a number of other top shipowners of the time, including the American Daniel Ludwig, the Norwegian Erling Dekke Naess, and the Greek Stavros Niarchos, have indicated that they introduced this method, the banking and shipping market attributes it to Aristotle Onassis.[32] Onassis himself mentions that in July 1946 he persuaded Citibank and Metropolitan Life Insurance to provide him with financing to purchase war surplus ships, Liberties, and T2 tankers from MARCOM and order new ships from US shipyards.[33] The Onassis Archives verify the loans taken from National City Bank of New York since 1946, and the books of the loan agreements themselves indicate that from 1946 to 1958 Onassis had received $90.4 million for the purchase of eighty-four war-built or new vessels in US and European shipyards on charter-backed finance guaranteed by Metropolitan Life Insurance and himself personally (Table 7.6). According to the CEO of National City Bank, he was the one who opened up the ship finance market to the American banks:

> Ship loans were invented by Onassis ... he used to come in the Bank and stand at the door and wait till what he called "the pope" was free – it was Howard Shepherd. Shep sat in the catbird's seat on the East Platform and Onassis would go over to see him, and Shep would kid him along the way Shep does ... I eventually got in the act. And he (Onassis) came up with a Texaco bare-boat charter, signed by ... [the] chairman of Texaco. And he said he'd assign that Texaco and his personal guarantee, with great trepidation. And that was the first ship loan as far as I know. Everybody

[31] Vlassopoulos, *Pages of a Life*, 86–87.
[32] Ibid., 86–88. For Ludwig see Shields, *The Invisible Billionaire*; for Erling Dekke Naess, see *Autobiography*; for Stavros Niarchos, see Carlisle, *Sovereignty for Sale*, 131, 171.
[33] Onassis, "Our Postwar Shipping," March 20, 1953.

takes credit for it, but the facts are that to my knowledge Onassis invented the concept and we all were pretty wise after the event.[34]

How profitable was the Onassis business? The Onassis Archives reveal, for the first time, the income and profits of his business. The business of shipping depends on the level of world trade, which is affected by international trends, world economic crises, wars, and political turmoil. As the demand for shipping services is a derived demand, the price of sea transport – freight rates – suffers from severe fluctuations. Profits can be stable and relatively low, but sometimes have bursts of incredible gains. The account books of Onassis's three "grandmothers," the Miraflores, Ariona, and Aristotelis, reflect the sharp fluctuations of freight rates and the spectacular income that Onassis's business enjoyed, particularly during the periods 1946–1956 and 1967–1975 (Table 9.5 and Figure 9.2).

Table 9.5 and Figure 9.1 confirm the gross income of the three main "grandmothers": the A-companies of the Onassis group of companies from 1946 to 1975. From an income of about $1 million in 1946, the Miraflores income rose spectacularly to $40 million in 1949, $80 million in 1951, and $116 million in 1953. As we have seen, this was the result of Onassis's particular purchase and sales strategy, and the operation of his newly built or acquired ships in the high-freight-rate environment of 1947 to 1954. The closure of the Suez Canal in 1956 by Egyptian President Gamal Abdel Nasser more than doubled the Miraflores income from 1953 to 1957, when it reached $270 million. However, low freight rates from 1958 to 1967 brought a dramatic decrease of earnings in the 1960s, during which period the income of the company varied between $25 and $50 million. Nonetheless, the quadruple increase in freight rates, which again occurred after the closure of the Suez Canal at the beginning of the Six Day War between Israel and Egypt in June 1967, and the timely investments in a newly built fleet of VLCCs at the end of the 1960s, increased the income to almost $1 billion in 1970.

Ariona, which owned the twenty-four vessels of the US flag fleet as well as the US-built new tankers from the Bethlehem shipyards, also experienced astronomical earnings growth: from $10 million in 1947 to $250 million in 1954. Evidence of income for Ariona between 1965 and 1970 is not available. From 1970 to 1975, however, its income remained at astonishing levels, indicating a sixfold increase; this was probably due to inner accounting and intercompany arrangements.[35]

[34] Harold van B. Cleveland and Thomas F. Huertas with Rachel Strauber, Joan L. Silverman, Mary Mongibelli, Mary S. Turner and Clarence L. Wasson, Jr., *Citibank, 1812–1970* (Cambridge, MA: Harvard University Press, 1985), 231.
[35] Evidence for *Aristotelis* is limited between 1951 and 1960, when its income does not appear to exceed $28 million.

Table 9.5 *Gross income from Onassis A-group of companies, 1946–1975 (in US dollars)*

	Sociedad Armadora Miraflores	Sociedad Industrial Maritima Financiera Ariona	Sociedad Armadora Aristotelis
1946	936,315		
1947	13,082,786	10,235,979	
1948	22,426,636	26,307,273	
1949	38,337,012	71,044,736	
1950	54,612,794	88,894,627	
1951	79,659,151	127,534,263	4,582,098
1952	103,887,642	182,780,170	1,018,425
1953	116,104,032	209,446,927	867,432
1954		249,434,627	8,120,936
1955			2,482,405
1956			15,621,462
1957	263,380,156		23,982,573
1958			28,295,966
1959			
1960			28,898,841
1961	24,740,191		
1962	39,103,008		
1963	25,027,235		
1964	50,460,368		
1965	29,028,722		
1966			
1967			
1968			
1969	266,416,389		
1970	883,194,375	88,622,939	
1971	345,157,128	105,823,953	
1972		198,887,279	
1973		350,206,403	
1974		273,185,722	
1975	335,080,606	553,446,007	

Source: Processed data from Onassis Business Archive, Alexander S. Onassis Foundation, *Olympic Maritime SA*, June 1955–June 1970, "Libro Diario," 26 vols.; Sociedad Industrial Maritima Financiera Ariona, "Libro Diario" 1952–1955, 1970–1974, 5 vols., *Sociedad Maritima Miraflores Panama S.A.*, "Libro Diario," December 1946–December 1957, January 1961–January 1966, October 1969–December 1975, 10 vols.; Libro Diario Aristotelis *Sociedad Maritima Panama S.A.* "Libro Diario," 1951–1958, 1960, 5 vols.

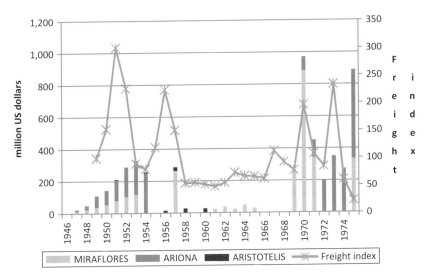

Figure 9.1 Gross income of the three Onassis A-companies in comparison with the
fluctuation of freight rates, 1946–1975
Source: See Table 9.5.

As it is not clear to what extent there is double counting of the multiple
holding companies in the ledgers of these companies, I have presented the
yearly results of each company's accounts separately. The unification of the
group's outcome was done internally every year, and the overall balance results
of the group's excess profit over losses was the combined work of the accounting offices in Montevideo and Monte Carlo. Until now, however, I found only
the overall results of 1975 in the Onassis Archives. These indicate that the
Onassis Group's excess profits over losses, as of December 31, 1975, amounted
to $513 million. For that same year, for Miraflores and Ariona alone, the gross
income is calculated as almost $900 million (Table 9.6).

Contribution to the Development of Ship Technology and Gigantism

Aristotle Onassis was a world leader in the shift towards ship gigantism, and in
advancing shipping technology in general. By the time of his death, his fleet
was composed of tankers whose sizes today are considered the standard types.
According to today's ship terminology, the vessel size groups are indicated in
Table 9.6.[36]

By the late 1930s oil transported by sea had reached fully 20 percent of total
world seaborne trade. By the 1950s, this number had doubled to 40 percent, and

---

[36] *Review of Maritime Transport* (New York: UNCTAD, 2015), 22.

Table 9.6 *Types and sizes of tankers, 2016*

Very large crude carrier	200,000 deadweight tons (dwt)
Suezmax crude tanker	120,000–200,000 dwt
Aframax crude tanker	80,000–119,999 dwt
Panamax crude tanker	60,000–79,999 dwt

Source: *Review of Maritime Transport* (New York: UNCTAD, UN 2015), 22.

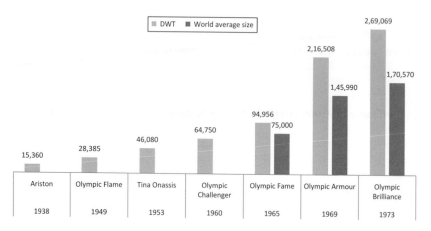

Figure 9.2   From the supertanker to the VLCCs in the Onassis fleet (deadweight tons)
Source: Tables 7.1–7.8; for the world average size of tankers *Review of Maritime Transport* (1976): Table 10, 20.

by the early 1970s 55 percent of all seaborne trade worldwide was oil. The size of vessels required to serve this trade also exploded between the late 1940s and the 1970s. The aim was to achieve economies of scale: the larger the tanker, the lower the cost of transport, the higher the profits. Such economies of scale would not have been possible without technological advancements in shipbuilding. These also related to the speed of loading and discharging operations. For example, in 1969 tankers of 200,000 dwt and over were able to load and discharge 12,000 tons per hour, double the performance of a 90,000 dwt tanker a few years earlier. There were further improvements in the engines, hull design, propulsion, rudder, navigation aids, and even new kinds of hull paints. Technical advances were made inside the hull too; gradually automation reduced the number of crew from over fifty to about thirty seamen. Aristotle Onassis was ordering larger and more technologically advanced tanker ships in each wave of shipbuilding orders.

   The largest vessels Onassis ordered are depicted in Figure 9.2. His first tanker was the *Ariston*, of 15,360 dwt, which was ordered from the Swedish shipyards; it was one of the biggest and most technologically advanced tankers of its time. Ten years later, in 1949, his second tanker almost doubled the size: *Olympic Flame*, built in US shipyards at 28,385 dwt. In Germany, four years later, he built the largest tanker in the world and the first to take the name "supertanker": *Tina Onassis*, 46,080 dwt (the term denoted a new type of tanker that was, at the time, between 50,000 and 70,000 dwt). He continued building supertankers in the German shipyards and his *Olympic Challenger*, built in 1960, was 64,750 dwt. As larger ships kept being built, the industry invented more superlatives, like the "mammoths" of 100,000 dwt;[37] Onassis's "mammoth" *Olympic Fame* was built in 1965 in French shipyards. Eventually the industry ran out of colorful superlatives; the largest category of tankers, of above 200,000 dwt, began to be called Very Large Crude Carriers (VLCCs). When the shipyards could build VLCCs Onassis was one of the first to order them; he received his first VLCC *Olympic Armour* of 216,508 dwt in April 1969 from the Hitachi shipyards in Japan. From 1969 to 1973 he built fourteen VLCCs in Japanese, French, and British-Irish shipyards; his last VLCC, *Olympic Brilliance* (269,069 gwt), was built in Britain and Ireland in 1973. Another two he had ordered were received in 1976, after his death.

The giganto-mania in tankers reached its limit in the 1970s with colossal ships of between 350,000 and 500,000 dwt; these were the Ultra Very Large Crude Carriers. The tendency to growth in the average size of tankers continued throughout the postwar period, but it seems that the rate of increase for the period 1965–1975 was higher than any other time. Onassis, although always at the top of the ship sizes, did not exceed the various limitations imposed on the size of tankers. These were, first, the terminal facilities. Large ships need deep waters at sea and in terminals: a fully loaded 200,000 dwt tanker needed 61 feet depth, and a 300,000 one needed 73 feet. In 1970 there were only eight ports in western Europe able to accept vessels more than 200,000 dwt, and outside western Europe, only Tokyo.[38] The other limitations were the world's main sea routes, the Suez and Panama canals, hence the terms "Suezmax" and "Panamax."

Onassis was always above the average size of the world fleet (see Figure 9.2 and Table 9.7). In 1960 he owned a tanker fleet of 1.4 million dwt, representing just over 2 percent of the world tanker fleet. That same year 14 percent of his fleet's tankers was above 65,000 dwt, whereas only 2 percent of the world tanker fleet was above 65,000 dwt. In the next tanker category, between 25,000 and 65,000 dwt, the percentage of his fleet was almost the same as the world fleet (43 percent for Onassis, 40 percent for the world fleet). In the smaller tankers, under 25,000, his percentage was way below the world fleet. However, it was in 1975 that the difference was tremendous, indicating his leadership; that year he owned nearly 3 percent of the world's tanker fleet, but 64 percent

---

[37] Mike Ratcliffe, *Liquid Gold Ships* (London: Lloyd's of London Press, 1985), 19–120.

[38] *Review of Maritime Transport* (1976).

Table 9.7 *Onassis and world tanker fleet in sizes of ships (in million deadweight tons)*

Size of tanker	Onassis tankers		World tanker fleet	
1960	Onassis (million dwt)	% of total	World fleet (million dwt)	% of total
Above 205,000	–		–	–
65,000–205,000	0.2	14	1.3	2
25,000–65,0000	0.6	43	25.9	40
under 25,000 dwt	0.6	43	36.8	58
Total	1.4	100	64.0	100
1975				
Above 205,000	3.2	64	28.7	18
65,000–205,000	0.5	10	48.8	31
25,000–65,0000	1.1	20	49.9	32
under 25,000 dwt	0.3	6	28.3	18
Total	5.0	100	155.7	100

Source: Tables 7.1–7.8; Ratcliffe, *Liquid Gold Ships*, 123.

of his fleet was above 205,000 dwt, whereas in the world tanker fleet only 18 percent was above that size.

Moreover, Onassis ships were known to be in excellent condition, due to frequent repairs and good-quality spare parts. His technical department in Monte Carlo was divided into the new-build and repair departments and was managed by an efficient team with good working relations.[39] The new-build team, headed by Andrea Spyrou, studied and proposed developments in ship gigantism. The Onassis tankers were easily distinguishable at sea by their bright white paint scheme, unusual because it was so costly to keep the color fresh (the usual practice was to paint ships black or green). He was particular with his ships, and his staff had strict orders to keep the external and internal parts of his vessels and engines in immaculate condition. He was known to build all his ships with luxurious crew accommodation, regardless of the cost.[40]

Aristotle Onassis was a shipowner in the traditional sense: attached and committed to his vessels. There was a relationship between man and ship. He was very proud of his fleet and knew every single one of his ships by their name, characteristics, condition, and "birthday." Recurring anecdotes from his close collaborators indicate that he considered them as living beings and often

[39] Interview with Thanos Krassaris, March 30, 2016.
[40] Papadimitriou, "The Other Onassis"; Vlassopoulos, *Pages of a Life*, 123; Dimitris Paizis-Danias, Θαλάσσης Μνήμες [*Memories of the Sea*] (Athens: Finios, 2008), 38.

compared them to cows that should be known by their names, implying that they produced the "milk" that was needed for his business.[41]

Management

The management of the Onassis companies was highly complex. The fleet was large, ranging between sixty and eighty vessels that sailed around the globe. He had between 3,500 and 5,000 employees at sea and in offices, staffing roughly 200 companies operating from six countries on three continents. For the management of its resources, a shipping company develops systems that have to do with capital, people, and information.[42] To that end the operations of a shipping company and the departments involved include: (1) selection and acquisition of ships; (2) employment of ships (chartering); (3) ship operation (constant communication between ship and office); (4) technical administration; (5) Support of the ship operation (supplies); (6) manning of ship and office; (7) insurance; (8) administration of information and communication; (9) financial administration; (10) communication with client-charterers and the rest of social and business partners; and (11) quality and education.[43] Table 9.8 reflects the system of organization of the management of the Onassis shipping business from 1954 to 1975. Its mainstay was the mobility and the constant control by Onassis at all levels, a group of trusted managers in key positions, and a large number of staunch and loyal employees.

From 1946 to 1975 the operation of the vessels took place from his agencies established in New York, Monte Carlo, London, Paris, Piraeus, and Montevideo (see Table 9.8). From 1946 to 1954 the central offices of the Onassis shipping group were divided between New York and Montevideo. The operation of the vessels in New York took place through the Central American Agency. After 1954, the year when Onassis was sued by the American government, Olympic Maritime SA became the principal agent and Central American Agency acted as a subagency of the Onassis group of companies, but was in fact also the agency of his American company Victory Carriers Inc., established in New York in the neighboring offices. This was the holding company of the US-flag vessels of the Onassis fleet as things were formulated after the settlement agreement of December 1954 between Onassis and the US Justice Department.

During this period more than half of Onassis's ships were under an American flag (see Table 7.2). Onassis himself dealt with the purchases, sales, and finance, and his managers, Nicholas Cokkinis and Costas Gratsos, dealt with the chartering, operation of ships, technical support, and supplies, along with another three trusted men, Creon Broun, William A. Preusch, and Thomas

---

[41] Vlassopoulos, *Pages of a Life*, 121; Papadimitriou, "The Other Onassis."
[42] Theotokas, *Management of Shipping Companies*, 118–140.   [43] Ibid.

Table 9.8 *The geographic location of Onassis shipping operations and management, 1954–1975*

Aristotle Onassis

General Directors (in Monte Carlo)
1954–1965 Nicolas Cokkinis
1965–1971 Nikos Konialidis
1971–1977 Stelio Papadimitriou

Where based	Name of company/agency	Departments	Directors
Monte Carlo	Olympic Maritime (1951)	Chartering	1954–1985 Costas Vlassopoulos
		Sales and Purchase	
		Technical Dept	a) New-builds
			1950–1986 Andrea Spyrou
			b) Maintenance
			George Koutsouvelis
			1953–1986 Gerasimos Dragonas
		Ship Operation	Constantine
		Supplies	Michalis Dologlou, Hadjiconstantis, Costas Papas
		Economic Department	P. Nikolaides
		Insurance	Astoin and Dracoulis
		Computer	Charles Girard
		Director	1946–1981 Costas Konialidis
		Accounting	Guillermo Mc Clew
		Legal	Eduardo Albanell Mc Coll, Lorenzo W. Hayter
Montevideo	Constantino Konialidis Holding		
	Olympic Maritime Agencies		

252

Location	Company (year)	Function	Director
Piraeus	Springfield (1961)	Crewing Port captains	1963–1973 Captain Dimitri Vlismas
New York	Central American Agency (1947)	Manager Financial Accounting Supplies Accounting Insurance Crewing Legal	1947–1975 Nicolas Cokkinis Creon Broun William A. Preusch Thomas Lincoln
	Victory Carriers (1948)	Manager	George Gratsos (1963–1983)
London	Olympic Agencies		
Paris	Olympic Maritime (1952)		
Hamburg	Olympic Maritime (1951–1959)	Manager	1951–1959 Kurt Reiter
Jeddah	Saudi Arabian (1954–1960)	Management Legal	Michael Dologlou Stelio Papadimitriou

Dates for directors stated when known

Source: Onassis Archive, Alexander S. Onassis Foundation, Corporate Books, Central American Steamship Agency, Springfield Shipping Co., Olympic Maritime SA, Victory Carriers Inc.; Interviews with Thanos Krassaris April 30, 2016 and Paul Ioannidis April 18, 2016, May 16, 2016.

Lincoln, who was a lawyer. It is worth noting that the latter was the son of Leroy A. Lincoln, who was president of the Metropolitan Life during the time Onassis obtained his initial financing there.[44]

In the post–World War II period, the Buenos Aires office lost its importance. It was headed by Nikos Konialidis, but there was no shipping activity run from there. In its stead, the Montevideo office acquired a central position in the management of the companies, running two extremely important departments of the Onassis business: the Legal Department and the main Accounting Department. Costas (or Constantinos) Konialidis, who proved the most trusted of Onassis's cousins, headed the office from 1934 until at least 1956. He remained, at least nominally, the head of the office there until 1975; he moved to Athens after 1956, where he was appointed General Manager of *Olympic Airways S.A.* He still, however, traveled once a year for a couple of months to Montevideo after the move, to supervise the Montevideo office.[45]

The first European office that Onassis established was Olympic Maritime Panama SA in Paris in 1952; the company was formed and incorporated in 1951. But it was in 1954, after he moved Olympic Maritime SA to Monte Carlo, that the company became the main agency, the window to the world and the head office of his shipping conglomerate until his death. It has been reported by many that the main aim of transferring his business to Monaco was because the Principality was a tax haven, but this was only partly true. The establishment of the Onassis offices in Monaco did not affect the taxation obligation of his Panamanian agency, Olympic Maritime SA. The company, apart from paying its tax obligations to the country of its nationality, paid 30 percent of its agency income to the Monaco tax authorities, since it operated ships from Monte Carlo.[46]

The departments operating in Olympic Maritime SA were the chartering, sales and purchases, finance, operation, the technical department, the supplies, and the port captains. The technical department had two important sections: the new-build section and the maintenance section. Onassis's company was well known for the excellent condition of the ships. Thanos Krassaris, a shipbuilding engineer who studied in Germany and worked until 1969 in the Howaldtwerke shipyards in Hamburg, joined the company in 1969 in the ship maintenance section; his brother Panos Krassaris, a shipbuilding

---

[44] "How the Empire was Run," *New York Times*, June 15, 1975.

[45] Interview with Ritsa Konialidis, December 22, 2016. According to the wife of Constantino Konialidis, they kept a house in Montevideo and also had a coffee plantation in the north of the country. While correspondence to Montevideo was addressed to "Constantino Konialidis, 1481 Missiones, Montevideo, Uruguay," and all correspondence from Montevideo to Monte Carlo includes the typed name of "Constantino Konialidis," it was signed on his behalf either by Lorenzo W. Hayter, Eduardo Albanell Mac Coll, or Guillermo McClew. Therefore, one can safely assume that the "directorship" of Constantine Konialidis (actually a citizen of Uruguay) was only nominal; staff did all the real work.

[46] Vlassopoulos, *Pages of a Life*, 96.

engineer, worked for the company from 1955. According to the testimony of Thanos Krassaris, there was an excellent team spirit and team work in the technical department in Monte Carlo.[47]

In Piraeus, the Onassis agency Springfield Shipping Co. was established in 1962–1963 and was used as a subagency of Olympic Maritime for recruiting crew. It was formed and incorporated in Panama in 1961.[48] There were various other offices around the world. In Paris, Olympic Maritime's first office in Europe in 1952 was kept to serve Onassis when he visited his home in Paris. In London, Onassis kept an office, Olympic Agents, in Bond Street, in a building that also housed the offices of Olympic Airways. Until early 1960s the group's business was outsourced there to the British shipbrokers Lambert Brothers and Simpson Spence Young. Onassis had offices in Hamburg from 1951 to 1959, in charge of building of his ships in the German shipyards; there was also a Saudi office (Saudi Arabian Tankers) in Jeddah from 1954 to 1960.[49] About 4,500 people were working for the Onassis shipping business in 1970; at least 230 staffed the Onassis offices around the world; the rest were on his eighty ships.

From an Island Maritime Culture to a Business Maritime Culture

If this was a global company, how international were his employees? Onassis certainly hired people of many nationalities: Greeks, Americans, Uruguayans, Germans, Norwegians, English, French, Armenians, and others. Still, most of his employees were Greek, so this was a global company with a Greek character. What is more, Onassis built a distinct maritime corporate culture. Recruitment and selection of human resources was one of his strengths, which made it possible for the Onassis shipping business to continue beyond his death. Onassis built sound human and professional relations with top executives and office employees alike, as well as with the seamen of his ships; mutual loyalty characterized his relations with most of his Greek employees. He invested in his people, spent time with them, and was able to establish a culture of trust and pride, based on hard work and efficiency.

[47] Interview with Thanos Krassaris, March 30, 2016.
[48] Onassis Archive, Alexander S. Onassis Foundation, United States District Court, Southern District of New York, "Rosemary Nelson against Central American Steamship Agency, Springfield Shipping Co., Olympic Maritime SA, Olympic Trading Co., Victory Carriers Inc., Victory Development Corp., Victory shipping and Trading Inc. and Williston S.A.," 89 Civ. 5872 (RO), "Testimony of Michael Cleoudis."
[49] In the meeting of Sociedad Maritima Miraflores on August 19, 1959, "the Chairman then stated that as the sale of the real estate situated at 13 Harvestehuderweg, Hamburg that was owned by the Company had been now concluded, it was necessary to appoint an Attorney in Fact to act on behalf of the Company to settle tax matters with the German tax authorities." Onassis Archive, Alexander S. Onassis Foundation, Corporate Books, Sociedad Maritima Miraflores.

As Ioannis Theotokas has pointed out, in Greek shipping the business philosophy and culture that characterizes an entrepreneur determines the management and organization of his material and human resources.[50] It is known that the leader sets the pace. "If the owner lacks integrity, it will quickly become apparent to employees," and vice versa.[51] As Michael Miller has recently reemphasized, maritime culture matters enormously in the shipping business.[52] A unique culture permeated the Onassis organization, originating with its head. In Greek shipping circles, he is the only shipowner recognized as a legendary boss.

Choosing the right people is not easy. Onassis prized loyalty and long-term relationships; for example, he knew most of the CEOs of his businesses from the beginning of his career, and many remained in their posts during and after his lifetime. Although he usually did not believe in kinship but hired based on merit, his first cousins, with whom he started and developed his businesses, remained his close collaborators; they were regarded as bosses only superseded by Onassis himself.[53] Onassis's relationship with Nikos Konialidis, with whom he was very close up to the 1930s, was not an easy one; various testimonies describe Nikos Konialidis as erratic.[54] Onassis gave him the lead only for short intervals (see Table 9.8). In contrast, Costas Konialidis remained throughout as one of Onassis's right-hand men. Costas Gratsos, "Onassis' closest friend,"[55] whom he met in Buenos Aires in the 1920s, introduced him to shipping through the Ithacan London office of Dracoulis, and to Ithacan seamen. Creon Broun was a Greek American employed in the Central American Steamship Agency, first hired in 1947. He acted as chief operating officer, responsible for its day-to-day management. Nicolas Cokkinis, whom Onassis met in New York in the 1940s, and Costas Vlassopoulos, whom he met in London in the 1930s, also remained in this inner circle, as the main managers of his fleet.[56]

This was the old guard. By the late 1960s, however, some of its members were aging or stepping outside the bounds of their authority. What is more, in

---

[50] Theotokas, "On the Top of World Shipping"; Mark Casson, *Economics of Business Culture: Game Theory, Transaction Costs, and Economic Performance* (Oxford: Oxford University Press, 1991).

[51] Frank Hoy and Trudy G. Verser, "Emerging Business, Emerging Field: Entrepreneurship and the Family Firm," *Entrepreneurship: Theory and Practice* 19 (Fall 1994): 9–23.

[52] For a recent analysis on maritime business culture see Miller, *Europe and the Maritime World*, 176–210.

[53] Interview with Thanos Krassaris, March 30, 2016; S. Papadimitriou, "The Other Onassis"; Papinianos, *Ο δικηγόρος* [*The Lawyer*] (Athens: Estia 2013), 27–34. The latter book are the memoirs of Tryphon Koutalidis, a Greek lawyer who used the pseudonym "Papinianos" to write this book, which is mainly about his relationship with Aristotle Onassis and Olympic Airways.

[54] Papinianos, *The Lawyer*; Vlassopoulos, *Pages of a Life*; Alexandra Papadimitriou, *Αλεξάνδρεια-Αθήνα* [*Alexandria-Athens*] (Athens: Kastaniotis, 2010).

[55] Vlassopoulos, *Pages of a Life*, 42–43.   [56] Ibid., 82.

Figure 9.3 Stelio Papadimitriou (1930–2005), a lawyer, was one of Onassis's youngest recruits in 1954 in one of the most difficult missions, the Saudi Arabian deal. In 1971 he was selected as General Director of all Onassis's businesses, and became his right-hand man. He proved fundamental for the execution of Onassis's will and for the creation of the Alexander S. Onassis Foundation, of which he was President (1988–2005)
Source: Courtesy of the Onassis Archive. © 2018 Onassis Archive/Onassis Foundation.

1966 after his conflict with Prince Rainier, Onassis did not set foot in Monte Carlo for the next six years; during his absence there were suspicions of mismanagement and breach of trust in the business there.[57] It was at this stage that Aristotle Onassis felt the need to introduce younger men to take the lead. His instinct proved right and his decision to clean the house at this stage proved fundamental for the future of his business.

The new guard were younger people who had worked and collaborated with Onassis for a number of years and had proven their abilities and trustworthiness. His way of working with his younger executives has been described as the "Onassian University."[58] It was an education in negotiations, drawing up of

---

[57] The suspicions concerned Nikos Konialidis, CEO of the shipping business. See Papadimitriou, *Athens-Alexandria*, 416–417. Vlassopoulos characterizes Nikos Konialidis as a "dictator," implying problems at Monte Carlo; see Vlassopoulos, *Pages of a Life*, 158–159. Same does Papinianos, *The Lawyer*. The above were verified by an interview with Paul Ioannidis, April 18, 2016.

[58] Papinianos, *The Lawyer*, 27–34.

INNOVATION IN GLOBAL SHIPPING

contracts and agreements, financial analysis of contracts, and dealing with laws and legal institutions.[59] The member of the new guard selected and appointed to run his business in 1971 was Stelio Papadimitriou.

Stelio Papadimitriou (1930–2005) was one of Onassis's youngest recruits and had to complete one of the most difficult missions in the Onassis business. He had just graduated from the University of Alexandria in Egypt as a young lawyer when he was selected by Onassis in 1954 at only twenty-four as his personal lawyer for the Saudi Arabian agreement. Papadimitriou had grown up in Egypt and, apart from Greek, was fluent in Arabic, French, and English; he also knew the Arabic and western European law. What is more, Papadimitriou had a common background with Onassis. They were both raised in the multiethnic, multicultural, and multilingual cities of Alexandria and Smyrna, which had large Greek populations along with French, Italians, Armenians, Jews, Turks, and Arabs. Under Onassis's employment, Papadimitriou was established in Jeddah from 1954 until 1960 and went through the Saudi Arabia-Aramco ordeal.[60] After the agreement was concluded, despite Onassis proposing to move him to Monte Carlo or New York, Papadimitriou decided to continue independently, first in Alexandria from 1960 to 1965 (with the Egyptian law firm Abdel Hadi & Yansouni, which specialized in maritime law) and then in Piraeus, Greece independently after 1965.[61] In 1970, Onassis asked Papadimitriou to work with him again; this time Papadimitriou accepted.[62] In 1971 he became the CEO of Onassis's shipping business, replacing Nikos Konialidis. Onassis entrusted Stelio Papadimitriou with the training of his twenty-three-year-old son, Alexander, in the shipping business. After Alexander's tragic accident on January 22, 1973, Onassis prepared the future of his business after his own death and trusted Papadimitriou to guide his daughter; Stelio Papadimitriou became his right-hand man. Onassis chose well. Papadimitriou proved worthy of everything Onassis hoped for: he was able, shrewd, insightful, loyal, and trustworthy.

Apart from his own people, Onassis kept a large network of foreign collaborators. He relied highly on trust to coordinate his collaborations worldwide. It all worked on personal, oral agreement. After all, trust is the way the shipping industry works, and the rule is "my word is my bond," as the London maritime market very well knows.[63] Aristotle Onassis was far from perfect.

---

[59] Ibid., 35.

[60] Alexandra Papadimitriou, Τζέντα [Jeddah] (Athens: Kastanioti Publications, 2008), 34, 47.

[61] Papadimitriou, Alexandria-Athens, 175. For Abdel Hadi & Yansouni see http://eldibadvocates.com/about/history/ (accessed August 28, 2016).

[62] Papadimitriou, Alexandria-Athens, 341.

[63] For the development of the institutions in shipping see Boyce, "The Development of Commercial Infrastructure."

However, as an employer he was extremely successful; testimonies of all who worked with him talk about a charismatic personality, hardworking, open to suggestions, creative, friendly, and a passionate businessman. Stelio Papadimitriou wrote that Onassis had an "unbelievable fascination, attraction, warmth and ability to communicate with anybody."[64]

Onassis's ships' agencies were manned mainly by seamen from Ithaca.[65] In fact, Onassis reinvented the maritime culture of the island of Ithaca, shaping it around his distinct corporate culture. "After our families, it is the Onassis Company," Captain Gerasimos Barkas from Ithaca told me. "In 1975 I passed the door of Springfield [Onassis's company in Piraeus] and ever since it became my home"; today he is head of the Marine Department of Springfield, agency of the Onassis shipping company of the Alexander S. Onassis Foundation. Onassis reinvented the traditional bond of a Greek shipping firm to the seafaring population of a Greek island, transforming and modernizing it into a bond that tied a global shipping group to its employees. Maritime culture and pride in being the best is part of the productivity and efficiency of a company and it is highly important in shipping. It is part of the nature of shipping, where small groups of people spend their lives in closed floating societies thousands of miles away from the company's headquarters, and their line of communication with the world is the office. But if it is "their" office – if they have a strong bond to it – then they do the job as best as they can.

Ithaca, with centuries of maritime tradition, was a seafarers' hotbed. One of the traditional methods in Greek shipping to keep the home office closely connected with its ship is that many departments of the company (such as the Crewing Department, the Marine Department, the Operation Department, or the Technical Department) are manned by shipmasters and ship engineers who have served at sea for a number of years within the company. The most able ones are hired eventually to serve in administrative capacities. This tradition has been followed in the Onassis group of companies from its very beginning. For example, in the Marine Department of the Onassis group of companies from 1951 to 1975, eleven out of the fifteen port captains, or 73 percent of the total number, who served in the Onassis offices in Greece, France, Monte Carlo, and the United States were Masters from Ithaca who had served on Onassis ships (Appendix 4.D). Equally, 70 percent of all 140 vessels that Onassis purchased in his lifetime were commanded at one point or another by Ithacan Masters.[66]

---

[64] Papadimitriou, "The Other Onassis."

[65] The wider region of Ithaca included a number of small islands like Kalamos and Kastos, along with the villages on the opposite mainland like Mytikas. Seamen from Cephalonia and Lefkas were also hired.

[66] Marine Department, Springfield/Olympic Shipping and Management. I would like to thank Captain Gerassimos Barkas for making available the archives of the Department.

Figure 9.4   The mainstay of Onassis's crews were Greek. Pictured: the Master and officers of the tanker *Olympic Ice*, on the day of its launching in 1954 at Howaldtswerke, Hamburg, Germany
Source Courtesy of the Onassis Archive. © 2018 Onassis Archive/Onassis Foundation.

Figure 9.5   *Olympic Ice*, 13,655 grt, 21,337 dwt, built in 1954 at Howaldtswerke, Hamburg, Germany
Source Courtesy of the Onassis Archive. © 2018 Onassis Archive/Onassis Foundation.

For example from 1953 to 1966 Captain Dimitris Paizis-Danias from Ithaca served on six tankers and one refrigerator ship of the Onassis group of companies: *Tina Onassis, Olympic Sun, Orfeus, Olympic Falcon, Olympic Thunder, Olympic Challenger*, and *Olympic Armour*.[67] His case is typical of the opportunities shipping gave to young Greek Masters. He became a chief executive in other Greek shipping companies and a shipowner himself. Other Onassis Masters who became shipowners were Dimitri Vlismas and Erikos Kertsikoff. The latter, with Apostolos Hadjieleftheriadis, Grigoris Hadjieleftheriadis, and Ioannis Karastamatis (all former ship captains), formed the Eletson company, a Piraeus-based business that emerged in the late 1960s

---

[67] Paizis-Danias, *Memories of the Sea, passim*. In his book, Paizis-Danias describes his work and crew and mentions anecdotal incidents on all the ships on which he served.

and was established in the 1990s.[68] Eletson today consists of twenty-two double-hull tankers with a combined capacity of 1,489,931 dwt.[69]

In the Piraeus shipping market there is no shipowner other than Onassis who is known to have been such a legendary boss or such a model employer. It was known that "Onassis is a gentleman, he pays well and respects the people that work for him."[70] In an industry where rich shipowners were known to pinch pennies – they "have crabs in their pockets" – he was known to be gallant, and a source of inspiration for his employees; he often visited his ships whenever he could. He was not bragging when he wrote in 1947: "I always had much higher victualling and wage costs than anybody, to the point of being regarded as ignorant and a fool."[71] Onassis paid well but was also very demanding. Orders from the Monte Carlo headquarters were that his vessels should be model ships: "impeccable appearance, quick and efficient procedure in ports and good maintenance."[72] According to his seamen, "he brought civilization to Greek shipping"; seamen worked on brand-new vessels that had heating, refrigerators, hot and cold showers, and comfortable accommo-dation – a spectacular difference from the World War I-era ships in which Greek seamen were called to serve until the end of World War II.[73]

From being proud to be Ithacans, crews of Onassis's ships became proud to be "Onassis men" – a unique corporate culture. What is more, they "adopted Onassis as one of them and considered his ships as 'their own.'"[74] These were considered Greek ships. They may have flown flags of convenience, but the Greek flag always waved honorably on the middle mast; these ships "had a Greek soul, with a foreign hat."[75] It is interesting to note that the port authorities of Rotterdam and Hamburg knew the "Greek soul" of Onassis' ships. In Hamburg, for example, since 1952, the "Willkomm-Höft" ("welcome point") was established and ships were greeted on entering and leaving the Elbe with their national anthem. Every time an Onassis ship left, under a Panamanian, Liberian, or Honduran flag, out of respect for their Greek crews, the Greek national anthem was played to bid them farewell.[76]

Conclusions

Onassis was a prime mover after World War II exclusively in instituting offshore companies, with their flags of convenience, in the rapidly globalizing

[68] Theotokas and Harlaftis, *Leadership in World Shipping*, 145.
[69] www.eletson.com (accessed September 28, 2016).
[70] Papadimitriou, *Alexandria-Athens*, 322.   [71] Onassis, "Our Postwar Shipping."
[72] Paizis-Danias, *Memories of the Sea*, 93.   [73] Ibid., 76–77, 81.   [74] Ibid., 99.
[75] Ibid., 98.
[76] Ibid., 51. See also www.hamburg-travel.com/attractions/hamburg-maritime/willkomm-hoeft/ (accessed September 15, 2016).

shipping industry. In the 1950s it was mainly the Greeks that used them; today two-thirds of the world fleet flies a flag of convenience. One can safely say that Greeks, although steeped in the European maritime tradition, were the first to respond to and to lead the transformation of global shipping.

In this way Onassis was a pioneer global entrepreneur. He conducted his business in the 1940s in ways that anticipated modern business practices, not least its globalization. Onassis innovated on four levels. First, he pioneered the modern model of ownership and management of global shipping companies, based on offshore companies, flags of convenience, and multiple holding companies. Second, he was the one to first open the US financial markets to ship finance. Third, by building tankers in US, European, and Asian shipyards, he contributed to the evolution of ship technology and gigantism. And fourth, he reinvented Greek island maritime culture into a corporate shipping culture. In this way he converted the old-school Greek shipping practice in bulk trades to a new global shipping practice.

Onassis developed and refined the ownership and management of vessels, something that contributed dramatically to the formation of the global shipping company. From the 1930s he implemented the concept of the division between companies of ownership and companies of management, something quite usual in the practice of shipping. What was unusual in the 1930s and 1940s was his extensive use of (almost exclusively) Panamanian companies and, even more important, the multiple layers of holding companies and management companies that protected the owner from legal entanglements. Onassis had learned his lessons well, and desired never again to be so exposed to judicial attack or political conflicts.

10

Diachronic Presence

An Epilogue

The unique success of the Greeks was that they created a global shipping business while still retaining the traditional family and national character that had characterized Greek shipping for hundreds of years. When the ship steward Christos Triantis died in 2000 in the town of Mytikas in the Ionian Sea only eleven miles from Skorpios, the Onassis island, his coffin was wrapped in the Onassis shipping flag before it was interred. Five or six years earlier, he had asked Captain Gerassimos Barkas, head of the Marine Department of Springfield Shipping Company of the Onassis shipping business, for such a flag (Figure 10.1); he told his relatives that, after his death, everyone should remember that he was "an Onassis man."[1] In 1975, the Onassis businesses employed roughly 11,500 people in sea and air transport, almost all Greeks. Aristotle Onassis was by far Greece's largest and most popular private employer.

Forty years after Onassis's death, in the yearly event of Lloyd's List Shipping Awards 2015, Onassis's shipping business, the Olympic Shipping and Management SA, was voted tanker company of the year. It was the first time the shipping company received a prize that did not have to do with the Onassis legacy, but was earned on its own merits. The Onassis shipping group is a unique case in Greek shipping: the private shipping business of one man that successfully continued its shipping activities after his death, without immediate descendants and without being listed on the stock market. What Onassis did was to create a business family that not only still remembers him and honors his name, but also continues his business and operates tankers that fly the Onassis flag.

In 2008 – 106 years after his death – Panagi Vagliano was inducted into the Greek Shipping Hall of Fame, as one of the founders of the modern Greek-owned fleet.[2] The Greek shipping world had retained its knowledge of the Vagliano Brothers' importance to the country's maritime tradition in its collective memory, passed down through the generations. In 1975, the shipowner-historian Andrea Lemos wrote: "humble and plain was Panagi

---

[1] Interview with Captain Gerassimos Barkas, March 30, 2016.
[2] http://greekshippinghalloffame.org (accessed January 25, 2019).

Figure 10.1   The Onassis shipping logo on the funnel of *Tina Onassis*. The same logo is on the flags hoisted on all Onassis ships to the present day
Source: Courtesy of the Onassis Archive. © 2018 Onassis Archive/Onassis Foundation.

Vagliano's office in London, from which he directed one of the largest businesses of his time. This was what Panagi Vagliano was: the Patriarch of our modern merchant shipping."[3]

What happened to the Vagliano and Onassis businesses after their deaths? Why and how were they able to continue successfully their legacy, and what was their effect on Greece, Greek shipping, European shipping, global shipping? This chapter will explore their diachronic presence in all four levels.

The Wills

Although they were not succeeded by their immediate offspring in business, the Vaglianos and Onassis both ensured a multigenerational diachronic presence. Both included bequests for public benefit foundations in their wills: remarkably, they both left fortunes of roughly similar amounts. The three Vaglianos left about $2.1 billion and Onassis $2.7 billion in 2018 US dollars (see Table 10.1). In 1902, when the last Vagliano died, the brothers' bequest was £12.4 million; this was, even more remarkably, equivalent to half of Greece's Gross National Product (GNP), which was £25.5 million at that time.[4] Even if we take just Panagi Vagliano's fortune of £2.9 million, it would equal 11 percent of Greece's GNP in 1902. When Onassis died in 1975, Greece's GNP was about $17 billion; this would make Onassis' fortune 3 percent of the whole country's Gross National Product. It is no wonder that they became such legendary figures; this was public largesse on a grand scale.

---

[3] Lemos, *Modern Greek Eternal Seamen*, 82–83.

[4] George Kostelenos, Dimitrios Vasileiou, Emmanouil Kounaris, Socrates Petmezas, and Michael Sfakianakis, *Ακαθάριστο Εγχώριο Προϊόν, 1830-1939* [*Gross Domestic Product 1830-1939*] (Athens: KEPE and Historical Archives of the National Bank of Greece, 2007).

Table 10.1 *The Vagliano and Onassis inheritances*

	Value of assets from inheritance (contemporary prices[a])	Pounds sterling (1902 pound sterling purchasing power)	Pounds sterling [b] (2018 pound sterling purchasing power)	US dollars[c] (2018 US dollars purchasing power)
Andreas Vagliano (d. 1887)	36,000,000 *French francs*	1,540,465	185,994,405	246,182,194
Mari Vagliano (d. 1896)	200,000,000 *drachmas*	8,000,000	1,045,458,823	1,383,769,298
Panagi Vagliano (d. 1902)	2,886,420 *Pounds sterling*	2,886,420	348,503,841	461,279,684
All Vagliano brothers		**12,426,885**	**1,579,957,069**	2,091,231,177
Aristotle Onassis (d. 1975)	**$500,000,000** **£244,750,000**		**2,016,827,151**	2,669,472,417

[a] 1975 US dollar = 0.4895 pounds sterling. Conversion of 1 pound sterling to US dollar, Mid Exchange Rate: 1.3236 on July 16, 2018, www.poundsterlinglive.com/best-exchange-rates/best-british-pound-to-us-dollar-history-2018.
[b] For conversion of pounds sterling to 2018 purchasing power, www.bankofengland.co.uk/monetary-policy/inflation/inflation-calculator.
[c] for conversion of dollars to today's purchasing power, http://data.bls.gov/cgi-bin/cpicalc.pl.
Sources: For Andreas Vagliano, *Deltion Estias*, May 31, 1887; for Mari Vagliano, *Epitheorisis*, Greek newspaper, January 27, 1896; for Panagi Vagliano, Vagliano Archive GSA, Cephalonia Archive, file 1, "The Will of Panagi Athanasse Vagliano." For Aristotle Onassis, interview with Paul Ioannidis, April 18, 2016.

Of course, there was plenty left for family members. The first Vagliano to die, Andrea Vagliano in 1886 in Marseilles, distributed 36 million French francs or $246 million (in 2018 US dollars) in his will. Andrea bequeathed 5 million French francs (about $35 million in 2018 US dollars) for each of his three surviving sons, Marino, Alexandros, and Christoforos. He also took care of the women of his family; he left 4 million French francs to his wife Eurphrosyne, 2.5 million to his unmarried daughters, and 2 million to the married ones. About 100,000 francs were sent to Greece for philanthropic activities and 10,000 for the poor of Marseilles.[5]

Mari Vagliano died in Taganrog in 1896. He was the richest of the three Vaglianos, but there is no will extant for him. The level of his fortune was probably exaggerated; estimates vary between £8 and £17 million. According to Russian sources it was estimated at 148 million rubles; this makes it worth £17 million in 1902.[6] According to some Greek sources it was £10 million;[7] while according others it was 200 million drachmas, which makes it £8 million in 1902.[8] I chose the latter, smallest amount as the estimate of his fortune. The Russian sources stress the fact that he did not leave any philanthropic dona-tion in Taganrog or anywhere else in Russia. His two sons, Alcibiades based in London and Athanasse in Paris, inherited his estate and became the richest of all the Vagliano second generation.

Panagi Vagliano died in 1902 (Figure 10.2). He left £2.8 million (£348 million in 2018) or about half a billion US dollars in 2018 purchasing power (Table 10.1) in his will. Almost one-fifth of his fortune (£500,000, or £60.4 million in 2018 value) went to his home island, Cephalonia, and founded the Panagi Vagliano Bequest. The rest of his money went to his nine nephews, as he had no surviving children.[9] All of the Vagliano inheritance was comprised of ships, real estate, and, most importantly, portfolio investments.

Aristotle Onassis died in 1975 (Figure 10.3). His fortune was estimated at $500 million, divided between his daughter and the Foundation that was to be formed bearing his lost son's name. So Onassis left $250 million (or $1.35 billion in 2018 value) to the Alexander S. Onassis Foundation, and an

[5] *Deltion Estias*, May 31, 1887.
[6] Four Russian sources agree on the amount of 148–150 million rubles. The first one is in "The Will of the Lost M. A. Vagliano," in the newspaper *Taganrog Vestnik*, January 31, 1896. The second is the Альманах-справочник по Городу Таганрог и его okrugi [*Guide-Catalogue of the City of Taganrog and its Region*], 1912, 145–148. The third is found in the Rostov Archives, GARO P-2557.2.20, which includes the unpublished study by V. Anensky, "The History of Rostov, 1749–1944," which mentions the same amount for the Vagliano fortune. In that same file it is noted that V. Anensky was working for the Archives of the Secret Police Service of the Russian Empire which was later merged in GARO. The fourth source is the recent book by Oleg Pavlovich Gabrioushkin, *Мари Вальяно и другие (Хроника обывательской жизни)* [*Mari Vagliano and the Others (Chronicles of a Local Society)*] (Taganrog: Editions MIKM, 2001), 272.
[7] E. I. Kapsabelis, *Τι οφείλει η Ρωσία εις την Ελλάδα* [*What Russia Owes to Greece*] (Athens: n.p., 2003), 105.
[8] *Athinaiki Epitheorisis*, January 27, 1896.
[9] Vagliano Archive GSA, Cephalonia Archive, file 1, "The Will of Panagi Athanasse Vagliano."

Figure 10.2   Panagi Vagliano, the "Patriarch" of Greek shipping
Source: Nursery Home-Charity Foundations of Lixouri, Cephalonia.

Figure 10.3.   Aristotle Onassis, March 28, 1955
Photo credit: Bettmann.
Source: Getty Images.

equivalent amount to his daughter Christina. Apart from his shipping business and banking accounts, this sum included real estate in Greece, such as the houses and the island of Skorpios, along with assets in the United States, such as half of the Olympic Tower and the yacht *Christina*.[10] While this study concentrated on Onassis's shipping business, it is worth noting at this point that he had significant investments in other sectors too. His Olympic Airways, which he proudly used to call the only private airline in the world apart from Howard Hughes's TWA, had developed from a small local airline to a world-wide giant by 1975. In 1975, Olympic Airways had a fleet of thirty airplanes of the latest technology, carrying more than 3 million passengers and with a total of 7,500 employees.[11]

For his 11,500 employees (in shipping and Olympic Airways), Onassis was their famed boss. For people in Ithaca, Lefkas, and Cephalonia, Onassis and the Vaglianos were local heroes and, for many others, national stars. For the first half of the twentieth century the Vagliano Foundation functioned as the social safety net for the population of the island of Cephalonia, providing social security, health, and education. From the mid-1970s to the present day the Onassis Foundation has become a renowned model of international philanthropy, providing education, culture, and health care in Greece and promoting Greek culture in Greece and abroad.

The Vaglianos' business was not continued by their immediate descendants after the death of the founders. Nevertheless, their impact on Greek shipping was immense, disseminated through their collaborators and other relatives like the Lykiardopoulos family. The Vaglianos managed to create a maritime business network and a nodal ship-management office that provided the springboard for numerous other businesses to develop. The Onassis business continues to the present day but, again, not by Onassis's descendants. Onassis managed to create a corporate business family and culture that survived him. What is interesting is that none of the descendants of either family today speaks Greek, and most refute or have refuted their Greekness. However, the legacy of both is nowhere as evident as it is in Greece and in the Greek shipping business, an economic sector where Greeks excel internationally and which the Vaglianos and Onassis marked with their activities.

The traces left by such people are not just money invested in business, real estate, institutions, or bloodlines. Such people formed part not only of a national but an international heritage, business culture, and image. They became part of an international elite: followed by the press and inspiring fictional characters on page, stage, and screen. The legend of Onassis, one of the "world's most

---

[10] Interview with Paul Ioannidis, April 18, 2016.
[11] Athanassios E. Papageorgiou, Ελληνικές Δημόσιες Αερομεταφορές [*Greek Public Airlines*] (Athens: Free Thinking, 1987).

sympathetic rich,"[12] a modern Greek Croesus, is well known thanks to the thousands of articles and dozens of books, films, TV series, documentaries, and songs written about him. In their time, the Vaglianos were also part of the international elite, albeit in a less popularly visible way.

Panagi Vagliano left almost one-fifth of his fortune to a bequest for charitable purposes for the island of Cephalonia. The bequest was to be under the control of the Charity Commission in London and a permanent Committee of Trustees in Cephalonia; the sum of £500,000 (or £60.4 million in 2018 purchasing power) and its investments were to be left with his bank, the London and National Westminster Bank. Health, education, religion, and relief of poverty were his prime concerns. Thus, the Vagliano Hospital was built: a complex of buildings including pathology, cardiology, and pediatrics clinics, run by the so-called Philanthropic Brotherhood of Cephalonia. The hospital became a prototype medical institution in Greece during the interwar period and it supported excellent doctors and staff. In addition, a series of schools were built and administered to promote education. The Mercantile Marine School and the Practical Agricultural School in Argostoli, as well as the Technical and Professional School of Lixouri for training technicians and marine engineers, were established and started functioning in the 1920s.[13] As a result, Cephalonians received good education and health care on their home island and were considered the aristocracy among Greek seafarers.[14] In a sense, the Panagi Vagliano Bequest defined the character of Cephalonia.

However, in 1953 there was a devastating earthquake in the Ionian islands that mostly destroyed Cephalonia, Ithaca, and Zante. Almost all the buildings constructed by the Vagliano Bequest were destroyed. The Vagliano Hospital was demolished. The Mercantile Marine School at Argostoli was also destroyed; in its place, at the heart of Argostoli, is still an empty space called the "White Earth." The buildings of the Agricultural School were also wrecked, along with the school in Kerameies. What remained standing were the church of St. Basil and the Technical Professional School in Lixouri, which has become the Department of Sound and Musical Instruments Technology in Lixouri.[15] And

---

[12] Papadimitriou, "The Other Onassis."

[13] Ioannis Antonopoulos and Ourania C. Kalouri, "Το Βαλλιάνειο κληροδότημα στις Κεραμειές της Κεφαλονιάς: Η συνάντηση Κοσμοπολιτισμού Και τοπικής Κοινωνίας" ["The Vagliano Bequest in Kerameies of Cephalonia: The Meeting of Cosmopolitanism and Local Society"], www.eriande.elemedu.upatras.gr/eriande/synedria/synedrio3/praltika%2011/antonopoulos-kalouri.htm (accessed August 10, 2016); A. Debonos, "Εμποροναυτική Σχολή Αργοστολίου" ["Commercial and Maritime School of Argostoli"], Κυμοθόη 4 (1994): 35–43.

[14] Lemos, Modern Greek Eternal Seamen, 407.

[15] Spyros P. Kouloumbakis, Βαλλιάνειος Επαγγελματική Σχολή Ληξουρίου (Β.Ε.Σ.): ιστορική αναδρομή 1900–2000 [Vaglianos Professional School of Lixouri (VES): A History] (Arta: n. p., 2002).

of course, far more broadly influential than the Cephalonian-based Panagi Vagliano Public Benefit Foundation, the legacy of the three Vaglianos still lies in the center of Athens: the Vagliano National Library, built by the famous Danish architect Baron Theophil Edvard von Hansen, which has served Athenians and Greeks more generally in continuing and preserving Greek culture. A total donation of 2.8 million drachmas in the 1890s ($13.3 million in 2018 purchasing power) has served the country well for the last 120 years.

Aristotle Onassis left half of his fortune to the public benefit foundation named after his lost son, Alexander S. Onassis.[16] The headquarters of the Alexander S. Onassis Public Benefit Foundation today are situated in the beautiful neoclassical mansion in Plaka on Amalias Avenue 56, in downtown Athens. A replica of Onassis's Monte Carlo office is touchingly set up in the building with all the original *boiserie* and the Louis XV furniture. Visitors can see his desk, complete with his amber worry beads, and behind it his large library with its (read and annotated) books. In 1999, the affiliated Alexander S. Onassis Public Benefit Foundation was established in the Olympic Tower in New York, opposite the Rockefeller Center, in order to promote Greek culture and education in America. It supports a large number of programs of exchange of Greek professors in the United States, neo-Hellenic programs in American universities, and organizes exhibitions on Greek culture.

The first main contribution of the Alexander Onassis Public Benefit Foundation was to education. The Foundation has sponsored prestigious scholarships for graduate and doctoral studies for thousands of Greek and young foreign scholars since 1978, along with a valuable library, which is being provided with Greek books from the period of Renaissance until the late years of the Neo-Hellenic Enlightenment. Also after 1978, the international prizes program was set up according to Onassis's will. Another important contribution is in medical care, the "Onasseio" as the Greeks commonly call it. This is the Onassis Cardiac Surgery Centre (OCSC) completed in 1992. A more recent focus is on art, the Onassis Cultural Centre inaugurated in December 2010, a new vibrant cultural site with the mission to promote modern cultural expression.

From 1977 to the end of 2011, the Onassis Public Benefit Foundation offered more than $1 billion (in 2018 purchasing power) and has become one of world's leading public benefit foundations.[17] All this money has been mainly provided from the Onassis shipping business that is operated by the Alexander Onassis Foundation. The Onassis Public Benefit Foundation has continued a long line of

---

[16] Stelios Papadimitriou, President, Alexander S. Onassis Foundation, "The Workings of a Public Benefit Foundation. The Alexander S. Onassis Foundation: Problems and Solutions," lecture held at the City University Business School, Department of Shipping, Trade and Finance, London, Monday, November 11, 1996.

[17] Paul J. Ioannidis, *Destiny Prevails: My Life with Aristotle, Alexander, Christina Onassis and Her Daughter, Athina* (Athens: Livani Publishing, 2013), 313.

Greek traditional national benefactors, diaspora merchants, and shipowners who, since the nineteenth century, have formed foundations to channel funds either to their home islands, villages, towns, or cities in the Greek provinces, or to Athens. The Onassis Public Benefit Foundation was the first Greek foundation, however, to acquire such national and international prestige, due to its spread of activities and amount of financial funds.

In a kind of metaphysical form of continuation of the Onassis-Niarchos "rivalry" the public loved so much, the Stavros Niarchos Foundation followed on the same scale. It was formed after the death of Stavros Niarchos in 1996, twenty years after Aristotle Onassis. It has also shown remarkable activity that has culminated in the completion in 2016–2017 of the Stavros Niarchos Foundation Cultural Centre, an impressive complex lying on Greece's former National Race Course, where now stands the new National Library of Greece, the new Greek National Opera, as well as the Stavros Niarchos Park. There is symbolism in the proximity of some of these institutions. The Stavros Niarchos Foundation Cultural Centre lies next to the Onassian Cardiac Surgery Centre. And the new Niarchos National Library replaces, after 120 years, the old Vagliano National Library. What is lacking in this remarkable new institution is its shipping dimension. Despite the existence of a large family and descendants, there is no longer a Niarchos shipping business.

The Vagliano Family and the Business: Diachronic Presence

Panagi Vagliano wrote his will on January 16, 1900 and it was supplemented in May 1901.[18] He describes himself as "Panagi of Athanassios Vagliano, merchant of the City of London." He left about one-sixth of his fortune to a Vagliano trust fund for the education, health care, and needs of the people of Cephalonia and the rest to eight of his nephews, sons of his brothers who ran the business with him.[19] His fortune was invested in government bonds and railway stock all over the world.[20]

---

[18] Vagliano Archive GSA, Cephalonia Archive, file 1, "The Will of Panagi Athanasse Vagliano."

[19] Alcibiades and Athanasse, sons of Mari, inherited at least £4 million each in 1896 (£523 million in 2018 purchasing power) upon the death of their father, and another £297,000 (£36 million in 2018 purchasing power) from their uncle. Marino, son of Andrea, after the death of his father in 1886, inherited 5 million francs (or $25 million in 2018 purchasing power), and another £197,000 from Panagi. Panagi left £197,000 (£24 million in 2018 purchasing power) to each of his three nephews, Michael, Athanasse, and Christoforos, sons of his brother Spyridon; and £197,000 each to Basil and Athanasse, sons of his brother Metaxas.

[20] Ibid., and Gelina Harlaftis, "Μεγιστάνες του Ιονίου: Ο οίκος των Αδελφών Βαλλιάνου" [Ionian Tycoons: The House of the Vagliano Brothers"], *Ionios Logos* 1 (2007): 303–346.

Although Panagi Vagliano had a plethora of nephews, he did not make any of them minor or major partners in the Vagliano Bros. Company after the death of his brothers, but retained total control over all business, signing all correspondence himself to the very end. As a result, after his death, the Vagliano Bros. Company had to be dissolved. Alcibiades and Basil were the two nephews established in London who collaborated closely with their uncle Panagi. After his inheritance from his father Mari, who died in 1896, Alcibiades must have withdrawn from the business. It was mainly Basil who ran the London office until 1902 and was Panagi's most likely successor in operating a new, similar office. He and his wife lived in London in the house next to their uncle Panagi.[21] But Basil passed away suddenly in 1903, at the age of fifty-seven.[22] Just a few years after his death, his only daughter Danae married her second cousin Marinos (of Athanasse, son of Mari) Vagliano and they lived in Paris until World War I.

Both sons of Mari Vagliano, Alcibiades (1850–1924) and Athanasse (1854–1936), were born in Taganrog (Figures 10.4 and 10.6). They both must have left home after they turned eighteen and never lived in Russia again. After the death of their father Mari, they inherited his immense fortune and became millionaires. Alcibiades settled in London in 1868 and in 1875 was naturalized as a British citizen.[23] He married the beautiful Angeliki (1855–1912), daughter of the merchant Xenophon Balli, in July 1873.[24] In 1881 they settled in fashionable Kensington, at 68 Holland Park, where they kept five servants.[25] They did not have any children and Angeliki, known as Madame Vagliano, mingled in London high society, where she was recognized as a beautiful and elegant socialite always in the front line of new social trends (see Figure 10.5).[26] Athanasse Vagliano (1854–1936), son of Mari, made an excellent marriage in the Anglo-Greek "commercial aristocracy" around the early 1880s (Figure 10.6). He married Katina Ralli (1861–1941), the daughter of Stephen Ralli, relative of the mighty Ralli brothers (see Figure 10.7).

The Vagliano second generation and their children and grandchildren formed part of an international *haute bourgeoisie* dispersed among many

---

[21] They lived at 21 Dawson Place, whereas Panagi Vagliano lived at 16 Dawson Place, Kensington (later Bayswater); 1881, English Census-Ancestry.co.uk.
[22] With a letter to John Hollams, on March 19, 1907 Alcibiades announced the closure of the office of Basil Vagliano in London. Vagliano Archive, GSA, Cephalonia Archive, Letterbook, 1904 Private no. 9 (1904–1914).
[23] "Naturalisation of Alcibiades Vagliano," General Archives HO45/9385.
[24] *The Pall Mall Gazette (London)* (2619, July 8, 1873).
[25] 1881, English Census-Ancestry.co.uk.
[26] Lady Violet Greville, "Place aux Dames," *The Graphic*, 1894.

Alcibiades Vagliano,
1851-1924

Figure 10.4   Alcibiades (1850–1924), son of Mari Vagliano
Source: Timotheos Catsiyannis, *The Greek Community of London* (London: 1993).

countries, from Russia to the United States, from the United Kingdom and Switzerland to Egypt.[27] Athanasse and Katina Vagliano made sure their sons and daughters married into French nobility and abnegated their Greek line, although the faded memory survived somewhere in the family history (Appendix 1.A). Their children, grandchildren, and great-grandchildren lived on large French estates, in castles, and lavish mansions. Of their four children, their firstborn, Marino (1883–1960), married a Greek; his second cousin, Basil M., married Vagliano's only daughter, Danae. Their family lived between Paris, Cannes, and Switzerland, while during World War I they lived in England. Their sons, Stephan and Francis, never worked, nor did they have any children. Stephan Vagliano was a dilettante writer and collector, and he was the one who became interested in and indicated sensitivity to the Vagliano family's island of origin, Cephalonia.[28] The ninety-two-year-old Francis Vagliano narrated the faded memory of the origins of the family in 2004, from his residence in Switzerland:

---

[27] Théodore Zarifi and Stéphane Zarifi, eds., "Zarifi & Cie. 150 ans d'histoire (Récits et témoignages)," typescript. I would like to thank Sonia de Panafieu for making it available to me.

[28] Collection of Stephan and Frances Vagliano, Korgialeneio Historical and Folklore Museum of Cephalonia.

Figure 10.5   Angeliki Vagliano, daughter of Xenophon Balli, wife of Alcibiades
Vagliano. Her portrait was done by James Lafayette in 1899.
© Lafayette Portrait Archive / Victoria and Albert Museum, London.

My brother was interested in the family in Greece in particular, Cephalonia where the Vaglianos come from. They were shipping people, you
see. We are a family that came from Cephalonia and we became a
shipping people bringing wheat from various countries in Europe ... they
sold the wheat to all over the world.[29]

The descendants of Andrea Vagliano, based in Marseilles, formed the other
French branch of the Vagliano family, and it was a big family: Andrea and
Euphrosyne Vagliano had nine surviving children (Appendix 1.A). The firstborn, Marino A. Vagliano (1851–1928), was fully involved in shipping and
shipowning until 1902. In the mid-1890s he married a lovely young wife,
Liola (1873–1967), daughter of the Douma and Petrokockino family, who had
been brought up in Greece (see Figure 10.8). Their son André (1896–1971)
became a French and international golf champion between the 1920s and
1930s and established the Vagliano Trophy, a regular international contest in

---

[29] Interview of Frances Vagliano by Jason Vagliano, June 11, 2004, available on YouTube.
I would like to thank Jason Vagliano and his father Andre Vagliano for uploading the
interview and making it available.

Figure 10.6   Athanasse Vagliano (1854–1936), son of Mari Vagliano
Source: Collection of Stephan and Frances Vagliano, Korgialeneio Historical and Folklore Museum of Cephalonia.

women's golf.[30] His daughters Lally and Sonia also excelled in golf, with Lally becoming an international golf star. His sister, Sonia Vagliano (1898–1990), continued the new Vagliano tradition by marrying into the French aristocracy: she married Raoul de La Poëze, marquis d'Harambure, and her children too married into French aristocratic families (Appendix 1.A).

The son of the champion golfer André M. Vagliano, and great-grandson of the first Andrea and Euphrosyne Vagliano, Alexander A. Vagliano (1927–2003), graduated in law from Harvard University and made the first male breakout from this indolent line of the family. Working in law and in banking by 1969, at the age of forty-one, he became Senior Vice President of Morgan Guaranty Trust Co. and President of the Bank's subsidiary Morgan Guarantee International.[31] It was only the great-great-grandsons, the fifth Vagliano generation, that launched into independent business in the United States and France, in publishing, wine exports, and marketing.[32]

---

[30] André M. Vagliano, "Golf in France," in J. S. F. Morrison, ed., *Around Golf* (London: Arthur Baker Limited, 1939); *Autobiography of Lally Vagliano-de St. Sauver on Her Life in Golf in Lally* (Morfontaine: n.p., 2011). Her sister, Sonia Vagliano-Eloy, also wrote a biography, *Les Mademoiselles de Gaulle, 1943–1945* (Paris: Hachette littératures, 1999) about her service during World War II.

[31] "Alexander Marino Vagliano," *Hartford Courant*, November 17, 2003.

[32] Correspondence with Andre Marino Vagliano, November 11, 2016.

Figure 10.7   Katina Ralli (1861–1941), daughter of Stephen Ralli, wife of Athanasse Vagliano
Source: *Femina* no. 69, December 1, 1903.

Figure 10.8   The engagement of Marinos Andrea Vagliano (1851–1928) and Eleni (Liola) (1873–1967), daughter of Ioannis Doumas and Sophia Petrokockino, in Athens, 1895. Third from the left in the third row is Marinos and next to him is Liola. Fifth from the left in the second row (the lady in black) Euphrosyne Vagliano
Source: Private collection of Marina Eloy, Paris.

Figure 10.9   Athanasse S. Vagliano and his nephew Panagi N. Lykiardopoulo whom
he financed. The Lykiardopoulos, closely related to the Vaglianos, continued their
legacy. Their firm is today among the top tanker shipping firms
Source: Private collection of Athanassios Akrivos.

The six daughters of Andrea and Euphrosyne Vagliano, who grew up in
Marseilles, were all married by their parents into the Greek merchant diaspora
aristocracy; these were collaborators with the brothers Vagliano, mostly based
in Constantinople, Odessa, Alexandria, and Marseilles (Appendix 1.A).
A large number of their descendants eventually lived in Athens and constituted the Athenian upper bourgeoisie – its old money.

Apart from the sons of Mari and Andrea, Panagi left significant sums of money
to the sons of his brother Spyridon, Michael, Athanasse, and Christoforos. The
first two, Michael (1857–1939) and Athanasse (1865–1927), were in the Vagliano
business established in Russia; Michael in Rostov-on-Don and Athanasse in
Novorossiysk.[33] After the death of his uncle, Michael operated eight of the family
steamships, which he ran from Piraeus with his brothers Athanasse and Christoforos until 1905. His brother Athanasse S. Vagliano collaborated closely with
him (see Appendix 1.D). After working hard in the trade and shipping business
for thirty years, in the last ten years of his life, from 1918 to 1927, as a millionaire
Athanasse enjoyed life as much as he could, marrying a much younger wife and
becoming a sort of a legend in the casino of Monte Carlo. He also invested in the
steamships of his nephew Panagi Lykiardopoulo (see Figure 10.9).

The Lykiardopoulos family are the descendants of the Vaglianos; it is through
the Vagliano women that the bloodline of the Vagliano shipowning business
continues to the present day. The granddaughters of Metaxas and Spyros
Vagliano married into the Lykiardopoulos family (Appendix 1.A). On the eve
of World War II, the Lykiardopulos, who were employed and eventually
financed by the Vaglianos, were operating eight steamships of 36,000 tons and
in the post-World War II period entered the tanker market. Panagis's son Photis
(born 1924) continued the family shipping business successfully. The

---

[33] Bundesarchiv Berlin, R 9331/13. I would like to thank Wolfgang Sartor for this reference.

Lykiardopoulo Company, Neda Maritime Agency, was able to survive the 1980s crisis. In the 1990s the Lykiardopoulo group updated its fleet, entering the forefront of international shipping though the innovative building of the VLCC *Arosa*, the first double-hull, double-bottom supertanker, after the passing of the Oil Pollution Act of 1990 (OPA90).[34] In 2016, Neda Maritime owned twenty-five vessels, VLCCs and bulk carriers of more than 4 million dwt.[35]

Onassis: A Will Like the Business

Aristotle Onassis died on March 15, 1975. Fifteen months before, on January 3, 1974, on his flight from Acapulco to New York, he wrote out his will by hand in Greek. It was an amazing will, like his business. At first glance, it appeared simple. He divided his fortune into two parts, one for his deceased son Alexander and one for his surviving daughter Christina, while he provided an annual allowance for his wife Jaqueline and her children, his sisters, his relatives, and his close collaborators (Figures 10.10–10.11).

But what Onassis really did was construct the administration of his inheritance and the continuation of his business when he was gone, as he had constructed his business edifice while he was alive. Just as the whole concept of his business group was based on multiholding offshore companies of an A-, B- and C-type, his will was multilayered.

The Alexander S. Onassis Foundation inherited 50 percent of the Onassis shipping fleet and assets and was to operate the shipping and other businesses; this foundation had no other owner and was completely independent from the estate of Christina and her descendants (Figures 10.12 and 10.13). The executors formed two foundations, a business one and a public benefit one. The business one, Alexander S. Onassis Foundation, would direct 40 percent of its profits to the second, charitable, foundation: the Alexander S. Onassis Public Benefit Foundation, which was also its ultimate beneficiary. Another 40 percent would be directed to run the business and 20 percent would be channeled to investments. Following Onassis's testament, the executors created another two companies: an A (Alpha) company named ASO Financiera, Panama SA and a B (Beta) company, ASO Naviera, Panama SA, which in turn would own all the other C-companies (Figure 10.14).

The Alexander S. Onassis Foundation, and its main beneficiary, the Alexander S. Onassis Public Benefit Foundation, were right on target. The achievement of this creation was a personal success of the man Onassis had appointed as the CEO of his businesses in the last five years of his life, the lawyer Stelio Papadimitriou. He proved to be the pillar of both foundations, fully supported

---

[34] Theotokas and Harlaftis, *Leadership in World Shipping*, 217–218.
[35] www.nedamaritime.gr (accessed July 7, 2016).

Figure 10.10   Aristotle Onassis sitting on the side of the pier in front of his yacht *Christina*, April 16, 1956
Photo Credit: Bettmann. Source: Getty Images.

Figure 10.11   Aristotle and Jacqueline Onassis relax during their ten-day tour of Egypt, March 28, 1974
Photo Credit: Bettmann. Source: Getty Images.

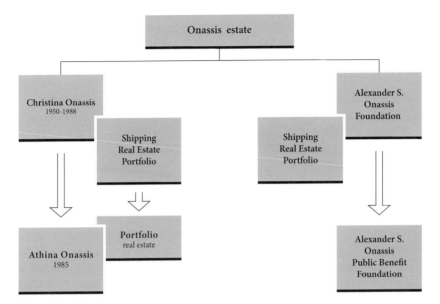

Figure 10.12   The final division of the Onassis estate

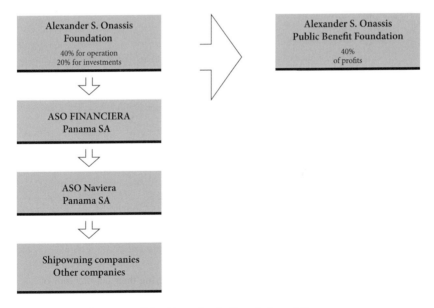

Figure 10.13   Structure of the Alexander S. Onassis Foundation

Figure 10.14   The offices of Olympic Shipping and Management SA in P. Phalero, Athens

Photo credit: N. Daniilidis. Source: Courtesy of the Onassis Archive. © 2018 Onassis Archive/ Onassis Foundation.

by Paul J. Ioannidis, General Director of Olympic Airways,[36] Apostolos Zambelas, an executive accountant of Olympic Airways, and a few others, who "stood by, like faithful and devoted guardians of Thermopylae."[37] For the next few decades it was these people who set the pace: an ethos of loyalty, trust, and respect for the Onassis legacy and memory. They had all gone through the "Onassis University" and run parts of the Onassis business family. Business after all, was Onassis's life. And business did not mean just money, profit, and bank accounts. It meant a business family, with all its relations, daily discussions, and plans amongst family members. As Stelio Papadimitriou noted, "above all the wives, lovers, children, friends, and collaborators, Aristotle Onassis (in my opinion) loved most his business that was an extension of himself."[38]

---

[36] Paul Ioannidis was born in 1922. He became a pilot and joined TAE, Greece's first postwar passenger airline, in 1947. He met Aristotle Onassis in 1956, and became the leading pilot of the new Olympic Airlines: he inaugurated new routes, like the one from Athens to New York, trained in all the newly purchased airplanes, and trained young pilots. An excellent pilot, and a man of few words and great integrity, Paul Ioannidis was characterized by loyalty and passion for his work; by 1966 he had become one of Onassis's trusted men in Olympic Airways. In 1968 he became head of the Flight Operations Department and in 1971 he was appointed by Onassis as Director General of Olympic Airways. It is interesting to note that even in this position he did not stop flying.

Furthermore, Onassis had also entrusted Ioannidis with the supervision and education of his son Alexander, who had become a pilot of small airplanes and had developed a passion for flying. In 1968, with Alexander's initiative, a new Department of Light Aircraft and Helicopters at Olympic Airways was formed. See Ioannidis, *Destiny Prevails*, 107–108, 136, 176–180, 157–158, 173–183.

[37] Anthony S. Papadimitriou, "Introduction," in Ioannidis, *Destiny Prevails*, 15.

[38] Papadimitriou, "The Other Onassis."

Becoming and remaining part of the business family was not easy for the trusted Onassis men. They had to confront turbulent waters in the post-Onassis era. The first President of the Board of Directors of the Alexander S. Onassis Foundation was Christina Onassis (1975–1988).[39] After her death, the Presidency of the two Foundations was shared by Stelio Papadimitriou and Professor Ioannis Georgakis (1988–1992), and then Papadimitriou (1992–2005) by himself. Upon his death in 2005, his son Anthony S. Papadimitriou was unanimously elected next President. This was a business family and perceived as such; but this family was related by merit rather than blood. The great achievement of Onassis was that he created a unique corporate culture – a corporate culture *a la grecque*. The three Vaglianos did not manage their succession well but, as it has turned out, Onassis chose his business family, and the family business chose well.

The family businesses that manage to choose successors from the most able sons (or daughters) are the ones that succeed in passing the business from generation to generation. The custodians of the Onassis legacy who formed the executive committee of the Board of Directors of the Alexander S. Onassis Foundation – Stelio Papadimitriou, Paul Ioannidis, and Apostolos Zambelas – passed the torch gradually to a new generation of managers: their sons, Anthony Papadimitriou, John Ioannidis, and George Zambelas. The new generation was well educated and had been part of the Alexander S. Onassis Foundation since their youth. This threesome constituted the new executive committee starting in 1998 and worked harmoniously together for a number of years. Each one had a different task. Anthony Papadimitriou[40] was responsible for the legal and economic section of the Foundation, John Ioannidis[41] for shipping and George Zambelas[42] for the real estate.

---

[39] For all the turbulent meta-Onassis times see Ioannidis, *Destiny Prevails*.

[40] Anthony Papadimitriou (born in 1954) graduated in Law at the National Kapodistrian University of Athens Law School where later he received his PhD. He did further graduate studies in France, at the University of Aix-en-Provence, and in the UK, at the London School of Economics. A managing partner of the legal firm of S. & A. Papadimitriou and Partners, since 1986 he has served as legal advisor to the Onassis Group of companies.

[41] John Ioannidis (born in 1954) was admitted to the Oxford Air Training School in England in 1974 and trained as a commercial pilot. Subsequently, he joined Olympic Airways SA and remained with the airline for fourteen years. In the meantime he took degrees in economics and shipping. He joined the Onassis group in 1988. In January 1992 he became Director General of Springfield Shipping Co. Panama SA, and in 1998 he became the Managing Director of Olympic Shipping and Management SA, replacing his father. Interview with John Ioannidis, December 22, 2016.

[42] George Zambelas trained as an architect; he joined the Board of Directors of the Alexander S. Onassis Foundation in 1988.

In 2005, after the death of his father, Anthony Papadimitriou was elected President of the Board of Directors of the Alexander S. Onassis Foundation and the Alexander S. Onassis Public Benefit Foundation. Anthony Papadimitriou took the lead, and has proven an excellent leader; he is also cultivated and widely read, understanding art, literature, history, and education. This is a man who remembers the words of his own father: "Loyalty has been the key to success," emphasized Stelio Papadimitriou. "Onassis always told newcomers seeking a job with the group: 'Look my friend, I am most impressed with your qualifications but with the kind of money I have, I could buy people with even more qualifications than yours. But I cannot buy people with loyalty, which is what I want if you come with us.'"[43]

The Onassis Shipping Business after Onassis

The Onassis shipping business today, owned by the Alexander S. Onassis Foundation, is situated in Paleo Phalero, the first coastal suburb of Athens to the south on the coastline (see Figure 10.14). The main management company of the Onassis group of companies today is called Olympic Shipping and Management SA; it replaced Olympic Maritime SA. It operates the ships and does the chartering, insurance, and accounting. Springfield Shipping Panama SA, traditionally headquartered in Greece, is a subagency of Olympic Shipping and Management SA, domiciled under the same roof; it handles manning, purchasing, supplies, the Marine Department, and the technical management of the fleet, while the other subagency, Olyship SA in London, is involved with insurance.

In November 2016, the Onassis Olympic fleet of the Alexander S. Onassis Foundation consisted of twenty-seven ships of 5.3 million dwt, with an average age of eight years. Forty years before, it had inherited 25.5 vessels with a carrying capacity of 2.7 million dwt and of a similar average age. As at the time of Aristotle Onassis, it is still mainly a tanker fleet, half of which consists of the largest possible vessels, VLCCs, as was the case in the past. Half of the fleet sails under the Greek flag. The ships' crews comprise more than 600 seafarers, of whom one-third are Greek, 15 percent Russian (mostly officers), and the rest other foreign seafarers.[44]

All heads of the departments that operate and run the ships have been selected from among those that Aristotle Onassis trusted. What is more, the maritime corporate culture has continued and has been disseminated. From the interviews I carried out, I sensed a stable, healthy working environment in

---

[43] Papadimitriou, "The Other Onassis"; Nigel Lowry, *Onassis and his Legacy* (Athens: Alexander S. Onassis Public Benefit Foundation, Lloyd's List, 2003), 85.
[44] www.onassis.org/en/business-foundation.php (accessed September 9, 2016).

Table 10.2 *The Onassis fleet, 2016*

Vessel name	DWT	Type	Year built
1. *Olympic Legacy*	302,789	Tanker VLCC	1996
2. *Olympic Spirit II*	96,773	Tanker Arfamax	1997
3. *Olympic Liberty*	309,449	Tanker VLCC	2003
4. *Olympic Legend*	309,270	Tanker VLCC	2003
5. *Olympic Future*	155,039	Tanker Suez max	2004
6. *Olympic Flag*	155,009	Tanker Suez max	2004
7. *Olympic Leader*	306,997	Tanker VLCC	2005
8. *Olympic Loyalty II*	306,997	Tanker VLCC	2005
9. *Olympic Gemini*	82,992	Bulk carrier	2006
10. *Olympic Peace*	55,709	Tanker Supramax	2006
11. *Olympic Pride*	55,705	Tanker Supramax	2006
12. *Olympic Sea*	104,402	Tanker Arfamax	2008
13. *Olympic Sky*	104,215	Tanker Arfamax	2008
14. *Olympic Galaxy*	81,383	Bulk carrier	2009
15. *Olympic Lion*	319,541	Tanker VLCC	2010
16. *Olympic Trophy*	319,869	Tanker VLCC	2010
17. *Olympic Trust*	319,869	Tanker VLCC	2010
18. *Olympic Luck*	319,106	Tanker VLCC	2010
19. *Olympic Leopard*	319,368	Tanker VLCC	2011
20. *Olympic Target*	319,869	Tanker VLCC	2011
21. *Olympic Light*	317,106	Tanker VLCC	2011
22. *Olympic Glory*	84,091	Bulk carrier	2011
23. *Olympic Pegasus*	56,726	Tanker Supramax	2011
24. *Olympic Pioneer*	54,443	Tanker Supramax	2012
25. *Olympic Progress*	54,439	Tanker Supramax	2012
26. *Olympic Hope*	182,631	Bulk carrier	2016
27. *Olympic Harmony*	182,631	Bulk carrier	2016

Source: *Olympic Shipping and Management SA.*

the whole building; unpretentious, with great respect for and pride in where they work, and with a sense of continuity and stability that permeates from the top officers to the lower-rank employees. The General Manager of Springfield is Dimitris Patrikios, hired by Paul Ioannidis back in 1988. Patrikios, a graduate from the University of Athens, received an MBA from Imperial College, London. He eventually succeeded Thanos Krassaris, who had joined the Onassis business in the 1960s.[45]

[45] Interview with Dimitris Patrikios, December 9, 2016.

The company continues the traditional Greek shipping practices. The most able captains eventually come ashore to head the various Departments of the company. In November 2016, head of the Operations Department was Captain Dionysis Siganakis, forty years in the Onassis shipping business.[46] Head of the Manning Department is Captain Thanasis Apostolopoulos, from Piraeus. He joined the Onassis shipping company in 1982 and traveled on Olympic ships from 1982 to 2006, of which he served ten as a Master.[47] Head of the Marine Department is Captain Gerasimos Barkas from Ithaca. Captain Barkas graduated from the Nautical High School of Ithaca in 1970; out of his thirty classmates, twenty-two went to sea, and out of those, twelve were employed in the Onassis shipping company.[48] Head of the Technical Department is naval architect Dimitris Makris, from Corfu. He studied in Scotland and did postgraduate studies at University College London.[49] Out of the twenty-seven Greek captains now serving, half come from traditional maritime islands and five are still from Ionian islands (Cephalonia, Ithaca, Lefkas, and Kalamos). The maritime culture of the Greek islands has penetrated the Onassis corporate culture. The success of the Onassis business family was that it guarded its know-how and its tradition, which ran not only from the top down, but also from the bottom up.

Creating Global Business: An Epilogue

This book is about the creation of global bulk shipping by the Greeks. It narrates the transformation of the island shipping companies of the Ionian and Aegean seas into international trading companies, then London shipping and ship-management offices, and finally to global shipping groups. The story unfolds through the paradigms of two main Greek shipping firms, that of the Vagliano Brothers, whose business life spans from the 1820s to 1900s, and that of Onassis from the 1920s to the 1970s. The book indicates how the Vagliano and Onassis enterprises followed and, at the same time, reinvented the evolution of Greek shipping and how their innovations led to the creation of global shipping. It was in large part due to their pioneering activities that, at the beginning of the twenty-first century, Greek shipowners still have the largest fleet in the world.

During the nineteenth and twentieth centuries, the Greeks, who carried with them the European maritime tradition, transcended the local, and connected the local and regional with the international and global. In the twentieth century, they evolved as agents of globalization, following but also

---

[46] Interview with Captain Dionysis Siganakis, December 9, 2016.
[47] Interview with Captain Thanassis Apostolopoulos, December 9, 2016.
[48] Interview with Captain Gerassimos Barkas, December 9, 2016.
[49] Interview with Captain Dimitris Makris, December 9, 2016.

reinventing shipping practices on a global scale, yet retaining locally based maritime traditions. Onassis belonged to this group of shipowners, which changed the face of shipping in the post–World War I era, replacing the British, the world's largest shipping companies of the first half of the twentieth century. The Vagliano and Onassis firms opened new markets, pioneered the adaptation of new technology, operated with network firms in many states, and survived confrontations with political regimes in Russia and the United States. They managed to be competitive in the international economy by creating new business methods and organizational models that ultimately led to the creation of global shipping firms; they also added to these new creations the reinvention of their own maritime business culture and the development of local institutions to fit global norms. Their paradigms reflect and explain the success of the Greek shipping firms. The reasons can be traced within two large categories: exogenous and endogenous factors.

The exogenous factors have to do with the political, economic, and social environment that prevailed during their lifetimes. The Vaglianos served both the British and Russian empires in their colonial expansion in the Black Sea; they also benefited from the formation of the Greek state. For the British, they were citizens of a British semicolony, of the state of the Ionian islands, which lasted from 1815 to its union with Greece in 1864. The Black Sea was a desirable area to access and the British urged and supported the Ionians to penetrate the Russian grain markets. The firm Vagliano Brothers was registered in the City of London from 1858, and became one of the largest British trading houses involved in the Black Sea trade. However, the Vaglianos also served the Russian Empire well. They became among Russia's largest grain exporters, fulfilling the expectations of the imperial policy makers in attracting Greek merchants and shipowners to the south. Since the Vaglianos were based in Taganrog, on the Azov Sea – an area that was an export gateway for the grain production of the cultivated vast steppe hinterland – their shipping and trading activities were pivotal for opening and connecting this frontier land and transforming it into a prime exporting zone of the whole empire. What is more, the formation of the Greek kingdom after 1830 gave the Vaglianos a state to whose protection they could turn at times when they were in danger in their host countries. For the young Greek state, the Vaglianos, along with all the economically powerful Greek diaspora merchants outside its jurisdiction, were the capitalists they would support in exchange for reciprocal actions.

The Vaglianos were products of the Industrial Revolution, during which Europe imposed on the world the economic system that still prevails to the present day: raw materials and foodstuffs from developing to developed countries, and industrial goods from developed to developing countries. World trade between 1800 and 1900 increased twenty times and the need for transportation by sea exploded. It was during this period that the transport revolution took place on land and sea, by the introduction of railways and steamships. These developments brought significant changes to the world shipping market, including its sharper division into liner shipping (which carried industrial and processed goods and people) and tramp shipping (which carried raw materials and foodstuffs). It also brought specialization to the profession of the shipowner. The Vaglianos, with the British and the Russians as partners, along with the large Greek maritime network they led, were able to exploit the opportunities offered by the new era, and became pioneers in the shipping business of the eastern Mediterranean and the Black Sea, by carrying grain from the east and coal from the west using both sailing ships and steamships.

Aristotle Onassis's life was marked by the political developments in the eastern Mediterranean where he was born, and he was able to benefit from the interwar economies of Argentina and Greece to form his initial capital. However, ultimately it was his relationship with the United States, the leading economy of the post–World War II period, that gave him the opportunities for the great leap forward in his own business and world shipping. He and his family were among the victims of the Greco-Turkish war that followed World War I and was the cause of the forced uprooting of Christian and Muslim populations from centuries-long homelands; but Onassis's father, remarkably, was able to start a new trading company almost immediately after his establishment in Greece based in Piraeus. Young Aristotle, with a refugee passport, decided to leave Greece and seek his luck elsewhere. In Argentina, he was able to exploit the opportunities and, in collaboration with his father, was involved in importing tobacco to Buenos Aires.

Onassis entered shipping in the 1930s, a transitional era for both shipping and the world economy. Two world wars, the economic crisis of the 1930s, and the decolonization of the British Empire fractured the status quo, and dealt a deathblow to many British shipping groups that had traditionally reigned. Moreover, the rise of oil as the world's energy source changed sea transport systems and opened new possibilities in a globalizing era. Onassis seized these opportunities. Taking advantage of surplus from the massive US shipbuilding program during World War II, he rode the crest of the spectacular rise of the oil trade from 1945 to 1973.

Furthermore, the postwar period was characterized by the increased use of offshore companies and flags of convenience. "Flagging out" from traditional registers of national fleets to flags of convenience was a major feature of interwar and particularly of post-World War II international shipping. The flags of convenience of Panama, Honduras, and Liberia – known as the PanHoLib fleet – were cheap flags with low taxes, which provided cheap sea transport for large US corporations like the oil companies. Onassis and the other Greek shipowners were among those that were able to take advantage of this opportunity. The breaking of the genuine link between flag and nationality opened the route to the global fleet of the flags of convenience. Onassis made the United States, the world's new economic power, his main trading partner, as the Vaglianos had done with Russia and Great Britain in an earlier period. He was able to exploit the opportunities presented in the new era and became the pioneer of the global shipping business, carrying oil in gigantic tankers owned by offshore companies and adopting flags of convenience. This was the advantage of the cross-traders and of tramp owners: by serving international trade rather than the needs of a particular nation, they were able to adjust to changes in the world environment.

The endogenous factors behind the success of the Vaglianos and Onassis lie in their entrepreneurship. In order to trace entrepreneurship historically, one has to trace a businessman's entrepreneurial activities within the market system and within his own business. The Vaglianos and Onassis made smart decisions as to the markets in which they were engaged, the types of ships they used in these markets, the timing of their investments in new ship technology, their choice of shipyards, their mobilization of finance and human capital, and the kind of administration and institutional framework they followed. They also innovated, not just by adopting new technology, but by creating new institutional frameworks. As indicated, the path to the top was certainly not easy for them. It took these entrepreneurs years of trial and error amid fierce competition in all the business and political environments where they were active, which culminated in legal confrontations in Russia for Mari Vagliano in the 1880s, and in the United States for Aristotle Onassis in the 1950s. The other important element that characterized both cases was their business philosophy and the culture that determined the management and organization of their material and human resources.

The Vaglianos and Onassis mostly made the right decisions and chose their markets well. They both used the maritime skills and practices of the islands of Cephalonia and Ithaca as the springboard to start and expand their businesses. The Vaglianos recognized the shipping and trade opportunities stemming from grain production in Russia, and were able to exploit the wartime opportunities provided by Russian colonization schemes along the eastern coast of the Black Sea during the Crimean War in 1854–1856, which marked their apogee. For the first thirty years their business was characterized by their constant mobility as merchant captains and traders within the Black Sea and eastern Mediterranean. But in the late 1850s, they chose to expand into the main ports of northern and southern Europe, especially London and Marseilles. Their knowledge of the markets in the world's main economic centers gave them the opportunities to proceed to institutional innovations. By establishing a chain of agencies in the main European port cities linking eastern and western European sea trade and shipping on the one hand, and penetrating the European interlocking financial circuits from the Russian port cities to Constantinople and London on the other, they were able to connect the local to the global.

Onassis recognized the opportunities offered by Greek tobacco exports and promoted tobacco imports to Argentina, something that gave him his first capital in Argentina and financed his timely entry into shipping in the early 1930s. As an outsider in shipping, he was able to recognize and harness the strengths of traditional Greek and Norwegian shipping practices and reinvent the business of shipping in oil transport, using the infrastructures of London and New York, respectively the traditional and emerging world financial and maritime centers. He exploited opportunities and experimented in every sector of shipping: dry cargo, tanker shipping, tramp shipping, liner shipping, coastal shipping, secondhand ships, new ships, small, medium, and gigantic ships. However, what marked him as special was his final decision to invest in tankers and the transportation of oil.

Innovation in ship technology and timely investments in new ship technology characterized both cases. Both the Vaglianos and Onassis led the way in investing in new ship technology. The Vaglianos invested in an unprecedented (for Greek shipping) shipbuilding program of steamships in British shipyards in the 1870s and 1880s. Their investment in steamships took place twenty years before the transition from sail to steam in the Greek-owned fleet. Equally, Aristotle Onassis was the first Greek shipowner to invest in tankers in the 1930s and proceeded with an unprecedented (for world shipping) shipbuilding program of new large tankers in the 1940s and 1950s in US, German, and French shipyards. He negotiated deals and assembled resources to promote his strategy of ship gigantism, and he was one of the prime movers in postwar ship gigantism that established the main tanker types that prevail today.

They both mobilized resources to draw finance and invented or expanded existing methods of ship finance through effective social networking, developing connections within all the economic and political environments in which they worked. The Vaglianos invested in their own ships but also invented a method to finance other shipowners and Greek shipmasters, which secured them control of ship tonnage for their trading activities. In this way, they combined the financial resources of island shipping communities with their own financial resources to promote ship investment. Onassis's success story is his entrepreneurial ability to open the US financial market to ship finance and to expand the method of charter-backed finance, which has been established as a usual practice today.

However, the main contribution of both the Vaglianos and Onassis was in developing the institution of the shipping firm. The element that characterized them was innovation in management and in the creation of new institutional frameworks in shipping business at critical moments of transition of the Greek shipping industry. The Vaglianos invented the "London shipping office," a new form of organization, a hybrid form of shipowning and ship-management office that led Greek shipping firms into the twentieth century. In a way, the London office was the predecessor of the modern ship-management company, which became the new organizational form in international shipping after the 1950s.

Onassis pioneered the modern model of the global shipping company, which had three components. First, he used multiple offshore companies, mainly Panamanian and Liberian, to render the owner of a ship practically invisible. Second, his ships usually sailed under flags of convenience (or open registries). Third, he managed the shipping group from many locations, which meant that there was not a domicile in only one particular country, but businesses run by agencies in different locations. These practices, which were very much frowned upon at the time, have been consolidated and are today considered the proper and usual way of organizing and running shipping companies around the world. Although these practices were not invented by Onassis, he was among the first worldwide, and certainly the first in Greek-owned shipping, to put them all together and consolidate them.

Conflict with host countries and their particular politics is an embedded ingredient of international business. Vagliano and Onassis were both attacked for fraud and corruption, and, despite the seventy-year difference and the different countries, many similarities can be found. Both cases are examples of an old story: governmental accusations of fraud and corruption against foreign entrepreneurial elites. It is indicative of how national interests try to restrict global economic activities, using foreign businessmen as scapegoats for their internal political and economic problems. Both cases reveal the ability of global businesses to overcome government restrictions with the assistance of local economic elites. They indicate the ability of international shipping entrepreneurs to confront governments through official institutions relying on local, national, and international networks. The use of offshore companies has become the ultimate tool to provide the flexibility and adaptability necessary for international shipping companies to survive competition and the protectionist measures of national governments.

The other important element that characterized both cases was their business philosophy. The business philosophy of an entrepreneur determines the management and organization of their material and generates distinct business cultures. The Vaglianos and Onassis have, as entrepreneurs, both left their mark on the culture of Greek shipping. The Vaglianos were nurtured in Cephalonia, an island community with a long maritime tradition and culture. They used and profited from the abundant sources of human seafaring labor of the island, but what they did was to expand further the Ionian maritime and commercial network. By marrying into the existing entrepreneurial network of the Chiot and Ionian merchants, the Vaglianos became part of Greek entrepreneurial network in which they were the leading company during the last decades of the nineteenth century. They also went beyond serving their compatriots from the Ionian islands, a role that had been sufficient until then for the large diaspora Greek trading companies. They in effect built an agency of agencies, providing services through their company to all Greek shipping companies, and thus linking the shipping companies of the Aegean with those of the Ionian islands. Through their London office, they were the first to facilitate access to the London shipping market to all Greek islands shipping companies. It is this practice that made the Vaglianos recognized as "Patriarchs of Greek shipping."

Onassis was able to transform the island maritime culture into a corporate business culture. Onassis's business philosophy determined the management of his human resources both ashore and at sea: this was the famous "Onassis University." He chose young men to collaborate with and conducted his business by both educating them and listening to their views. Most of his seamen came from the island of Ithaca, which had a long maritime culture and a seafaring tradition. He managed to reinvent their local maritime culture into a distinctive corporate culture. His seamen, proud Ithacans for the most part, also became proud of being Onassis seamen. As he was able to create a corporate culture, he ensured its continuation in the Onassis shipping group, forty years after his death. The Alexander S. Onassis Public Benefit Foundation, which was founded posthumously, according to his will, and to which he left half his fortune, continued his shipping business, initially run by his trusted men and today by their offspring. A number of his managers and seamen are still from Ithaca, while all officers onboard the ships are Greek.

Greek shipping families remained in the shipping business, sometimes for multiple generations. Their success lay to a large extent in the fact that they were family businesses that retained an important connection to their local island maritime communities, which provided their human resources and preserved their maritime cultural tradition. They expanded geographically to form solid entrepreneurial networks showing flexibility, versatility, and adaptability. The Vaglianos' case indicated how, from the second stage of the evolution of the sailing shipping firm, they made the transition to the third stage of the international trading firm and then led the way to the formation of a ship-management firm. The Onassis case indicates how from the third stage of the ship-management firm a great leap forward was made to the creation of the new form of the global shipping firm.

The stories of the two businesses indicate the use of the local to reach the global. They are paradigms of how local European maritime culture led to world trade during the nineteenth and twentieth centuries. Shipping has been one of the most dynamic sectors of the European economy since the early-modern period and has constantly generated economic growth. European shipping emerged from regional maritime development and contributed to the process of globalization from its first wave in the last third of the nineteenth century to the beginning of the twenty-first century. By developing transport systems in local maritime regions in areas that transcended state borders, the Greeks expanded during the Industrial Revolution through articulated networks and sea-transport production systems in a wider peripheral maritime region in the nineteenth century, as the Vagliano Brothers case reveals. This led to a new form of global maritime business in the second half of the twentieth century, as shown by the Onassis case. The evolution of Greek business can be seen as an integral part of Europe's maritime history. In the twentieth century the shipping firms of southern Europe took the lead from those of northern Europe; of the traditional northern European shipping powers only the Danish (in liner shipping) and Norwegians are left.

The Vagliano Brothers, a pivotal actor during the transitional stage from sail to steam, were able to adapt to the exponential increase in world trade and sea transport in the second half of the nineteenth century, and to pave the way, with their London office, to a new era for other Greek shipping firms. Aristotle Onassis, then, was the archetype of that new era – a global businessman attached to no country. By building on human relations and mobility on a global scale, he transformed himself into a global entrepreneur, a cosmopolitan, and a citizen of the world. He became the symbol, the face, of the shipping tycoon of the new globalized era. But at the same time, his global activities were interwoven with the local maritime culture of the Greek islands; they depended on the Greek (and Ithacan) men that he had chosen. Aristotle Onassis, who was not from the Ionian Sea but from the Aegean Sea, blended the Ionian maritime tradition into his business, just as the Vaglianos had, and he was able to retain and expand Greek maritime business culture onboard and ashore. If people like their job, if they are proud of it and of who they are, then the business flourishes and survives.

The ships with the Olympic prefix to their names and the Onassis Olympic flag still sail today across the world's oceans, run by global crews – Greeks, Russians, Filipinos, and many more. However, their captains and officers are still Greek and some are still from Ithaca and the Ionian Sea. In November 2016, Captain Fotios Sakarelis was with his tanker *Olympic Leopard*, from the Onassis fleet, anchored in China loaded with 2 million barrels of crude oil from Brazil waiting to discharge. He said:

> I started my career as cadet up to Master with Springfield. I am ten years at sea and if I were young, I would follow the same career. Shipping is a unique career. It separates and joins people. I was privileged to visit many countries and visit many people of different cultures and nationalities. We are Greek officers and Filipino ratings on this vessel … Thanks to company's initiatives we keep in touch with our families despite being tens of thousands of miles apart … We are very proud to continue thousands of years of Greek tradition at sea. God bless Greek shipping.[50]

---

[50] Video/skype interview of Captain Fotios Sakarellis by Captain Gerassimos Barkas in November 2016, given to me by Captain Barkas on December 9, 2016.

SELECT BIBLIOGRAPHY

Archives
Greece

- Archives of the National Bank of Greece
  - Series XXI Correspondence IA, Foreign Correspondence, Vagliano Brothers
- ELIA [Hellenic Literary and Historical Archive]
  - Arvanitis Archive
  - Syrmas Archive
- General State Archives, Archive of the Prefecture of Cephalonia
  - Vagliano Archive
- General State Archives, Syros
  - Archive of Notary Maximos Talaslis
- Onassis Business Archive, Alexander S. Onassis Foundation
  - Corporate Books and Board Meetings of Onassis companies
- Private Archive of Coutsis family, Spetses
- Private Collection of Elias M. Kulukundis, Athens, Logbook *Anastasia*.

France

Bureau Veritas (1830–1900)

Italy

Lloyd Austriaco (1861–1890)

Russia

- State Archives of Rostov Region (GARO)
  - 579.1, Greek Magistrate of Taganrog
  - 584.1.1, Taganrog Port Customs
  - 577.1, Architectural Plans of Taganrog
- *Государственная внешняя торговля в разных ее видах* [*State Foreign Trade in different categories*] (St. Petersburg: Department of Foreign Trade, 1860)

- *Первая всеобщая перепись населения Российской империи 1897 года, 1897* [The first all-Russian population census of 1897] XLVII, Chersonskaya Gubernia, Odessa (Moscow, 1904).
- *Первая всеобщая перепись населения Российской империи 1897 года* [The first all-Russian population census of 1897], *oblast' voiska Donskogo* (Moscow, 1905).
- *Статистический обзор железных дорог и внутренних водных путей* [*Statistical Review of Railways and internal Waterways of Russia*], Министерство путей сообщения, Отдел статистики и картографии, [Ministry of Transport, Department of Statistics and Cartography] (St. Petersburg, 1900)
- *Альманах-справочник по Городу Таганрог и его okrugu* [Guide-catalogue of the city of Taganrog and its region], 1912

Ukraine

- Central Historical Archives of Ukraine, Kiev (TsDIAK)
  - 1072, 3, 1504–1508, "Харьковская судебная палата" [Kharkov Court] "О беспошлинном пропуске заграничных товаров Таганрогской таможней. Январь 1885–1 июня 1887" [On the Imports of Foreign Goods from the Custom House of Taganrog: January 1885–June 1, 1887].

United Kingdom

- Archives of the Bank of England
  - C30/4, "Discount Office Analyses and Summaries: Greek Accounts 1848–1852"
  - "Drawing Office: Customer Account Ledgers," C98/3618 (1858), C98/3646 (1859), C98/3674 (1860), C98/3702 (1861), C98/3729 (1862), C98/3758 (1863), C98/3786 (1864), C98/3815 (1865), C98/3846 (1866), C98/3878 (1867), C98/3906 (1868), C38/3932 (1869), C98/3959 (1870), C98/3985 (1871), C98/4011 (1872), C98/4038 (1873), C98/4064 (1874), C98/4090 (1875), C98/4116 (1876), C98/4142 (1877), C98/4168 (1878), C98/4196 (1879), C98/4223 (1880), C98/4248 (1881), C98/4276 (1882), C98/4305 (1883), C98/4335 (1884), C98/4362 (1885), C98/4394 (1886), C98/4425 (1887)
  - "The Governor and Company of the Bank of England vs Vagliano Bros," Freshfields papers: records of Civil Court Actions, 1798–1903; F13.33–F13.40
- British Customs Bills of Trade, 1830–1910
- *Lloyd's Register of Shipping*, 1880–1975
- National Archives, London
  - Foreign Office, Reports of Consuls from Taganrog, 1860s–1880s
  - English Census, 1861, 1871, 1880, 1881, 1890, 1891, 1901
- *Report on the Financial, Commercial and Industrial Situation of Argentina, Department of Overseas Trade* (London: His Majesty's Stationary Office, 1932)

United States of America

- Federal Bureau of Investigation

○ "Aristotle Onassis," part 1, Bufile 100-125834 and parts 2, 3, and 4, Bufile 46-17783

UNCTAD

Review of Maritime Transport (New York: UNCTAD, UN, 2018)
Review of Maritime Transport (1976)

Newspapers
Russia

- *Южный Край* [Iuznii Krai], Kharkov
- *Кіевлянинъ* [Kievlianin], Kiev
- *Московский листок* [Moskovskii Listok], Moscow
- *Московские Ведомости* [Moscovskie Vedomosti], Moscow
- *Таганрог Правда* [Taganrog Pravda], Taganrog
- *Таганрог Вестник* [Taganrog Vestnik], Taganrog

Greece

- *Ακρόπολις* [Akropolis], Athens
- *Άστυ* [Asty], Athens
- *Αθηναϊκή Επιθεώρησις* [Athinaiki Epitheorisis], Athens
- *Δελτίον Εστίας* [Deltion Estias], Athens
- *Επιθεώρησις* [Epitheorisis], Athens
- *Εθνικός Κήρυξ* [Ethnikos Kyrix], Athens
- *Ελλάς* [Hellas], Athens
- *Ναυτικά Χρονικά* [Nautika Chronika], Athens
- *Οικονομικός Ταχυδρόμος* [Oikonomikos Tachydromos], Athens
- *Πατρίς* [Patris], Athens

United States of America

- *New York Times*
- *The Man's Magazine*
- *The Washington Post*

United Kingdom

- *Hearth & Home: An Illustrated Weekly Journal for Gentlewomen*
- *Horse and Hound: A Journal of Sport and Agriculture*
- *The County Gentleman: Sporting Gazette, Agricultural Journal*
- *The Graphic*
- *The Pall Mall Gazette*
- *The Telegraph*

France

- Commercial and Shipping Journal *Semaphore de Marseilles, 1830–1910*
- *Femina*
- *Le Figaro*

Documentaries

"Aristotle Onassis, The Golden Greek," TV movie, written and directed by William Cran, BBC 1992

Interviews

Interview with Marino Andre Vagliano April 10, 2016; correspondence with Andre Marino Vagliano, November 11, 2016.

Interviews with Marina Eloy, Sonia de Panafieu and Jean Marc de le Bédoyère, Paris, June 23, 2014.

Interviews with Sophia Kostomeni, Thanassis Akrivos, Ioannis Vaglianos-Dimitriadis and Eleni Lykiardopoulou, December 2016.

Interview of Frances Vagliano by Jason Vagliano, June 11, 2004, YouTube.

Interview of Thanos Krassaris, March 30, 2016.

Interview with Paul Ioannidis, Athens, April 11, 2016, April 18, 2016, June 23, 2014.

Interview with John Ioannidis, December 22, 2016.

Interview with Dimitris Patrikios, December 9, 2016.

Interview with Captain Gerassimos Barkas, March 30, December 9, 2016.

Interview with Captain Dionysis Siganakis, December 9, 2016.

Interview with Captain Thanassis Apostolopoulos, December 9, 2016.

Interview with Captain Dimitris Makris, December 9, 2016.

Interviews with George Hartofilakidis and Ritsa Konialidis, December 22, 2016.

Interview with Nicolas Const. Konialidis, March 2019; correspondence with Marios Chrysostomos Konialides, April, June and July 2018

Secondary Sources

Agriantoni, Christina and Aggeliki Fenerli, *Ερμούπολη-Σύρος. Ιστορικό Οδοιπορικό* [*Hermoupolis-Syros: Historical Travelogue*] (Athens: EIE, 2000).

Amatori, Franco and Geoffrey Jones, eds., *Business History around the World at the End of the 20th Century* (Cambridge: Cambridge University Press, 2003).

Ananich, Boris, "The Russian Private Banking Houses, 1870–1914," *The Journal of Economic History* 48 (2), The Tasks of Economic History (June 1988): 401–407.

Anderson Jr., Irvine H., *Aramco, the United States, and Saudi Arabia: A Study of the Dynamics of Foreign Oil Policy, 1933–1950* (Princeton: Princeton University Press, 1981).

Argenti, Philip P., *Libro d'oro de la noblesse de Chio* (London: Oxford University Press, 1955).

Argyros, Leonidas, *Burrel and Son of Glasgow: A Tramp Shipping Firm, 1861–1930* (Unpublished PhD thesis, Memorial University of Newfoundland, 2012).

Armstrong, John and David M. Williams, "Technological Advances in the Maritime Sector: Trade, Modernization and the Process of Globalization in the Nineteenth Century," in Maria Fusaro and Amelia Polonia, eds., *Maritime History as Global History*, Research in Maritime History 43 (St. John's Newfoundland: International Association of Maritime Economic History, 2010), 177–202.

"The Steamship as an Agent of Modernisation, 1812–1840," *International Journal of Maritime History* 19 (1) (2007): 145–160.

Barthelmess, Klaus, "A Century of German Interests in Modern Whaling, 1860s–1960s," in Bjørn L. Basberg, Jan Erik Ringstad, and Einar Wexeilsen, eds., *Whaling and History: Perspectives on the Evolution of the Industry* (Sandefjord: Sandefjordmuseene, 1993), 121–138.

Barty-King, H., *The Baltic Exchange* (London: Hutchinson Benham, 1977).

Black Sea Pilot, *The Dardanelles, Sea of Marmara, Bosporus, Black Sea and Sea of Azov* (Washington, DC: Washington Printing Office, 1927).

Boyce, Gordon, *Information, Mediation and Institutional Development: The Rise of Large-Scale Enterprise in British Shipping, 1870–1919* (Manchester: Manchester University Press, 1995).

"Network Structures, Processes, and Dynamics," in Lewis R. Fischer and Even Lange, eds., *International Merchant Shipping in the Nineteenth and Twentieth Centuries: The Comparative Dimension* (St. John's, Newfoundland: International Maritime Economic History Association, 2008).

"The Development of Commercial Infrastructure for World Shipping," in Gelina Harlaftis, Stig Tenold, and Jesus Valdaliso, eds., *'World's Key Industry', History and Economics of International Shipping* (London: Palgrave Macmillan, 2012), 106–123.

The Growth and Dissolution of a Large-Scale Business Enterprise: The Furness Interest 1892–1919 (St. John's, Newfoundland: International Maritime History Association, 2012).

Broeze, Frank, "Shipping Policy and Social-Darwinism: Albert Ballin and the *Weltpolitik* of the Hamburg-America Line, 1886–1914," *Mariner's Mirror* 79 (4) (1993): 419–436.

The Globalisation of the Oceans: Containerisation from the 1950s to the Present, Research in Maritime History 23 (St. John's, Newfoundland: International Maritime Economic History Association, 2003).

Butterworth, Arthur, *The Vagliano Case in Australia* (London: Stevens and Sons, 1894).

Cafruny, Alan, *Ruling the Waves: The Political Economy of International Shipping* (Berkeley: University of California Press, 1987).

Carlisle, Rodney, *Sovereignty for Sale: The Origins and Evolution of the Panamanian and Liberian Flags of Convenience* (Annapolis, MD: Naval Institute Press, 1981).

Carvounis, Christos, *Efficiency and Contradictions of Multinational Activity: The Case of Greek Shipping* (Unpublished PhD thesis, New School for Social Research, New York, 1979).

Casson, Mark, *Enterprise and Competitiveness: A Systems View of International Business* (Oxford: Oxford University Press, 1990).

Economics of Business Culture: Game Theory, Transaction Costs, and Economic Performance (Oxford: Oxford University Press, 1991).

"Entrepreneurship and Business Culture," in Jonathan Brown and Mary B. Rose, eds., *Entrepreneurship, Networks, and Modern Business*, (Manchester: Manchester University Press, 1993), 30–54.

"An Economic Theory of the Free-Standing Company," in Mira Wilkins and Harm Schröter, eds., *The Free Standing Company in the World Economy, 1830–1996* (Oxford: Oxford University Press, 1998), 116–121.

The Entrepreneur. An Economic Theory (Cheltenham: Edward Elgar, 2003).

Caty, R. and E. Richard, *Armateurs Marseillais au XIXe siecle* (Marseilles: Chambre de Commerce et d'Industrie de Marseilles, 1986).

Celik, Zeynep, *The Remaking of Istanbul: Portrait of an Ottoman City in the Ninenteenth Century* (Seattle: University of Washington Press, 1993).

Chalmers, Mackenzie D., "Vagliano's Case," *The Law Quarterly Review* 27 (1891): 216–223.

Chandler, Alfred D., *The Visible Hand: The Managerial Revolution in American Business*, (Cambridge, MA: Harvard University Press, 1999).

Chapman, Stanley, *Merchant Enterprise in Britain: From the Industrial Revolution to the World War I* (Cambridge: Cambridge University Press, 1992).

The Rise of Merchant Banking (London: Allen & Unwin, 1984).

Chatziioannou, Maria Christina, "Greek Merchants in Victorian England," in Dimitris Tziovas, ed., *Greek Diaspora and Migration since 1700: Society Politics and Culture* (Farnham: Routledge, 2009).

Chatziioannou, Maria Christina and Gelina Harlaftis, "From the Levant to the City of London: Mercantile Credit in the Greek International Commercial Networks of the Eighteenth and Nineteenth Centuries," in Philip L. Cottrell, Even Lange, and Ulf Olsson, eds., *Centres and Peripheries in Banking: The Historical Development of Financial Markets* (Aldershot: Ashgate, 2007), 13–40.

Chekhov, Anton, *Plays*, translated by Marian Fell and Julius West (London: Duckworth & Co., 1912).

Chekhov, Mikhail, *A Brother's Memoir*, translated by Eugene Alper (Basingstoke: Palgrave Macmillan, 2009).

Chlomoudis, Constantinos, Συνεργασία και συμπλοιοκτησία στην ελληνική φορτηγό ναυτιλία: Η περίοδος του Μεσοπολέμου [*Collaboration and Co-ownership in Greek Cargo Shipping: The Interwar Period*] (Athens: MIET, 1996).

Chudakov, Alexander, "Dr Chekhov: A Biographical Essay (29 January 1860–15 July 1904)," in Vera Gottlieb and Paul Allain, eds., *The Cambridge Companion to Chekhov* (Cambridge: Cambridge University Press, 2000), 3–16.

Chumakhova, Z., "Σύντομη ανασκόπηση αρχειακού υλικού του Κρατικού Αρχείου της περιφέρειας του Ροστόφ που περιέχει έγγραφα για την Ελληνική διασπορά του Ντον και της Αζοφικής" ["Brief Review of the State Archives of the Rostov Region Containing Documents for Greek Diaspora of the Don and the Azov"], in Evrydiki Sifneos and Gelina Harlaftis, eds., Οι Έλληνες της Αζοφικής, 19ος αιώνας [The Greeks of the Azov, 19th Century] (Athens: Institute for Neohellenic Research / NHRF, 2015).

Clay, Christopher, Gold for the Sultan: Western Bankers and Ottoman Finance, 1856–1881 (London: I. B. Tauris, 2000).

Cleveland, Harold van B. and Thomas F. Huertas with Rachel Strauber, Joan L. Silverman, Mongibelli, Mary, Mary S. Turner and Clarence L. Wasson, Jr., Citibank, 1812–1970 (Cambridge: Cambridge University Press, 1985).

Colli, Andrea, The History of Family Business 1850–2000 (Cambridge: Cambridge University Press, 2003).

Colli, Andrea and Mary Rose, "Family Firms in Comparative Perspective," in Franco Amatori and Geoffrey Jones, eds., Business History Around the World at the End of the 20th Century (Cambridge: Cambridge University Press, 2003).

Corrales, Eloy Martín, "Greek-Ottoman Captains in the Service of Spanish Commerce in the Late Eighteenth Century," in Maria Fusaro, Colin Heywood and Mohamed-Salah Omri, eds., Trade and Cultural Exchange in the Early Modern Mediterranean: Braudel's Maritime Legacy (London: I. B. Tauris, 2009), 203–222.

Craig, Robin, The Ship. Steam Tramps and Cargo Liners, 1850–1950 (London: HMSO, 1980).

——— ed., British Tramp Shipping, 1750–1914, Research in Maritime History 24 (St. John's, Newfoundland: International Economic History Association, 2003).

da Silva Lopes Teresa, Christina Lubinski, and Heidi Tworek, eds., The Routledge Companion to Global Business (London: Routledge, 2019).

Damilakou, Maria, Η ελληνική μετανάστευση στην Αργεντινή:. διαδικασίες συγκρότησης και μετασχηματισμοί μιας μεταναστευτικής κοινότητας, 1900–1970 [Greek Immigration in Argentina: Formation Procedures and Transformations of an Immigrant Community, 1900–1970] (Athens: Historical Archive of the Commercial Bank of Greece, 2004).

——— "Μικρασιάτες πρόσφυγες στην Αργεντινή: μεταναστευτικές διαδρομές και στοιχεία ταυτότητας" ["Refugees from Asia Minor to Argentina: Immigration Routes and Identity Clues"], Ιστορικά [Istorika], 42 (July 2005): 177–202.

Davies, Peter N., The Trade Makers: Elder Dempster in West Africa (London: George Allen and Unwin, 1973).

——— Sir Alfred Jones: Shipping Entrepreneur par Excellence (London: Europa Publications, 1978).

——— Henry Tyrer: A Liverpool Shipping Agent and his Enterprise 1879–1979 (London: Croom Helm, 1979).

"Nineteenth Century Ocean Trade and Transport," in Peter Mathias and John A. Davis, eds., *International Trade and British Economic Growth from Eighteenth Century to the Present Day* (Oxford: Blackwell, 1996), 56–75.

Davis, Ralph, *The Rise of the English Shipping Industry in the Seventeenth and Eighteenth Centuries*, (London: Macmillan, 1962).

Debonos, A., "Εμποροναυτική Σχολή Αργοστολίου" ["Commercial and Maritime School of Argostoli"], *Κυμοθόη* [*Kymothoi*] 4 (1994): 35–43.

Dedichen, Ingeborg, *Onassis mon amour* (Paris: Éditions Pygmalion, 1975).

Delis, Apostolos, *Ερμούπολη (Σύρος): το ναυπηγικό κέντρο της ιστιοφόρου ναυτιλίας, 1830–1880* [*Hermoupolis (Syros): The Shipbuilding Centre of the Sailing Merchant Marine, 1830–1880*] (Unpublished PhD thesis, Ionian University, 2010).

"Shipping Finance and Risks in Sea Trade during the French Wars: Maritime Loan Operations in the Republic of Ragusa," *International Journal of Maritime History* 24 (1) (2012): 229–242.

"Τύποι πλοίων της ναυτιλίας των Ελλήνων, 1700–1821" ["Types of Ships of Greek Shipping, 1700–1821"], in Gelina Harlaftis and Katerina Papakonstantinou, eds., *Greek Shipping, Η ναυτιλία των Ελλήνων: Η ακμή πριν την επανάσταση, 1700–1821* [*Greek Shipping, 1700–1821: The Heyday before the Greek Revolution*] (Athens: Kedros Publications, 2013), 469–540.

Mediterranean Wooden Shipbuilding. Economy, Technology and Institutions in Syros in the Nineteenth Century (Leiden: Brill, 2016).

Donovan, Robert J., *Conflict and Crisis: The Presidency of Harry Truman, 1945–1948* (Columbia, MO: University of Missouri Press, 1996).

Eden, R., M. Posner, R. Bending, E. Crouch and J. Stanislaw, eds., *Energy Economics: Growth, Resources and Policies* (Cambridge: Cambridge University Press, 1981).

Eldem, Edhem, "La circulation de la lettre de change entre la France et Constantinople au XVIII siécle," in H. Batu and J. L. Bacque-Grammont, eds., *L'Empire Ottoman, la Republique de Turquie et la France* (Istanbul: Isis, 1986), 87–97.

French Trade in Istanbul in the Eighteenth Century (Leiden: Brill, 1999).

A History of the Ottoman Bank (Istanbul: Ottoman Bank Historical Research Center, 1999).

Emets, S. I., "Мемориал одесских присяжных поверенных" ["Records of Lawyers in Odessa"], *Вестник Одесской адвокатуры* [*Messenger of Odessa Lawyers*] 2 (2008).

Exertzoglou, Harris, *Greek Banking in Constantinople, 1850–1887* (Unpublished PhD thesis, King's College London, 1986).

Προσαρμοστικότητα και πολιτική ομογενειακών κεφαλαίων: Έλληνες Τραπεζίτες στην Κωνσταντινούπολη: το κατάστημα Ζαρίφης Ζαφειρόπουλος, 1871–1881 [*Adjustment and Policy of Diaspora Capital: Greek Bankers in*

Constantinople: The 'Zarifi-Zafeiropoulos, 1871–1881] (Athens: Commercial Bank of Greece, 1989).

Feys, Torsten, *The Battle for the Migrants: The Introduction of Steam Shipping on the North Atlantic and Its Impact on the European Exodus*, Research in Maritime History 50 (St. John's: International Maritime Economic History Association, 2013).

Filefsky, P., *История города Таганрога* [*History of the City of Taganrog*] (Taganrog: n.p., 1898).

Filippidis, Platon, *Εμπορικός και Κοινωνικός Οδηγός των Ελλήνων της Νοτίου Αμερικής* [*Commercial and Social Guide of the Greeks of South America*] (Buenos Aires: n.p., 1938).

Fischer, Lewis R. and Nordvik, Helge W., "Maritime Transport and the Integration of the North Atlantic Economy, 1850–1914," in Wolfram Fischer, R. Marvin McInnis and Jurgen Schneider, eds., *The Emergence of a World Economy, 1500–1914* (Wiesbaden: Franz Steiner Verlag, 1986), 519–544.

Flerianou, Aikaterini, ed., *Χαρίλαος Τρικούπης: Η ζωή και το έργο του* [*Harilaos Trikoupis: His Life and Work*] (Athens: Greek Parliament, 1999).

Foustanos, George, *Onassis: Pioneer in Shipping* (Athens: Argo, 2009).

Foustanos, Georgios M., *Hellenic Lines, όραμα δίχως τέλος* [*Hellenic Lines, Vision without End*] (Syros: Argo Publishing, 2010).

Frangakis-Syrett, Elena, *The Commerce of Smyrna in the Eighteenth Century (1700–1820)* (Athens: Centre for Asia Minor Studies, 1992).

——— *Οι Χιώτες έμποροι στις διεθνείς συναλλαγές (1750 – 1850)* [*The Chiot Merchants in International Transactions (1750–1850)*] (Athens: Agricultural Bank of Greece, 1995).

——— "Networks of Friendship, Networks of Kinship: Eighteenth-Century Levant Merchants," *Eurasian Studies* 1 (2) (2002): 189–212.

Fraser, Nicholas, Philip Jacobson, Mark Ottaway and Lewis Chester, *Aristotle Onassis* (New York: Ballantine Books, 1977).

Gabriushkin, Oleg, *Гуляет старый Таганрог: Исторический очерк* [*Walking Old Taganrog: Historical Study*] (Taganrog: AI MIKM, 1997).

Galani, Katerina, *British Shipping and Trade in the Mediterranean in the Age of War, 1770–1815* (Unpublished PhD thesis, University of Oxford, 2011).

——— "Έλληνες έμποροι-τραπεζίτες στο City του Λονδίνου: η πρώτη εγκατάσταση (αρχές 19ου αιώνα) [Greek merchant and bankers in the City of London: the first settlement (early 19th century)]", in British-Greek Relations. Aspects of their Recent History (Hellenic Parliament Foundation for Parliamentarism and Democracy: Athens, 2016), 237–256.

——— "Η Ελληνική κοινότητα του Λονδίνου τον 19ο αιώνα: Μια Κοινωνική και οικονομική προσέγγιση" ["The Greek Community in London in the 19th Century: A Social and Economic Approach"], *Τα Ιστορικά* [*Ta Istorika*] 63 (April 2016): 43–68.

Getty, Jean Paul, *As I See it: The Autobiography of J. Paul Getty* (Los Angeles, CA: The Paul Getty Museum, revised edn 2003).

Gibson, Andrew and Arthur Donovan, *Abandoned Ocean: A History of United States Maritime Policy* (Columbia, SC: University of South Carolina Press, 2000).

Gifford, D. J. and John Salter, *How to Understand an Act of Parliament* (London: Cavendish, 1996).

Glasmeier, Amy K., "Economic Geography in Practice: Local Economic Development Policy," in Gordon L. Clark, Maryann P. Feldman and Meric S. Gertler, eds., *The Oxford Handbook of Economic Geography* (Oxford: Oxford University Press, 2000), 559–579.

Gorton, Lars, Patrick Hillennius, Rolf Ihre and Arne Sandevärn, *Shipbroking and Chartering Practice*, 7th edn (London: Informa, 2009).

Graham, Gerald S., "The Ascendancy of the Sailing Ship, 1850–85," *The Economic History Review* 9 (1) (1956): 74–88.

Green, Edwin and Michael Moss, *A Business of National Importance: The Royal Mail Shipping Group, 1902–1937* (London: Methuen, 1982).

Greenhill, Robert G., "Competition or Co-operation in the Global Shipping Industry: The Origins and Impact of the Conference System for British Shipowners before 1914," in D. J. Starkey and G. Harlaftis, eds., *Global Markets: The Internationalization of the Sea Transport Industries since 1850*, Research in Maritime History 14 (St. John's, Newfoundland: International Maritime Economic History Association, 1998), 53–80.

Gromov, Mikhail, in Anton Chekhov, *Полное собрание сочинений и писем в 30-ти томах: Сочинения* [*All the Works and Letters in 30 Volumes*], vol. 1 (Moscow: Nauka, 1974–1982).

Harlaftis, Gelina, "Greek Shipowners and State Intervention in the 1940s: A Formal Justification for the Resort to Flags-of-Convenience?," *International Journal of Maritime History* 1 (2) (December 1989): 37–63.

"The Role of the Greeks in the Black Sea Trade, 1830–1900," in Lewis R. Fischer and Helge W. Nordvik, eds., *Shipping and Trade, 1750–1950: Essays in International Maritime Economic History* (Pontefract: Lofthouse, 1990), 63–95.

"Εμπόριο και ναυτιλία τον 19ο αιώνα, το επιχειρηματικό δίκτυο των Ελλήνων της διασποράς, η 'χιώτικη' φάση (1830–1860)" ["Trade and Shipping in the 19th Century: The Entrepreneurial Network of the Diaspora Greeks, the 'Chiot' Phase (1830–1860)"], *Μνήμων* [*Mnemon*] 15 (1993): 69–127.

Greek Shipowners and Greece: From Separate Development to Mutual Interdependence, 1945–1975 (London: Athlone, 1993).

Greek Seamen and Greek Steamships on the Eve of the First World War (Athens: Aegean Maritime Museum, 1994).

A History of Greek-Owned Shipping: The Making of an International Tramp Fleet, 1830 to the Present Day (London: Routledge 1996).

"The Greek Shipping Enterprise: Investment Strategies, 1900–1939," in M. Dritsas and T. Gourvish, eds., *European Enterprise. Strategies of Adaptation* (Athens: Trochalia Publications, 1997), 139–159.

"Mapping the Greek Maritime Diaspora from the Early Eighteenth to the Late Twentieth Century," in Ina Baghdiantz McCabe, Gelina Harlaftis and

Ioanna Minoglou, eds., *Diaspora Entrepreneurial Networks: Five Centuries of History* (Oxford: Berg Publications, 2005), 147–169.

"From Diaspora Traders to Shipping Tycoons: The Vagliano Bros," *Business History Review* 81 (2) (Summer 2007): 237–268.

"Μεγιστάνες του Ιονίου: Ο οίκος των Αδελφών Βαλλιάνου" ["The Tycoons of the Ionian Sea: The House of the Vagliano Brothers"], *Ιόνιος Λόγος* [*Ionios Logos*] 1 (2007): 303–346.

"Η ακμή του ναυτεργατικού κινήματος της 'Ελευθέρας Ελλάδος'" ["The Rise of the Seafaring Labour Movement during World War II"], in Christos Hadjiiosif and Papastratis, Prokopis, eds., *Ιστορία της Ελλάδος του 20ού αι.* [*History of Twentieth-Century Greece*] vol. 3 (Athens: Vivliorama, 2007), 261–283.

"From the Levant to the City of London: Mercantile Credit in the Greek International Commercial Networks of the Eighteenth and Nineteenth Centuries," in Philip L. Cottrell, Even Lange and Ulf Olsson, eds., with Iain L. Fraser and Monika Pohle Fraser, *Centres and Peripheries in Banking: The Historical Development of Financial Markets* (Aldershot: Ashgate, 2007), 13–40 (in collaboration with Maria Christina Chatziioannou)

"The Greek Shipping Sector c. 1850–2000," in Lewis R. Fischer and Even Lange, eds., *International Merchant Shipping in the Nineteenth and Twentieth Centuries: The Comparative Dimension* vol. 37 (St. John's, Newfoundland: International Maritime Economic History Association, 2008), 79–103.

"The 'Eastern Invasion': Greeks in the Mediterranean Trade and Shipping in the Eighteenth and Early Nineteenth Centuries," in Maria Fusaro, Colin Heywood and Mohamed-Salah Omri, eds., *Trade and Cultural Exchange in the Early Modern Mediterranean: Braudel's Maritime Legacy* (London: I. B. Tauris, 2010), 223–252.

"The Fleet 'Dei Greci': Ottoman and Venetian Greeks in the Mediterranean Sea Trade of the Eighteenth Century," in Michela d'Angelo, Gelina Harlaftis and Carmel Vassalo, eds., *Making the Waves in the Mediterranean: Sulle onde del Mediterraneo*, Proceedings of the 2nd Conference of the Mediterranean Maritime History Network, Messina and Taormina, May 4–7, 2006, vol. 12 (Messina: Istituto di Studi Storici Gaetano Salvemini, 2010), 492–526.

"Aristotle Onassis and FBI archives in the 1940s," *Enterprises et Histoire* 2 (2011): 80–85.

"Ο 'πολυεκατομμυριούχος κύριος Μαράκης' Βαλλιάνος, το σκάνδαλο του Τελωνείου Ταγκανρόκ και οι 144 καταστροφές του Αντόν Τσέχωφ" ["The 'Multi-Millionaire Mr. Marakis' Vagliano, the Scandal of the Taganrog Customs Office and 144 Disasters of Anton Chekhov"], *Ιστορικά* [*Istorika*] 54 (2011): 79–122.

"Maritime Transport Systems in Southeastern Mediterranean," in Edhem Eldem and Socrates Petmezas, eds., *The Economic Development of Southeastern Europe in the Nineteenth Century* (Athens: Historical Archives Alpha Bank, 2011), 397–446.

"Το κατηγορώ του Αριστοτέλη Ωνάση προς τους εφοπλιστές Και την ελληνική κυβέρνηση το 1947" ["The 'J'accuse' of Aristotle Onassis to the Shipowners and the Greek Government in 1947"], *Ιόνιος Λόγος* [*Ionios Logos*] 4 (2013): 325–400.

"The Onassis Global Shipping Business: 1920s–1950s," *Business History Review* 88 (2) (Summer 2014): 241–271.

Harlaftis, Gelina and Costas Chlomoudis, "Greek Shipping Offices in London in the Interwar Period," *International Journal of Maritime History* 5 (1) (June 1993): 1–40.

Harlaftis, Gelina and Vassilis Kardasis, "International Bulk Trade and Shipping in the Eastern Mediterranean and the Black Sea," in Jeffrey Williamson and Sevket Pamuk, eds., *The Mediterranean Response to Globalization* (London: Routledge, 2000), 233–265.

Harlaftis, Gelina and Sophia Laiou, "Ottoman State Policy in Mediterranean Trade and Shipping, c. 1780–c. 1820: The Rise of the Greek-Owned Ottoman Merchant Fleet," in Mark Mazower, ed., *Networks of Power in Modern Greece* (London: Hurst 2008), 1–44.

Harlaftis, Gelina and Katerina Papakonstantinou, eds., *Η ναυτιλία των Ελλήνων: Η ακμή πριν την επανάσταση, 1700–1821* [*Greek Shipping, 1700–1821: The Heyday before the Greek Revolution*] (Athens: Kedros Publications, 2013).

Harlaftis, Gelina and John Theotokas, "Maritime Business during the 20th Century: Continuity and Change," in C. T. Grammenos, ed., *Handbook of Maritime Economics and Business* (London: Lloyd's of London Press, 2002), 9–34.

"European Family Firms in International Business: British and Greek Tramp-Shipping Firms," *Business History* 46 (2) (April 2004): 219–255.

Harlaftis, Gelina, and Nikos Vlassopoulos, eds., *Ιστορικός νηογνώμονας, Ποντοπόρεια: Ποντοπόρα Ιστιοφόρα Και Ατμόπλοια 1830–1939* [*Pontoporeia: Historical Registry Book of Greek Cargo Sailing Ships and Steamships, 1830–1939*] (ELIA/Niarchos Foundation: Athens, 2002).

Harlaftis, Gelina, Helen Beneki and Manos Haritatos, eds., *Πλωτώ: Έλληνες Εφοπλιστές από το τέλος του 18ου έως την παραμονή του Β' Παγκοσμίου Πολέμου* [*Ploto: Greek Shipowners from the Late Eighteenth Century to the Eve of World War II*] (Athens: ELIA/Niarchos Foundation, 2003).

Harlaftis, Gelina, Stig Tenold and Jésus M. Valdaliso, eds., *"World's Key Industry". History and Economics of International Shipping*, (London: Palgrave/MacMillan, 2012).

Harlaftis, Gelina, Helen Thanopoulou and Ioannis Theotokas, *Το Παρόν και το Μέλλον της Ελληνικής Ναυτιλίας*, [*The Present and the Future of Greek Shipping*] (Athens: Research Study no. 10, Office of Economic Studies, Academy of Athens, 2009).

Harley, C. Knick, "The Shift from Sailing Ships to Steam Ships, 1850–1890," in D.N. McCloskey, ed., *Essays on a Mature Economy: Britain after 1840* (Princeton, NJ: Princeton University Press, 1971), 215–234.

"Coal Exports and British Shipping, 1850–1913," *Explorations in Economic History* 26 (3) (February 1989): 311–338.

Herlihy, Patricia, "Russian Grain and the Port of Livorno, 1794–1865," *Journal of European Economic History* 5 (1976): 184–195.

Odessa: A History, 1794–1914 (Cambridge, MA: Harvard University Press, 1986).

Hoy, Frank and Trudy G. Verser, "Emerging Business, Emerging Field: Entrepreneurship and the Family Firm," *Entrepreneurship: Theory and Practice* 19 (Fall 1994): 9–23.

Hutchins, John G. B., "United Merchant Marine Policy and Surplus Ships," *Journal of Political Economy* 59 (2) (April 1951): 117–25.

Hyde, Francis E., *Blue Funnel: A History of Alfred Holt and Company of Liverpool, 1865–1914* (Liverpool: Liverpool University Press, 1957).

Cunard and the North Atlantic, 1840–1914 (Liverpool: Macmillan, 1975).

Shipping Enterprise and Management, 1830–1939: Harrisons of Liverpool, (Liverpool: Harrison of Liverpool 1967).

Ioannidis, Paul J., *Destiny Prevails: My Life with Aristotle, Alexander, Christina Onassis and her Daughter, Athina* (Athens: Livani Publishing, 2013).

Iversen, Martin Jes and Lars Thue, "Creating Nordic Capitalism: The Business History of Competitive Periphery," in Susanna Fellman, Martin Jes Iversen, Hans Sjögren and Lars Thue, eds., *Creating Nordic Capitalism: The Business History of a Competitive Periphery* (Houndmills, Basingstoke: Palgrave Macmillan, 2008), 1–19.

Jackson, Gordon and David M. Williams, *Shipping, Technology and Imperialism* (Hans: Scolar Press, 1996).

Jacobsen, Alf R., *Eventyret Anders Jahre* (Oslo: Forlaget, Oktober A/S, 1982).

Jones, Geoffrey, *The Evolution of International Business: An Introduction* (Oxford: Oxford University Press, 1996).

Merchants to Multinationals: British Trading Companies in the Nineteenth and Twentieth Centuries (Oxford: Oxford University Press, 2000).

Jones, Geoffrey and Paul Gomopoulos, "Aristotle Onassis and the Greek Shipping Industry," 9-805-141, rev. October 18, 2008, Harvard Business School.

Jones Geoffrey and Andrea Lluch, eds., *The Impact of Globalization on Argentina and Chile: Business Enterprises and Entrepreneurship* (Cheltenham: Edward Elgar, 2015).

Jones, Geoffrey and Mary Rose, eds., *Family Capitalism* (London: Frank Cass, 1993).

Jones, Geoffrey and Jonathan Zeitlin, eds., *The Oxford Handbook of Business History* (Oxford: Oxford University Press, 2008)

Jones, R. E., "Opening a Window on the South: Russia and the Black Sea, 1695–1792," in L. Hughes and M. di Salvo, eds., *A Window on Russia: Papers from the V International Conference of the Study Group on Eighteenth-Century Russia* (Rome: La Fenice, 1996).

Jones, Stephanie, *Trade and Shipping: Lord Inchcape 1852–1932* (Manchester: Manchester University Press, 1989).

Kahan, Arcadius, *Russian Economic History: The 19th Century* (Chicago: University of Chicago Press, 1989).

Kapetanakis, Panayiotis, *Ο ποντοπόρος εμπορικός στόλος των Επτανήσων κατά την διάρκεια της βρετανικής κατοχής και προστασίας και η κεφαλληνιακή υπεροχή (1809/1815-1815)* [*The Deep-Sea Going Merchant Fleet of the Seven Islands of the Ionian Sea during the Time of British Conquest and Protection and the Cephalonian Prominence (1809/1815-1864)*] (Unpublished PhD thesis, Ionian University, 2010).

Kapsabelis, E. I., *Τι οφείλει η Ρωσία εις την Ελλάδα* [*What Russia Owes to Greece*] (Athens: 2003).

Kardasis, Vassilis, *Σύρος: Το σταυροδρόμι της Ανατολικής Μεσογείου, 1832-1857* [*Syros: Crossroads of the Eastern Mediterranean (1832-1857)*] (Athens: Cultural Foundation of the National Bank, 1987).

Diaspora Merchants in the Black Sea: The Greeks in Southern Russia, 1775-1861 (Lanham, MD: Lexington Books, 2001).

Kasunmu, B. and S. A. Omabegho, "Provocation as a Defence Under the Nigerian Criminal Code," *International and Comparative Law Quarterly* 14 (1965): 1399-1410.

Katakouzinos, Simon, *Το εμπόριον, η ναυτιλία και αι μεταναστεύσεις των Ελλήνων* [*Trade, Shipping and the Immigration of the Greeks*], 2nd edn (Athens: n.p., 1908).

Katsiardi-Hering, Olga, "Central and Peripheral Communities in the Greek Diaspora: Interlocal and Local Economic, Political, and Cultural Networks in the Eighteenth and Nineteenth Centuries," in M. Rozen, ed., *Homelands and Diaspora: Greeks, Jews and their Migrations* (London: I. B. Tauris, 2008), 169-180.

Katsomalos, Vassilios, *Αργεντινή, Χιλή, Ουρουγουάη, Βραζιλία και οι Έλληνες* [*Argentina, Chile, Uruguay, Brazil and the Greeks*] (Buenos Aires: n.p., 1972).

Kaukiainen, Yrjö, "Coal and Canvas: Aspects of the Competition between Steam and Sail, c. 1870-1914," *International Journal of Maritime History* 4 (2) (1992): 175-191.

A History of Finnish Shipping (New York: Routledge, 1993).

Kiouzes-Pezas, S., "Εκθεσις περί γεωργίας, εμπορίας, βιομηχανίας και ναυτιλίας ανά την προξενικήν περιφέρειαν Ταϊγανίου" ["Report on Agriculture, Trade, Industry and Shipping in the Consular Region of Taganrog"], *Δελτίον επί των Εξωτερικών Β. Υπουργείου* [*Bulletin of the Greek Foreign Ministry*], second part, Studies and Reports 9 (Athens: Ministry of Foreign Affairs, 1912).

Kirkaldy, Adam W., *British Shipping: Its History, Organisation and Importance* (London: David & Charles Reprints, 1970).

Kostelenos, George, Dimitrios Vasileiou, Emmanouil Kounaris, Socrates Petmezas and Michael Sfakianakis, *Ακαθάριστο Εγχώριο Προϊόν, 1830-1939* [*Gross Domestic Product, 1830-1939*] (Athens: KEPE and Historical Archives of the National Bank of Greece, 2007).

Kucherov, Samuel, *Courts, Lawyers and Trials under the Last Three Tsars* (New York: Frederick A. Praeger, 1953).

Laffitte, Sophie, *Chekhov: 1860–1904* (London: Angus and Robertson,1974).

Landes, David S., *Dynasties: Fortunes and Misfortunes of the World's Great Family Businesses* (London: Penguin Books, 2006).

Lane, Frederic C., *Ships for Victory: A History of Shipbuilding under the U.S. Maritime Commission in World War II* (Baltimore, MD: Johns Hopkins University Press, 1951).

Lemarchand, Yannick, Cheryl McWatters and Laure Pineau-Defois, "The Current Account as Cognitive Artefact: Stories and Accounts of La Maison Chaurand," in Pierre Gervais, Yannick Lemarchand and Dominique Margairaz, eds., *Merchants and Profit in the Age of Commerce, 1680–1830* (London: Pickering and Chatto, 2014), 33–52.

Lemos, Andreas, *Η εμπορική ναυτιλία της Χίου* [*The Commercial Shipping of Chios Island*] (Chios: Epimeleies, 1963).

——— *Το ναυτικόν του γένους των Ελλήνων: Η ιστορία του* [*The Shipping of the Greeks: Its History*], vol. A' (Athens: Tsikopoulos, 1968).

——— *The Greeks and the Sea: A People's Seafaring Achievements from Ancient Times to the Present Day* (London: Cassell, 1970).

——— *Νεοέλληνες αειναύται* [*Modern Greek Eternal Seamen*] (Athens: Kostas Tsikopoulos, 1971).

——— *Παγκόσμιο Βιογραφικό Λεξικό* [*World Biographical Dictionary. Educational Greek Encyclopedia*] (Athens: Athens Publishing House, 1984).

Lincoln, W. Bruce, *The Great Reforms: Autocracy, Bureaucracy, and the Politics of Change in Imperial Russia* (DeKalb, IL: Northern Illinois University Press, 1990).

Long, Ann and Russel, *A Shipping Venture: Turnbull Scott and Company, 1872–1972* (London: Hutchinson Benham, 1974).

Lowry, Nigel, *Onassis and his Legacy* (Athens: Alexander S. Onassis Public Benefit Foundation, Lloyd's List, 2003).

Lyberatos, Andreas, "The Usury Cases of the Black Sea Region: State Legitimation and Bourgeois Rule of Law in 19th Century Dobrudzha," *Études Balkaniques* 49 (3–4) (2013): 59–94.

Mantidis, Yannis, *Όταν ο Ωνάσης συγγένευε με το Πήλιο: Οι δυο ζωές της άγνωστης ανηψιάς του* [*When Onassis Was Related to Pelion: The Two Lives of His Unknown Niece*] (Thessaloniki: Adelpoi Kyriakides Publishers, 2009).

Marchese, Ugo, "L'industria armatoriale ligure dal 1816 al 1859," *Archivio Economico dell' Unificazione Italiana* 6 (1) (1957): 1–32.

Margari, D., Template "Vaglianos," in Constantinos Vovolinis, *Μέγα Ελληνικόν Βιογραφικόν Λεξικόν* [*Grand Greek Biographical Dictionary*], vol. 1, (Athens: Publication of Industrial Review, 1958).

Marriner, Sheila and Hyde, Francis E., *The Senior: John Samuel Swire 1825–98. Management in Far Eastern Shipping Trades* (Liverpool: Liverpool University Press, 1967).

Marx, Daniel Jr, "The Merchant Ship Sales Act," *The Journal of Business of the University of Chicago* 21 (1) (January 1948): 12–28.

Melas, Andreas, *Los griegos en la Argentina* [*The Greeks in Argentina*] (Buenos Aires: Pellegrini Editions, 1954).

Metaxas, Basil N., *The Economics of Tramp Shipping*, 2nd edn (London: Athlone Press, 1981).

Flags of Convenience (London: Gower Press, 1985).

Metaxas-Laskaratos, Dionyssios, Ελληνικαί παροικίαι Ρωσσίας και Ρωμουνίας [*Greek Communities of Russia and Romania*] (Braila: Universala of Con. P. Nikolaou, 1900).

Metaxas-Laskaratos, Spyridon Efst., Εμποροπροξενικοί καταδιωγμοί [*Commercial-Consular Prosecutions*] (Athens: n.p., 1882).

Miller, Michael, "Review on Leadership in World Shipping: Greek Family Firms in International Business. By Ioannis Theotokas and Gelina Harlaftis," *Business History Review* 86 (1) (2012): 173–175.

Europe and the Maritime World: A Twentieth-Century History (Cambridge: Cambridge University Press, 2012).

Milne, Graeme J., "North East England Shipping in the 1890s: Investment and Entrepreneurship," *International Journal of Maritime History* 21 (1) (2009): 1–26.

Moon, David, *The Plough that Broke the Steppes: Agriculture and Environment on Russia's Grasslands, 1700-2014* (Oxford: Oxford University Press, 2015).

Mordaunt Crook, J., *The Rise of Nouveaux Riches* (London: John Murray, 1999, repr. 2000).

Morozan, B. B., "Деятельность Азовско-Донского коммерческого банка на Юге России в конце XIX в. Исторический факультет МГУ, 31 января 2007 г." ["The Activities of the Commercial Bank of Azov-Don in South Russia at the End of the Nineteenth Century"], *III Научные чтения памяти профессора В.И.Бовыкина* [*III Scientific Readings dedicated to the Memory of Professor B. I. Bovikina*], Department of History of the State University of Moscow, January 31, 2007], www.hist.msu.ru/Science/Conf/01_2007/Morozan.pdf, accessed February 15, 2009.

Morozan, Vladimir, *Деловая жизнь на юге России в XIX - начале XX века* [The Entrepreneurial Life in Southern Russia, 19th–Beginning of 20th Century] (St. Petersburg: Dmitrii Bulanin, 2014).

Morris, Charles R., *The Tycoons* (New York: Times Books, 2005).

Moschona, Panayota, *Παναγής Α. Βαλλιάνος: Από τη μυθοπλασία στην ιστορία* [*Panagis A. Vagliano: From Myth to History*] (Athens: Foundation of Panagi A. Vagliano 2008).

Moss, Michael S. and John R. Hume, *Shipbuilders to the World: 125 Years of Harland and Wolff, Belfast 1861-1986* (Belfast: Blackstaff Press, 1986).

Munro, Forbes J., *Maritime Enterprise and Empire: Sir William Mackinnon and his Business Network, 1823-1893* (Woodbridge: Boydell, 2003).

Munro, Forbes J., and Tony Slaven, "Networks and Markets in Clyde Shipping: The Donaldsons and the Hogarths, 1870-1939," *Business History* 43 (2) (April 2001): 19–50.

Naess, Erling D., *Autobiography of a Shipping Man* (Colchester: Seatrade Publication, 1977).

Napier, Christopher J., "Allies or Subsidiaries? Inter-Company Relations in the P&O Group, 1914–39," *Business History* 39 (1997): 67–93.

Necla Geyikdagi, V., "French Direct Investments in the Ottoman Empire Before World War I," *Enterprise & Society* 12 (3) (September 2011): 525–561.

Nemirovsky, Irene, *A Life of Chekhov* (London: The Grey Walls Press, 1950).

Nordvik, Helge, "The Shipping Industries of the Scandinavian Countries," in Lewis R. Fischer and Gerald E. Panting, eds., *Change and Adaptation in Maritime History: The North Atlantic Fleets in the Nineteenth Century* (St. John's, Newfoundland: International Maritime History Association, 1985).

North, Douglass, *Institutions and Economic Growth: An Historical Introduction* (London: Elsevier, 1989).

Onassis, Aristotle, "Η ναυτιλία μας μετά τον πόλεμον και η δράσις των Ελλήνων εφοπλιστών" ["Our Postwar Shipping After the War and the Activities of the Greek Shipowners"], Memorandum to the President of the Greek Shipowners in New York, M. Kulukundis in 1947, published in *Ethnikos Kyrex* (*National Herald*). The memorandum was published in thirteen parts on March 8, 10, 11, 12, 13, 15, 17, 18, 19, 20, 22, 24, 25. 1953. It has been republished with an introduction in Gelina Harlaftis, "Το 'κατηγορώ' του Αριστοτέλη Ωνάση προς τους εφοπλιστές και την ελληνική κυβέρνηση το 1947" ["The 'J'accuse' of Aristotle Onassis to the Shipowners and the Greek Government in 1947"], *Ionios Logos* (2013): 325–400.

O'Rourke, Shane, *Warriors and Peasants: The Don Cossacks in Late Imperial Russia* (Oxford: MacMillan/St. Antony's College, 2000).

Osborn, S., "On the Geography of the Sea of Azov, the Putrid Sea, and Adjacent Coasts," *Journal of the Royal Geographical Society of London* 27 (1857): 133–148.

Oshri, Ilan, Julia Kotlarsky and Leslie P. Willcocks, *The Handbook of Global Outsourcing and Offshoring*, 3rd edn (Basingstoke: Palgrave Macmillan, 2015).

Owen, Thomas C., "Entrepreneurship and the Structure of the Enterprise in Russia, 1800–1880," in Gregory Guroff and Fred Carstensen, eds., *Entrepreneurship in Imperial Russia and the Soviet Union* (Princeton, CT: Princeton University Press, 1983).

Pagratis, Gerassimos, "Οργάνωση και διαχείριση της ναυτιλιακής επιχείρησης στην Κέρκυρα στο πρώτο ήμισυ του 16ου αιώνα" ["Organisation and Administration of the Shipping Firm in Corfu in the First Half of the 16th Century"], *Μνήμων* [*Mnemon*] 30 (2009): 9–35.

"Η ναυτιλιακή επιχείρηση τον 18° αιώνα: η περίπτωση των Ελλήνων υπηκόων της Βενετίας" ["The Shipping Business in the 18th Century: The Greek Case"], in Gelina Harlaftis and Katerina Papakonstantinou, eds., *Η ναυτιλία των Ελλήνων: Η ακμή πριν την επανάσταση, 1700–1821* [*Greek Shipping, 1700–1821: The Heyday before the Greek Revolution*] (Athens: Kedros Publications, 2013), 445–466.

"Εμπόριο και ναυτιλία στα νησιά του Ιονίου Πελάγους στα χρόνια της Επτανή-
σου Πολιτείας, 1800–1807" ["Trade and Shipping in the Islands of the Ionian
Sea during the Years of the Septinsular Republic, 1800–1807"], in Gelina
Harlaftis and Katerina Papakonstantinou, eds., Η ναυτιλία των Ελλήνων:
Η ακμή πριν την επανάσταση, 1700–1821 [Greek Shipping, 1700–1821: The
Heyday before the Greek Revolution] (Athens: Kedros Publications, 2013),
631–649.

Κοινωνία και οικονομία στο βενετικό "Κράτος της Θάλασσας": Οι ναυτιλιακές
επιχειρήσεις της Κέρκυρας (1496–1538) [Society and Economy in the Venetian
Stato del Mar: The Shipping Firms of Corfu (1496–1538)] (Athens: Pedio,
2013).

Paizis-Danias, Dimitris, Θαλάσσης Μνήμες [Memories of the Sea] (Athens: Fimios,
2008).

Palmer, Sarah, "Investors in London Shipping, 1820–1850," Maritime History 2
(1973): 46–68.

"The British Industry Shipping Industry 1850–1914," in Lewis R. Fischer and
Gerald Panting, eds., Change and Adaptation in Maritime History: The
North Atlantic Fleets in the Nineteenth Century (St. John's, Newfoundland:
International Maritime Economic History Association, 1985).

"British Shipping from the Late 19th Century to the Present," in Lewis, R.,
Fischer and Evan Lange, eds., International Merchant Shipping in the Nine-
teenth and Twentieth Centuries: The Comparative Dimension, Research in
Maritime History 37 (St. John's, Newfoundland: International Maritime
Economic History Association, 2008).

Pamuk, Sevket, A Monetary History of the Ottoman Empire (Cambridge: Cambridge University Press, 2000).

Panzac, Daniel, Les Corsaires Barbaresques : La fin d'une epoqee, 1800–1820 (Paris:
CNRS editions, 1999).

Papadimitriou, Alexandra, Τζέντα [Jeddah] (Athens: Kastanioti Publications, 2008).
Αλεξάνδρεια-Αθήνα [Alexandria-Athens] (Athens: Kastaniotis, 2010).

Papadimitriou, Stelios A., "Ο άλλος Ωνάσης" ["The Other Onassis"], Lecture at the
Museum of Cycladic Art, November 27, 1995, Αργώ [Argo] (January 1996).

Papadimitriou, Stelios A. and President, Alexander S. Onassis Foundation, "The
Workings of a Public Benefit Foundation: The Alexander S. Onassis Foun-
dation, Problems and Solutions," lecture held at the City University Business
School, Department of Shipping, Trade and Finance, London, Monday
November 11, 1996.

Papadopoulou, Alexandra, Ναυτιλιακές επιχειρήσεις, διεθνή δίκτυα και θεσμοί στη
σπετσιώτικη εμπορική ναυτιλία, 1830–1870: Οργάνωση, διοίκηση και στρατηγική [Maritime Businesses, International Networks and Institutions in the
Merchant Shipping of the Island of Spetses: Organisation, Management and
Strategy] (Unpublished PhD thesis, Ionian University, Corfu, 2010)

"From Local to Global: The Evolution of Greek Island Shipping Business
Groups," (Unpublished ms).

Papageorgiou, Athanassios E., *Ελληνικές Δημόσιες Αερομεταφορές* [*Greek Public Airlines*] (Athens: Free Thinking, 1987).

Papakonstantinou, Katerina, "Θαλάσσιες και χερσαίες μεταφορές και διακινούμενα φορτία τον 18° αιώνα: η συγκρότηση μεταφορικών συστημάτων στην Ανατολική Μεσόγειο" ["Sea and Land Transport and the Movement of Cargoes in the 18th Century: The Formation of Transport Systems in the Eastern Mediterranean"], in Gelina Harlaftis and Katerina Papakonstantinou, eds., *Η ναυτιλία των Ελλήνων: Η ακμή πριν την επανάσταση, 1700-1821* [*Greek Shipping, 1700-1821: The Heyday before the Greek Revolution*] (Athens: Kedros Publications, 2013), 283-351.

Papinianos, *Ο δικηγόρος* [*The Lawyer*] (Athens: Estia 2013).

Paris, Erato, "Les Grecs de Marseilles dans la deuxième moitié du XIXe siècle: une perspective nationale et transnationale," *Revue européenne des migrations internationales* 17 (3) (2001): 23-42.

Pedraja, René de la, *Rise and Decline of US Merchant Shipping in the Twentieth Century* (New York: Maxwell Macmillan International, 1992).

Per Sebak, Kristian, *A Transatlantic Migratory Bypass – Scandinavian Shipping Companies and Transmigration through Scandinavia, 1898-1929* (Unpublished PhD thesis, University of Bergen, 2012).

Perry, Hobart S., "The Wartime Merchant Fleet and Post War Shipping Requirements," *The American Economic Review* 36 (2) (May 1946): 520-546.

Petersen, Kaare, *The Saga of Norwegian Shipping* (Oslo: Dreyers Forlag, 1955).

Polemis, Demetrios, *Τα ιστιοφόρα της Άνδρου* [*Sailing Ships of Andros*] (Άνδρος: Kaireios Library, 1991).

Polodny, Joel and Karen Page, "Network Forms of Organisation," *Annual Review of Sociology* 24 (1998): 57-76.

Pomeranz, William, "'Profession or Estate'? The Case of the Russian Pre-Revolutionary 'Advokatura'," *The Slavonic and East European Review* 77 (2) (April 1999): 240-268.

Porter, Michael, "Location, Competition and Economic Development: Local Clusters in a Global Economy," *Economic Development Quarterly* 14 (1) (2000): 15-34.

"Locations, Clusters and Company Strategy," in Gordon L. Clark, Maryann P. Feldman and Gertler, Meric S., eds., *The Oxford Handbook of Economic Geography* (Oxford: Oxford University Press, 2000), 253-274.

Proskurnin, D., "Хищники (Изъ воспоминаній)" ["The 'Voulchers' (From Memories)"], *Istoricheskiy Vestnik* 110 (1907): 137-150.

Ratcliffe, Mike, *Liquid Gold Ships* (London: Lloyd's of London Press, 1985).

Rieber, Alfred J., *Merchants and Entrepreneurs in Imperial Russia* (Chapel Hill, NC: University of North Carolina Press, 1982).

Rizo Rangabe, Eugene, *Livre d'or de la noblesses Ionienne*, 3 vols. (Athens: Eleftheroudakis, 1925-1927).

Roberts, Richard, *Schroders. Merchants and Bankers* (London: Macmillan, 1992).

"What's in a Name? Merchants, Merchant Bankers, Accepting Houses, Issuing Houses, Industrial Bankers and Investment Bankers," *Business History* 35 (3) (July 1993): 22–38.

The City: A Guide to the London's Global Financial Centre (London: The Economist, 2004)

Roberts, William Johnson, *The Bills of Exchange Act, 1882, with a Copious Index* (Dublin: John Falconer, 1882).

Roth, Almon E., "Sea Transportation," *Proceedings of the Academy of Political Science* 21 (2) (January 1945): 4–16.

Rubinstein, W. D., "British Millionaires, 1809–1949," *Bulletin of the Institute of Historical Research* 48 (1974): 202–223.

Sawyer, L. S. and W. H. Mitchell, *The Liberty Ships: The History of the Emergency Type Cargoships Constructed in the United States during the Second World War*, 2nd edn (London: Lloyd's of London Press, 1985).

Scheltjens, Werner, *Dutch Deltas: Emergence, Functions and Structure of the Low Countries' Maritime Transport System, ca. 1300–1850* (Leiden: Brill, 2015).

Scholl, Lars U., "German Whaling in the 1930s," in Lewis R. Fischer, Helge W. Nordvik and Walter E. Minchinton, eds., *Shipping and Trade in the Northern Seas 1600–1939* (Bergen: n.p., 1988), 103–121.

Schwebel, Judge Stephen M., "The Kingdom of Saudi Arabia and Aramco Arbitrate the Onassis Agreement," *The Journal of World Energy Law and Business* 3 (3) (2010): 2–12.

Sedgwick, Stanley and Raymond F. Sprake, *London and Overseas Freighters Limited, 1949–1977* (Kendal: World Ship Society, 1977).

Seton-Watson, Hugh, *The Decline of Imperial Russia* (London: Methuen, 1952).

Sheppard, Eric and Trevor J. Barnes, eds., *A Companion to Economic Geography*, 2nd edn (Oxford: Blackwell Publishing, 2003).

Sherry, Dana, "Social Alchemy on the Black Sea Coast, 1860–65," *Kritika: Explorations in Russian and Eurasian History* 10 (1) (Winter 2009): 7–30.

Shields, Jerry, *The Invisible Billionaire: Daniel Ludwig* (Dublin: Houghton Mifflin, 1986).

Sidorov, Vladimir, *Энциклопедия старого Ростова и Нахичевани-на-Дону* [*Encyclopedia of Old Rostov and Nachichevan-on-Don*], vol. 3 (Rostov-on-Don: Gefesy, 1995).

Sifneos, Evrydiki, "Εθνικός αυτοπροσδιορισμός σε ένα οικονομικά μεταβαλλόμενο περιβάλλον: Η μαρτυρία ενός έλληνα εμποροϋπαλλήλου από το ρώσικο εμπόριο σιτηρών" ["National Self-Determination in an Economically Changing Environment: The Testimony of a Greek Trading Employee from the Russian Grain Trade"], in M. A. Stasinopoulou and M.-C. Chatziioannou, eds., *Diaspora–Networks – Enlightenment*, Tetradia Ergasias 28 (Athens: INE/EIE, 2005).

"The Dark Side of the Moon: Rivalry and Riots for Shelter and Occupation between the Greek and Jewish Populations in Multi-ethnic Nineteenth Century," *The Historical Review/La Revue Historique* 3 (2006): 189–204.

"Merchant Enterprises and Strategies in the Sea of Azov Ports," *International Journal of Maritime History* 22 (1) (June 2010): 259–268.

Sifneos, Evrydiki and Gelina Harlaftis, "Entrepreneurship at the Russian Frontier of International Trade: The Greek Merchant Community/*Paroikia* of Taganrog in the Sea of Azov, 1780s-1830s," in Viktor Zakharov, Gelina Harlaftis and Olga Katsiardi-Hering, eds., *Merchant "Colonies" in the Early Modern Period (15th–18th Centuries)* (London: Chatto & Pickering, 2012), 157–180.

Οι Έλληνες της Αζοφικής, 18ος-αρχές 20ού αιώνα. Νέες προσεγγίσεις στην ιστορία των Ελλήνων της νότιας Ρωσίας [Greeks in the Azov, 18th-beginning of 20th century. New approaches in the history of the Greeks in South Russia], National Research Foundation, Institute of Historical Research, Athens 2015.

Sifneos, Evrydiki and Sophronis Paradisopoulos, "Οι Έλληνες της Οδησσού το 1897: διαβάζοντας την πρώτη επίσημη ρωσική απογραφή" ["The Greeks in Odessa in 1897: Rereading the First Official Russian Census"], Τα Ιστορικά [*Ta Istorika*] 44 (June 2006): 81–122.

Slinn, Judy, *A History of Freshfields, 1743–1993* (London: Freshfields, 1993).

Sphyroeras, Vasilis, Anna Avramea, and Spyros Asdrahas, *Maps and Map-Makers of the Aegean* (Athens: Olkos, 1985).

Starkey, David J., "Ownership Structures in the British Shipping Industry: The Case of Hull, 1820–1916," *International Journal of Maritime History* 8 (2) (December 1996): 71–95.

Stopford, Martin, *Maritime Economics* (London: Routledge, 1997).

Sturmey, Stanley G., *British Shipping and World Competition* (London: Athlone Press, 1962).

Suss, Esther C., Oral Williams and Chandima Mendis, "Caribbean Offshore Financial Centers: Past, Present, and Possibilities for the Future," *The World Economy* 28 (8) (August 2005): 1173–1188.

Swyngedouw, Erik, "Elite Power, Global Forces, and the Political Economy of 'Glocal' Development," in Gordon L. Clark, Maryann P. Feldman and Meric S. Gertler, eds., *The Oxford Handbook of Economic Geography* (Oxford: Oxford University Press, 2000), 541–558.

Sydorenko, Anna, *The Economic and Social Development of the Crimean Ports in the Second Half of the 19th Century* (Unpublished PhD thesis, Ionian University, Corfu, 2017).

Syngros, Andreas, Απομνημονεύματα [*Memoirs*], Alkis Aggelou and Maria Christina Chatziioannou, eds., 2 vols. (Athens: Estia, 1998).

Tenold, Stig, "Crisis? What Crisis? – The Expansion of Norwegian Shipping in the Interwar Period," in Lars U. Scholl and David M. Williams, eds., *Crisis and Transition – Maritime Sectors in the North Sea Region – 1790–1940* (Bremen: Verlag H.M. Hauschild GmbH, 2005), 117–134.

Tankers in Trouble: Norwegian Shipping and the Crisis of the 1970s and 1980s, Research in Maritime History 32 (St. John's, Newfoundland: International Maritime History Association, 2006).

Norwegian Shipping in the 20th Century. Norway's Successful Navigation of the World's Most Global Industry (Cham, Switzerland: Palgrave: 2018).

Tenold, Stig, Odfjell:, The History of a Shipping Company (Bergen: Odfjell ASA, 2016).

Thanopoulou, Helen A., "Anticyclical Investment Strategies in Shipping: The Greek Case," World Transport Research, Proceedings of the 7th World Conference on Transport Research, Transport Management 4 (Sydney: Pergamon, 1995), 209–219.

Theotokas, Ioannis, "Organizational and Managerial Patterns of Greek-Owned Shipping Companies and the Internationalization Process from the Postwar Period to 1990," in David J. Starkey and Gelina Harlaftis, eds., *Global Markets: The Internationalization of the Sea Transport Industries since 1850*, Research in Maritime History 14 (St. John's, Newfoundland: International Maritime History Association, 1998), 303–18.

"On the Top of World Shipping: Greek Shipping Companies' Organization and Management," in A. Pallis, ed., *Maritime Transport: The Greek Paradigm*, Research in Transportation Economics 21 (2007): 63–93.

Management of Shipping Companies (London: Routledge, 2018).

Theotokas, Ioannis and Gelina Harlaftis, *Leadership in World Shipping: Greek Family Firms in International Business* (Houndmills, Basingstoke: Palgrave Macmillan, 2009).

Thowsen, Atle, *Handelsflåten i krig 1939–1945: Nortraship: Profit tog patriotism* vol. 1 (Oslo: Grøndahl, Dreyer, 1992).

Toprak, Z., "The Financial Structure of the Stock Exchange in the Late Ottoman Empire," in Philip Cottrell, M. Pohle and Fraser I. Fraser, eds., *East Meets West: Banking, Commerce and Investment in the Ottoman Empire* (Aldershot: Ashgate, 2008), 145–150.

Tsitselis, Ilias A., *Κεφαλληνιακά Σύμμικτα: Συμβολαί εις την Ιστορίαν και Λαογραφίαν της Νήσου Κεφαλληνίας* [Cephallonian Papers: Contributions to the History and Ethnology of the Island of Cephalonia] vol. 1 (Athens: Paraskeua Leoni, 1904).

Tsymbal, Ala, "Греки, Таганрога" ["Greeks of Taganrog"], in *Энциклопедия Таганрога* [*Encyclopedia of Taganrog*] (Taganrog: Anton, 1998), 81–85.

"Οι Έλληνες ως επικεφαλής της Δημοτικής Δούμας του Ταγκανρόκ" ["Greeks at the Head of the Duma of Taganrog"], in E. Sifneos and G. Harlaftis, eds., *Οι Έλληνες της Αζοφικής, 19ος αι.Νέες προσεγγίσεις την ιστορία των Ελλήνων της Νότιας Ρωσίας* [*Greeks in the Sea of Azov, 19th c.: New Approaches in the History of the Greeks of Southern Russia*] (Athens: Hellenic Institute of Research/Institute of Historical Research, 2015).

Tzamtzis, Anastasios, *Τα Λίμπερτυ και οι Έλληνες: Το χρονικό μιας ειρηνικής αρμάδας* [*The Liberties and the Greeks: The Chronicle of a Peaceful Fleet*] (Athens: Estia, 1984).

Unger, Richard W., ed., *Shipping and Economic Growth, 1350–1850* (Leiden: Brill, 2011).

Valdaliso, Jesus M., "Spanish Shipowners in the British Mirror: Patterns of Investment, Ownership and Finance in the Bilbao Shipping Industry,

316 SELECT BIBLIOGRAPHY

1879–1913," *International Journal of Maritime History* 5 (2) (December 1993): 1–30.

"The Rise of Specialist Firms in Spanish Shipping and Their Strategies of Growth, 1860 to 1930," *Business History Review* 74 (Summer 2000): 268–300.

La familia Aznar y sus negocios (1830–1983): Cuatro generaciones de empresarios en la España contemporánea (Madrid: Marcial Ponts Historia, 2006).

Vellianitis, Theodoros A., "Οι Εν Ρωσσία Έλληνες" ["Greeks in Russia"], *Εστία* [*Estia*] 44 (1893): 273–276.

Ville, Simon P., *English Shipowning during the Industrial Revolution* (Manchester: Manchester University Press, 1987).

Vlassopoulos, Costas, Σελίδες μιας ζωής [*Pages of a Life*] (Athens: Zaharopoulos Editions, 1994).

Von Laue, Theodore H., *Sergei Witte and the industrialization of Russia* (New York: Atheneum, 1969).

Vourkatioti, Katerina, "The House of Ralli Bros (*c.* 1814–1961)," in Maria Christina Chatziioannou and Gelina Harlaftis, eds., *Following the Nereids: Sea Routes and Maritime Business, 16th–20th Centuries* (Athens: Kerkyra Publications, 2006), 99–110.

Wechsberg, Joseph, *The Merchant Bankers* (Mineola, NY: Dover, 2014).

Wilkins, Mira, *The History of Foreign Investment in the United States, 1914–1945* (Cambridge, MA: Harvard University Press, 2004).

Zakharov, V. N. "Внешнеторговая деятельность иностранных купцов в портах Азовского и Черного морей в середине и второй половине XVIII в." ["The Development of Foreign Trade by Foreign Merchants in the Azov and the Black Sea Ports in the Second Half of the Eighteenth Century"], *Vestnik Moskovskogo universiteta*, ser. 8, Istoria [*History*] 4 (2004): 85–102.

Zander, Michael, *The Law-Making Process*, 6th edn (Cambridge: Cambridge University Press, 2004).

Zipperstein, Steven J., *The Jews of Odessa: A Cultural History, 1794–1881* (Stanford, CA: Stanford University Press, 1986).

Zvantsev, Sergei, Дело Вальяно [*Vagliano Case*] (Rostov-on-Don: Rostidzat editions, 1959).

Миллионное наследство: Рассказы о Таганроге [*Inheritance of Millions: Novels on Taganrog*] (Rostov: Sov. Pisatel, 1965).

APPENDICES

Appendix 1.A

The Vagliano Genealogical Tree

Athanassios Vagliano (1775–1842) and **Kerasia Kambitsi** had eight children: 1) Santina, 2) Metaxas, 3) Nikolaos, 4) Spyridon, 5) **Marino, 6) Panagi, 7) Andrea,** 8) Maria

1) **Santina Vagliano** and Panaghis Rossolimos
2) **Metaxas Vagliano** (1800–18?) and Και Roubina Kambitsi of Theotoki
    a. *Diamantina and Lazaros Rossolimos*
        i. Katerina and Nikolaos D. Lykiardopoulos (1866–1963)
            1. Panagi Lykiardopoulos (1893–1983) and Penelope Kamillou (1888–1975)
                a. Diamantina and Evangelos Averoff
                    i. Natalia
                    ii. Tatiana
                b. Fotis and D. Serpieri
                c. Kate (1922–2002) and S. Monas
                    i. Alexandros
                    ii. Nikolaos
            2. Gerassimos Lykiardopoulo (1894–1982) and Angeliki (Antzouletta) Gianoulato (1903–1986)
        ii. Elisavet and ... Mazarakis
        iii. Athanassios Rossolimos
        iv. Loukas Rossolimos
    b. *Athanassios* (1844–1914) and Aglaia Foka
    c. *Basil* (1846–1903) and Chariklia Portocaloglou (1863–?)
        i. Danae (1885–1958) and Marinos A. Vagliano
    d. *Penelope* (1850–?) and George Inglessis
    e. *Christoforos* (1847–?)
    f. *Stamatoula and* George Mousouris
3) **Nikolaos Vagliano** (1801–1886) and Efthymia Vagelou
4) **Spyridon Vagliano (1802–1892)** and Eleni Sorbanou (1837–?)
    a. *Michael (1857–1939) and Vera Souzi*
    b. *Ekaterini (Kate) and Gerassimos Kamillos*
        i. Andreas

      1. Ekaterini
      2. Penelope and Benderley
    ii. Penelope Kamillou (1888–1975) and Panagis Lykiardopoulos
   iii. Panagis
   iv. Nikos and Katerina Lainaki
  c. *Maris*
  d. *Athanasse* (1864–1927) 1) Marousa
    i. Spiros
                      2) Silvia Nikolaidou (1903–1995)
    ii. Eleni (1925–?) and Nikos Dimitriadis
      1. Ioannis (1957)
   iii. Ekaterini (1927–2010) and Marios Akrivos
      1. Dimitrios (1960)
      2. Athanassios (1962)
      3. Alexander (1967)
   iv. Athanassia (1929)
  e. *Christoforos* (1870–1925*)* and Eleni Destouni
    i. Olympia and Georgios Zografos
      1. Ioannis
      2. Eleni
      3. Konstantinos
    ii. Ekaterini (1913–1979) and N. Kostomenis (1891–1972)
      1. Maria (1936) and Stephanos Rokanas
        a. Giorgos
      2. Eleni (1937) and Youli Rascheff
        a. Agapi (Liouba)
      3. Sophia (1939)
      4. Stephania (1939) and Stelios Karageorgis
        a. Nicolas
        b. Sonia
        c. Spyros
        d. Vassilis
   iii. Maria (1915–1936)
   iv. Kerasia and Haralambos Matiatos
      1. Dimitri and Marina
        a. Kerasia
      2. Irene and Jacques Facon
        a. Laetitia
      3. Christoforos
    v. Sophia and Giorgos Trikoupis
5) **Marino/Maris (1804/8–1896)** and Maria Krassa (1814–1894)
  a. *Aspasia* (1842–1859)
  b. *Alcibiades* (1850–1924) and Angeliki Xen. Balli (1855–1912)
  c. *Athanassios* (1854–1936) and Katina Steph. Ralli (1861–1941)

   i. Marinos (1883–1960) and Danae Vagliano (1885–1958)
     1. Stephan (1908–1988?)
     2. Helene (1909–1944)
     3. Francis (1911–2006?)
   ii. Stephanos/Stephane (1884–?)
   iii. Andreas/André (1885–?) and Julie de Zogheb
     (?–1934 Lausanne) daughter of Georges Vicomte de de
     Zogheb
   iv. Maria/Marie (1887–1939) and Vicomte Henri de Kersaint
     (1881–1949)
     a. Jacques de Kersaint (1907–1979)
     b. Yvonne de Kersaint (1909–2005) and Antoine de la
       Bédoyère (1903–198?)
       1. Jean Marc (1946)
     c. Guy de Kersaint (?–1979)
     d. Marie-Claire de Kersaint (1910–?)
6) **Panagi Vagliano (1814–1902)** and Klara Bagdatopoulou (1839–1878?)
   a. *Christoforos*, died at a young age
7) **Andrea Vagliano (1827–1887)** and Euphrosyne George Mela
   (1837–1908)
   a. *Marinos* (1851–1928) and Eleni (Liola) (1873–1967) (daughter of
     Ioannis Doumas and Sophia Petrokockino)
     i. Andreas (1896–1971) and Barbara Allen (1897–1951)
       1. Dorothée (Lally) (1921) and Jacques Edmond Vicomte de
         Rafelis Saint Sauver
         a. Evelyn Marina (1940–2016)
           i. Armelle (1965)
         b. Alain Armand (1942–1995) and Daphné Corvinne de
           Turckheim
           i. Charles (1971)
           ii. Marc (1972)
       2. Sonia (1922–2002) and Philippe Eloy (1921–2010)
         a. Marina (1947) and 1) Eric le Tourneur d'Ison
           i. Alexandra (1969)
           ii. Julien (1972)
               and 2) Bertrand Jacquillat
         b. Bernard Andre Pierre(1949) and Princesse Natalie
           Poniatowska
           i. Eloise (1976)
           ii. Sebastien (1978)
           iii. Pauline (1987)
       3. Alexandre Vagliano (1927–2003) and 1) Shirley Lynch
         a. Barbara (1951)
           i. Sonia Fielding Vagliano (1982)

    ii. Sheena Fielding Vagliano (1988)
  b. Andre-Marino Vagliano (1953) and Leslie Shansky (1953–2002)
    i. Jason Bellamy Alexander (1982)
    ii. Raphael Stephen Marino (1987)

            and 2) Elizabeth Fly

            and 3) Sarah (Sally)
                Griesinger Findlay
  c. Justin Christopher Vagliano (1975)
    i. Andrew Fessenden (1998)
    ii. Alexander Kern (2004)

            and 4) Sara Ector Via Pais
ii. Sonia (1898–1990) and Raoul de La Poëze, marquis d'Harambure (1890–1952)
  1) Jean (1920–2011) and Anne d'Hespel (1927–2008)
    a. Diane (1956) and Axel Augier de Moussac (1953)
    b. Guillaume, *marquis d'Harambure* (1960) and Valérie Queyrat
    c. Laure(1961) and Emmanuel de Saboulin Bollena (1951)
    d. Alexandre (1968)
  2) Liolia (1923) and Étienne Le Gouz de Saint-Seine (1908–1986)
    a. Stephen (1945–2005) and Michaela Schultze
    b. Oriane (1946) and Alain-Charles Perrot
    c. François (1954) and Daniela Sonnino Sorisio (1957)
  3) May (1925–1995) and Guy de Moustier (1920–1994)
    a. Patrick (1949) and Béatrice Faguer (1955)
    b. Sonia (1951) and Christian de Panafieu (1946)
    c. Diane (1952) and Richard Brunner (1957)
    d. Philibert (1956) and Marie-Laure Ozoux (1960)
    e. Pierre-Etienne (1959) and Anne-Charlotte Gas (1962)
b. *Athanasse*
c. *Eleni/Helene* (1854–1927) and Menelaos Negreponte
d. *Maria/Marie* (1855–1856)
e. *Katerina/Catherine* (1858–1951) and Nikolaos Cuppas
  i. Euphrosyne/Fronia (1876–1961) and Stephan Zafiropoulos
    1. Georges (1903) and Maria Eugenidi Christine (1946)
  ii. Eleni/Helene (1877–1953) and Ioannis Choremis
    1. Andre
    2. Jenny and Jean Vlasto
    3. Eyphrosyne and Vassili Mostra

f. *Aspasia/Aspasie* (1859–1953) and Athanassios Moutsopoulos
   i. Alexandra (1878–1934) and Konstantinos Melas
   ii. Euprosyne (Fronieta) (1880–1935) and Nikolaos Paspattis
g. *Sophia/Sophie* (1862–1863)
h. *Alexandros/Alexandre* (1864–1890)
i. *Maria or Marika* (1867–1957) and Athos Romanos
   i. Ioannis Romanos (1896–?) and Virginia Alex. Benaki
      1. Alexandros (1928) and Maria Karayanaki
         a. Virginia (1957)
         b. Alexandra (1960)
         c. Ioannis (1966)
         d. Elli and Leonidas Zarifis
k. *Sophia* /**Sophie** (1870–1898) and Ioannis Ambanopoulos
   i. Nina (1893–1978) and Manolis Vucina
   ii. Marika (1894–1978) and Jacques Velten
   iii. George (1897–1918)
   iv. Andrea (1911–) and Reggina Ant. Vlastou
l. *Christoforos/Christophe* (1872–1954)
m. *Angeliki/Angelique* (1875–1923) and George Zarifi
   i. Stéphane Zarifi (1897–1939) and Marie (Mimi) Eugenidi
      1. Georges-Pericles (1928)
      2. Angelique-Helene
   ii. Fanny (1900–?) and Paul de Demandolx
8) **Maria Vagliano and Michael Kambitsis**

Sources: Interviews and e-mail communication with descendants of the Vagliano family in France, Marina Eloy, Sonia de Panafieu, Jean Marc de le Bédoyère; in the United States, Andre Marino Vagliano, Barbara Vagliano and Justin Vagliano; and in Greece Sophia Kostomeni, Athanassios Akrivos, Ioannis Vaglianos-Dimitriadis and Eleni Lykiardopoulou. The Vagliano genealogical tree by Sonia de Panafieu, typescript; Felix Vagliano, "Livre d'or de la Famille Vagliano" (typescript) (Athens, 1965); M. D. Sturdza, *Dictionnaire Historique et Genealogique des Grandes familles de Grece, d'Albanie et de Constantinople* (Paris: n.p., 1983); Timotheos Catsiyannis, *The Greek Community of London* (London: n.p., 1992) ; Ilias A. Tsitselis, Κεφαλληνιακά Σύμμικτα: Συμβολαί εις την Ιστορίαν και Λαογραφίαν της Νήσου Κεφαλληνίας [*Cephallonian Papers: Contributions to the History and and Ethnology of the Island of Cephalonia*] (Athens: n. p., 1904), vol. 1; Panayota Moschona, Παναγής Α. Βαλλιάνος: Από τη μυθοπλασία στην ιστορία [*Panaghi A. Vagliano: From Legend-Making to History*] (Cephalonia: Foundation Panaghi A. Vagliano, 2008); The National Archives, English Census-Ancestry.co.uk.; the Archives of the National Bank of Greece; Vladimir Morozan, *The Entrepreneurial Life in Southern Russia, 19th–Beginning of 20th Century*; Vagliano Archive GSA, Cephalonia Archive, file 1, "The Will of Panagi Athanasse Vagliano"; Newspaper *Taganrog Vestnik*, January 26, 1896, April 12, 1896, April 14, 1896; Cemetery of Keramies, Cephalonia.

Appendix 1.B

Table A1.1 *Voyages of the Vagliano brothers as Masters of sailing vessels, 1830–1850*

Date of voyage	Name of ship	Type of ship	Flag	Nrt	Captain	Port of origin	Port of arrival
July 21, 1830	*Achille*	Brig	Ionian	427	Vagliano Mari	Odessa	Marseilles
May 21, 1834	*Rosa*	Brig	Ionian	190	Vagliano Panagi	Taganrog	Constantinople
August 28, 1844	*Konstantinos and Eleni*	Brig	Russian	188	Vagliano Andrea	Con/ple	Zante
September 28, 1844	*Konstantinos and Eleni*	Brig	Russian	188	Vagliano Andrea	Zante	Zante
August 4, 1845	*Konstantinos and Eleni*	Brig	Russian	188	Vagliano Andrea	Corfu	Corfu
January 2, 1845	*Chios*	Brig	Russian		Vagliano Andrea	Corfu	Corfu
January 15, 1845	*Chios*	Brig	Russian		Vagliano Andrea	Corfu	Corfu
February 14, 1845	*Chios*	Brig	Russian		Vagliano Andrea	Zante	Zante
February 22, 1845	*Chios*	Brig	Russian		Vagliano Andrea	Lefkas	Cephalonia
February 23, 1845	*Chios*	Brig	Russian		Vagliano Andrea	Paxoi	Lefkas
March 19, 1845	*Chios*	Brig	Russian		Vagliano Andrea	Paxoi	Cephalonia
March 20, 1845	*Chios*	Brig	Russian		Vagliano Andrea	Paxoi	Cephalonia
December 5, 1845	*Chios*	Brig	Russian		Vagliano Andrea	Con/ple	Zante
February 4, 1846	*Chios*	Brig	Russian		Vagliano Andrea	Zante	Zante
February 7, 1846	*Chios*	Brig	Russian		Vagliano Andrea	Zante	Corfu

Table A1.1 (cont.)

Date of voyage	Name of ship	Type of ship	Flag	Nrt	Captain	Port of origin	Port of arrival
November 6, 1846	Agios Andreas	Barca		21	Vagliano Panagi	Cephalonia	Zante
April 20, 1847	Agios Andreas	Barca		21	Vagliano Panagi	Cephalonia	Lefkas-Zante
May 14, 1847	Agios Andreas	Barca		21	Vagliano Panagi	Cephalonia	Zante
June 12, 1847	Agios Andreas	Barca		21	Vagliano Panagi	Zante	Cephalonia
July 29, 1848	Agios Andreas	Barca		21	Vagliano Panagi	Zante	Cephalonia
May 25, 1849	Agios Andreas	Barca		21	Vagliano Panagi	Cephalonia	Fiscardo-Lefkas
July 2, 1849	Agios Andreas	Barca		21	Vagliano Panagi	Patras	Cephalonia
January 14, 1850	St. Nickolas	Brig	Ιονική		Vagliano Andrea	Zante	Zante
June 11, 1850	Sophia	Brig	Russian	92	Vagliano Marinos	Zante	Zante
June 17, 1850	Sophia	Brig	Russian	92	Vagliano Marinos	Con/ple	Zante
June 23, 1850	Sophia	Brig	Russian	92	Vagliano Marinos	Zante	Cephalonia
July 1, 1850	Sophia	Brig	Russian	92	Vagliano Marinos	Zante	Cephalonia
July 6, 1850	Sophia	Brig	Russian	92	Vagliano Marinos	Cephalonia	Cephalonia

Sources: Return of British and Ionian vessels in the Port of Taganrog during the year ending June 30, 1834, indicating Captain Panagi Vagliano. Source: FO 257/3, "Report of Consul in Taganrog William Yeames." Database Odysseus, 1809–1864, based on the the governmental newspaper of the British-protected Ionian state, Gazzetta Degli Stati Uniti Delle Isole Jonie. This database was formed by Panayotis Kapetanakis for his PhD thesis titled "The Deep-Sea Going Merchant Fleet of the Seven Islands of the Ionian Sea during the Time of British Conquest and Protection and the Cephalonian Prominence (1809/1815–1864) (Corfu: Ionian University, 2010). The database and the thesis were part of the research project "Greek Maritime Centres in the 19th Century," Ionian University of the programme PENED financed by the Greek Ministry of Development/EU, 2005–2008 with Gelina Harlaftis as project leader. See also G. N. Moschopoulos and S. Zapanti, Άδειες ελευθεροκοινωνίας 1846–1864 [Free Pratique Permissions 1846–1864] (Argostoli: General State Archives – Archives of Cephalonia, 1997); Semaphore de Marseilles, 1830, 1835, 1840, 1845, 1850.

~

Appendix 1.C

Table A1.2 *Current account for Mr. George Coutsis of Spetses, office of Mari Vagliano, Taganrog*

		Debit					Credit		
			Silver rubles					Silver rubles	
1870 May	26	Insurance in Marseilles francs 1428 @ 3.10		463.63	1870 April	1	From older accounts		1,302.08
"	30	Invoice of hard wheat with *Antonios*		14,590.08	April	310	Remittance to the Masters of Antonios from Palermo to Marseilles of 1,800 francs @ 3.12		576.95
July	4	Invoice of hard wheat with *Genesis*		34,282.20		25	Transfer to Mrss Mavro of Odessa		4,008
August	15	Invoice of hard wheat with *Agios Ioannis Theologos*		28,860.90	May	4	Transfer to Mrss Mavro of Odessa		14,811
September	19	20,15 francs @ 6.46 to Malokini in Constantinople		96.90		16	Remittance to Marseilles insurance francs 118.25 @ 3.10		38.39
October	6	Flour to the Master of *Antonios*		106.75		18	Cash from Master of *Antonios*		6950
"	17	Invoice of hard wheat with *Komna*		23,873.89		29	Cash from Master of *Antonios*		50
"	23	Invoice of wheat Girca with *Eleftheria*		26,451.66		30	Remitance of Mavros from Odessa		17,184
"	"	Cash at various times to Mr Geor. Koutsis		1,910	June	6	Remittance of Mavros from Odessa		4,000
"	"	Accounts of Masters of *Eleftheria*		1,168.76		15	Remittance of Mavros from Odessa		3,777
"	"	Telegraphic expenses for Spetses and Marseilles and letter transfer expenses		40	July	3	Remittance of Mavros from Odessa		14,232

325

Table A1.2 (*cont.*)

Debit		Credit	
	21	1,150 Remitance to Moscow	9,555
	25	Remitance of Ottoman Lira of Constantinople 301.08	2,317.6
	"	20 francs notes 1825 in various prices	11,749.55
	August 25	Accounts of Master of *Antonios*	1,645
	29	628 francs gave Isaias to Skouzes in Athens @ 3.20	196.25
	September 4	In 20 fr. notes 1095	7,171.20
	October 10	In 20 fr. notes, 140	906.15
	23	In 20 fr. notes 1,000 transfer to Constantinople	6,468
	"	Balance billing in new accounts	24,905.55
131,844.77			131,844.77

The balance of the billing as above 24,905.55

Taganrog, October 23, 1870.
Source: Private Archive of Coutsis family, Spetses.

~~

Appendix 1.D

Calculation of the sailing ship fleet of the Vaglianos has been a complex procedure. Frequently sailing ships bore the name of Andrea Vagliano or Mari or Panagi Vagliano but belonged to other shipowners. The tables that follow include all sailing ships and steamships that have either Mari, Panagi, or Andrea as shipmasters or as shipowners. Ships of other masters they financed were not kept more than ten years. Information on one ship has been derived from many sources and hence the span of their life under the Vaglianos has been calculated. When the information was of one year and we had the construction date available, the period of ownership has been calculated as an average of twenty years after its construction.

The sources from which information on their ships has been derived are a) Russia: State Archives of the Rostov-on-Don Region, 584.1.284 (1867), 584.1.28 (1880–1914), 579.1.100 (1881–1898), *Russki kommercheski flot po 1-e ianvaria 1858 goda* [Russian Commercial Fleet on January 1, 1858], St. Petersburg, 1858, *Russki torgovyi flot: Spisok sudov k 1 ianvaria 1903 g.* [Russian Merchant Fleet: List of Ship on January 1, 1903), St. Petersburg, 1903–1918, b) Great Britain: *Lloyd's Register of Shipping*, 1860–1930, National Archives, Foreign Office, Reports of Consuls from Taganrog, c) France: *Bureau Veritas* (1830–1900), *Semaphore de Marseilles* (1830–1914), d) Italy: *Lloyd* Austriaco (1861–1890), e) Greece: classification society *Archangelos* (1870–1885), State General Archives of Syros, *Gazzetta Degli Stati Uniti Delle Isole Jonie*, Greek Port Authorities, Piraeus Ship Register 1880–1939. Information has also been derived from two databases. The first one published as Gelina Harlaftis and Nikos Vlassopoulos, Ιστορικός νηογνώμονας, Ποντοπόρεια: Ποντοπόρα Ιστιοφόρα και Ατμόπλοια 1830–1939 [*Pontoporeia: Historical Registry Book of Greek Cargo Sailing Ships and Steamships, 1830–1939*] (Athens: ELIA/Niarchos Foundation, E.Λ.Ι.A, 2002); it is based on information derived from the classification societies, Lloyd Austriaco, Bureau Veritas, and Archangelos. The second database is *Odysseus*, 1809–1864, formed by Panayotis Kapetanakis based on the governmental newspaper of the British-protected Ionian state, *Gazzetta Degli Stati Uniti Delle Isole Jonie*.

Table A1.3 *The sailing ship fleet of the Vagliano Bros., 1825–1900*

Name of ship	Shipowner	Master	NRT	Type of ship	Flag	Year built	Place built	Port registered
[No name]	Vagliano Mari		62	Martigo	Ionian	1825		
Achilles	Vagliano Mari	Vagliano Mari	422	Brig	Ionian	1828	Syros	Cephalonia
Adelphotis	Vagliano Andrea	Rosolymos T.	240	Brig	Greek	1855		Cephalonia
Adelfoi Vagliano	Vagliano Mari		282	Brig	Russian	1852		Kherson
Agioi Petros and Pavlos	Vagliano Mari		134					
Agios Andreas	Vagliano Panagi	Vagliano Panagi	21	Barca	Ionian			Cephalonia
Agios Andreas	Vagliano Mari		56	Schooner	Russian	1859		Rostov
Agios Constantinos and Agia Eleni	Vagliano Andrea	Vagliano Andrea	188	Brig	Russian	1840		Taganrog
Agios Gerassimos	Vagliano Mari	Syrigos M.	118	goleta	Greek	1871	Syros	Syros
Agios Ioannis	Vagliano Bros		272			1893		
Agios Nikolaos	Vagliano Andrea		242	Brig	Ionian	1843	Syros	Cephalonia
Agios Nikolaos	Vagliano Mari		64	Schooner		1854		Kherson
Agios Nikolaos	Vagliano Mari		64	schooner	Russian	1854		Kherson
Agios Nikolaos	Vagliano Andrea		261	Wbn		1868	Syros	Cephalonia
Agios Petros	Vagliano Andrea	Rosolymos P.	206	Brig	Greek	1857		Cephalonia

Name	Owner	Captain	Tonnage	Rig	Flag	Year	Port 1	Port 2
Aglaia Vagliano	Vagliano A.M.		338			1889	Syros	
Alexandr	Vagliano Mari	Gershos G.	170	Schooner	Russian		Rostov	Rostov
Alexandr	Vagliano Mari	Metaxa A.	191	Schooner	Russian		Tatianovka	Rostov
Alexandros Vaglianos	Vagliano	Mantzavino G.	197	Brig	Greek	1868		Cephalonia
Alexandros Vaglianos	Vagliano M.A.		485			1889	Marseilles	
Alkibiades	Vagliano Andrea	Kambitsis P.	212	Brig	Greek	1856	Korkoula	Zante
Alkibiades Vaglianos	Vagliano Andrea	Michalitsianos Zannis	314	Brig	Greek	1872	Galaxidi	Galaxidi
Analipsis	Vagliano Andrea	Sklavounos N.	203	Brig	Greek	1858	Galaxidi	Zante, Cephalonia
Anastasia*	Vagliano Mari		64	Schooner	Russian	1859		Rostov
Andrea Vagliano	Bagdatopoulos George	Vagliano George K.	192	Brig	Ionian	1853	Syros	Cephalonia
Andreas	Vagliano Mari		62	Schooner	Russian	1859		Rostov
Sviatoi Arkhangel Mikhail	Vagliano Mari	Granitski	102	trabacolo	Russian	1864	Taganrog	Taganrog
Aspasia	Vagliano Andrea	Tsitsilianis P.	206	Brig	Greek	1864	Syros	Cephalonia
Athanassios Vaglianos	Vagliano A. sons		683	Brig				Cephalonia
Azofiki	Vagliano Mari		64	Schooner	Russian	1858		Rostov
Berdyansk	Vagliano Mari	Lavrenti Ivan	172	Schooner	Russian	1869	Rostov	Rostov

Table A1.3 (cont.)

Name of ship	Shipowner	Master	NRT	Type of ship	Flag	Year built	Place built	Port registered
Cephalonia	Vagliano Andrea	Lykiardopoulo Z.	237	Brig	Greek	1861		Hydra
Chios	Vagliano Mari	Vagliano Andrea	204	Brig	Russian			Taganrog
Eirini	Vagliano sons	Cuppa Panagi M.	190	Brig	Greek	1832	Syros	Syros
Ekaterina	Vagliano Mari	Simonovich S.	163	Schooner	Russian	1868	Donets river	Rostov
Eleni Vaglianou	Vagliano Andrea	Ambatiellos E.	261	Brig	Greek	1865	Pirano	Zante
Elisaveta Svorono	Vagliano Mari	Pankov Fedorov	186	Tug	Russian	1883	England	Taganrog
Enosis	Vagliano Mari	Kordias I.	244	Brig	Russian	1862	Charlotte Town	Taganrog
Enotis	Vagliano Andrea	Ambatiellos E.	346	Gabara	Greek	1860	England	Cephalonia
Eptanissos	Vagliano Andrea	Lykiardopoulo F.	185	Brig	Greek	1864		Cephalonia
Eugenia	Vagliano Andrea	Vucina G.	210	Brig	Greek	1866	syros	Zante
Euphrosyne Vagliano	Vagliano Andrea	Kambitsis A.	282	Brig	Greek	1870	Syros	Cephalonia
Hawkeye	Vagliano A. A.		505			1878		
Iako s nami Bog [God is with us]	Vagliano Mari	Svorono N.	91	Schooner	Russian	1879	Pavlovsk	Rostov

330

Ios	Vagliano Mari	Lalis Mario	265	Schooner	Russian	1879	Syros	Taganrog
Karnilon	Vagliano Mari	Platio Petr	202	Schooner	Russian	1870	Borisoglebsk	Rostov
Kefallinia	Vagliano A.		210	Brig	Russian	1866	Constantinople	Corfu
Kefalonia	Vagliano Mari	Mussuri P.	120	steamship	Russian	1879		Taganrog
Keramies	Vagliano Andrea	Vagliano G. A.	206	Brig	Greek	1869	Syros	Cephalonia
Kimon	Vagliano Andrea	Parisianos Georg	316	Brig	Russian	1846	Malta	Syros
Leon	Vagliano Andrea	Focas G.	360	Gabara	Greek	1873	Kassos	Melos
Maria	Vagliano Mari	Livirados Andrea	236	Schooner	Russian	1876	Syros	Berdyansk
Marika	Vagliano Andrea	Kambitsis G.	147	Goleta	Greek	1861	England	Cephalonia
Marika	Vagliano Andrea	Frangopoulos C.	320	Brig	Greek	1863	Constantinople	Constantinople
Marina	Vagliano Andrea		168		Greek	1869	England	Cephalonia
Marionka	Vagliano Mari	Kambitsis	230	Brig	Russian	1868	Syros	Cefalonia
Maris A Vaglianos	Vagliano Mari	Kambitsis A.	201	Brig	Ionian	1858		Cephalonia
Mariupol	Vagliano Mari	Karmanis M.	172	Schooner	Russian	1869	Rostov	Rostov
Mellon	Vagliano Andrea	Cambitis A.	228	Brig	Greek	1867	Syros	Cephalonia
Nea Elpis	Vagliano Mari		90	Brig		1856		Taganrog
Olga	Vagliano Andrea	Vergottis G.	298	Brig	Greek	1855	England	Syros, Constantinople
P. Focas	Vagliano P.		196	Brig		1868	Sunderland	Cephalonia

Table A1.3 (*cont.*)

Name of ship	Shipowner	Master	NRT	Type of ship	Flag	Year built	Place built	Port registered
Panagis Vaglianos	Vagliano Andrea	Lykiardopoulo E.	283	Brig	Greek	1868	Syros	Piraeus
Panayota	Vagliano Andrea	Rosolymos T.	285	Brig	Greek	1868	Castellamare	Cephalonia
Rosa	Vagliano Mari and Panagi		196		Ionian	1830		
Sophia	Vagliano Mari	Vagliano Mari	92	Brig	Russian			Taganrog
Sophoula	Vagliano Andrea	Rosolymos P.	285	Brig	Greek	1867	Napoli	Poros, Corfu
Sviatoi Mitrofani	Vagliano Mari	Mussuri P.	129	Schooner	Russian	1869	Pavlovsk	Rostov
Sviataia Elena	Vagliano Mari	Gerasimatos Str.	162	Brig	Russian	1868	Rostov	Rostov
Sviatoi Alexandr	Vagliano Mari	Fodinov F.	93	Schooner	Russian	1863	Trebizond	Poti
Sviatoi Andrei	Vagliano Mari	Gerasimatos Gr.	166	Schooner	Russian	1872	Mt Athos	Rostov
Sviatoi Luca	Vagliano Mari		116	Schooner	Russian	1868	Sukhodol	Rostov
Sviatoi Nicolai	Vagliano Mari	Chrisoluri N.	196	Schooner	Russian	1874		Taganrog
Sviatoi Petr	Vagliano Mari	Russo M.	190	Schooner	Russian	1857	Rostov	Rostov
Sviatoi Spyridon	Vagliano Mari	Lengopulo Andrei	171	Schooner	Russian	1865	Taganrog	Taganrog
Taganrog	Vagliano Mari	Benet Sarlo	167	Schooner	Russian	1869	Rostov	Rostov
Tagiri Bakh	Vagliano Mari	Kambitsis	104	Schooner	Russian	1869	Taganrog	Taganrog
Theotokos	Vagliano Mari		42	Schooner		1857		Rostov

Table A1.4 *The steamship fleet of the Vaglianos, 1876-1919*

Name of ship	Shipowner	Nrt	Grt	Date of built	Place of built	Port registered	Date of purchase
Vagliano	Vagliano Bros.		276	1869	UK, Rutherglen, Thomas B. Seath & Co	Cephalonia	1869
Cephalonia	Valliano and Co	37	114	1865	UK, North Shields	Braila	1876
Vagliano Brothers	Vagliano Bros	832	1280	1878	UK, Sunderland, Bartram, Haswell & Co	Cephalonia	1878
Vagliano A	Vagliano Bros		394	1880	UK, Rutherglen, Thomas B. Seath & Co	Cephalonia	1880
Vagliano B	Vagliano Bros	188	320	1880	UK, Rutherglen, Thomas B. Seath & Co	Cephalonia	1880
Adelphi Cuppa	Vagliano Bros	890	1380	1880	UK, Sunderland, Shipyards W. Pickersgill and son	Cephalonia	1880
Mari Vagliano	Vagliano Bros	948	1461	1880	UK, Sunderland, Bartram, Haswell & Co	Cephalonia	1880
Andrea Vagliano	Vagliano Bros	1045	1622	1880	UK, Sunderland, Bartram, Haswell & Co	Cephalonia	1880
P.A. Vagliano	Vagliano Bros	964	1482	1880	UK, Sunderland, Shipyards J. Laing	London	1882
Ekaterini Coupa	Vagliano A., Vagliano M.A.	883	1387	1878	UK	Cephalonia	1882
Adelphi Vagliano	Vagliano Bros	1087	1677	1883	UK, Sunderland, Shipyards W. Pickersgill and son	Cephalonia	1883
Nicholas Vagliano	Vagliano Bros	1101	1693	1883	UK, Sunderland, Bartram, Haswell & Co	Cephalonia	1883
Spyridon Vagliano	Vagliano Bros	1111	1708	1883	UK, Sunderland, Bartram, Haswell & Co	Cephalonia	1883
Cephalinia	Vagliano Ath.	299	562	1880	UK, Greenock	Piraeus	1886
Ithaka	Vagliano S.P.	703		1873	UK	Syros	1887
Alcibiades	Vagliano M.	265				Taganrog	1890
Cephalonia	Vagliano P.A., Vagliano A.A. and sons	710	929			Cephalonia	1890

Table A1.4 (cont.)

Name of ship	Shipowner	Nrt	Grt	Date of built	Place of built	Port registered	Date of purchase
Cephalonia	Vagliano M.S.	1137				Cephalonia	1890
Cephalonia	Vagliano A.A. sons (from G. Stathopulo)	929	1254	1878	UK, Middlesbrough, H. Dixon	Marseilles	1890
Danae	Vagliano Mari	126	290		UK	Rostov on Don	1890
Adelphi	Vagliano Bros	824	1271		UK, South Shields, Lawe Yard	Syros	1891
Despoina	Vagliano P.A.	770		1890	UK	Cephalonia	1891
Cephalonia	Vagliano A.A.	473				Cephalonia	1892
Zakynthos	Vagliano AA. Sons	973				Marseilles	1892
Aghios Ioannis	Vagliano Bros	1093					1893
Alexandros	Vagliano Bros	26				Marianople, Russia	1894
Flying Arrow	Vagliano M.	26	132	1882	UK, South Shields, J.T. Eltringham	Taganrog	1896
Vagliano	Vagliano Bros.	1753	2716	1895	UK, Sunderland, Bartram, Haswell & Co	Cephalonia	1895
Agios Gerassimos	Vagliano Bros	1093				London	1895
Ambatiellos	Vagliano P.A.	1074	1132			Cephalonia	1895
Astrea	Vagliano M.	789				Rostov-on-Don	1895
Christophoros	Vagliano and Co	550				Rostov-on-Don	1895
Aspasia	Vagliano Bros	454	547	1896	UK, North Shields, Edwards Brothers	Rostov-on-Don	1896
Eleni Millas	Vagliano Bros	1503					1897
Liolia	Vagliano M. and I. Frangopoulo	393				Rostov-on-Don	1897

Girda Ambatiellos	Vagliano Bros	1167				Corfu	1899
Maria	Vagliano Bros	1721	2643		UK, Palmer's, Shipbuilding & Iron Co	Piraeus	1901
Vassileios	Vagliano Bros	1407				Piraeus	1901
Photis	Vagliano Bros	1613	2518		UK, Glasgow, A Rodger & Company Port	Piraeus	1902
K. Paskhalidis	Vagliano A.S.	1674	1743	1883	UK, Campbell MacIntosh and Bowstead	Piraeus	1902
Athos Romanos	Vagliano A.S.	1567	2430	1902	UK, South Shields, West Yard	Cephalonia	1902
Lelia	Vagliano M.	1182	1616		UK	Rostov-on-Don	1903
Christophore	Vagliano M.S.	536	727	1904	UK, North Shields, Smith's Dock Co, Ltd	Rostov-on-Don	1904
Adelfotis	Vagliano A.S.	1471				Piraeus	1904
Panaghi Vagliano	Vagliano A.S.		3010	1904	UK, Middlesbrough, Robert Craggs & Sons, Ltd	Cephalonia/Piraeus	1904
Cephalonia	Vagliano M.S.	1137				Rostov-on-Don	1904
Demetrios	Vagliano M.S.	1220				Rostov-on-Don	1904
Ainos	Vagliano K.S. and A.S.	1458				Piraeus	1905
Keramiai	Vagliano K.S. and A.S.	3020	4702			Piraeus	1905
Spyridon Vagliano	Vagliano A.S.	2997	4471			Piraeus	1905
Cristoforo Vagliano	Vagliano A.S.	1822	3063	1896	UK. Sir WG Armstrong, Mitchell & Co, Ltd	Cephalonia	1905
Boiotia	Vagliano A.S.	1968				Athens	1910
Olympia	Vagliano Ath.	1897	3619			Piraeus	1914
Kentavros	Vagliano Sp.	483	856	1884	UK	Piraeus	1918
Gennadios	Vagliano Ath.	164	333	1891	UK, Glasgow	Piraeus	1919

~

Appendix 1.E

Table A1.5 *Selected Greek and non-Greek merchants and bankers collaborating with Vagliano Bros. in London, 1858–1887*

Greek merchant and bankers	Non-Greek merchant bankers	Banks
Abbot	Allen	Anglo-Egypt Bank
Acatos	Anderson	Bank of Australia
Agelasto	Aynard	Bank of Constantinople
Alexander	Barclay	Bank of Egypt
Alexiadi	Barff	Bank of Ireland
Ambatiello	Baring	Bank of Liverpool
Ameros	Barnett	Bank of London
Anagnostopoulo	Barnett	Bank of Romania
Analyti	Blydenstein	Colonial Bank
Andreades	Brown	Credit Lyonais
Aneilotti	Cohen	English Bank of Rio
Argenti	Courtauld	Imperial Bank
Avierino	Dixon	Ionian Bank
Bacca	Engelhardt	London Bank
Bagdatopoulo	Fruchling	National Bank of Greece
Balli	Gibbs	Ottoman Bank
Benaki	Gillett	Union Bank
Caragianachi	Glyn	
Caralis	Goldberger	
Carra	Goldsmith	
Cassavetti	Hambro	
Cavafy	Harris	
Cefalla	Heath	
Chefalino	Hill	
Choleva	Horeley	
Cicelli	Houghton	
Corgalegno	Huth	

Table A1.5 (*cont.*)

Greek merchant and bankers	Non-Greek merchant bankers	Banks
Coronio		
Couvelas	Jackson	
Cremidi	James	
Cuppa	Kleinwort Benson	
Delta	Lambert	
Doresa	Lure	
Dracopulo	Melbrough	
Eustathiadi	Mendl	
Fachiri	Mercier	
Franghiadi	Mitchell	
Frangopulo	Mogley	
Galai	Murton	
Georgacopulo	Palmer	
Georgiades	Payworth	
Geralopulo	Peabody George & Co.	
Gerussi	Prescott	
Giannacopulo	Ranking	
Homere	Raphael	
Ionides	Robinson	
Lambrinidi	Rothchild N. M. & Sons	
Lascaridi	Samuel	
Margetti	Schroeder	
Mavro	Stern	
Mavrocordato	Thomas	
Melas	Wadall	
Mercuri	Warburg	
Mesimeri	Yeames	
Negreponte		
Nicolopoulo		
Nomico		
Pana		
Paparitor		
Papayanni		
Paspatti		
Petrokockino		
Protopazzi		
Ralli		
Rodocanachi		

Table A1.5 (*cont.*)

Greek merchant and bankers	Non-Greek merchant bankers	Banks
Salvago		
Scaramanga		
Schilizzi		
Sevastopoulo		
Spartali		
Tamvaco		
Theologo		
Vucina		
Xenos		
Zarifi		
Ziffo		
Zizinia		
Zucco		
Zygomala		

Sources: Archives of the Bank of England, C98/3674, C98/3959, C98/4248.

Table A1.6 *Network of agents and collaborators of Vagliano Bros., 1901–1902*

Name	Place of company
Achillopoulos E. C.	Cairo
Achillopoulos S. C.	Cairo
Alonzo & Consoli	Catania
Ambanopulo N. G.	Grans, Bouches-du-Rhone
Ambatiellos Eust.	Cephalonia
Ambatiellos G.	Cephalonia
Ambatiellos P.	Cephalonia
Anastasiadi	Smyrna
Anralhs	Dusseldorf
Assani	Marseilles
Bank Amsterdam	Amsterdam
Banque Anglo-Egyptien	Alexandria
Banque Anversoise	Anvers
Banque Comptoir National d'Escompte de Paris	Paris
Banque et Compagnie de l'Azoff Don	Taganrog
Banque Francaise pour le commerce et d'Industrie	Paris
Banque Internationale de Paris	Paris
Bassias A. I.	Galatz

Table A1.6 (*cont.*)

Name	Place of company
Buttigieg G. e figli	Malta
Callivoca G.	Corfu
Callivokas G. S.	Corfu
Calvocoressis I.G.	Syros
Camilo G. P.	Cephalonia
Capt. A. L. Vatis	Syros
Capt. C. Mazarachi, s. *Photis*	Cephalonia
Capt. E. Comnino, s. *Girda Ambatiello*	Cephalonia
Capt. G. Moraiti	Andros
Captain A. Cosmas, s. *Mari Vagliano*	Syros
Captain C. A. Polemis	Andros
Captain C. Cochinos, s. *Ambatiellos*	Onboard
Captain D. K. Callimeri, s. *Avra*	Onboard
Captain D. Vergotis, s. *And. Vergottis*	Cephalonia
Captain G. B. Moustakas, s. *Vassilios*	Onboard
Captain Lykiardopoulo, s. *Photis*	Cephalonia
Captain Mazarachis	Cephalonia
Captain Michalitziano, s. *Sidney Thomas*	Onboard
Captain Paul Ambatiello, s. *Georgios Ambatiellos*	Onboard
Caruzos C. D.	Trieste
Catacuzino S. D.	Smyrna
Catziyeras	Cephalonia
Charokopos P. A.	Athens
Choidas A.	Patras
Chrussachi M.	Smyrna
Cicelis P. G., P. L	Marseilles
Cohen F.	Rotterdam
Costa A. C.	Genoa
Cuppa Nik.	Marseilles
Coutsis I. G.	Piraeus
Couvielos D. S.	Syros
Cozzifachi A. C.	Syra
Credit Lyonnais	Paris
Dendrias Bros.	Constantinople
Destounis Bros.	Constantinople
Di Pasquale Agap Michele & Sons	Malta
Diamantindis D. Sons	Taganrog
Dimopoulos D. G.	Nafplion
Foka A. J.	Cephalonia

Table A1.6 (*cont.*)

Name	Place of company
Fokas A. G.	Cephalonia
Fokas G. A.	Athens
Foscolo Mango	Constantinople
Foustanos P. A.	Syros
Gangos A.	Syra
Garafallo J. A.	Cairo
Gentilinis P. M.	Cephalonia
Georgiades D.	Paris
Goulandris A. L.	Andros
Goulandris G. L.	Andros
Goulandris I. P.	Andros
Hadjopoulos S.	Manchester
Kallinicos P. A.	Constantinople
Kallinicos P. A.	Constantinople
Kambitsis Ger.	Constantinople
Kambitsis G. M.	Cephalonia
Kamilos G. P.	Cephalonia
Karadzaev	Mariupol
Katakouzinos S. D.	Smyrna
Katsigeras C. and G. C.	Cephalonia
Katsigeras L.	Cephalonia
Koninkly Ke Nederlandsche	Amsterdam
Kornilakis	Syros
Kotsifakis A. C.	Syros
Koundouris C.	Cephalonia
Krinos G.	Paris
Kulukundis E. G.	Syros
La Banque d'Escompte de St. Petersburg	Petersburg
La Banque d'Escompte de St. Petersburg	Taganrog
Liberopulo A. D.	Patras
Lippmann Rosenthal	Amsterdam
Livierato freres	Marseilles
Livieriatos	Aden
London Coal	Gibraltar
Lyberopoulos I. D.	Patras
Manolatos S. G.	Antwerp
Mandakas G. & S.	Andros
Manthos D.	Syros
Margaroni P and Sons	Chios

Table A1.6 (*cont.*)

Name	Place of company
Mascaro Franco	Barcelona
Mavrocordato A. E.	Syros
Mazarakis C.	Constantinople
Mercati D.	Zante
Meyer M. C.	Cologne
Michalinos	Piraeus
Michalinos Co.	London
Michalitsianos M. E.	Piraeus
Mikroulakis S. E.	Marseilles
Millas J. D.	Braila
Milona N.	Leghorn
Mitropoulos C. D.	Burgas
Mitzis D. L.	Alexandria
Momferatos G. S.	Alexandria
Moraitis D. G.	Andros
Moumoutzis I. P.	Syros
Mussuri A. D.	Taganrog
National Bank of Greece	Athens
Negreponti A. Z., Z. P.	Syros
Negroponte D. A.	Athens
Nicolachi G. fils	Piraeus
Nicolaides J.	Cyprus, Paphos
Nicolaidis Ch. & Sons	Syros
Nikolaidis Sons	Syros
Ortenzato I. G.	Cephalonia
Ortenzatos M. and Bros.	Nikolaiev
Owners of *Katina*	Kassos, Syros
Panas G. A.	Galatz
Papageorgiou G. V.	Athens
Paracachis D.	Smyrna
Parikatsis G. V.	Smyrna
Patrikios N.	Cephalonia
Pellerini fils & Co.	Christiania
Petritsis G. Sons	Syros
Pieridis	London
Pieridis I.	Larnaca
Pignatore A.	Constantinople
Prault M.	Paris
Pringos V. A.	Alexandria

Table A1.6 (*cont.*)

Name	Place of company
Ralli S. P.	Athens
Retsina Freres	Piraeus
Romanos A.	Athens
Rosolymos L. L.	Cephalonia
Rosolymos C.	Constantinople
Rousos N. P.	Syros
Saliaris A. C.	Chios
Seiklounas G.	Cephalonia
Sfaello E. A.	Taganrog
Sinodinos Freres	Piraeus
Skouzes G. P.	Athens
Sloman R. M.	Hamburg
Stathatos Bros.	Braila
Stathatos O. A.	Athens
Stefano A.	Athens
Suclima J. et fils	Malta
Svorono C. & Son	Taganrog
Svorono J. E.	Vathy, Samos
Svoronos F. G.	Cephalonia
Svoronos Sons	Taganrog
Tas. Erzu	Amsterdam
Theodorides C. G.	Rodosto
Theofani T.	Rostov
Theophilatos A. N.	Athens
Thomopoulo	Patras
Tsiropinas C. A.	Syros
Tsiropinas P.	Marseilles
Valadov C. & Co.	Paris
Vasileiadis A. G.	Marseilles
Vatis I. Z.	Syros
Vejas P.	Cephalonia
Zouros D. M.	Marseilles

Source: Foreign Letter Books, 1901–1902, Vagliano Archive, General State Archives, Archive of the Prefecture of Cephalonia.

Appendix 1.F

Table A1.7 *Vagliano Bros., Schröder, and Rothschild assets, 1858-1887*

Year	Vagliano	Schroder	Rothschild
1858	139,008		
1859	554,363		
1860	1,072,227		
1861	1,053,420	2,017,000	
1862	620,810	1,681,000	
1863	1,216,913	1,893,000	
1864	1,169,107	2,150,000	
1865	1,894,846	2,191,000	
1866	1,333,129	2,725,000	
1867	2,404,368	2,537,000	
1868	2,963,869	3,616,000	
1869	2,980,695	3,761,000	
1870	2,618,690	5,213,000	
1871	3,866,324	4,414,000	
1872	4,852,302	5,843,000	
1873	6,278,515	6,514,000	15,595,035
1874	4,805,596	5,828,000	14,755,232
1875	3,715,579	6,680,000	18,487,727
1876	3,711,715	5,571,000	13,389,106
1877	4,804,019	4,813,000	13,592,698
1878	6,548,246	3,655,000	13,592,698
1879	5,841,584	3,705,000	13,022,317
1880	6,763,535	3,576,000	10,857,738
1881	7,865,769	3,926,000	12,177,367
1882	4,259,668	3,818,000	12,511,291
1883	6,485,791	3,626,000	12,734,390
1884	5,497,419	3,526,000	13,491,790
1885	5,994,254	3,533,000	11,446,012

Table A1.7 (*cont.*)

Year	Vagliano	Schroder	Rothschild
1886	3,392,161	3,742,000	14,126,858
1887	3,513,831	5,066,000	16,984,901

I define "assets" as the aggregate transactions including commercial bills, cash, securities, advances, etc., along with customers' liabilities for acceptances.
Sources: For Vagliano, see Archives of the Bank of England, Vagliano Bros. account in "Drawing Office: Customer Account Ledgers," C98/3618 (1858), C98/3646 (1859), C98/3674 (1860), C98/3702 (1861), C98/3729 (1862), C98/3758 (1863), C98/3786 (1864), C98/3815 (1865), C98/3846 (1866), C98/3878 (1867), C98/3906 (1868), C38/3932 (1869), C98/3959 (1870), C98/3985 (1871), C98/4011 (1872), C98/4038 (1873), C98/4064 (1874), C98/4090 (1875), C98/4116 (1876), C98/4142 (1877), C98/4168 (1878), C98/4196 (1879), C98/4223 (1880), C98/4248 (1881), C98/4276 (1882), C98/4305 (1883), C98/4335 (1884), C98/4362 (1885), C98/4394 (1886), C98/4425 (1887). For Schroder see Roberts, *Schröders: Merchants and Bankers*, appendix IV(i). For Rothschild, Niall Ferguson, *The House of Rothschild* (New York: Viking, 2000).

Appendix 2.A

Genealogical Tree, Onassis Family

Charalambos Onassoglou (1848–1914) and **Gesthimani Antoniadou (c. 1858–c. 1922)** had seven children: 1) Kyriakos, 2), Ioannis, 3) Socrates, 4) Vasileios, 6) Alexandros, 7) Maria, 8) Omiros

1) **Kyriakos Onassis (1870–1916)**
2) **Ioannis Onassis (1872–1930) and Penelope Abramoglu**
   a. *Charalambos Onassis (1899–1922)*
   b. *Georgia Onassi (1901–1995) and K. Katsoulis*
   c. *Iraklis Onassis (1908–1975) and 1) Eleni Stergiou*
      i. Penelope (1948–1989)
      ii. Charalambos (1949) and 1) Miria Mires
         1. Marianna Carolina (1977)
         2. Elena Florencia (1982)
                        2) Maria Bustamente
         1. Sofia Penelope (1994)
      iii. Spyros (1959–1994) and L. Maldonado
         1. Valeria Soledad (1986)
         2. Franco Federico (1991)
   d. *Kimon Onassis (1910–1996) and Maria Papantoniou*
      i. Ioannis (1957)
         1. Kimon (1989)
      ii. Jason (1962)
   e. *Aris Onassis (1912–1972) and Mary Xenakis*
      i. Veronica (1961) and Ricardo Chain
         1. Alejandro (1983)
         2. Federica (1986)
      ii. Annabella (1955) and Carlos Ibichian
         1. Stefania (1993)
         2. Nicolas (1998)
   f. *Maria Onassis (1922) and Andreas Dimopoulos*
      i. Andreas (1955) and A. M. Caramano
         1. Andreas (1985)
         2. Maria (1986)
      ii. Marina (1967) and M. Ramirez

3) **Socrates Onassis (1874–1932) and 1) Penelope Dologlou (c. 1881–1911)**
and 2) Eleni Tzortzoglou (1887–1962)

a. *Artemis Onassis (1902/1903–1981) and 1) Pantelis Papaniko-laou (1892–1972)*
   i. Penelope Papanikolaou (1924–1954)
                                    2) *Theodoros Garofalidis*
b. *Aristotle Onassis (1904/1906–1975) and 1) Athina Maria Livanos*
                                    (1929–1975) married in 1946
                                    and 2) Jaqueline Bouvier-
                                    Kennedy (1929–1994)
                                    married in 1968

   i. Alexander (1948–1973)
   ii. Christina (1950–1988) and 1) Joseph Bolker (b. 1923)
                                    (m. 1971–div. 1972)
                                    2) Alexander Andreadis
                                    (b. 1944)
                                    (m. 1975–div. 1977)
                                    3) Sergei Danilovich Kauzov
                                    (m. 1980–div. 1980)
                                    4) Thierry Patrick F.Roussel
                                    (b. 1953)
                                    (m. 1984–div. 1987)
      a. Athina Helen Onassis (1985)
c. *Meropi Onassis (1913–2012) and Nikolaos Konialidis*
   i. Marios Chrysostomos (1940–2019)
   ii. Giorgos Socrates (1942)
d. *Calliroe Onassis (1918–2007) and Gerassimos Patronikolas (1904–1969)*
   i. Marilena Patronikola (1948) and Panagiotis Drakos
      a. Alexandra
      b. Giorgos (1969)
4) **Vasileios Onassis (1876–1945) and Magdalini**
   a. *Themistocles Onassis (1910–1980)*
   b. *Georgios Onassis (1916–1982) and Olga*
      i. Kostas (1950)
      ii. Vasileios (1954)
   c. *Evangelia Onassis (1920–?) and Zissis Tiamkaris*
      i. Andreas
5) **Alexandros Onassis (1878–1922) and Ifigeneia Lazarides**
   a. *Anastasia (Stasa) Onassis (1912–?) and Stamatis Voivodas*
      i. Lita Voivodas and George S. Livanos (1934)
         1. Arietta (1968) and Georgios Vardi Vardinoyannis

2. Eugenia (1971) and Nicholas Clive-Worms
3. Marina (1976) and Andreas Ioannis (Kiko) Martinos
4. Stavros (1980)
5. Christina (1988)
ii. Alexandros (1951)
b. **Nikos Onassis (1914–1984)**
i. Vyron
ii. Lyda
c. **Eleftherios Onassis (1919–1994)**
i. Lydia
ii. Monica
iii. Alexander
6) **Maria Onassi (1880–1919) and Chrysostomos Konialidis (?-1923)**
a. **Antiopi Konialidis (1904–1923)**
b. **Nikolaos Konialidis (1908–1990) and Meropi Onassis**
i. Marios Chysostomos (1939-2019) and Ann-Christin Kordel (1941)
1. Nicolas Chrisostomo (1974)
2. Andreas Chrisostomo (1977)
3. Elena Christina (1979)
ii. Giorgos Socrates (b. 1942) and Zografia (Zita) Yannagas
1. Alexandra (1965) and Dimitris Fafalios
a. Ralia
b. Zita
c. John
2. Nicolas Giorgos (1970) and Athina
a. Emilia Meropi
b. Giorgos
3. Catherine (1979) and Vasilios Katsikis
a. Giannis
b. Giorgos
c. Euphrosyne
c. **Charalambos Konialidis (1910–1925)**
d. **Constantinos Konialidis (1913–1981) and Ritsa Hartofilakidis (1928–)**
i. Pavlos (1950-1987)
ii. Nicolas (1953)
1. Adriano Constantino (1981)
2. Rafaela (1984)
3. Lorenzo (1987)
7) **Omiros Onassis (1885–1946) and Anna Voutsnoglou**

Sources: Handwritten Onassis family genealogical tree by George Hartofilakidis and Ritsa Konialidis, 2011; Ioannidis, *Destiny Prevails*; Mantidis, *When Onassis was Related to Pelion*, 171–172, 177–178, 183–184; e-mail correspondence with Nicolas (of Marios) Konialidis; www.genealogy.com/ftm/g/o/u/Alkiviadis-L-Goulandris/WEBSITE-0001/UHP-0251.html; www.linkedin.com/in/nicolas-a-konialidis-2432b01/

Appendix 2.B

Table A2.1 *The Onassis fleet, 1945–1975*

Year	Ships	GRT
1945	6	51,318
1950	55	437,608
1955	77	791,324
1960	62	900,260
1965	80	1,444,641
1970	76	2,224,859
1975	61	2,555,463

Sources: Lloyd's Register of Shipping, 1946–1975; Onassis Archive, Alexander S. Onassis Foundation, S.A., Corporate Books and Minutes of Meeting of the Board of Directors of owned companies.

Appendix 2.C

Forfeitures of Greek-Owned Ships by the United States Government, 1953–1954

Table A2.2 *American companies and vessels involved in the* United States *v.* Onassis

Owning company/ agency	Name of ship	Type of ship	grt	dwt	Year built	Purchased from	Financed by	Chartered to	Seized by the US government
	1. *Arickaree*	TSH-T2	10,532	16,460	1943	MARCOM	Chase National Bank	Socony Vacuum Oil Company	New York, April 1, 1953
	2. *Battle Rock*	TSH-T2	10,448	16,640	1944	MARCOM	Chase National Bank	Socony Vacuum Oil Company	New York, March 27, 1953
	3. *Camas Meadows*	TSH-T2	10,172	16,460	1943	MARCOM	National City Bank	Socony Vacuum Oil Company	Sold
	4. *Camp Namanu*	TSH-T2	10,511	16,460	1944	MARCOM	Chase National Bank	Socony Vacuum Oil Company	New York, March 27, 1953
	5. *Fort Bridger*	TSH-T2	10,172	16,460	1944	MARCOM	National city Bank	Socony Vacuum Oil Company	Mobile, Alabama, Dec. 5, 1955
	6. *Lake George*	TSH-T2	10,582	16,460	1943	MARCOM	National City Bank	Socony Vacuum Oil Company	Wilmington, Delaware, March 24, 1953
	7. *Stony Point*	TSH-T2	10,506	16,460	1943	MARCOM	Chase National Bank	Socony Vacuum Oil Company	New York, , April 2, 1953
	8. *Republic*	TSH-T2	10,581	16,748	1944	MARCOM		Transatlantica	Port Arthur, Texas, Sept. 23, 1953
	9. *Federal*	TSH-T2	10,599	16,460	1944	MARCOM			Not seized

Olympic Whaling Co. SA								
10. Olympic Challenger	TSH-T2-CONVERTED WHALING	10,448	16,576	1943	MARCOM			Not seized
11. Mckittrick Hills	TSH-T2	10,521	16,539	1944	MARCOM	National City Bank	Transatlantica	Los Angeles, June 15, 1953
12. Montebello Hills	TSH-T2	10,521	16,539	1944	MARCOM	National City Bank	Transatlantica	Not seized
13. William A. M. Burden	TSH-T2	10,642	16,656	1943	MARCOM	National City Bank	Socony Vacuum Oil Company	Not seized
14. Olympic Games	TSH-T2				MARCOM	National City Bank	Time-chartered to Transatlantica and then to Socony Vacuum Oil Company	Not seized
15. Ames Victory	CSH-VICTORY	7,644	10,757	1945	MARCOM	National City Bank	Transatlantica	Los Angeles, Aug. 6, 1953
16. Coe Victory	CSH-VICTORY	7,643	10,757	1945	MARCOM	National City Bank	Transatlantica	San Francisco, Aug. 10, 1953
17. Coeur D' Alene Victory	CSH-VICTORY	7,645	10,745	1945	MARCOM	National City Bank	Transatlantica	San Francisco Sept. 14, 1953
18. Heywood Broun	CSH- LIBERTY	7,643	10,767	1945	MARCOM	National City Bank	Transatlantica	Tacoma, Wash., Sept. 28, 1955
19. Jefferson City Victory	CSH-VICTORY	7,643	10,767	1945	MARCOM	National City Bank	Transatlantica	Philadelphia, Aug. 30, 1953
20. Lewis Emery Jr	CSH- Liberty	7,238	10,920	1943	MARCOM	National City Bank	Transatlantica	San Francisco, July 31, 1953

Table A2.2 (cont.)

Owning company/ agency	Name of ship	Type of ship	grt	dwt	Year built	Purchased from	Financed by	Chartered to	Seized by the US government
	21. *Longview Victory*	CSH-VICTORY	7,639	10,745	1945	MARCOM	National City Bank	Transatlantica	Los Angeles, Aug. 17, 1953
	22. *Mankato Victory*	CSH-VICTORY	7,645	10,745	1945	MARCOM	National City Bank	Transatlantica	San Francisco, Sept. 28, 1953
	23. *Northwestern Victory*	CSH-VICTORY	7,628	10,733	1945	MARCOM	National City Bank	Transatlantica	New York, Aug. 6, 1953

Sources: FBI, "Aristotle Onassis," part 2, Bufile 46-17783, 'Fraud against the government'. New York office 46-2507 report, May 10, 1952, http://vault.fbi.gov/Aristotle% 20Onassis (accessed September 29, 2008); *Current Merchant Marine Problems*, Hearings before the Committee on Merchant Marine and Fisheries, House of Representatives, Eighty-fifth Congress, first session, February 6 and 7, 1957, United States Government Printing Office, Washington, 1957, 188.

Table A2.3 *American companies and vessels involved in the case of the* United States *v.* Kulukundis

Company	Type	Name of vessel	Place and date of seizure
Seatrade Group			
	Tanker	1. *Risano*	
	Tanker	2. *Krussa*	
	Tanker	3. *Else Basse*	
	Tanker	4. *Daniela Borchard*	
	Tanker	5. *Ramapo*	
	Tanker	6. *Tagalam*	Los Angeles, Jan. 10, 1955
	Tanker	7. *Queenston Heights*	New York, Jan. 28, 1954
	Victory	8. *San Angelo*	
	Victory	9. *Newberry*	
Aegean Marine Corp.	Liberty	10. *Trojan Trader*	
Tramp Shipping &	Liberty	11. *W.L. McCormick*	
Oil Transportation	Tanker	12. *Pytheas*	
	Tanker	13. *Poseidon*	
Veritas Steamship Co., Inc.	Liberty	14. *Shinnecock Bay*	Norfolk, Jan. 7, 1955
	Tanker	15. *Amphitrite*	
American Tramp Shipping Development Corp.	Tanker T-2	16. *Stony Creek*	
U.S. Waterways Corp. (sold to Los-Pezas)	Liberty	17. *Compass*	Baltimore, March 17, 1955
Philadelphia Marine Corp.	Liberty	18. *National Servant*	
	Liberty	19. *Seaglorius*	
	Tanker T-2	20. *Potrero Hills*	
Potrero Corp.	Tanker T-2	21. *Oleum*	
Clenega Tanker Corp.	Tanker T-2	22. *Santa Paula*	
	Tanker T-2	23. *Lompoc*	
	Tanker	24. *Paul M. Gregg*	
	Tanker	25. *L.P.St. Clair*	
	Tanker	26. *A.C. Rubel*	

Table A2.3 (*cont.*)

Company	Type	Name of vessel	Place and date of seizure
Metro Petroleum Shipping Co., Inc.	Tanker T-2	27. *Sweetwater*	Wilimington, Jan. 4, 1954
	Liberty	28. *Ragnar Maess*	
Metro Steamship Corp.	Liberty	29. *Gulfwater*	Philadelphia, Dec. 17, 1954
	Liberty	30. *Atlantic Water*	
Elam Shipping Corp.	Liberty	31. *Santa Venetia*	

Source: Current Merchant Marine Problems, Hearings before the Committee on Merchant Marine and Fisheries, House of Representatives, Eighty-fifth Congress, first session, February 6 and 7, 1957, United States Government Printing Office, Washington, 1957, 186.

Table A2.4 *American companies and vessels involved in the case of the* United States *v.* Niarchos

Company	Type	Name of vessel	Place and date of seizure
North American Shipping and Trading Co., Inc.	T2 tanker	1. *Seven Seas*	San Francisco, March 14, 1953
	T2 tanker	2. *Jeanny*	San Francisco, March 21, 1953
	T2 tanker	3. *Memory*	Wilmington, March 15, 1953
	T2 tanker	4. *Merrimac*	Delaware River, March 5, 1953
	T2 tanker	5. *Monitor*	Paulsboro, Feb. 16, 1953
	T2 tanker	6. *Mermaid*	Wilimington, March 9, 1953
	Liberty	7. *Mohawk*	Philadelphia, July 29, 1953
	Liberty	8. *Mojave*	Wilmington, Aug. 7, 1953
	Liberty	9. *Mohican*	New York, Aug. 31, 1953

Table A2.4 *(cont.)*

Company	Type	Name of vessel	Place and date of seizure
American Pacific Steamship Co.	T2 tanker	10. *Ampac California*	New Bedford, Aug. 4, 1953
	T2 tanker	11. *Ampac Washington*	Baltimore, Sept. 11, 1953
	Liberty	12. *Ampac Oregon*	Boston, Nov. 9, 1953
	Liberty	13. *Ampac Idaho*	New York, Aug. 24, 1953
	Liberty	14. *Ampac Nevada*	Philadelphia, Aug. 31, 1953
Ventura Steamship Co.	T2 tanker	15. *Ventura*	Port Arthur, May 23, 1953
American Overseas Tanker Co.	T2 tanker	16. *Owyhee*	Orange, Aug. 27, 1954
	T2 tanker	17. *Fort George*	Orange, Feb. 10, 1956
	T2 tanker	18. *Umatilla*	Orange, Dec. 15, 1955
	T2 tanker	19. *Yarnhill*	Orange, Dec. 15, 1955
	T2 tanker	20. *Gervais*	Beaumont, Aug. 15, 1954

Source: Current Merchant Marine Problems, Hearings before the Committee on Merchant Marine and Fisheries, House of Representatives, Eighty-fifth Congress, first session, February 6 and 7, 1957, United States Government Printing Office, Washington, 1957, 187.

Table A2.5 *American companies and vessels involved in the case of the* United States *v.* Los-Pezas Group

Company	Type	Name of vessel	Place and date of seizure
Compass Steamship Co.	*Liberty*	*Compass*	Baltimore, Dec. 1, 1954
Pegor Steamship Co.	*Liberty*	*Pegor*	Not seized
Paroh Steamship	*Liberty*	*Annioc*	Not seized
Are Steamship Co.	*Liberty*	*Chian Trader*	Not seized
Steelcraft Steamship Co.	*Liberty*	*Chian Breeze*	Not seized

Source: Current Merchant Marine Problems, Hearings before the Committee on Merchant Marine and Fisheries, House of Representatives, Eighty-fifth Congress, first session, February 6 and 7, 1957, United States Government Printing Office, Washington, 1957, 187.

Table A2.6 *American companies and vessels involved in the case of the* United States v. Kallimanopoulos Group

Company	Type	Name of vessel	Place and date of seizure
Transfuel Co.	*Liberty*	*William H. Carruth*	Not seized
Drytrans, Inc.	*Liberty*	*Cecil N. Bean*	Not seized
Drytrans, Inc.	*Liberty*	*Frederic C. Collin*	Not seized
Drytrans, Inc.	*Liberty*	*Catherine*	Not seized
Drytrans, Inc.	*Liberty*	*Albion*	Not seized

Source: Current Merchant Marine Problems, Hearings before the Committee on Merchant Marine and Fisheries, House of Representatives, Eighty-fifth Congress, first session, February 6 and 7, 1957, United States Government Printing Office, Washington 1957, 188.

Appendix 2.D

Table A2.7 *Port captains of Onassis group of companies*

Name	Place of birth	Born	Office	Period of service
J. Kallimanis	–	1894	France	1951–1953
E. Vaglianos	Ithaca	1908	France/Monaco	1952–1962
J. Paizis	Ithaca	1921	Germany/Monaco	1952–1965
G. Koutsouvelis	Ithaca	1904	Greece	1953–1963
F. Maroudas	Ithaca	1895	Greece	1954–1968
E. Romais	Ithaca	1912	United States	1954–1970
D. Vlismas	Ithaca	1925	Greece	1963–1973
P. Pierros	Ithaca	1920	Greece	1963–1979
G. Tsaganeas	–	1911	Greece	1966–1967
G. Yfantidis	Ithaca	1930	Greece-United States	1967–1983
J. Patrinos	Ithaca	1918	United States	1968–1982
X. Verykios	Ithaca (Kalamos)	1920	Greece	1969–1974
S. Theodorou	–	1922	Greece	1971–1972
J. Artemiou	Ithaca	1931	Greece	1972–1988
S. Savanis	Patra	1924	Greece	1973–1989
P. Giannakopoulos	Piraeus	1929	Greece-United States	1974–1997
P. Nambouris	Athens	1931	Greece	1979–1997
S. Lourandos	Ithaca	1936	Greece	1980–2005
P. Katravas	Ithaca	1932	Greece/Japan	1982–1999
A. Anastasiadis	–	1936	United Kingdom	1985–1996
D. Nannos	Aegina	1936	Greece	1986–1988
K. Anastasiadis	Athens	1921	Greece	1986–1996
P. Papazoglou	–	1934	Greece	1987–1989
D. Raptis	Trikala	1935	Greece	1988–1993
D. Iliopoulos	Patra	1947	Greece	1992–2013

Table A2.7 (*cont.*)

Name	Place of birth	Born	Office	Period of service
G. Barkas	Ithaca (Kalamos)	1952	Greece	1995–
D. Siganakis	Crete	1950	United Kingdom/ Greece	1996–
D. Barbounis	Chalkida	1947	Greece	1996–2014
N. Mendrinos	Athens	1940	Greece	1999–2006
B. Giannoutsos	Ithaca	1959	Greece	2004–
A. Angeletos	Lakonia	1960	Greece	2004–
A. Apostolopoulos	Piraeus	1963	Greece	2004–
K. Lemos	Athens	1953	Greece	2013–
T. Isiris	Athens	1972	Greece	2014
F. Mitromaras	Volos	1968	Greece	2015

Source: Springfield, SA, Archives of Marine Department.

INDEX OF NAMES

Note: The index reflects the names that Greek individuals used overseas, where they often dropped the 's' (included in this index in parenthesis) from the end of their surname.

INDEX OF PLACES

INDEX OF TERMS